Tasmania

a Lonely Planet Australia guide

John Chapman
Monica Chapman

A.D
1823

Tasmania

1st edition

Published by
Lonely Planet Publications
Head Office: PO Box 617, Hawthorn, Vic 3122, Australia
Branches: 155 Filbert St, Suite 251, Oakland, CA 94607, USA
10 Barley Mow Passage, Chiswick, London W4 4PH, UK
71 bis rue du Cardinal Lemoine, 75005 Paris, France

Printed by
Colorcraft Ltd, Hong Kong

Photographs by

Glenn Beanland	Lindsay Brown	John Chapman
Monica Chapman	Adrienne Costanzo	Charlotte Hindle
Chris Klep	Ray Stamp	Tasmanian Department of Tourism
Olegas Truchanas/Wilderness Society		

Front cover: Crayfish pots, Constitution Dock, Hobart (Glenn Beanland)
Title page: Richmond Bridge, the oldest bridge in Australia (Chris Klep)

Published
September 1996

Although the authors and publisher have tried to make the information as accurate as possible, they accept no responsibility for any loss, injury or inconvenience sustained by any person using this book.

National Library of Australia Cataloguing in Publication Data

Chapman, John, 1953 - .
Tasmania.

Includes index.
ISBN 0 86442 384 5.

1. Tasmania – Guide-books. I. Chapman, Monica. II. Title.
(Series: Lonely Planet Australia guide).

919.460463

text & maps © Lonely Planet 1996
photos © photographers as indicated 1996

John Chapman

John has used many years of experience of walking and travelling in Tasmania to write this book and to update the Tasmania chapter of Lonely Planet's current *Australia* guide. His main interest is bushwalking, and he has written magazine and newspaper articles and several bushwalking guidebooks, including Lonely Planet's *Bushwalking in Australia*. He enjoys both colour and black & white photography, and has exhibited internationally. John is also a keen ski tourer and rockclimber who has led many treks in the Himalayan regions of Nepal and India.

Monica Chapman

In her 'spare time', Monica has joined forces with John to research and write various travel and bushwalking guides. Her main interest is also bushwalking, and she has been involved in local bushwalking clubs for many years. She has led numerous bushwalks, and is a member of a search & rescue organisation. Monica is a keen photographer, enjoys ski touring and occasionally even rockclimbs!

From the Authors

John & Monica would like to thank everyone who provided assitance, hospitality and advice during their travels in Tasmania – in particular the Tasmanian Travel & Information Centres, various tour operators and the friendly staff at many B&Bs.

From the Publisher

This book was edited at the Lonely Planet office in Melbourne by Liz Filleul, with much help from Lindsay Brown, and from Brigitte Barta and Kirsten John at proofreading stage. The maps and illustrations were superbly drawn by Anthony Phelan and Lyndell Taylor, and Anthony was also responsible for the design and layout. The help given by Mary Neighbour and Michelle Stamp at layout was much appreciated. David Kemp and Adam McCrow designed the cover. Thanks to Steve Womersley for computer assistance.

Warning & Request

Things change – prices go up, schedules change, good places go bad and bad places go bankrupt – nothing stays the same. So if you find things better or worse, recently opened or long since closed, please write and tell us and help make the next edition better.

Your letters will be used to help update future editions and, where possible, important changes will also be included in an Update section in reprints.

We greatly appreciate all information that is sent to us by travellers. Back at Lonely Planet we employ a hard-working readers' letters team to sort through the many letters we receive. The best ones will be rewarded with a free copy of the next edition or another Lonely Planet guide if you prefer. We give away lots of books, but, unfortunately, not every letter/postcard receives one.

Contents

Map Legend

BOUNDARIES

.... International Boundary

.... Regional Boundary

ROUTES

.... Freeway

.... Highway

.... Major Road

.... Unsealed Road or Track

.... City Road

.... City Street

.... Railway

.... Underground Railway

.... Tram

.... Walking Track

.... Walking Tour

.... Ferry Route

.... Cable Car or Chairlift

AREA FEATURES

.... Parks

.... Built-Up Area

.... Pedestrian Mall

.... Market

.... Cemetery

.... Reef

.... Beach or Desert

.... Rocks

HYDROGRAPHIC FEATURES

.... Coastline

.... River, Creek

.... Intermittent River or Creek

.... Rapids, Waterfalls

.... Lake, Intermittent Lake

.... Canal

.... Swamp

SYMBOLS

✪ CAPITAL	.... National Capital	
◉ Capital	.... Regional Capital	
☁ CITY	.... Major City	
● City	.... City	
● Town	.... Town	
● Village	.... Village	
■ ▼	.... Place to Stay, Place to Eat	
☎ ♟	.... Cafe, Pub or Bar	
✉ ☎	.... Post Office, Telephone	
❸ ❾	.... Tourist Information, Bank	
⬤ 🅿	.... Transport, Parking	
⛫ ⌂	.... Museum, Youth Hostel	
🏕 ⚑	Caravan Park, Camping Ground	
✝ ➡	.... Church, Cathedral	
☪ ✡	.... Mosque, Synagogue	
卍 卐	Buddhist Temple, Hindu Temple	
✚ ★	.... Hospital, Police Station	

◯ 🄿	.... Embassy, Petrol Station	
✈ ✝	.... Airport, Airfield	
▭ ✿	.... Swimming Pool, Gardens	
❖ ➤	.... Shopping Centre, Zoo	
⚲ ♔	...Winery or Vineyard, Picnic Site	
← A25	One Way Street, Route Number	
⛪ ⚱	.... Stately Home, Monument	
⚑ ⚐	.... Golf Course, Ski Field	
⌒ ⌂	.... Cave, Hut or Chalet	
▲ ☀	.... Mountain or Hill, Lookout	
⚓ ⚓	.... Lighthouse, Shipwreck	
)(◎	.... Pass, Spring	
♪ ♝	.... Beach, Surf Beach	
∴	...... Archaeological Site or Ruins	
	.... Ancient or City Wall	
⟿ ⟸	.... Cliff or Escarpment, Tunnel	
	.... Railway Station	

Note: not all symbols displayed above appear in this book

Introduction

Tasmania is Australia's smallest state, and the only island state. Usually referred to by Australians as 'Tassie', it is a place of great contrasts – of wild ocean beaches and thick rainforests, rugged mountain ranges and delicate alpine moorlands.

The state was originally known as Van Diemen's Land, and became notorious as a British penal colony during the mid-19th century. Reminders of its convict heritage can be seen in various places: the ruins of the penal settlement at Port Arthur, the many convict-built bridges, and in the beautifully preserved Georgian sandstone buildings in more than 20 historic towns.

Tasmania's pristine wilderness areas are also known worldwide. The battles for the conservation of wilderness areas and wild rivers have attracted international attention

and many visitors come to see these beautiful areas. About one quarter of Tasmania is contained in national parks and most of this – about 20% of the state – has World Heritage status.

The beaches on the east coast of Tasmania offer a diversity of water sports. In the north, there are wineries, patchwork hillsides and magnificent coastal scenery (especially around Stanley and Table Cape). Over in the west, the lunar landscape of Queenstown provides a stark contrast to the tall rainforests of the Gordon River. Also in the west is the world-famous Cradle Mountain and walks (even short ones) in this area are a must.

Hobart, Tasmania's capital, has historic buildings, a lively market and a magnificent waterfront. The Tasman Peninsula has spectacular sea cliffs, which tower some 300

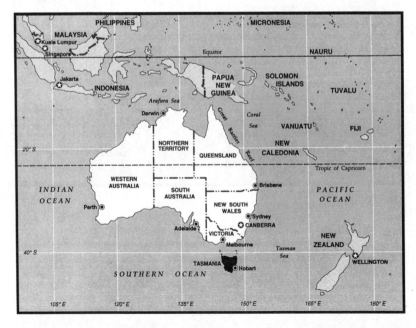

metres above the ocean. South of Hobart, in the Huon Valley, are some culinary surprises; good food at reasonable prices in an area not often discovered by visitors. Further south are beaches and even more rugged coastline.

Tasmania has something for everyone.

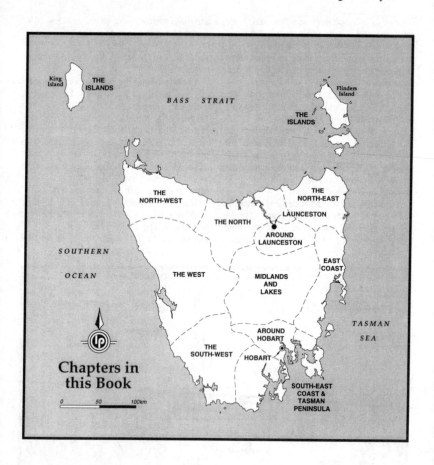

Facts about Tasmania

HISTORY
Aboriginal People

Since European settlement, the story of Australia's Aboriginal people has not been a happy one, and nowhere has it been more tragic than in Tasmania. Here the Aboriginal people were removed so quickly that almost nothing of their history, culture or language was recorded. Slowly, pieces of their history have been discovered in various caves and other sites around the state. Among the discoveries are early rock paintings in caves, carvings on rocky outcrops, middens which are the remains of meals, and quarries where stone tools were created.

Tasmania was settled by the Aboriginal people at least 35,000 years ago, when they probably migrated across the land bridge that joined Tasmania to the rest of Australia. The sea level was much lower then and the Tasmanian climate was much drier and colder. The Aboriginal people at that stage seem to have settled the western side of the state, where extensive grasslands supported the animals they hunted. The eastern half of the state was probably too barren and dry for settlement.

When the last Ice age ended and the glaciers retreated, sea levels rose and, about 10,000 years ago, Tasmania became separated from mainland Australia. From that time on, the culture of the Tasmanian Aboriginal people diverged from that of their mainland counterparts. While the mainland people developed more specialised tools for hunting like boomerangs and spear-throwing holders, the Tasmanian people stayed with simpler tools like the ordinary spear, wooden waddie and stones.

With the change of climate the vegetation of the western half of the state altered, tall forests covered the landscape, and in the east rainfall increased and extensive grasslands developed. The Aboriginal people abandoned their caves and shelters and followed the animals they hunted, moving to the more open eastern side of the state. Some still lived in the west but primarily along the coast.

They lived by hunting, fishing and gathering, and sheltered in bark lean-tos. Despite Tasmania's cold weather, they went naked apart from a coating of grease and charcoal. Their society was based on sharing and exchange – a concept with which the European invaders failed to come to terms. It was estimated there were about 4000 Aboriginal people in Tasmania when the Europeans arrived.

European settlers first arrived in 1803 and found Tasmania fertile and fenced it off to make farms. They settled the same areas that the Aboriginal people occupied and as the Aboriginals lost more and more of their traditional hunting grounds, they slowly realised that the Europeans had come to steal their land, not share it, and began to fight for what was rightfully theirs. By the 1820s the killing on both sides was out of control and this period became known as the Black War. The Aboriginal people speared shepherds and their stock, and, in turn, were hunted and shot. Europeans abducted Aboriginal children to use as forced labour, raped and tortured Aboriginal women, gave poisoned flour to friendly tribes, and laid steel traps in the bush.

In 1828 martial law was proclaimed by Governor Arthur, giving soldiers the right to arrest or shoot on sight any Aboriginal found in an area of European settlement. Finally, in 1830, in an attempt to flush out all Aboriginals and corner them on the Tasman peninsula, a human chain, known as the Black Line, was formed by the settlers, and this moved for three weeks through the settled areas of the state. Ultimately unsuccessful (only two Aboriginals were captured) it disturbed the Aboriginal people so much that, soon afterwards, many gave themselves up.

Those who were captured or had given themselves up were kept in a camp on Bruny

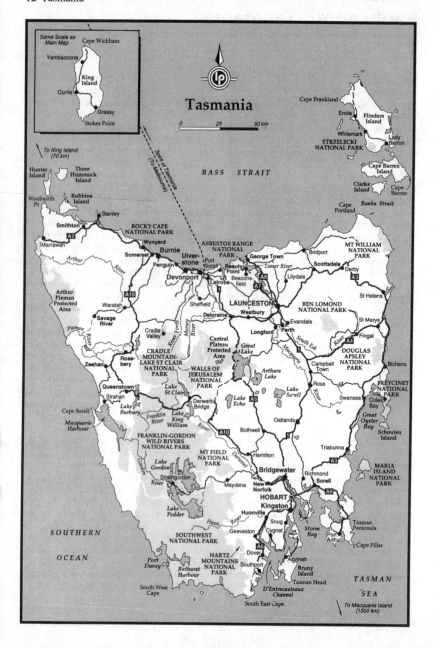

Tasmania

Island. In 1830 George Robinson, who was in charge of the camp, suggested that he run an expedition to 'conciliate' the remaining Aboriginal people and bring them into the settlement. Governor Arthur gave permission and Robinson followed the native tracks around the coastline of the south-west. He was initially unsuccessful even though the Aboriginal people called him 'the good white man'. Over the next three years Robinson travelled over most of the state and collected virtually all remaining Aboriginals. His last journey in 1833 was again to the south-west and this time he used force to capture the last tribe.

A few small bands of Aboriginals still existed in the bush and refused to surrender. They lasted until 1842 when the last free family gave themselves up near the Arthur River in the north-west.

To placate the captured and surrendered Aboriginal people, a verbal treaty of sanctuary and recompense was agreed to and the remnants of this once proud and peaceful race were resettled on the Furneaux Islands in Bass Strait. The treaty never really worked as the Aboriginals expected sanctuary and to be given trusteeship of some land, while the government attempted to 'civilise' them by turning them into Christians and making them work for the government. After several moves around the islands, Settlement Point on Flinders Island became the Aboriginals' new home. Initially they were treated well, but soon were regarded as pensioners of the state and were supported in the cheapest way possible.

With nothing to do but exist, most of them died of despair, homesickness, poor food or respiratory disease. Of the 135 who went to the island, after 13 years only 47 survived. The Aboriginals petitioned Queen Victoria, complaining of poor treatment, and in 1847 they were transferred to Oyster Cove, south of Hobart, which made little difference to their plight. With restrictions being placed on their movements, they could not follow their traditional way of living and at the same time were neglected by being given inadequate rations. The end was inevitable and in 1876 Truganini, the last full-blood Aboriginal, died. It's hard to believe, but during those first 35 years of European settlement, 183 Europeans and nearly 4000 Aborigines were killed.

Furneaux Islands European sealers had been working in Bass Strait since 1798, and

Truganini

Truganini was the last surviving full-blooded Tasmanian Aboriginal. She was born on Bruny Island in 1812 as a daughter of Mangana, the chief of the Nuenanne tribe. She left her island home to travel with G A Robinson on his mission to round up the remaining Aboriginal people and twice saved his life. Robinson was one of the few Europeans who tried to befriend the Aboriginal people and had lived with them on Bruny Island. The remainder of Truganini's life was spent on Flinders Island and then at Oyster Cove, near Hobart.

Truganini died on 8 May 1876 and with her went the last opportunity for Europeans to receive eye-witness accounts about the life of her people. For many years her skeleton was displayed as a public exhibit in Hobart. One hundred years after her death, her wishes were granted when her ashes were finally scattered in the channel beside her beloved Bruny Island. ■

although they occasionally raided tribes along the coast, on the whole their contact with the Aboriginal people was based on trade. Aboriginal women were traded for or stolen in raids, and many sealers settled down on the Bass Strait islands with these women and had families.

By 1850 a new Aboriginal community, with a lifestyle based mainly on European ways, had emerged on the Furneaux group of islands, saving the Tasmanian Aboriginals from total extinction. The people were based mainly on Cape Barren Island and were initially treated as slaves. They lived as peasant farmers and soon came to be regarded with some respect by the white Australians living on the islands.

The 20th Century brought new technology to farming, and the wealth of white Australians quickly improved while the Aboriginal Islanders' wealth remained unchanged. This economic inequality led to their rejection by the European community, and the group has associated itself with the Australian Aboriginals who also face the same problems of inequality.

Today There are more than 6500 descendants of the Tasmanian Aboriginals still living in Tasmania. Aboriginal people all across Australia are claiming rights to land and compensation for past injustices. The Tasmanian group is seeking fulfilment of the obligations which the treaty of the 1830s promised them: namely rights to land and compensation. Increasing awareness of the plight of Aboriginal people by white Australia has resulted in the recognition of native title to land, but there is still much to be reconciled.

European Discovery

The first European to see Tasmania was the famous Dutch navigator Abel Tasman, who arrived in 1642 and called it Van Diemen's Land after the governor of the Dutch East Indies. Between 1770 and 1790, Tasmania was sighted and visited by a series of famous European sailors, including captains Tobias Furneaux, James Cook and William Bligh.

Abel Tasman

They all visited Adventure Bay on Bruny Island and believed it to be part of the Australian mainland rather than an island off Van Diemen's Land. In 1792 Admiral Bruni D'Entrecasteaux explored the south-eastern coastline more thoroughly, mapping and naming many of the features. Most major landmarks still bear names from this expedition.

European contact with the Tasmanian coast became more frequent after the soldiers and convicts of the First Fleet settled at Sydney Cove in 1788, mainly because ships heading to the colony of New South Wales from the west had to sail around the island.

In 1798 Lieutenant Matthew Flinders circumnavigated Van Diemen's Land and proved that it was an island. He named the rough stretch of sea between the island and the mainland Bass Strait, after George Bass, the ship's surgeon. The discovery of Bass Strait shortened the journey to Sydney from India or the Cape of Good Hope by a week.

Founding of Hobart

In the late 1790s, Governor King of New South Wales decided to establish a second settlement in Australia, south of Sydney Cove. Port Phillip Bay in Victoria was initially considered, but was this was rejected due to a lack of water on the Mornington Peninsula; so, in 1803, Risdon Cove in Tasmania was chosen for settlement. One year later, the settlement was moved to the present site of Hobart. The threat of other nations gaining a foothold by starting settlements prompted more expansion, and in 1804 the first settlement on the Tamar River was made at George Town.

Convicts

Although convicts were sent out with the first settlers, penal colonies were not built until later, when free settlers demanded to be separated from convicts. The initial penal colony was established in 1821 in as far away and inhospitable a place as possible, Macquarie Harbour. The actual site was on the small Sarah Island and prisoners who were sent there had committed further crimes after arrival in Australia. Their punishment was hard, manual labour, cutting down Huon pines in the rainforest.

As the number of prisoners grew, another penal colony was established on Maria Island in 1825. Here, prisoners were treated more humanely. A third colony was established at Port Arthur in 1832. Each of these colonies were chosen because they were naturally escape-proof.

In the British Isles, Van Diemen's Land was the most feared destination for prisoners for more than three decades. During those years, a total of 74,000 convicts were transported to Tasmania. The majority of them served out their sentences and afterwards remained in the state.

Much opposition to the transportation of convicts came from free settlers, and in 1856 the punishment was abolished. That same year parliamentary elections for Tasmania took place, and the government decided to rename the state Tasmania – after Abel Tasman – in a bid to escape its dreadful reputation.

Exploration & Expansion

After Hobart and George Town were established, they attracted new settlers, resulting in demand for more land. Initially the spread was along the southern coast towards Port Arthur (Richmond and Sorell), along the east coast and around the Launceston area. By 1807 an overland route from Hobart to Launceston had been discovered. The earliest buildings were rough timber huts, but as towns developed, settlers with stone masonry skills arrived. Stone was readily available, and many of the early stone buildings have survived.

The big unknown was the rugged hinterland, where difficult mountainous country barred the way. The first Europeans to cross the island were escapees from Macquarie Harbour; many escaped but only a few survived the journey across to Hobart Town. A significant early explorer was George Robinson, who in 1830 set out on his historic journey to placate and capture the Aboriginal people and so became the first European to walk across much of the state.

In 1828 George Frankland was appointed surveyor-general of Tasmania. He was determined to map the entire state and, during the 1830s, sent many surveyors out on epic journeys, often accompanying them. By 1845, when Frankland died, most of the state was roughly mapped and known.

Building roads across the mountainous west was difficult, and many were surveyed across all sorts of difficult country before being abandoned. Finally, in 1932, the Lyell Highway from Hobart to Queenstown was opened, linking the west coast to Hobart.

Mining

In the 1870s gold was discovered near the Tamar River and tin was found in the north-east. These discoveries prompted rushes, with prospectors coming from around the world. In the north-east a number of Chinese miners arrived and brought their culture with them. Mining was a tough and dangerous way of life and most people did not make a fortune. The story of Tasmania's mines are similar to those elsewhere in Australia. Individual prospectors grabbed the rich, easily-found surface deposits. Once these were gone, the miners formed companies and larger groups to mine the deeper deposits and eventually these either ran out or became unprofitable to work. Remains of the mine workings at Derby and Beaconsfield can still be seen today.

Once it was realised that there was mineral wealth to be found, prospectors randomly explored most of the state. Over on the west coast they discovered rich deposits of silver and lead and another boom occurred in the 1880s, with a rush at Zeehan. This was an extremely rich mineral area and many other mines have since been developed, creating towns at Rosebery, Tullah and Queenstown. Exploitation of the area was unchecked and, by the 1920s, the hills around Queenstown had been stripped bare of timber to feed the smelters. In an area with a rainfall of three metres, the pollution was so bad that nothing grew and this situation continued until the 1960s.

The rich belt of land from Queenstown through to the northern coast is still being mined in several places, but this is now being done with more regard for the environment and the effects of these operations are less visible than in the past. Undoubtedly new finds will continue in this mineral-rich belt and mining will remain an important industry to Tasmania.

The 20th Century – Conservation Issues

Tasmania is renowned worldwide for its pristine wilderness areas and, during the last 20 or so years, for the essential role it has played in world environmental and conservation issues. The most dominant dispute has been between the proponents of hydroelectricity and the conservation movement, and the history of this issue best sums up the change in politics towards conservation.

Electricity is one of the prime energy sources of today's cities. In Tasmania they solved its generation problem by making use of one of Tasmania's most generous resources, water. A series of hydroelectric stations, along with associated dam works and pipelines, was built on the Central Plateau and the Derwent River.

In the 1960s the large government depart-ment responsible for electricity production, the Hydro Electric Commission (HEC), decided the next dam scheme would be in the middle of the undeveloped region of the state. It proposed flooding the only national park in the region, Lake Pedder, to create a much larger lake for electricity generation.

At this stage a small number of people, mainly bushwalkers, had begun to realise that much of Tasmania's natural environment was being altered and that the remaining wilderness should be kept as it was for future generations to see. A bitter fight developed over Lake Pedder with dubious tactics being used – for example, Bills were pushed through Parliament in the early hours of the morning. As more information was published, it became clear that flooding Lake Pedder was not even necessary for the hydroelectricity scheme.

Lake Pedder was flooded in 1972, and the HEC began working on the next grand power scheme even though there was no real demand for the electricity. It started work on the lower Gordon and Franklin rivers and, despite protests from the HEC that nothing was planned, the public began to realise what the government was really up to. Polls in 1980 revealed that the public were opposed to any dam by two to one.

Experience over Lake Pedder had shown the conservationists that they had to be organised. The Tasmanian Wilderness Society (TWS) was created and succeeded in having the Wild Rivers National Park declared in 1980. The TWS then pushed the premier of the state to nominate the area for World Heritage listing. The premier thought these concessions would not effect the dams. The federal government announced in 1981 that the entire region had been officially nominated for World Heritage listing.

In 1981 the state government attempted to resolve the issue by holding a referendum asking the public to choose between two different dam schemes. Despite telling the public that informal votes were illegal, 46% of voters wrote 'no dams' on the ballot papers; it was clear that public opposition was very strong.

While this referendum was happening, parliament was in turmoil with the premier and opposition leader being dumped over the issue and some leaders ended up sitting on the cross benches. The issue forced a state election where power changed hands, but once elected, the former opposition party also supported the HEC dam project on the Gordon and Franklin Rivers. When the World Heritage Committee eventually announced the World Heritage listing for the area and expressed concern over the dam construction the new premier attempted to have the listing withdrawn. The fact that the main newspaper in Hobart didn't even report such a significant event has been attributed to political interference.

Realising that resolving the issue by democratic means in Tasmania was impossible, the TWS and other conservation groups switched attention to federal politics. In May 1982, at a by-election in Canberra, 41% of voters wrote 'no dams' on their ballot papers and politicians began to take the issue seriously. Later that year at another by-election, 40% of voters again declared 'no dams' on the ballot papers, but still the federal government refused to intervene.

Construction work began in 1982 and protesters set off from Strahan in what became known as the 'Franklin River Blockade'. They protested peacefully, realising that they could only hinder work not prevent it. The Tasmanian government then passed special laws to arrest, fine and jail protesters and 1400 were arrested over the summer of 1982-83. The arrests appalled the public and the confrontation was publicised internationally.

A federal election was held in early 1983 – the Franklin River became a major election issue and the government changed hands. As promised, the new Labor government acted promptly with new laws to protect the World Heritage status of the region and stop the dam scheme. The state premier disagreed and, after several months, the high court (which oversees the constitution in Australia) ruled that the federal government did have the power to stop the dam scheme because of the World Heritage status of the region.

After its victory the TWS was renamed the Wilderness Society and became involved in conservation issues throughout Australia. Some conservationists have entered politics. (See the Government section later in this chapter).

GEOGRAPHY

Tasmania is the only island state in Australia and is also its smallest state, with an area of 67,800 sq km. It is located about 200 km south of Victoria, across the stormy treacherous seas of Bass Strait.

Although its highest mountain is only 1600 metres (about 5300 feet) high, the island has an extremely mountainous interior and much of it is not suitable for agriculture. The only large, relatively flat area is the undulating broad plain that extends from Launceston south towards Hobart. The coast is very beautiful, with attractive coves and beaches, shallow bays and broad estuaries, which have resulted from river valleys being flooded when the sea levels rose after the last Ice age.

The lack of flat land around the island is readily seen in the two largest cities, Hobart and Launceston, where there are some extremely steep hills very close to the city centres.

The centre of the state is dominated by a high, relatively flat region called the Central Plateau. This was covered in a single sheet of ice during the Ice ages and even today the weather is too bleak and the soil too barren for agricultural purposes.

Most of the western half of the state is covered with a maze of mountain ranges and ridges which bear signs of recent glaciation. Cliffs, lakes and rainforest are dominant features which many come to see. The rugged country discouraged settlement and today forms one of the world's last great wilderness areas. The climate in the west is inhospitable and, for much of the year, raging seas batter the west coast, and rainfall is high, being more than three metres.

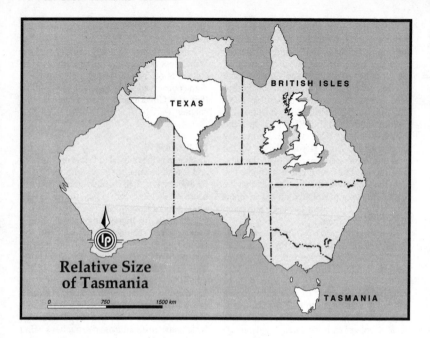

Relative Size of Tasmania

0   750   1500 km

BRITISH ISLES

TEXAS

TASMANIA

CLIMATE

Australia's seasons are the opposite of the northern hemisphere's, with January being the middle of summer and July the depths of winter.

Tasmania is located in the Roaring Forties, a notorious band of wind that encircles the world and produces very changeable weather conditions. Being small and surrounded by the sea, Tasmania has a maritime climate and is rarely extremely cold or extremely hot.

The majority of the weather comes from the west or south-west; these regions receive around three metres of rain per year. The one-sided flow of air has left a rain shadow, and rainfall decreases as you cross the state to the east coast, which receives less than one metre per year. The weather on the east coast is nearly always warmer and milder than the rest of the state and it is claimed by the Tasmanian Weather Bureau that towns like Swansea and Bicheno receive more hours of sunshine than the other coastal resort areas of Australia. Hobart is Australia's second-driest capital after Adelaide.

Tasmania has four distinct seasons, although storms can bring winter conditions at any time of year. Summer has warm weather, sunny days that are not too hot, and mild nights. This is the most pleasant time of year, and the weather gets better as summer progresses with February and March often being the best months. As autumn approaches, temperatures drop and there are some frosty nights and cool but sunny days.

Winter provides wet, cold weather characterised by regular storms particularly on the western side of the state. In the east, there is a lot less rainfall but the weather is often cloudy and overcast. Snow lies on the higher peaks but is usually not deep enough for skiing; the two ski resorts operate spasmodically.

Spring is the windy season when the winter pattern of storms still sweep across

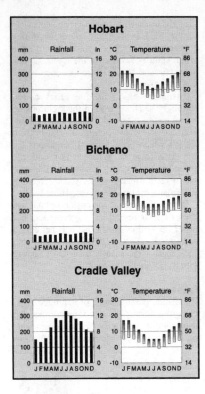

Tasmania's best known marsupial, the Tasmanian tiger, has been extinct since earlier this century; the last one was captured in 1933. It resembled a large dog or wolf and had dark stripes and a stiff tail. It is rumoured that tigers still exist, but despite many recent intense searches, there have been no official sightings.

Flora

Many of the trees are unique to the state, with native pines being very distinctive. The now rare Huon pine is the best known for its oily yellow timber which was valued for shipbuilding and furniture making and makes beautiful wood turnings. It grows very slowly and there are a few trees around 2500 years old; one this age can be seen from the cruises on the Gordon River. Its habit of sending up new shoots from the fallen trunks of old trees has resulted in a small stand of trees near the west coast believed to be clones of a single tree which germinated about 10,500 years ago. Other distinctive pines which are also slow-growing are King Billy pine, Pencil pine and celery-top pine. These pines are commonly found in the higher regions and live for about 500 years.

The dominant tree of the wetter forests is myrtle beech, which is similar to the beeches of Europe. A notable plant of the understorey in Tasmanian forests is the infamous horizontal scrub. This slender tree has very thin trunks that readily fall over; when they do fall, new vertical growth starts from the old

the state, but in between the sun shines and gradually the state warms up. The seasons often overlap and in some years the stormy spring weather continues well into summer.

FLORA & FAUNA

Tasmania's landscape ranges from the dry forests of the east through the alpine moorlands of the centre, to the rainforests of the west, so the flora is quite diverse. Many of the plants are different to those found in the rest of Australia and have ties with plants which grew millions of years ago when the southern continents were joined together as Gondwanaland – similar plants are found in South America and as fossils in Antarctica. The fauna is not as diverse as in the rest of Australia, and there are fewer large animals.

●●●●●●●●●●●●●●●●●●●●●●●●●

Horizontal can sometimes be vertical!
Anodopetalum biglandulosum – a real mouthful. This plant, commonly known as 'horizontal' is found only in Tasmania. The plant sends up thin, vigorous growth when an opening in the forest canopy occurs. The old branches become heavy and fall; they then put up shoots of their own. This continual process of growth and collapse creates dense, tangled thickets; a notorious obstacle to bushwalkers who venture off the beaten track. ■

●●●●●●●●●●●●●●●●●●●●●●●●●

horizontal trunk, and in time the tree becomes a dense thicket of vertical and horizontal trunks which can be impossible to get through. There are some good examples of this plant on the nature walks in the south-west and at Hartz Mountains.

Many of the trees flower but the most distinctive is the leatherwood tree. The tree itself is not notable except when it is in flower – then it is covered with a mass of white and pale pink flowers. These flowers are the source of a unique and fragrant honey which is highly prized by beekeepers.

While many of the eucalyptus trees are not unique to Tasmania (the same species are also found on mainland Australia) you can see plenty of extremely tall examples. The swamp gum (*Eucalyptus regnans*; known as mountain ash on the mainland) grows to around 100 metres in height and is the tallest flowering plant in the world. It is readily seen in the forests of the south-east along with the state's floral emblem, the Tasmanian blue gum.

In autumn you might see the deciduous beech, the only truly deciduous native plant in Australia. It usually grows as a rather straggly bush with bright green leaves. In autumn the leaves change colour, becoming golden and sometimes red, providing a bright splash of colour in the forest. Cradle Mountain and Mt Field are locations where it is easily seen.

Tasmania has a unique grass called buttongrass. This grows in thick clumps up to two metres high and likes swampy plains. The Ice ages left plenty of flat-bottom valleys which provide ideal conditions for this grass to grow. Where it is found, the ground is usually very muddy and unpleasant to cross; many of the tracks crossing these plains are now on elevated boardwalks.

In the alpine areas the cushion plants are interesting. It resembles a green rock, but closer inspection shows that it is actually a very tough, short plant which grows into thick mats – the plant's method of coping with its severe living conditions.

Fauna

The distinctive mammals of mainland Australia, the marsupials and monotremes, are also found in Tasmania. Marsupials including wallabies and pademelons give birth to

Despite being officially extinct since the 1930s, Tasmanian tigers are still much sought after by animal enthusiasts who insist they still exist

partially developed young which they then protect and suckle in a pouch. Monotremes – platypuses and echidnas – lay eggs but also suckle their young. Most are nocturnal and the best time to see them in the wild is around dusk. The smaller mammals can be very difficult to find in the bush, but there are plenty of wildlife parks around the state where they can be seen.

Kangaroos & Wallabies The species found in Tasmania are related to those found on the mainland, but are usually smaller. The largest marsupial is the Forester kangaroo, which at one stage looked like becoming extinct because it favoured farmland for grazing. National parks at Asbestos Range and Mt William have been set aside to preserve this kangaroo.

In the colder regions, the Bennett's wallaby thrives and this is the animal you are most likely to see begging for food at the Cradle Mountain-Lake St Clair national park. Do not give it bread as this causes a terrible disease called 'lumpy jaw' which kills the animal. You can feed it healthier food, which is available at the kiosks in the park. This very friendly animal stands just over one metre in height – but be careful as these and other native animals are not tame, and can sometimes be aggressive.

If you spy any shorter, rounder wallabies hiding in the forest, then you will have seen either a rufous wallaby or a pademelon. These smaller species are shyer than their larger relatives.

Tasmanian Devil This marsupial is mainly a scavenger, its diet consists of carrion, insects and small birds and mammals. With its ill-temper and unpleasant odour, you will know when you meet one. It's about 75 centimetres long, has a short, stocky body covered in black fur with a white stripe across its chest. You'll spot plenty in the wildlife parks around the state.

Possums These friendly creatures show little fear of humans and can at times be very cheeky, stealing food from tents and camping grounds. They live and sleep in the trees, but will come down to ground in search of food. The most common and boldest is the brushtail possum. There are several types of possum and one of the more interesting is the sugar glider, which has developed webs between its legs, enabling it to glide from tree to tree.

Wombats These are very solid and powerfully built marsupials with broad heads and short stumpy legs. They live in underground burrows which they excavate. Most of the time they seem very slow moving animals, but then they do not have any natural predators to worry about. Startle one and you will be surprised at how fast they can run.

Platypus & Echidna The platypus and the echidna are the only living representatives of the monotreme mammals. Monotremes are often regarded as living fossils, and although they display some intriguing features from their reptile ancestors, such as laying eggs, they are now recognised as a distinct mammalian lineage rather than a primitive stage in mammalian evolution. Although they lay eggs as reptiles and birds do, they suckle their young on milk secreted from mammary glands.

The platypus lives in water and has a duck-like bill, webbed feet and a beaver-like body. You are most likely to see one in a stream or lake, searching out food in the form of crustaceans, worms and tadpoles with its electrosensitive bill. They are common but not easy to find as they are shy animals, hiding if there is any noise around.

The echidnas are totally different and look similar to a porcupine, being covered in sharp spikes. They primarily eat ants and have very powerful claws which are useful for digging out their food and digging into the dirt to protect themselves when threatened. Usually all you will see is a round brown spiky ball as they hide in the ground. If you are lucky enough to see one, keep quiet and don't move. They have poor eyesight and will sometimes walk right past your feet.

Southern Right Whales These majestic creatures migrate annually from Antarctica to southern Australia to give birth to their calves in the shallow waters. So named because they were the 'right' whale to kill, they were almost hunted to the point of extinction. They are sometimes seen off the Tasmanian coast and occasionally beach themselves.

Rare Birds Some extremely rare birds are found in Tasmania – one of the best known is the orange-bellied parrot of which only a small number survive on the buttongrass plains of the south-west. They winter on the mainland and must make the treacherous crossing of Bass Strait to reach their breeding grounds in Tasmania. More common, but also under threat of extinction, is the ground parrot. To see this you will need to fly to Melaleuca in the south-west and wait in the specially constructed bird hide.

On the eastern side of Tasmania many birdwatchers come to catch a glimpse of the very rare forty-spotted pardalote, which is mainly found on Bruny Island and in Mt William National Park.

Black Currawong You will often see this large, black, fearless bird around picnic areas. With its large beak it can look threatening, but is actually very friendly and easily tamed.

Mutton Birds An interesting bird is the mutton-bird which is more correctly called a short-tailed shearwater. This little bird lives in burrows in sand dunes and migrates annually to the northern hemisphere. These birds provide spectacular displays as they fly back to their burrows in their thousands at dusk.

Penguins The little fairy penguin is the smallest penguin in the world and lives in burrows in the sand dunes. There are plenty of penguin rookeries around Tasmania where you can see them waddle from the ocean to their nests just after sunset. Bruny Island, Bicheno, Penguin and King Island all have rookeries you can visit to see these birds.

Other Birds There is a very wide variety of sea birds, parrots, cockatoos, honeyeaters and wrens. Birds of prey such as falcons and eagles are readily seen. There are many excellent publications available on Australian birds both in the form of field guides and large-format picture books.

Snakes There are only three types of snakes found in Tasmania and they are all poisonous. The most dangerous and largest are the tiger snakes which will sometimes attack, particularly in late summer. The other snakes are the copperhead and the smaller white-lipped whipsnake. Fortunately bites are very rare as most snakes are generally shy and try to avoid humans. If you do get bitten, do not try to catch the snake as there is a common antivenene for all three – instead get to hospital for treatment. See the section on Health in Facts for the Visitor.

NATIONAL PARKS & RESERVES

About one quarter of the state falls inside reserves and parks. Because the largest parks are considered to be of international importance, the federal government provides financial assistance.

National Parks

There are 14 national parks in the state and they are all worth visiting. The 10 parks outside the World Heritage Area of the south-west are all small and easily accessed by vehicle. Mt Field, Maria Island, Freycinet and Rocky Cape are the most popular of the smaller parks. They all have interesting scenery and marked, maintained walking tracks of a few minutes to several hours in duration.

National parks are managed by the Department of Parks, Wildlife and Heritage, and fees apply to all of them, even when there is no rangers office.

There are two types of fees: per vehicle and per person. For vehicles with up to eight people the charge per day is $8; a holiday pass which is valid for two months is $25 and an annual pass is $40. For individuals who arrive by bus, bicycle, motor bike or boat, entry fees are $2.50 per day, $10 for a two-month holiday pass or $15 for an annual pass.

The fees are fairly high if you are only spending a day or two in the park, but if you're staying longer or visiting several parks, then the multiple-entry passes provide worthwhile savings. For most visitors the holiday pass is the best value. Passes are available at any park entrance, at many tourist offices, and at the National Parks head office at 134 Macquarie St, Hobart.

World Heritage Area

Covering 20% of the state, this is a huge and significant area. It contains the four largest national parks in the state – South West, Wild Rivers, Cradle Mountain-Lake St Clair and the Walls of Jerusalem national parks – plus the Hartz Mountains National Park and the Central Plateau Protected Area.

The region was first accepted for listing as a world heritage area (WHA) in 1982. To be accepted, a nomination must satisfy at least one of the criteria for listing. The Western

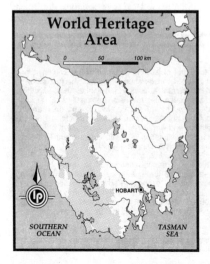

World Heritage Area

0   50   100 km

SOUTHERN
OCEAN

HOBART

TASMAN
SEA

Tasmania WHA was deemed to have outstanding natural and cultural values, and satisfied a record seven categories out of the 10 possible criteria. In 1989 the WHA was enlarged to 1.38 million hectares and renominated as the Tasmanian Wilderness World Heritage Area.

The area is managed by the same government agency that runs the national parks, the Department of Parks, Wildlife and Heritage. Most of the area is managed as a wilderness which the public are allowed to visit. However, being so large, most of it is accessible only to bushwalkers who can carry at least one week's food. One excellent and easy way to obtain a quick look over the area is to take a joy flight on a light aeroplane. Regular flights operate from Strahan and Hobart over the WHA.

Other Protected Areas

Parks, Wildlife and Heritage also manages a set of conservation areas and state reserves around the state. These reserves usually have one feature which is to be protected – often wildlife – but allow activities such as mining, farming, forestry and tourism development. Many of these places are very small and include caves, waterfalls, historic sites and some coastal regions. Usually there are no entry fees to these areas, except those where the government has actively restored or developed the area, such as at Port Arthur.

Forest Reserves

Forest reserves are usually small areas which have been given some protection inside larger regions of state forests. These forests are on crown land and their primary purpose is for timber production. Many of the waterfalls and picnic areas on the scenic forest drives are in this type of reserve. One major area in this category is the Cape Pillar State Reserve, which contains the spectacular coastal scenery around Port Arthur. None of these reserves have real protection from future alterations. During weekdays some forestry roads are closed to private vehicles; if the roads are open, drive slowly and give way to logging trucks. There are no entry fees to the forests.

GOVERNMENT

Australia has a federal system of government with elements of both the US and Westminster systems. The federal government controls areas of national importance such as defence and foreign affairs. It collects income tax and shares a portion of this revenue with the states. The state government controls all internal affairs within the state. If there is a dispute between the two levels of government, then the high court studies the problem and the constitution and makes a ruling.

The government in Tasmania has two houses. The House of Assembly is elected and has five seats with seven members in each seat for a total of 35 members. Members are elected by a complicated voting system, but, basically, candidates who poll around 15% of the vote will be elected. This system has encouraged smaller parties and independent candidates to run for parliament. This House of Assembly is the state government, with the leader of the majority party becoming premier of the state. Elections are held every four years.

The other house is the Legislative Council, members of which review government legislation. It isn't democratically elected. Generally this house makes few changes, but exercised its political muscle during the Franklin River debate, by rejecting legislation. This house has real power in that it can force a government to call an election without having to face an election itself. Full democracy does not yet exist in Tasmania.

Political Parties

There are three main parties. The Liberal Party isn't that liberal – it's usually very conservative and stands for free enterprise, law and order, business and the like.

The other main party is the Labor Party, which grew out of the shearers' strikes on the mainland in the 19th Century. Its origins are socialist but has taken a more middle road in politics in recent years and at times there is little to distinguish the two parties.

In Tasmania, Dr Bob Brown's Green Independents gain around 10 to 15% of the vote, and have become a real political force. With the Tasmanian election system supplying multiple members in each seat, the Greens are guaranteed representation in parliament; they have held the balance of power since 1989. In the 1996 state elections, the Greens

•••

Dr Bob Brown
Australia's leader of the Green Party is undoubtedly the most famous figure in the conservation movement in the country. A qualified doctor, his interest in conservation began after he rafted down the Franklin River in 1976. This event changed him into a strong advocate for the wilderness. Together with friends, he made films about the Franklin and soon became a television personality.

He became the Wilderness Society's director and a leading figure in the battle to save the Franklin River. During the 1970s he stood for parliament, but was not successful. At the height of the Franklin River Blockade in 1983 he was arrested as a protester and went to jail. In a strange turn of fate he went directly from jail to parliament because, with the resignation of green independent Dr Norm Saunders, the seat passed to the runner-up at the previous election, who was Bob.

Once he was in the state parliament he became a strong but solitary voice as an independent. Bob eventually formed his own political party and by 1989 his Green Independents held seven of the 35 seats in parliament and had become a significant political force. After many years in the state parliament, Bob followed his mentor, Dr Norm Saunders, and stood for Federal Parliament. He just made it, winning his seat by only a handful of votes and joins the other green independents (who aren't members of Bob's Green Party) in the Upper House of Parliament. As minor parties such as the Democrats and the independents hold the balance of power, it is expected that Bob will remain a force in Australian politics. ■

•••

returned six members to the House of Assembly.

ECONOMY

Tasmania's economy is based primarily on mining and agriculture. There are only a couple of heavy industries, and they employ only a small proportion of the population. Tasmania has difficulty encouraging large industry, because the major markets are on the Australian mainland and Bass Strait is a real obstacle (and expense) to cross.

Mineral production has always been an important part of the economy. With the mineral-rich belt on the western side of the state, mining should continue to be a significant income earner for a long time.

The other main earner has been agricultural products and Tasmania's economy has always been affected by price trends on the competitive world market. In the 1960s Tasmania was the primary supplier of apples to Europe, but when prices plummeted the economy suffered. Farmers have learnt from that experience and the state produces a diverse range of products – including cheese, pickled onions, fruit and lavender – many of which are of a very high quality.

Tasmania has some of the cleanest air and water in the world, and now exports pollution-free, bottled rainwater. The clean ocean waters support a healthy fishing industry. A recently developed industry which has become a major export earner is fish farming. Atlantic Salmon from these farms is now sold around the world. Dairying is a major industry, with King Island cheese being world famous. Vegetables and potatoes are major crops in the north, with the produce being mainly sold to mainland Australia.

Another recent industry is tourism, now making a major contribution to the economy. Tasmania has come to realise it has in abundance what is now rare: huge, undeveloped areas which are wild and beautiful. The industry is dominated by many small family style businesses which offer good value for money as well as friendly personal service.

POPULATION & PEOPLE

The population of Tasmania is around 453,000. One quarter of the population lives in Hobart, the state's capital, and about one eighth live in Launceston, the other large city. There are only eight other towns with more than 5000 residents. Most Tasmanians live in small towns, either close to Hobart or along the northern coastline.

Most people have a British background, and there are fewer non-British migrants here than in the other states of Australia. Chinese restaurants have long been a part of Tasmania's eating scene, ever since the Chinese arrived last century for mining. More recently Vietnamese and other Asians have arrived and have established restaurants in North Hobart and become a feature of the Salamanca Market in Hobart.

Tasmanians regard themselves as different to other Australians, and in fact call anyone from elsewhere 'mainlanders'. Those from the mainland who live here are often quietly discriminated against and are not regarded as locals until they have been there for many years. This parochialism is slowly changing as more Tasmanians travel to the mainland for holidays and to work.

ARTS & CULTURE
Aboriginal Arts & Crafts

Unfortunately, relatively little is known about the arts and culture of the Tasmanian Aboriginal people, which included rock engravings (petroglyphs), body decoration and possibly some bark painting. Some Aboriginal 'craft' traditions have survived and have been revitalised in recent years, notably basketry and shell necklace making.

The Tasmanian Aboriginal Culture & Art Centre (Tiagarra) (☎ (03) 6424 8250) in Devonport was set up to preserve the art and culture of the Tasmanian Aboriginal people. It has artefact exhibits, a rare collection of more than 250 rock engravings, and sales of contemporary craftwork.

Painting & Sculpture

Tasmania's art scene flourished from colonial times, particularly in the early 19th century under the governorship of Sir John Franklin and the patronage of his wife Lady Jane Franklin. One of the first artists to successfully capture the Australian landscape's distinctive forms and colours was John Glover, an English artist who migrated to Tasmania in 1830. English sculptor Benjamin Law also arrived in Tasmania in the 1830s, and he sculpted busts of two of the last full-blood Tasmanian Aboriginal people, Truganini and Woureddy.

Benjamin Duterrau is best known for his somewhat coarse paintings of Tasmanian Aboriginals, including *The Conciliation*, which commemorated the rounding up of the Aboriginal people by George Robinson. Successful convict artists included portraitists T G Wainewright (a convicted forger and reputed poisoner) and Thomas Bock, and W B Gould, who executed charmingly naive still-lifes.

Hobart-born William Piguenit has been called 'the first Australian-born professional painter'. He painted romantic Tasmanian landscapes including Lake St Clair and Lake Pedder in the 1870s, and his works were among the first exhibited by the Art Society of Tasmania, founded in 1884. Other early exhibitors were J. Haughton Forrest, who painted 'chocolate-box' landscapes and maritime subjects, and Belgian-born modernist Lucien Dechaineux, who also founded the art department at Hobart Technical College.

Major mainland Australian artists who visited Tasmania for inspiration early this century included Tom Roberts, Arthur Streeton and Frederick McCubbin.

In 1938 the Tasmanian Group of Painters was founded to foster the work of local artists. Founding members included Joseph Connor, a Hobart-born landscape watercolourist who was one of the early Australian modernists. Other innovators of the time were the under-recognised women artists Edith Holmes and Dorothy Stoner.

Since the 1940s a strong landscape watercolour school has developed in Tasmania, with artists such as Max Angus and Patricia Giles among the best known.

Launceston-born artist and teacher Jack Carington Smith won Australia's coveted Archibald Prize for portraiture in 1963. Tasmanian sculptor Stephen Walker has produced many bronze works that adorn Hobart's public spaces. Renowned Australian landscape painter Lloyd Rees spent his final years living and working in Tasmania, where he was also involved in the conservation movement.

Notable contemporary artists include Bea Maddock, whose serialised images incorporate painting and photography, and Bob and Lorraine Jenyns, both sculptors and ceramicists. Since the early 1980s Tasmania's art culture has been revitalised, and the new wave includes printmaker Ray Arnold, painter David Keeling, photographer David Stephenson and video-maker Leigh Hobbs.

The Tasmanian Museum & Art Gallery (☎ (03) 6235 0777) in Hobart has a good collection of Tasmanian colonial art, and exhibits relating to Tasmanian Aboriginal culture. Also worth visiting are the Queen Victoria Museum & Art Gallery in Launceston and the Gallery & Arts Centre in Devonport.

Crafts

A strong crafts movement has existed in Tasmania since the turn of the century. Studio potters Maude Poynter and Mylie Peppin were active in the 1940s, and furniture making has been particularly important, with cedar pieces from colonial times highly prized today. Contemporary furniture designers such as Leslie Wright, John Smith, Gay Hawkes and Peter Costello are nationally recognised for their highly refined and often sculptural use of Tasmania's superb native timbers, such as Huon pine and sassafras.

The Design Centre of Tasmania (☎ (03) 6331 5506) in Launceston displays and sells work by Tasmanian artists and craftspeople.

In Hobart, visitors are welcome to watch designers at work with timber, metal, ceramics and other media at the Hunter Island Design Centre. The galleries, shops and craft market at Salamanca Place also show and sell a range of crafts.

Literature

Tasmania's unique culture and landscape and its tragic convict and Aboriginal history have inspired writers of both fiction and non-fiction.

Marcus Clarke, a prolific writer who was born in London but spent most of his life in Australia, visited Tasmania in the 1870s and wrote *For the Term of His Natural Life*, an epic novel about convict life.

Queensland-born poet Gwen Harwood lived in Tasmania from 1945 until her death in 1996, and much of her work, such as *The Lion's Bride* (1981) and *Bone Scan* (1988), explores the island's natural beauty and the tragic history of its Aboriginal population.

Robert Drewe's novel *The Savage Crows* (1976) also explores the oppression of Tasmanian Aborigines by the Europeans, while Hal Porter's *The Tilted Cross* (1961) is a novel set in old Hobart Town.

Christopher Koch is a Hobart-born author of novels including *The Boys in the Island* (1958), an acclaimed account of growing up in Tasmania, and *The Year of Living Dangerously* (1978) which was made into a film directed by Peter Weir.

Carmel Bird, born in Launceston but now living in Melbourne, is known for the quirky black humour of her stories and novels, including *Cherry Ripe* (1985) and *The Bluebird Cafe* (1990), which is set in a fictional Tasmanian mining ghost-town.

James McQueen's novels include *Hook's Mountain* (1982), which has as its background the struggle to save Tasmania's forests.

Down Home: Revisiting Australia (1988) by academic Peter Conrad is an evocative recollection of the author's childhood in Tasmania and describes the island's cultural isolation and the sense of displacement of its people.

Tasmanian author Amanda Lohrey's novels include *Morality of Gentlemen* (1984), set against the backdrop of Tasmania's waterfront disputes, and *Camille's Bread* (1995).

Hobart author Richard Flanagan's award-winning novel *Death of a River Guide* (1995) weaves together Tasmanian history and myths in a story set on the Franklin River that makes an excellent introduction to Tasmanian history and life.

The Potato Factory (1995), by Bryce Courtenay (author of the blockbuster *The Power of One*) is a fictionalised account of the life of a famous Tasmanian convict, Ikey Solomon.

Tasmania has a thriving literary scene, with annual events such as the Salamanca Writers' Weekend (Hobart, in March) and Tasmanian Poetry Festival (Launceston, in October) providing opportunities for discussion and readings. The Writers' Weekend is organised by the Tasmanian Writers' Union, in the Salamanca Arts Centre, Salamanca Place, Hobart (☎ (03) 6224 0029). Local writers' work is published in the literary magazine *Island*.

Performing Arts

Tasmania's symphony orchestra is highly regarded, and there are regular concerts at Hobart's ABC Odeon or Launceston's Silverdome. Venues for theatrical events include Hobart's Playhouse and Theatre Royal (the oldest theatre in Australia), and the Princess Theatre in Launceston.

Facts for the Visitor

VISAS & EMBASSIES

All visitors to Australia need a visa, the only exception to this rule being New Zealand nationals.

Visa application forms are available from either Australian diplomatic missions overseas or travel agents, and you can apply by mail or in person. There are several different types of visas, depending on the reason for your visit.

Australian Embassies

Australian consular offices overseas include:

Canada
Suite 710, 50 O'Connor St, Ottawa K1P 6L2 (☎ (613) 236 0841; fax 236 4376)
also in Toronto and Vancouver

China
21 Dongzhimenwai Dajie, Sanlitun, Beijing 100600 (☎ (10) 532 2331; fax 532 6959)
also in Guangzhou and Shanghai

Denmark
Kristianagade 21, DK 2100 Copenhagen (☎ 3526 2244; fax 3543 2218)

France
4 Rue Jean Rey, 75724 Paris Cedex 15 Paris (☎ (01) 4059 3300; fax 4059 3310)

Germany
Godesberger Allee 107, 53175 Bonn (☎ (0228) 81 030; fax 810 3130)
also in Frankfurt and Berlin

Greece
37 Dimitriou Soutsou, Ambelokipi, Athens 11521 (☎ (01) 644 7303; fax 646 6595)

Hong Kong
23/F Harbour Centre, 25 Harbour Rd, Wanchai, Hong Kong Island (☎ 2827 8881; fax 2827 6583)

India
Australian Compound, No 1/50-G Shantipath, Chanakyapuri, New Delhi 110021 (☎ (11) 688 8223; fax 688 5199)
also in Bombay

Indonesia
Jalan H R Rasuna Said Kav C 15-16, Jakarta Selatan 12940 (☎ (021) 522 7111; fax 522 7101)
Jalan Prof Moh Yamin 51, Renon, Denpasar, Bali (☎ (0361) 23 5092; fax 23 1990)

Ireland
Fitzwilton House, Wilton Terrace, Dublin 2 (☎ (01) 676 1517; fax 678 5185)

Italy
Via Alessandria 215, Rome 00198 (☎ (06) 852 721; fax 8527 2300)
also in Milan

Japan
2-1-14 Mita, Minato-ku, Tokyo 108 (☎ (03) 5232 4111; fax 5232 4149)
Twin 21 MID Tower, 29th Floor, 2-1-61 Shiromi, Chuo-ku, Osaka 540 (☎ (06) 941 9271; fax 920 4543)
7th Floor, Tsuruta Keyaki Bldg, 1-1-5 Akasaka Chuo-ku, Fukuoka City 810, Kyushu (☎ (092) 734 5055; fax 724 2304)
8th Floor, Ikko Fushimi Bldg, 1-20-10 Nishiki, Naka-ku, Nagoya 460 (☎ (052) 211 0630; fax 211 0632)
also in Sapporo and Sendai

Malaysia
6 Jalan Yap Kwan Seng, Kuala Lumpur 50450 (☎ (03) 242 3122; fax 241 5773)
also in Kuching and Penang

Netherlands
Carnegielaan 4, 2517 KH The Hague (☎ (070) 310 8200; fax 310 7863)

New Zealand
72-78 Hobson St, Thorndon, Wellington (☎ (04) 473 6411; fax 498 7118)
Union House, 32-38 Quay St, Auckland 1 (☎ (09) 303 2429; fax 377 0798)

Papua New Guinea
Independence Drive, Waigani NCD, Port Moresby (☎ 325 9333; fax 325 6647)

Philippines
Dona Salustiana Ty Tower, 104 Paseo de Roxas, Makati, Metro Manila (☎ (02) 817 7911; fax 817 3603)

Singapore
25 Napier Rd, Singapore 1025 (☎ 737 9311; fax 733 7134)

South Africa
292 Orient St, Arcadia, Pretoria 0083 (☎ (012) 342 3740; fax 342 4222)
also in Cape Town

Sweden
Sergels Torg 12, Stockholm (☎ (08) 613 2900; fax 24 7414)

Switzerland
29 Alpenstrasse, CH-3006 Berne (☎ (031) 351 0143; fax 352 1234)
also in Geneva

Thailand
37 South Sathorn Rd, Bangkok 10120 (☎ (02) 287 2680; fax 287 2029)

UK
>Australia House, The Strand, London WC2B 4LA (☎ (0171) 379 4334; fax 465 8210)
>also in Edinburgh and Manchester

USA
>1601 Massachusetts Ave NW, Washington DC 20036 (☎ (202) 797 3000; fax 797 3168)
>also in Atlanta, Boston, Chicago, Denver, Honolulu, Houston, Los Angeles, New York and San Francisco

Vietnam
>66 Ly Thuong Kiet, Hanoi (☎ (04) 25 2763; fax 25 9268)
>also in Ho Chi Minh City

Foreign Embassies & Consulates

The principal diplomatic representations to Australia are in Canberra. There are also representatives in various other major Australian cities – particularly from countries like the USA, UK and New Zealand, which have strong links with Australia. Visa applications, however, are generally handled in Canberra.

In Hobart there are consulates for Belgium, Finland, Germany, Greece, Italy, Japan, the Netherlands, Norway, the Philippines, Sweden and Switzerland. Their addresses can be found in the Hobart telephone directory.

Tourist Visas

Tourist visas are issued by Australian consular offices abroad; they are generally valid for a stay of either three or six months within a 12 month period. The three-month visas are free; for the six-month visa there is a $35 fee.

The visa is valid for use within 12 months of the date of issue and can be used to enter and leave Australia several times within those 12 months.

When you apply for a visa, you need to present your passport and a passport photo and sign an undertaking that you have an onward or return ticket and 'sufficient funds' to cover your stay – the latter is obviously open to interpretation.

You can also apply for a long-stay visa, which is a multiple-entry, four-year visa which allows for stays of up to six months on each visit. These also cost $35.

Working Visas

Young, single visitors from the UK, Canada, Korea, Holland and Japan may be eligible for a 'working holiday' visa. 'Young' is fairly loosely interpreted as around 18 to 25, although exceptions are made and people up to 30, and young married couples without children, may be given a working holiday visa.

A working holiday visa allows for a visit of up to 12 months, but the emphasis is meant to be on casual employment rather than a full-time job, so you are only supposed to work for three months. This visa can only be applied for outside Australia (preferably but not necessarily in your country of citizenship), and you can't change from a visitor visa to a working holiday visa.

Conditions attached to a working holiday visa include having sufficient funds for an onward ticket and taking out private medical insurance. (See the Health section for any reciprocal health care rights.) A fee of about $140 is payable when you apply for the visa.

See the section on Work later in this chapter for details of what sort of work is available and where.

Visa Extensions

The maximum stay allowed to visitors in Australia is one year, including extensions.

Visa extensions are made through Department of Immigration & Ethnic Affairs offices in Australia and, as the process takes some time, it's best to apply about a month before your visa expires. There is an application fee of $135 – and even if they turn down your application they can still keep your money! To qualify for an extension you are required to take out private medical insurance to cover the period of the extension, and have a ticket out of the country. Some offices are more strict in enforcing these conditions than others.

If you want to remain in Australia in the long term, the books *Temporary to Permanent Resident in Australia* and *Practical Guide to Obtaining Permanent Residence in Australia*, both published by Longman Cheshire, might be useful.

CUSTOMS

When entering Australia you can bring most articles in free of duty provided that Customs is satisfied they are for personal use and that you'll be taking them with you when you leave. There's also the usual duty-free per person quota of one litre of alcohol, 250 cigarettes and dutiable goods up to the value of A$400.

With regard to prohibited goods, there are two areas you need to pay particular attention to. Number one is, of course, dope – Australian Customs has a positive mania about the stuff and can be extremely efficient when it comes to finding it. Unless you want to make first-hand investigations of conditions in Australian jails, don't bring any with you. This particularly applies if you are arriving from South-East Asia or the Indian Subcontinent.

Problem two is animal and plant quarantine. You will be asked to declare all goods of animal or vegetable origin – wooden spoons, straw hats, the lot – and show them to an official. The authorities are naturally keen to prevent weeds, pests or diseases getting into the country – Australia has so far managed to escape many of the agricultural pests and diseases prevalent in other parts of the world. Flowers are also unpopular, along with fresh food, particularly meat, sausages, fruit and vegetables. There are also restrictions on taking fruit and vegetables between states.

Weapons and firearms are either prohibited or require a permit and safety testing. Other restricted goods include products (such as ivory) made from protected wildlife species, non-approved telecommunications devices and live animals.

MONEY

Currency

Australia's currency is the Australian dollar, which comprises 100 cents. There are coins for 5c, 10c, 20c, 50c, $1 and $2, and paper notes for $5, $10, $20, $50 and $100. Nasty little indestructible plastic notes have replaced the old paper notes except for the $100 note (so far).

Although the smallest coin in circulation is 5c, prices are still marked in single cents, and then rounded to the nearest 5c when you come to pay.

There are no notable restrictions on importing or exporting currency or travellers' cheques except that you may not take out more than $5000 in cash without prior approval.

Exchange Rates

The Australian dollar fluctuates quite markedly against the US dollar, but seems to stay pretty much around the 60c to 70c mark – a disaster for Australians travelling overseas but a real bonus for inbound visitors.

Canada	C$1	=	$0.94
France	FF 10	=	$2.54
Germany	DM 1	=	$0.86
Hong Kong	HK$10	=	$1.66
Japan	¥100	=	$1.19
New Zealand	NZ$1	=	$0.87
United Kingdom	UK£1	=	$1.96
United States	US$1	=	$1.28

Changing Money

Changing foreign currency or travellers' cheques is no problem at almost any bank. It's done quickly and efficiently.

Travellers' Cheques

There is a variety of ways to carry your money around. If your stay is limited then travellers' cheques are the most straightforward way, and they generally enjoy a better exchange rate than foreign cash in Australia.

American Express, Thomas Cook and other well-known international brands of travellers' cheques are all widely used in Australia. A passport will usually be adequate for identification; it would be sensible to carry a driver's license, credit cards or some other form of identification in case of problems.

Fees for changing foreign currency travellers' cheques seem to vary from bank to bank and year to year. Currently of the 'big four' (ANZ, Commonwealth, National and Westpac), ANZ and Westpac do not charge any fee, while at the National it's $5 and the Commonwealth $6 per transaction, regardless of the amount or number of cheques.

Buying Australian dollar travellers' cheques is an option worth considering. These can be exchanged immediately at the bank without being converted from a foreign currency and incurring commissions, fees and exchange rate fluctuations.

Credit Cards

Credit cards are widely accepted in Australia and provide an alternative to carrying large numbers of travellers' cheques. Visa, MasterCard, Diners Club and American Express are all widely accepted.

Cash advances from credit cards are available over the counter and from many automatic teller machines (ATMs), depending on the card.

If you're planning to rent cars while travelling around Australia, a credit card makes life much simpler; they're looked upon with much greater favour by rent-a-car agencies than nasty old cash, and many agencies simply won't rent you a vehicle if you don't have a card.

Banks

Banks exist in most towns in Tasmania, but in the smaller centres they are often only open one or two days a week. The most common bank is Tasmania's own Trust Bank. There are very few branches of the Commonwealth Bank, but as post offices act as agents an account with them can be useful; but, like banks, many post offices in the small towns are only open for a few hours on weekdays. Automatic teller machines (ATMs) are slowly starting to spread across the state. Apart from Hobart they mainly exist in Launceston and the major towns across the north coast. They are not yet available on the west coast and only in St Helens on the east coast.

Local Bank Accounts If you're planning to stay longer than just a month or so, it's worth considering other ways of handling money that give you more flexibility and are more economical. This applies equally to Australians setting off to travel around the country.

Most travellers these days opt for an account which includes a cash card, which you can use to access your cash from ATMs found all over Australia. You put your card in the machine, key in your personal identification number (PIN), and then withdraw funds from your account. Westpac, ANZ, National and Commonwealth banks have branches with ATMs in Hobart, Launceston, Devonport and Burnie.

ATM machines can be used day or night, and it is possible to use the machines of some other banks: Westpac ATMs accept Commonwealth Bank cards and vice versa; National Bank ATMs accept ANZ cards and vice versa. There is a limit on how much you can withdraw from your account. This varies from bank to bank but is usually $400 to $500 per day.

Many businesses, such as service stations, supermarkets and convenience stores, are linked into the EFTPOS system (Electronic Funds Transfer at Point Of Sale), and at places with this facility you can use your bank cash card to pay for services or purchases direct, and sometimes withdraw cash as well. Bank cash cards and credit cards can also be used to make local, STD and international phone calls in special public telephones, found in most towns throughout the country.

Opening an account at an Australian bank is not all that easy, especially for overseas visitors. A points system operates and you need to score a minimum of 100 points before being given the privilege of letting the bank take your money. Passports, driver's licenses, birth certificates and other 'major' IDs earn you 40 points; minor ones such as credit cards get you 20 points. Just like a game show really! However, if visitors apply to open an account during the first six weeks of their visit, just showing their passport will suffice.

If you don't have an Australian Tax File Number (see the section on Work later in this chapter), interest earned from your funds will be taxed at the rate of 48% and this money goes straight to our old mate, the Deputy Commissioner of Taxation.

Costs

Compared to the USA, Canada and European countries, Australia is cheaper in some ways and more expensive in others. Manufactured goods tend to be more expensive: if they are imported they have all the additional costs of transport and duties, and if they're locally manufactured they suffer from the extra costs entailed in making things in comparatively small quantities. Thus you pay more for clothes, cars and other manufactured items. On the other hand, food is both high in quality and low in cost.

The biggest expense in any visit to Tasmania is the cost of actually getting over Bass Strait. You only have two choices; to fly or catch the ferry. Either way you'll be a couple of hundred dollars out of pocket before arriving.

On average you can expect to spend about $30 per day if you budget fiercely and *always* take the cheapest option; $50 gives you much greater flexibility. Obviously if you stay for longer periods in each place and can take advantage of discounts given on long-term accommodation, this helps to keep your costs to a minimum.

Tipping

In Australia tipping isn't entrenched in the way it is in the USA or Europe. It's only customary to tip in more expensive restaurants and only then if you want to. If the service has been especially good and you decide to leave a tip, 10% of the bill is the usual amount. Taxi drivers don't expect tips (of course, they don't hurl it back at you if you decide to leave the change).

WHEN TO GO

Tasmania is most popular during the summer months, as it's warm enough for swimming and it's great to be outdoors. Most days are fine in the major towns and cities. The exception is the south-west and west where only about half the days are fine; the other days are often rainy and cloudy.

The summer months from December to February are the busiest times for tourism. Accommodation is heavily booked (and often more expensive) and the popular venues and restaurants are more crowded, but as compensation you can expect to see an amazing variety of sporting events, including the Hobart to Sydney yacht race.

Winter is often cold, wet and cloudy across much of the state. The best weather is then along the east and north-east coasts where sunny days are still common. The great advantage of winter is that it feels like you have the entire island state all to yourself as there are almost no tourists.

Spring is the windiest time in Tasmania. Temperatures in early September are still quite cold and the weather can be changeable. It is not unusual for the hills around Hobart, especially Mt Wellington, to experience the occasional snowfall at this time of year. Spring is highlighted by the profusion of colour from the many varieties of daffodils, tulips and lavender which are grown in the northern part of the state. The *Blooming Tasmania* brochure, available from Tasmania Travel & Information Centres, outlines all the floral festivals and horticultural events available at this time of the year.

Autumn is often pleasant, with mild temperatures, and is the time of year when many festivals take place (see the Cultural Events section of this chapter for more information). In late April to early May, the deciduous beech changes from mid-green to glorious gold and red. It can be seen in Mt Field and Cradle Mountain-Lake St Clair national parks. Towards the end of autumn, the days (even sunny ones) are usually quite cold and windy.

The other major consideration when travelling is school holidays. Australian families take to the road (and air) en masse at these times and many places are booked out (Tasmania is one of the popular destinations), prices rise and things generally get a bit crazy. Holidays vary somewhat from year to year, but the main holiday period is from mid-December to late January; the other two-week periods are roughly early to mid-

April, late June to mid-July, and late September to early October.

WHAT TO BRING

Generally, Australians are casual dressers (shorts and T-shirts are very common) and in most cases neat, casual clothes will suffice in most hotels and restaurants. The casinos and more expensive restaurants will however require long trousers, a neat shirt and shoes for men (ties and jackets are rarely needed).

You'll definitely need a warm jumper (pullover, sweater) or jacket, as well as something which is wind-proof and water-proof, no matter at what time of the year you visit Tasmania. The climate is quite cool (some call it freezing) even when the sun shines.

Tasmania gets a lot of UV radiation through a hole in the ozone layer, and you'll find that safe sun is as important a public issue as safe sex. When the sun does come out, it is very strong, so you'll need a good sunscreen (15+) or good old zinc cream, which comes in a multitude of colours to match any occasion. A hat and sunglasses are also essential.

If you are intending to bushwalk, you should bring a sturdy, comfortable pair of boots. The ubiquitous rubber sandals known as thongs (easily purchased here, and known as jandals or flipflops elsewhere) are suitable beach or casual wear, but aren't allowed in most pubs or restaurants and are not good for sightseeing or walking long distances.

TOURIST OFFICES
Local Tourist Offices

The Tasmanian Travel & Information Centres are privately run, and the Hobart centre is on the corner of Davey and Elizabeth Sts (☎ (03) 6230 8233). There are also centres in Launceston, Devonport and Burnie. As well as supplying brochures, price lists, maps and other information, they will often book transport, tours and accommodation for you. Unfortunately, information desks are not staffed at the airports and, furthermore, the opening hours of the city offices are very much of the 9 am to 5 pm weekdays and Saturday morning only variety.

The Department of Tourism publishes an invaluable, bi-monthly newspaper called *Tasmanian Travelways* which is available at all information centres around the state. Along with interesting articles, it is packed with information, including comprehensive listings of accommodation, visitor activities, public transport, connecting transport facilities and vehicle hire, all with an indication of current costs throughout the state and, best of all, it's free!

The travel centres also stock a host of free tourist literature, including the monthly magazine *This Week in Tasmania* and the excellent *Let's Talk About ...* leaflets, which provide in-depth information about particular towns or areas. The annual *Tasmania Visitors Guide*, which has a good fold-out touring map of Tasmania, is particularly useful and is also free.

The latest backpackers information is available from the magazine *For Backpackers By Backpackers*, available from some hostels and travel agents. While the Tasmania section is brief, it can be useful for discovering new budget accommodation.

One of the best maps of the island is produced by the Royal Automobile Club of Tasmania (RACT) and costs $3. It's available from any Tasmanian Travel & Information Centre or RACT office.

Interstate Tourist Offices

On the mainland, there are branches of the government-run Tasmanian Travel centre in:

Australian Capital Territory
  165 City Walk, Canberra 2601 (☎ (06) 209 2133)
New South Wales
  149 King St, Sydney 2000 (☎ (02) 9202 2022)
Queensland
  40 Queen St, Brisbane 4000 (☎ (07) 3405 4122)
South Australia
  32 King William St, Adelaide 5000 (☎ (08) 8400 5533)
Victoria
  256 Collins St, Melbourne 3000 (☎ (03) 9206 7922)

These travel centres have information on just about everything you need to know about Tasmania and are also able to book accommodation, tours and even airline, boat and bus tickets.

Overseas Reps

The Australian Tourist Commission (ATC) is the government body which informs potential visitors about the country. There's a very definite split between promotion outside Australia and inside it. The ATC is strictly an external operator; it does minimal promotion within the country and has little contact with visitors who are in Australia. Within the country, tourist promotion is handled by state or local tourist offices.

ATC offices overseas have a useful free booklet called *On the Loose* which details things of interest for backpackers around Australia.

The ATC also recently published *Australia Unplugged*, which is a good introduction to Australia for young people, giving some information about the country in general and snapshots of the major cities.

The ATC also publishes a number of fact sheets on various topics, such as camping, fishing, skiing, disabled travel and national parks – and these can be a useful introduction to the subject. It also provides a handy map of the country for a small fee. This literature is intended for distribution overseas only; if you want copies, get them before you come to Australia.

The ATC also maintains a number of helplines, which independent travellers can ring or fax to get specific information about Australia.

Addresses of the ATC offices for literature requests are:

Hong Kong
    Suite 1501, Central Plaza, 18 Harbour Rd, Wanchai (☎ 2802 7700)
    Helpline: ☎ 2802 7817; fax 2802 8211
Japan
    Australian Business Centre, New Otani Garden Court Bldg 28F, 4-1 Kioi-cho, Chiyoda-ku, Tokyo 102 (☎ (03) 5214 0720)
    Helpline: ☎ (03) 5214 0730; fax 5214 0719

    Twin 21 MID Tower 30F, 2-1-61 Shiromi, Chuo-ku, Osaka 540 (☎ (06) 946 2503)
    Helpline: (☎ (06) 946 2500; fax 946 2473
New Zealand
    Level 13, 44-48 Emily Place, Auckland 1 (☎ (09) 379 9594; fax 307 3117)
    Helpline: ☎ (09) 527 1629; fax 377 9562
Singapore
    Suite 1703, United Square, 101 Thomson Rd, Singapore 1103 (☎ 255 4555)
    Helpline: ☎ 250 6277; fax 253 8431
UK
    Gemini House, 10-18 Putney Hill, London SW15 6AA (☎ (0181) 780 2227; fax 780 1496)
USA
    Suite 1200, 2121 Ave of the Stars, Los Angeles, CA 90067 (☎ (310) 552 1988; fax 552-1215)
    25th floor, 100 Park Ave, New York, NY 10017 (☎ (212) 687 6300; fax 661 3340)
    Helpline: ☎ (708) 296 4900; fax 635 3718

USEFUL ORGANISATIONS

There are many organisations in Tasmania which you may find useful during your visit. Most have their head office in Hobart. If you are looking for a particular group, check in the Yellow Pages telephone book under 'Organisations'.

Automobile Associations

The Royal Automobile Club of Tasmania (RACT) is on the corner of Patrick and Murray Sts in Hobart (☎ 6238 2200). It provides an emergency breakdown service and has reciprocal arrangements with services in other Australian states and some from overseas. It also provides literature, excellent maps and detailed guides to accommodation and camping grounds.

Department of Environment & Land Management

The Department is located at 134 Macquarie St, Hobart and manages national and state parks, maps and literature. Also located at the same address is the Department's Land Information Sales Centre (☎ 6233 6191). You can obtain brochures and leaflets on parks from the ranger stationed here as well as buy detailed maps (TASMAP) and other useful information.

Australian Conservation Foundation

The Australian Conservation Foundation (ACF) (☎ 6223 8750) at 132 Davey St, Hobart, is the largest non-government organisation involved in conservation. It covers a wide range of issues, including the depletion of the ozone layer, preservation of rainforests, the problems of land degradation and protection of the Antarctic. It frequently works in conjunction with the Wilderness Society and other conservation groups.

Wilderness Society

The Tasmanian Wilderness Society was formed by conservationists who had been unsuccessful in preventing the damming of Lake Pedder in south-west Tasmania and who were determined to prevent the destruction of the Franklin River. In 1983, after the High Court decided against the damming of the Franklin, the group changed its name to the Wilderness Society because of its Australia-wide focus on wilderness issues.

The Wilderness Society is involved in issues concerning protection of the Australian wilderness, such as forest management and logging. Like the ACF, government funding is only a small percentage of its income, the rest coming from memberships, donations, the shops and merchandising. In Tasmania, it can be contacted at 130 Davey St, Hobart 7000 (☎ 6234 9366).

Australian Trust for Conservation Volunteers

This non-political, non-profit group organises practical conservation projects (such as tree planting, track construction and flora & fauna surveys) for volunteers to take part in. Travellers are welcome and it's an excellent way to get involved with the conservation movement and, at the same time, visit some of the more interesting areas of the country. Past volunteers have found themselves working in places such as Tasmania, Kakadu in the Northern Territory, and Fraser Island in Queensland.

Most projects are either for a weekend or a week and all food, transport and accommodation is supplied in return for a small contribution to help cover costs. Most travellers who take part in ATCV join a Banksia Package, which lasts six weeks and includes six different projects. The cost is $650, and further weeks can be added for $105.

Contact the head office (☎ (03) 5333 1483) at PO Box 423, Ballarat, Vic 3350 for details.

National Trust

The National Trust is dedicated to preserving historic buildings in all parts of Australia. The Trust actually owns a number of buildings throughout the country which are open to the public. Because of the large number of well-preserved buildings in Tasmania the National Trust has many sites around the state.

The National Trust also produces some excellent literature, including a fine series of walking-tour guides. These guides are often available from local tourist offices or from National Trust offices and are usually free whether you're a member of the National Trust or not. Membership is well worth considering, however, because it entitles you to free entry to any National Trust property for your year of membership. If you're a dedicated visitor of old buildings this could soon pay for itself. Annual membership costs $44 for individuals ($31 concession) and $62 for families ($44 concession), and includes the monthly or quarterly magazine put out by the state organisation that you join. The state head office is in Franklin House, 413 Hobart Rd, Launceston 7249 (☎ 6344 6233).

ANZSES

The Australian & New Zealand Scientific Exploration Society is a non-profit organisation which undertakes scientific expeditions into remote areas. It provides young people with the opportunity to participate in the collection of scientific data and the experience of living and working in areas generally not accessible to the average traveller. Each year over 100 volunteers are sent into the field, always under the guidance of an experienced leader.

Recent studies have included flora &

fauna gathering in south-west Tasmania and other areas. The ANZSES postal address and phone number is PO Box 174, Albert Park, Victoria 3206 (☎ (03) 9690 5455).

Federation of Tasmanian Walking Clubs

The Federation is the umbrella body that represents bushwalking clubs in Tasmania. The clubs themselves conduct programmed bushwalks (day, weekend and longer), and will allow visitors on some of their trips. You'll need to attend a meeting or write to the club to be able to book on a walk. Due to the popularity of bushwalking, the clubs and the Federation no longer answer queries about walking opportunities in the state. There is now a central enquiry point at the Department of Environment & Land Management at 134 Macquarie St, Hobart (☎ 6233 6191) which provides brochures and information booklets about walking in the state. The Department employs many experienced bushwalkers and the information is helpful and up-to-date. If you are staying for a longer period and wish to attend a club meeting, details of locations and times can be obtained from local bushwalking shops.

BUSINESS HOURS

Most shops close at 5 or 5.30 pm on weekdays, and either noon or 5 pm on Saturday. In some places Sunday trading is starting to catch on, but it's currently limited to the major cities. In the larger towns there is usually one late shopping night each week, when the doors stay open until 9 or 9.30 pm. Usually it's Thursday or Friday night.

Banks are open from 9.30 am to 4 pm Monday to Thursday, and until 5 pm on Friday, except in small towns where they may only open one or two days a week. Some city branches are open from 8 am to 6 pm Monday to Friday. Some are also open to 9 pm on Friday. Of course there are some exceptions to the unremarkable opening hours and all sorts of places stay open late and all weekend – particularly milk bars, convenience stores, supermarkets, delis and city bookshops.

HOLIDAYS

The Christmas holiday season is part of the long summer school vacation and the time you are most likely to find accommodation booked out and long queues. There are three other shorter school holiday periods during the year but they vary by a week or two from year to year, falling from early to mid-April, late June to mid-July, and late September to early October.

Like school holidays, public holidays vary quite a bit from state to state. The following is a list of the main national and state public holidays:

New Year's Day
    1 January
Australia Day
    26 January
Regatta Day
    second Tuesday in February (southern Tasmania)
Launceston Cup
    last Wednesday in February (Launceston only)
Eight Hour Day
    first Monday in March
King Island Show
    second Tuesday in March (King Island only)
Easter
    Good Friday, Easter Saturday, Sunday, Monday & Tuesday
Anzac Day
    25 April
Queen's Birthday
    second Monday in June
Burnie Show
    first Friday in October (Burnie only)
Launceston Show
    second Thursday in October (Launceston only)
Flinders Island Show
    third Friday in October (Flinders Island only)
Hobart Show
    fourth Thursday in October (southern Tasmania)
Recreation Day
    second Thursday in November (northern Tasmania)
Christmas Day
    25 December
Boxing Day
    26 December

CULTURAL EVENTS

Major annual festivals and events include the following:

January

Sydney to Hobart Yacht Race – The arrival (29 December to 2 January) in Hobart of the yachts competing in this annual New Year race is celebrated with a mardi gras. The competitors in the *Melbourne to Hobart Yacht Race* arrive on the same days.

Hobart Summer Festival – Starts with the completion of the yacht races and lasts for 10 days at Hobart's waterfront.

Huon Valley Folk Festival – Popular music festival in a great setting by the Huon River.

Australia Day – this national holiday, commemorating the arrival of the First Fleet, in 1788, is observed on 26 January.

Beating Retreat – A military theme festival held at Port Arthur which is very popular – bookings essential.

Forest Festival – Jackie's Marsh is the venue for this festival which is held over the Australia Day weekend and has become an important event for those interested in conservation.

February

Royal Hobart Regatta – This is the largest aquatic carnival in the southern hemisphere and is held over four days, with boat races and other activities.

National Penny Farthing Championships – Evandale holds the strangest of bicycle races when people on these tall bikes race around the town. There are plenty of spills and other entertainment.

Cradle Mountain Overland Run – A hardy band of people attempt to run the entire 80 kilometres of the Overland Track in one day. If you are walking it, don't get put off by the speeding runners – they don't get to enjoy the views.

March

Fingal Valley Coal Shovelling Festival – The small town of Fingal hosts this unusual festival. See some unusual events like roof bolting, coal shovelling and double-handed sawing.

Food and Wine Fun Festa – Held at Devonport, many of the better restaurants on the northern coast participate in this popular event which also has live music.

April

Anzac Day – This is a national public holiday, on 25 April, commemorating the landing of Anzac troops at Gallipoli in 1915. Memorial marches by the returned soldiers of both world wars and the veterans of Korea and Vietnam are held all over the country.

Three Peaks Race – A combined event where the competitors have to sail their yachts and also run up three of Tasmania's higher mountains. Starts from Beauty Point north of Launceston.

Targa Tasmania – A car rally for exotic cars which runs for one week around the whole state. It is popular and receives wide press coverage.

May

Bicheno Festival – Local festival held on May Day.

June

Suncoast Jazz Festival – The east coast has the mildest winter weather in the state and is further warmed by this popular three-day jazz festival.

July

Southern Cross Marathon – Richmond hosts a full and half marathon running race in early July.

September

Blooming Tasmania – Lasting for three months, this is more of a coordinated set of festivals and displays rather than a single event. A special brochure is produced every year detailing when each festival and garden is open to the public.

Tasmanian Football League Grand Final – A visit to a grand final is an exciting and interesting way to see this fast paced game. The final is held in North Hobart.

October

Royal Shows – The royal agricultural and horticultural shows of Hobart, Burnie, Flinders Island and Launceston are held during this month.

Herald Sun Tour – A major two week professional bicycle race around Victoria and Tasmania. The local section is mainly through tough hilly sections on the northern coast.

Melbourne to Burnie Yacht Race – The fourth largest race in Australia dashes across Bass Strait in early October.

Wynyard Tulip Festival – At this time of the year, the tulips are in flower and you can also visit the tulip farm at nearby Table Cape as well.

Derby River Derby – Around 10,000 people cram into this old mining town to watch the assorted fleet raft down the river. There are no rules to the race and everybody usually gets wet but has a great time.

November

Melbourne Cup – On the first Tuesday in November, the whole country comes to a virtual standstill for the three minutes or so when Australia's premier horse race is run (in Melbourne). Even Tasmania stops while the Cup runs.

Tasmanian Irish Festival – Runs for several weeks at Port Arthur and is celebrated with music, song and dances from Irish entertainers.

December

Carols by Candlelight – Evening services are held in both Hobart and Launceston before Christmas.

Latrobe Wheel & Latrobe Gift – Professional bicycle races held when most other towns are having Christmas meals.

POST & COMMUNICATIONS
Post

Major post offices are open from 9 am to 5 pm Monday to Friday. There are also many post office agencies in the small towns with variable opening hours; these are often open only a couple of hours daily or in some cases just two days a week. You can often buy stamps from newsagencies and local shops.

In the major towns the post offices also have stamp vending machines. You must have the correct change.

Sending Letters Australia's postal services are relatively efficient but not too cheap. It costs 45c to send a standard letter or postcard within Australia.

Air-mail letters/postcards cost 75/70c to New Zealand, 85/80c to Singapore and Malaysia, 95/90c to Hong Kong and India, $1.05/95c to the USA and Canada, and $1.20/1 to Europe and the UK.

Sending Parcels The rates for posting parcels are not too extortionate. By sea mail a 1/2/5 kg parcel costs $14.50/18/28.50 to New Zealand and India, $15/19/31 to the USA, Europe or the UK. Each kg over five kg costs $3.50 for New Zealand and India, $4 for the USA, Europe or the UK, with a maximum of 20 kg for all destinations. Air-mail rates are considerably more expensive.

Receiving Mail The poste restante service at the GPO in Hobart is quite good. While it can be busy, particularly in the summer months, you usually do not have to wait too long. The GPO will hold your mail for one month before returning it to the sender. Alternatively, you can pay a $5 monthly fee to have your mail forwarded to you within Australia (or by surface mail overseas). All post offices will hold mail for visitors, so it could be more convenient for you to have your mail sent to a suburban post office – just have it addressed care of that post office and include the postcode. If you have an American Express Card or buy Amex travellers' cheques, you can have mail sent to you care

of American Express Travel (☎ 6234 3711), 74a Liverpool St, Hobart 7000.

Telephone

Local Calls Local calls from public phones cost 40c for an unlimited amount of time. You can make local calls from gold or blue phones – often found in shops, hotels, bars, etc – and from payphone booths. Local calls from private phones cost 30c. Many public phones accept the convenient Telecom Phonecards. The cards come in $5, $10, $20 and $50 denominations, and are available from retail outlets such as newsagents and pharmacies which display the Phonecard logo. You keep using the card until the value has been used in calls.

Tasmanian Area Codes All Tasmanian telephone numbers have recently been changed to an eight digit number and there is no longer any need to add an STD number when ringing elsewhere within Tasmania. The STD prefix for Tasmania is now 03, the same as for Victoria. Numbers start with 62, 63 or 64 denoting the area in which they are located as follows: 62 is Hobart and Southern, 63 is Launceston and the north-east and 64 is the west and north-west.

STD Calls It's also possible to make long-distance (STD – Subscriber Trunk Dialling) calls from virtually any public phone. If you're not using a Telecom Phonecard, have plenty of coins handy and be prepared to feed them through at a fair old rate. STD calls are cheaper in off-peak hours – see the front of a local telephone book for the different standard rates. With deregulation of the telephone system there is a price war on and even larger discounts are offered at times – watch the media advertising for such specials.

Some public phones are set up to take only bank cash cards or credit cards, and these too are convenient, although you need to keep an eye on how much the call is costing as it can quickly mount up. The minimum charge for a call on one of these phones is $1.20.

STD calls are cheaper at night. In ascending order, calls cost:

Economy – from 6 pm Saturday to 8 am Monday; 10 pm to 8 am every night
Night – from 6 to 10 pm Monday to Friday
Day – from 8 am to 6 pm Monday to Saturday

International Calls From most STD phones you can also make ISD (International Subscriber Dialling) calls. Dialling ISD you can get through to overseas numbers almost as quickly as you can to local numbers and, if your call is brief, it needn't cost very much.

All you do is dial 0011 for overseas, the country code (44 for Britain, 1 for the USA or Canada, 64 for New Zealand), the city code (171 or 181 for London, 212 for New York, etc.), and then the telephone number. And have a Phonecard, credit card or plenty of coins to hand.

It's also possible to make ISD calls with Optus rather than Telstra. The fee structure varies slightly with the two companies, and if you are phoning one country constantly it may be worth comparing the two. This option is only available from private phones in certain areas. Phone Optus (☎ toll-free 1800 500 005) for details on how to access their services.

International calls from Australia are among the cheapest you'll find anywhere. A Telecom call to the USA or Britain costs $1.35 a minute ($1.03 off-peak); New Zealand is $1.09 a minute ($0.72 off peak). Off-peak times, if available, vary depending on the destination – see the back of any White Pages telephone book, or call ☎ 0102 for more details. Sunday is often the cheapest day to ring.

Country Direct is a service which gives travellers in Australia direct access to operators in nearly 50 countries, to make collect or credit card calls. For a full list of the countries hooked into this system, check any local White Pages telephone book. They include: Canada (☎ 1800 881 150), Germany (☎ 1800 881 490), Japan (☎ 1800 881 810), New Zealand (☎ 1800 881 640), the UK (☎ 1800 881 440) and the USA (☎ 1800 881 011).

Toll-Free Calls Many businesses and some government departments operate a toll-free service, so no matter where you are ringing from around the country, it's a free call. These numbers have the prefix 1800 and we've listed them wherever possible throughout the book. Many companies, such as the airlines, have six-digit numbers beginning with 13, and these are charged at the rate of a local call.

Mobile Phones Phone numbers with the prefixes 014, 015, 016, 018 or 041 are mobile or car phones. The three mobile operators are the government's Telstra, and the two private companies Optus and Vodaphone. Calls to mobile numbers are charged at special STD rates and can be expensive.

Information Calls Other odd numbers you may come across are numbers starting with 0055 and 190. The 0055 numbers, usually recorded information services and the like, are provided by private companies, and your call is charged in multiples of 25c (40c from public phones) at a rate selected by the provider (Premium 70c per minute, Value 55c per minute, Budget 35c per minute).

Numbers beginning with 190 are also information services, but they are charged on a fixed fee basis, which can vary from as little as 35c to as much as $30!

Telegram (Cable)

Local telegrams are no longer available. International telegrams cost a flat rate of $7.50 plus 60c per word, including the address. Delivery is normally by the country's postal system (usually next day), but in countries where a same-day courier delivery can be arranged, it costs an extra $16. It's almost always cheaper to send a fax.

Fax

All post offices (but few agencies) send faxes. If you send a fax to another fax machine it costs $4, which is also the rate for sending a fax to a postal address. For the latter, the fax is sent to the local post office and delivered in the normal mail service, usually the next day. You can send a same-day fax to a postal address if you deliver it by 1 pm ($12), and there's a two-hour courier delivery service open until 4 pm ($20). These rates apply to the first page of any fax. Subsequent pages cost $1 no matter which service you use.

E-mail

If you want to surf the Net, even if it's only to access your e-mail, there are service providers in all Australia's capital cities, and in many regional areas too. On-line costs vary, but a typical price structure is a $25 joining fee then $5 per hour on-line, with no minimum charge. Major players include:

Australia On Line
 (☎ toll-free 1800 621258;
  http://www.ozon-line.com.au)
On Australia (Microsoft Network)
 (☎ (02) 9934 9000)
Oz Email
 (☎ (02) 9391 0480;
  http://www.ozemail.com.au)
Pegasus Networks
 (☎ toll-free 1800 812 812;
  http://www.peg.apc.org)

CompuServe users who want to access the service locally should phone CompuServe (☎ toll-free 1800 025 240) to get the local log-in numbers.

TIME

Australia is divided into three time zones: Western Standard Time is plus eight hours from GMT/UTC (Western Australia), Central Standard Time is plus 9½ hours (Northern Territory, South Australia) and Eastern Standard Time is plus 10 (Tasmania, Victoria, New South Wales, Queensland). When it's noon in Western Australia it's 1.30 pm in the Northern Territory and South Australia and 2 pm in the rest of the country.

During the summer things get slightly screwed up as daylight saving time (when clocks are put forward an hour) does not operate in Western Australia or Queensland, and in Tasmania it starts a month earlier and finishes up to a month later than in the other states. The main problem occurs with airline schedules and it pays to read your ticket carefully as the time shown will be correct but might be different from the published schedules in the crossover months.

ELECTRICITY

Voltage is 220-240 V and the plugs are three-pin, but not the same as British three-pin plugs. Users of electric shavers or hairdryers should note that, apart from in fancy hotels, it's difficult to find converters to take either US flat two-pin plugs or the European round two-pin plugs. Adapters for British plugs can be found in good hardware shops, chemists and travel agents.

WEIGHTS & MEASURES

Australia uses the metric system. Petrol and milk are sold by the litre, apples and potatoes by the kg, distance is measured by the metre or km, and speed limits are in km per hour (km/h).

If you need help with metric there's a conversion table at the back of this book.

BOOKS

In almost any bookshop in Tasmania you'll find a section devoted to Australiana, with books on every Australian subject you care to mention. Hobart and Launceston have quite a good range of bookshops with Ellison Hawker, Fullers Bookshop and Birchalls being the largest and best known.

At the Wilderness Society shop in The Galleria, 33 Salamanca Place, Hobart you'll find a good range of wildlife posters, calendars and books.

History

For a good introduction to Australian history, read *A Short History of Australia*, a most accessible and informative general history by the late Manning Clark, the respected Aussie historian, or *The Fatal Shore*, Robert Hughes's bestselling account of the convict era.

Finding Australia, by Russel Ward, traces the story of the early days from the first Aboriginal arrivals up to 1821. It's strong on Aboriginal people, women and the full story of foreign exploration, not just Captain Cook's role. There's lots of fascinating detail, including information about the appalling crooks who ran the early colony for long periods, and it's intended to be the first of a series.

The Fatal Impact by Alan Moorehead begins with the voyages of James Cook, regarded as one of the greatest and most humane explorers, and tells the tragic story of the European impact on Australia, Tahiti and Antarctica in the years that followed Captain Cook's great voyages of discovery. It details how good intentions and the economic imperatives of the time led to disaster, corruption and annihilation.

Aboriginal People

There is plenty of literature available on the massacre of Tasmania's Aboriginal people – among the best reads is *Blood on the Wattle* by Bruce Elder. Brian Plomley's books are well researched – *The Tasmanian Aborigines* incorporates most of his writing and is available at the museums in Hobart and Launceston. In *Fate of a Free People* Henry Reynolds re-examines history from an Aboriginal perspective and puts a case for Tasmanian Aboriginal land rights.

For information on Australia's Aboriginal people as a whole, *The Australian Aborigines* by Kenneth Maddock is a good cultural summary. The award-winning *Triumph of the Nomads* by Geoffrey Blainey chronicles the life of Australia's original inhabitants, and convincingly demolishes the myth that Aboriginal people were 'primitive' people trapped on a hostile continent. They were in fact extremely successful in adapting to and overcoming the difficulties presented by the climate and resources (or seeming lack of them) – the book's an excellent read.

For a sympathetic historical account of what's happened to the original Australians since Europeans arrived, read *Aboriginal Australians* by Richard Broome. *A Change of Ownership* by Mildred Kirk covers similar ground to Broome's book, but does so more concisely, focusing on the land rights movement and its historical background.

The Other Side of the Frontier by Henry Reynolds uses historical records to give a vivid account of an Aboriginal view of the arrival and takeover of Australia by Europeans. His *With the White People* identifies the essential Aboriginal contributions to the survival of the early White settlers. *My Place*, Sally Morgan's prize-winning autobiography, traces her discovery of her Aboriginal heritage. *The Fringe Dwellers* by Nene Gare describes just what it's like to be an Aborigine growing up in a White-dominated society.

Don't Take Your Love to Town by Ruby Langford and *My People* by Oodgeroo Noonuccal (Kath Walker) are also recommended reading for people interested in the experiences of Aboriginal people.

Fiction

You don't need to worry about bringing a few good novels from home for your trip to Tasmania; the state has plenty of its own literature to dip into. See Literature in the Arts & Culture section of the Facts about Tasmania chapter for some suggestions.

Travel Accounts

The Ribbon and the Ragged Square by Linda Christmas is an intelligent, sober account of a nine-month investigatory trip around Oz – including Tassie – by a *Guardian* journalist from England. There's lots of background and history as well as first-hand reporting and interviews.

The journals of the early European explorers can be fairly hard-going but make fascinating reading. The hardships that many of these men (and they were virtually all men) endured is nothing short of amazing. These accounts are usually available in the main libraries. Men such as Calder, McKay, Sprent, Frankland, Gould, Innes and many others kept journals that make interesting reading. For a summary of what they achieved, read *Trampled Wilderness* by

Ralph & Kathleen Gowlland which is available in Tasmanian bookshops.

Surfing Guides

The *Surfing and Sailboard Guide to Australia* by Nat Young covers the whole country. Surfing enthusiasts can also look for the expensive coffee-table book *Atlas of Australian Surfing*, by Mark Warren.

Flora & Fauna

Australia's Wonderful Wildlife (Australian Women's Weekly) is the shoestringer's equivalent of a coffee-table book – a cheap paperback with lots of great photos of the animals you didn't see, or those that didn't stay still when you pointed your camera at them.

Bushwalking

Lonely Planet's *Bushwalking in Australia*, by John & Monica Chapman, describes over 35 walks of different lengths and difficulty in every state, including nine in Tasmania. These include easy two-day strolls through Mt Field National Park or around the beaches of Freycinet Peninsula, as well as the Overland Track and more difficult walks such as the 11 to 14 day coastal trek along the South Coast and Port Davey tracks, and three to four day walks to the summits of Frenchmans Cap and Mt Anne.

If you prefer shorter walks of one day or less, the books by Jan Hardy & Bert Elson are worth finding. They produce two books covering the Hobart area, one to Launceston and the north-east and also one to north-west Tasmania. Some other writers also produce some small books on specific areas, like the mines of the west coast, and the Tasman Peninsula.

One well-known book, *100 Walks in Tasmania* by Tyrone Thomas, describes walks around the entire state and includes a wide mixture of short walks and some multi-day longer walks.

If you are coming to Tasmania to complete multi-day walks in the World Heritage Area and wish to do walks other than the ones described in *Bushwalking in Australia*, there are two guides you should read. *South West Tasmania* by John Chapman, and *Cradle Mountain – Lake St Clair & Walls of Jerusalem* by John Chapman & John Siseman describe the major tracks and routes across the wilderness regions.

Souvenir Books

If you want a souvenir of Tasmania, there are always plenty of cheap, glossy books displaying photographs of the tourist regions. For pictures of the World Heritage Area, buy a coffee-table book like *South West Tasmania* by Richard Bennett or *The Mountains of Paradise* by Les Southwell. The Wilderness Shop always has a good range of the latest books about the Franklin River and Lake Pedder.

MAPS

There's no shortage of maps available, although many of them are of average quality. For road maps, the best has always been the map to the state published by the Royal Automobile Club of Tasmania (RACT). The Department of Environment & Land Management also publish an almost identical map which is available at the tourist information offices. Both have main city street maps on the back, making them adequate for most purposes.

If you need street maps of the towns then buy the *Tasmanian Towns Street Atlas* ($25) which is published by the Department of Environment & Land Management. It contains excellent clear maps of every town of significance and is available where TASMAPS are usually sold. There are some other commercially produced city street guides which are second-rate compared to the street atlas.

For bushwalking, ski-touring and other activities which require large-scale maps, the topographic sheets put out by TASMAP are the ones to get. Many of the more popular sheets are available over the counter at shops which sell specialist bushwalking gear and outdoor equipment. TASMAP also has special interest maps, such as daywalks and bushwalks in national parks.

NEWSPAPERS & MAGAZINES

In Hobart, the major daily is *The Mercury* newspaper while for northern Tasmania it's *The Advocate*. They are fairly small papers often with only 40 to 50 pages and have lots of local news as well as major events elsewhere. The major daily papers from the mainland are available at the larger newsagents in Hobart and Launceston.

Good outdoor and adventure magazines which regularly include articles about Tasmania are *Wild*, *Rock* and *Outdoor Australia*, all quarterly publications.

About every two years *The Tasmanian Tramp*, published by the Hobart Walking Club, appears. It is a journal of various trips undertaken by club members and contains valuable information on out-of-the-way walks and articles on conservation, history and humorous episodes.

RADIO & TV

The national advertising-free (so far) TV and radio network is the Australian Broadcasting Corporation (ABC). In most places there are a couple of ABC radio stations and a host of commercial stations, both AM and FM, featuring the whole gamut of radio possibilities, from rock to talkback to 'beautiful music'. Triple J is a government youth FM radio station which broadcasts nationally and is an excellent place to hear music (Australian and overseas) from outside the pop mainstream, and to plug into Australia's youth culture. One interesting station for visitors is the Information Station on the FM band; there is one for Hobart, Launceston and Devonport. It's useful for basic information when entering these towns, but you will soon turn it off as the same tape is repeated every hour.

In Hobart are the ABC, two commercial TV stations (run by Southern Cross and Win Television) and SBS, a government-sponsored multi-cultural TV station. Around the state, the number of TV stations varies from place to place; Tasmania is very hilly and reception of the commercial stations varies. In some remoter towns the ABC may be all you can receive.

ONLINE SERVICES

The World Wide Web is rapidly expanding to become one of the major sources of information on anything you care to name. Although things on the Net change rapidly, some sites which currently provide a range of information on Australia include:

Guide to Australia
> This site, maintained by the Charles Sturt University in NSW, is a mine of information, with links to Australian government departments, weather information, books, maps, etc.
> http://www.csu.edu.au/education/australia.html

The Aussie Index
> A fairly comprehensive list of Australian companies, educational institutions and government departments which maintain Web sites.
> http://www.aussie.com.au/aussie.htm

Australian Government
> The federal government has a site, which is predictably unexciting, but it is wide-ranging and a good source for things like visa information.
> http://www.gov.info.au

National Parks
> Details all the parks and current regulations and is a mine of information if you intend to bushwalk.
> http://www.parks.tas.gov.au

Lonely Planet
> Our own site is not specific to Australia but is still definitely worth a look. Well, we would say that, wouldn't we?
> http://www.lonelyplanet.com.au

FILM & PHOTOGRAPHY

Australian film prices are not too far out of line with those of the rest of the Western world. Including developing, 36-exposure Kodachrome 64 or Fujichrome 100 slide film costs around $25, but with a little shopping around you can find it for around $20 – even less if you buy it in quantity.

There are several camera shops in Hobart and Launceston and standards of camera service are good. Developing standards are also high, with many places offering one-hour developing of print film and similar service for repeat prints. Slide film takes about one week to return from the laboratory.

The best photographs are obtained early in the morning and late in the afternoon. As the sun gets higher, colours begin to appear washed out. You must also allow for the intensity of reflected light when taking shots at coastal locations. Especially in the summer, allow for temperature extremes and do your best to keep film as cool as possible, particularly after exposure.

As in any country, politeness goes a long way when taking photographs; ask before taking pictures of people. Note that many Aboriginal people do not like to have their photographs taken, even from a distance.

HEALTH

Australia is a remarkably healthy country to travel in, considering that such a large portion of it lies in the tropics.

So long as you have not visited an infected country in the past 14 days (aircraft refuelling stops do not count) no vaccinations are required for entry.

Medical care in Australia is first-class and only moderately expensive. A typical visit to the doctor costs around $35. If you have an immediate health problem, phone or visit the casualty section at the nearest public hospital. If you are bushwalking or rafting in remote areas in Tasmania, remember that help can be several days away, so be prepared to deal with your own medical emergencies.

Visitors from the UK, New Zealand, Malta, Italy, Sweden and the Netherlands have reciprocal health rights in Australia and can register at any Medicare office. This entitles them to free medical treatment at public hospitals.

Travel Insurance

Ambulance services in Australia are self-funding (ie, they're not free) and can be frightfully expensive, so you'd be wise to take out travel insurance for that reason alone. Make sure the policy specifically includes ambulance, helicopter rescue and a flight home for you and anyone you're travelling with, should your condition warrant it. Also check the fine print: some policies exclude 'dangerous activities' such as scuba diving, motorcycling and even trekking. If such activities are on your agenda, you don't want that policy.

Medical Kit

While facilities in cities and towns are generally of a very high standard, doctors and hospitals are few and far between in the remote areas. If you're heading off the beaten track into the western half of the state, at least one person in your party should have a sound knowledge of first-aid treatment, and in any case you'll need a first-aid handbook and a basic medical kit. Some of the items that should be included are:

- Aspirin or Panadol – for pain or fever
- Antihistamine (such as Benadryl) – useful as a decongestant for colds and allergies, to ease the itch from insect bites or stings, and to help prevent motion sickness. Antihistamines may cause sedation and interact with alcohol so care should be taken when using them
- Kaolin preparation (Pepto-Bismol), Imodium or Lomotil – for stomach upsets
- Antiseptic such as Betadine, which comes as impregnated swabs or ointment, and an antibiotic powder or similar 'dry' spray – for cuts and grazes
- Calamine lotion – to ease irritation from bites or stings
- Eye drops
- Sterile gauze bandages
- Triangular bandages to support limbs and hold dressings in place
- Other assorted bandages and Band-aids – for minor injuries
- Adhesive tape and cotton wool
- Scissors, tweezers and a thermometer (note that mercury thermometers are prohibited by airlines)
- Insect repellent, sunscreen, chap stick and water purification tablets

Optional items include:

- Cold and flu tablets
- Antacid indigestion tablets
- Ear drops

Health Precautions

The contraceptive pill is available on prescription only, so a visit to a doctor is necessary. Doctors are listed in the Yellow Pages phone book or you can visit the outpatients section of a public hospital. Condoms are available from chemists, many convenience stores such as 7-Eleven, and vending machines in the public toilets of many hotels and universities.

Water Tap water is safe to drink in towns and cities throughout the state. Always beware of water from rivers, creeks and lakes, as it may have been infected by stock or wildlife. If there's any doubt, the surest way to disinfect water is to thoroughly boil it for 10 minutes.

Health Problems

Sunburn You can get sunburnt surprisingly quickly, even through cloud, in Tasmania. Use a sunscreen and take extra care to cover areas which don't normally see sun – such as your feet. A hat provides added protection, and you should also use zinc cream or some other barrier cream for your nose and lips. Calamine lotion is good for mild sunburn.

Sexually Transmitted Diseases Sexual contact with an infected sexual partner spreads these diseases. While abstinence is the only 100% preventative, using condoms is also effective. Gonorrhoea and syphilis are the most common of these diseases; sores, blisters or rashes around the genitals, discharges or pain when urinating are common symptoms. Symptoms may be less marked or not observed at all in women. Syphilis symptoms eventually disappear completely but the disease continues and can cause severe problems in later years. The treatment of gonorrhoea and syphilis is by antibiotics.

There are numerous other sexually transmitted diseases, for most of which effective treatment is available. However, there is no cure for herpes and there is also currently no cure for AIDS.

HIV/AIDS HIV, the Human Immunodeficiency Virus, may develop into AIDS, Acquired Immune Deficiency Syndrome. Any exposure to blood, blood products or bodily fluids may put a person at risk. Transmission in Australia is mostly through contact between homosexual or bisexual males, or via contaminated needles shared by IV drug users. Apart from abstinence, the most effective preventative is always to practice safe sex using condoms. It is impossible to detect the HIV-positive status of an otherwise healthy-looking person without a blood test.

HIV/AIDS can also be spread through infected blood transfusions, although in Australia all blood is screened for HIV. It can also be spread by dirty needles – vaccinations, acupuncture, tattooing and ear or nose piercing can potentially be as dangerous as intravenous drug use if the equipment is not clean.

Fear of HIV infection should never preclude treatment for serious medical conditions. Although there may be a risk of infection, it is very small indeed.

EMERGENCY

In the case of a life-threatening situation dial 000. This call is free from any phone and the operator will connect you with either the police, ambulance or fire brigade. To dial any of these services direct, check the inside front cover of any local telephone book.

For other telephone crisis and personal counselling services (such as sexual assault, poisons information or alcohol and drug problems), check the Community pages of the local telephone book.

WOMEN TRAVELLERS

Tasmania is generally a safe place for women travellers, although it's probably best to avoid walking alone late at night in any of the major towns. Sexual harassment is unfortunately still second nature to many Aussie males, and it's generally true to say that the further you get from 'civilisation' (ie, the big cities), the less enlightened your average Aussie male is going to be about women's issues; you're far more likely to meet an ocker than a SNAG!

Female hitchers should exercise care at all times (see the section on hitching in the Getting Around chapter). In the event of misfortune, a useful contact is the Sexual Assault Support Service in Hobart (☎ 6231 1811).

GAY & LESBIAN TRAVELLERS

Tasmania is the only Australian state in which homosexuality is illegal. Homosexual acts can, in theory, land you with a 21 year prison term – but, in practise, no-one has actually been sentenced. However, the penalty has been criticised by Amnesty International and the United Nations Human Rights Commission. The Tasmanian Gay & Lesbian Rights Group, based in Hobart, (☎ (03) 6224 3556) has long been active in pressing for the repeal of this law, and it could well be successful in August 1996, when it presents its case before the Australian High Court in Canberra.

While Tasmania has the reputation of being a state of anti-gay bigots, a public survey in 1995 showed that 58% of Tasmanians disapproved of the government's anti-gay stance. However, anti-gay feeling can be evident in Tasmania, especially in the

Disabled Travellers in Tasmania

Tasmania is a great tourist destination with an improving awareness of access issues.There are a number of agencies which provide information and/or assistance to disabled travellers.

Transport Transport options are limited so it is best to take your own vehicle on TT Line's ferry *Spirit of Tasmania* (freecall ☎ 13 2010) which sails between Port Melbourne and Devonport. Four cabins are accessible with the 'flood step' removed, a wheel-in shower and grab-rails. TT Line staff will drive your vehicle on and off the vessel for you. Qantas and Ansett service the airports at Hobart and Launceston but there are no air bridges so wheelchair passengers are boarded and disembarked using forklifts.

Three wheelchair accessible maxi-cabs (☎ 6234 3633) are available in Hobart but these must be booked in advance as availability is limited. AVIS (freecall ☎ 1800 22 5533) provides hand-controlled vehicles at Hobart and Launceston. Mobility Maps and Eating Out Guides are available from Launceston City Council Access and Advisory Committee (☎6337 1201) and City of Devonport Mersey Access Advisory Committee (☎6424 0511). *Easy Access Australia – A Travel Guide to Australia* includes a chapter about Tasmania and is available from PO Box 218, Kew Vic 3101 for $24.85.The Royal Automobile Club of Tasmania (RACT), on the corner of Patrick and Murray Sts, Hobart, 7000 (☎ 6232 6300) can provide information on access to attractions and aircraft.

Information The Australian Council for Rehabilitation of the Disabled (ACROD), Hampden Rd, Battery Point, 7004 (☎ 6223 6086) is an information and referral service for travellers with disabilities. Together with ACROD, the Paraplegic and Quadriplegic Association (☎ 6238 1874) is the main information source in Tasmania. They have information on accommodation, accessible toilets, mobility maps and attractions, and can help with specific requests from travellers. ACROD's Access Committee (☎ 6227 8688) and the Aged & Disability Care Information Service (☎ 6242 2322/freecall 008 80 6656) also provide information on services available throughout the state. Other organisations to contact are the Tasmanian Society for the Deaf (☎ 6273 2422/TTY 6272 6569) and the Royal Guide Dogs for the Blind Association (☎ 6232 1299).

Attractions & Accommodation Collect from the Tasmanian Parks and Wildlife Service (☎ 6233 3275 or 6233 6047) *Tasmania's National Parks and Reserves – A Visitors' Guide* which indicates parks with accessible facilities. Mt Field National Park (ranger ☎ 6288 1149), about 80 km north-west of Hobart, has an accessible 500-metre-long bitumen track leading to spectacular Russell Falls. A Tall Tree walk takes visitors through some of the world's tallest flowering plants.

The convict settlement at the Port Arthur Historical Site is the most significant attraction in Tasmania. Management are making the site accessible with dedicated parking spaces, accessible toilets, a wheelchair available to borrow and accessible entrances to many historic buildings. There is also access on the nightly Ghost Tour and on the Isle of the Dead tour (the crew provide all the help on the boat and up the steps on the island).

Purpose built accommodation is available at Melaleucas, Woodbridge (☎ 6264 7877) and Helvetia Retreat (☎6491 1806) at Sheffield, each with two self-catering units. Cradle Mountain-Lake St Clair National Park is Tasmania's most famous national park and Cradle Mountain Lodge (☎ 6492 1303) has two accessible self-catering chalets. The Visitors Centre and Rangers Station (☎ 6492 1133) has an accessible toilet and a ramp leads to the Rainforest Pencil Pines Walking Track, a 500-metre, accessible boardwalk through some spectacular rainforest.

Bruce Cameron

island's north-west: in February 1996, police investigated the circulation of a poster advocating the killing of gays. The two-part poster featured a drawing of two apparently dead men, with the slogan 'Stop AIDS now – execute homos', and a picture of a grim-reaper figure with the words 'Ethnic cleansing is God's will'.

Tasmania is the only Australian state where organised anti-gay hate groups exist. The most vocal is Tas-Alert, whose supporters have included federal MPs.

For local information or assistance, call the Gay Information Line (☎ (03) 6234 8179) or the Lesbian Line (☎ (03) 6231 4228).

Gay & Lesbian Publications

The Tasmanian Gay & Lesbian Rights Group's stall at Salamanca Place (every Saturday morning) distributes newsletters and the Melbourne gay/lesbian newspapers, *Melbourne Star Observer* and *Brother Sister*, which list Tasmanian gay and lesbian venues.

Gay & Lesbian Tours

A number of tour operators cater exclusively or partly for gay and lesbian travellers. One such operator is Destination DownUnder at 40 Miller St, (PO Box 429) North Sydney, NSW 2060 (☎ (02) 9957 3811; 9957 1385). It also has offices in Europe, the UK and the USA.

DANGERS & ANNOYANCES
Snakes

The best-known danger in the Australian bush, and the one that captures visitors' imaginations, is snakes. Although all snakes in Tasmania are venomous, they are not aggressive and, unless you have the bad fortune to stand on one, it's unlikely that you'll be bitten. The tiger snake, however, will sometimes attack if alarmed.

To minimise your chances of being bitten always wear boots, socks and long trousers when walking through undergrowth where snakes may be present. Don't put your hands into holes and crevices, and be careful when collecting firewood or toileting.

Snake bites do not cause instantaneous death and antivenins are usually available. Keep the victim calm and still, place a pad on the bite site, wrap the bitten limb firmly (to compress the muscle tissues, but not constrict the blood flow), as you would for a sprained ankle, and then attach a splint to immobilise it – do not remove the splint or bandages once applied. Seek medical help. Do *not* try to catch the snake. Never wash, cut and suck the poison out or use tourniquets. These treatments are now comprehensively discredited.

Flies

March flies are large and very persistent. They are prevalent in the summer months and are attracted to blue clothing, so you're better off wearing other colours. They can viciously attack the unsuspecting traveller and bite any uncovered area, leaving behind large, red lumps (similar to leech bites). Repellents such as Aerogard and Rid go some way to deterring these pests, but it's better to cover up. Calamine lotion can soothe the bites.

Mosquitoes

Just when you think the flies have gone (around sunset) and it's safe to come out, the 'mossies' appear. Repellents usually keep them at bay.

Ticks

The common bush tick (found in the forest and scrub country) can be dangerous if left lodged in the skin, as the toxin the tick excretes can cause paralysis and sometimes death. Regularly check your body for lumps, particularly before retiring at night if you're walking in tick-infested areas. The tick should be removed by dousing it with methylated spirits or kerosene and levering it out intact.

Leeches

These are very common in the damp rainforest and marsh areas around the state. While they will suck your blood they are not dangerous and are easily removed by the application of salt or heat. Do not pull them off as the wound will continue to bleed for quite some time. A leech bite can be a very itchy, swollen lump, but will go down in a few days – apply calamine lotion or cream to soothe the itching and try not to scratch it! Insect repellent, such as Rid, seems to stop them from getting hold quickly and gives you a chance of removing them before they attach.

Bushfires

Bushfires happen almost every year in Tasmania, even with the higher average rainfalls in this state. Don't be the mug who starts one. In hot, dry, windy weather, be extremely careful with any naked flame – no cigarette butts out of car windows, please. On a Total Fire Ban day (listen to the radio or watch the billboards on country roads), it is forbidden even to use a camping stove in the open. The locals will not be amused if they catch you breaking this particular law; they'll happily dob you in, and the penalties are severe.

If you're unfortunate enough to find yourself driving through a bushfire, stay inside your car and try to park off the road in an open space, away from trees, until the danger's past. Lie on the floor under the dashboard, covering yourself with a wool blanket if possible. The front of the fire should pass quickly, and you will be much safer than if you were out in the open. It is very important to cover up with a wool blanket or wear protective clothing, as it has been proved that heat radiation is the big killer in bushfire situations.

Bushwalkers should take local advice before setting out. On a day of Total Fire Ban, don't go – delay your trip until the weather has changed. Chances are that it will be so unpleasantly hot and windy, you'll be better off anyway in an air-conditioned pub sipping a cool beer.

If you're out in the bush and you see smoke, even at a great distance, take it seriously. Go to the nearest open space, downhill if possible. A forested ridge is the most dangerous place to be. Bushfires move very quickly and change direction with the wind.

Blizzards

At the other end of the scale, blizzards can occur in Tasmania's mountain regions even in summer. A white Christmas is not unheard of in places like Cradle Mountain National Park. Some summer storms are severe enough to deposit snow on the Lyell and Murchison highways.

Bushwalkers in particular need to be prepared for Tasmania's infamous weather, particularly those venturing into the southwest. Take warm clothing such as thermals and warm jackets as well as wind and waterproof garments and be sure to eat, drink and rest regularly. High quality tents suitable for snow camping are advisable and the best preparation is to carry enough food for two extra days, allowing you to wait for better weather.

WORK

If you come to Australia on a 12-month 'working holiday' visa you can officially only work for three out of those 12 months. Working on a regular tourist visa is strictly forbidden, but many travellers on tourist visas do find casual work. It is very difficult to find a job in Tasmania as it has the highest unemployment level in the country at around 12%, with youth unemployment at around 35%.

With the current boom in tourism, casual work is sometimes easy to find in the peak season (summer) at the major tourist centres. Other good prospects for casual work include factories, bar work, waiting on tables or washing dishes, childcare, fruit-picking and collecting for charities.

If you are coming to Tasmania with the intention of working, make sure you have enough funds to cover your stay, or have a contingency plan if the work is not forthcoming. Jobs can be hard to find and there is a lot of competition from locals.

The Commonwealth Employment Service (CES) has offices around the state and the staff usually have a good idea of what's available where. Try the classified section of the daily papers under Situations Vacant too.

The various backpackers' magazines, newspapers and hostels are good information sources – some local employers even advertise on their notice boards. As with all short jobs be wary of those who are ripping off workers with low pay or attached conditions (such as stipulating you must stay at a particular place).

Tax File Number It's important to apply for a Tax File Number (TFN) if you plan to work (or open a bank account – see the Money section for details) in Australia, not because it's a condition of employment, but without it tax will be deducted from any wages you receive at the maximum rate, which is currently set at 48.5%! To get a TFN, contact the Tasmanian branch of the Australian Taxation Office at 200 Collins St, Hobart (☎ 13 2861) for a form. It's a straightforward procedure, and you will have to supply adequate identification, such as a passport and driving license. The issue of a TFN takes about four weeks.

Paying Tax Yes, it's one of the certainties in life! If you have supplied your employer with a Tax File Number, tax will be deducted from your wages at the rate of 29% if your annual income is below $20,700. As your income increases, so does the tax rate, with the maximum being 48.5% for incomes over $50,000. For non-resident visitors, tax is payable from the first dollar you earn, unlike residents who have something like a $6000 tax-free threshold. For this reason, if you have had tax deducted at the correct rate as you earn, it is unlikely you'll be entitled to a tax refund when you leave.

If you have had tax deducted at 48.5% because you have not submitted a Tax File Number, chances are you will be entitled to a partial refund if your income was less than $50,000. Once you lodge a tax return (which must include a copy of the Group Certificate all employers issue to salaried workers at the end of the financial year or within seven days

of leaving a job), you will be refunded the extra tax you have paid. Before you can lodge a tax return, however, you must have a Tax File Number.

Fruit & Vegetable Picking Seasons In Tasmania the main harvest times for the crops where casual employment is a possibility are: February to May in the Huon Valley and Tasman Peninsula (apples, pears), and December to January in the Huon Valley and Kingston (soft fruit). For more information, enquire at the local Commonwealth Employment Service (CES) office.

ACTIVITIES

Tasmania has plenty to offer by way of activities. You can do everything from swimming to sea kayaking or walking to camel riding. The choice is yours.

There are many small and some large adventure tour operators and most are members of the Tasmanian Licensed Guiding Operators Association (☎ 6426 9312), PO Box Latrobe, 7307 which can supply a current list of their members.

Bushwalking

Tasmania, with its many national parks, is a Mecca for bushwalkers from all over the world. It has some of the finest bushwalks in Australia, the most famous of which is the superb Cradle Mountain-Lake St Clair Overland Track. (See the Cradle Mountain-Lake St Clair section for details of this walk.)

On long walks, it's important to remember that in any season a fine day can quickly become cold and stormy, so warm clothing, waterproof gear, a tent and compass are vital. The Department of Parks, Wildlife & Heritage publishes a booklet called *Welcome to the Wilderness – Bushwalking Trip Planner for Tasmania's World Heritage Area*, which has sections on planning, minimal-impact bushwalking and wilderness survival. Also included is a very useful equipment checklist which is essential reading for bushwalkers who are unfamiliar with Tasmania's notoriously changeable weather.

If you write to the Department at GPO

Box 44A, Hobart, ring ☎ 6233 6191, or contact them on their World Wide Web site at http://www.parks.tas.gov.au, you'll be sent this booklet and other leaflets, including the Bushwalking Code, free of charge. You can also pick up all the department's literature from its head office at 134 Macquarie St, Hobart; from its office at Henty House, Civic Square, Launceston; or from any ranger station in the national parks. On the ground floor of the Department's building is the Land Information Sales Centre (☎ 6233 3382) where you can obtain all brochures, maps and other published material.

The Department of Environment & Land Management produces and sells an excellent series of maps; again, you can be sent these or pick them up from the Department office, or at most outdoor-equipment stores, Wilderness Society shops and newsagencies throughout the state.

As bushwalking is so popular in Tasmania, there are many excellent shops selling bush gear, as well as several youth hostels which hire out equipment or take bushwalking tours. In the former category, Paddy Pallin in Hobart and Launceston, Allgoods in Launceston and the Backpackers Barn in Devonport all have a very good range of bushwalking gear and plenty of invaluable advice.

There are plenty of companies offering guided walks which range from one-day excursions to multi-day camping trips. Well established companies are Craclair Walking Holidays (☎ 6424 7833), Peregrine Adventures (☎ 6225 0944 or 1800 124 801) and Tasmanian Expeditions (☎ 6334 3477) who all offer trips along the Overland Track plus some other popular destinations. If sleeping in a tent is too rough then Cradle Huts (☎ 6331 2006) can offer you a guided walk along the Overland Track staying in privately owned huts.

There are plenty of smaller companies which provide more personal service for small bushwalking groups. Taswalks (☎ 6363 6112) and Adventuremania (☎ 6334 7766) are two examples of smaller companies who cater for small groups. Good

books on the subject and places to buy maps are detailed in the recommended reading section earlier in this chapter. For more information on walks in individual national parks see the relevant chapter.

Skiing
There are two small ski resorts in Tasmania: Ben Lomond, which is 60 kilometres from Launceston; and Mt Mawson, in Mt Field National Park, 70 kilometres from Hobart. Both offer cheaper, although less-developed, ski facilities than the major resorts in Victoria and New South Wales — rope tows are still used on some runs. Despite the state's southerly latitude, snowfalls tend to be fairly light and unreliable. For more information see the sections on the Ben Lomond and Mt Field National Parks.

Birdwatching
The eastern and south-eastern regions are the most popular birdwatching areas because the forest cover is thinner and birds are more easily seen. There are interesting birds throughout the state, but in the rainforest you often hear them but rarely see them. The less visited places like Bruny Island in the south and the Mt William National Park in the north-east are excellent places for finding the rare spotted pardolote and for general birdwatching. If you want to see the orange-bellied parrot, one of the world's rarest birds, fly to Melaleuca in the south-west, where the special bird hide near the airstrip provides frequent sightings.

Cycling
You can cycle all around Tasmania, but the most popular routes are from the north through the centre or down the east coast. When cycling on the narrow, winding roads, always keep your eyes and ears open for traffic. Even if you're in the right, you'll be worse off if you're hit. Remember to always wear a helmet (they are compulsory) and try not to cycle at night.

There are bicycle tours which you can join. Brake Out Cycling Tours (☎ 6229 1999) run single-day trips around Hobart plus extended two, four and eight-day tours in the north-east of the state.

Horse Riding & Camel Trekking

Horse riding is allowed in some of the national parks and all of the protected areas. There are several companies which provide horse riding, ranging from hour-long trails to multi-day treks across the Central Plateau. Rates start at $20 per hour for short rides up to $150 per person per day (including all food) for guided treks across the high country. Central Highland Trail Rides (☎ 6369 5298), Saddletramp Horseback Tours (☎ 6254 6196) and Horseback Wilderness Tours (☎ 1800 128 405) all run short rides and overnight trips through different areas of the state.

You may think camel rides are a bit of a novelty in a place like Tasmania, given that camels are traditionally thought of as 'ships of the desert'. However, camel rides have caught on and are available on Bruny Island, in Swansea and near Rocky Cape on the north-west corner of the state. Rides start at $14 rising to $90 for a full day.

Rock Climbing

Dry weather is desirable for rock climbing, and Tasmania's weather is often wet. In spite of this, some excellent cliffs have been developed for rock climbing, particularly along the east coast where the weather is usually better. The Organ Pipes on Mt Wellington (above Hobart), the Hazards at Coles Bay and the cliffs on Mt Killiecrankie on Flinders Island provide excellent climbing on firm rock. The really keen climbers drag all their gear onto the huge cliffs of Frenchmans Cap on the western side of the state and wait for a break in the rain. There are many other cliffs around the state for experienced climbers to visit. Guide books exist to Frenchmans Cap, Coles Bay and Mt Killiecrankie – other information is by word of mouth.

If you want to try some climbing or abseiling with an experienced instructor, visit the outdoor shops in Hobart, Launceston or Devonport.

Caving

Tasmania's caves are regarded as being among the most impressive in Australia. The caves at Mole Creek, Gunns Plains and Hastings are open to the public daily, but gems such as the Kubla Khan and Croesus caves (near Mole Creek) and the extremely large Exit Cave are only accessible to experienced cavers. Permits are needed to enter any caves; they are not places for the inexperienced and most are locked. Apply through your speleological club or association in your own state or country for permits.

You can visit an underdeveloped (wild) cave with Exit Cave Adventure Tours (☎ 6243 0546) from Hobart or with Wild Cave Tours (☎ 6367 8142) from Mole Creek. Costs are around $90 to $120 per person per day and include safety equipment and lunch. Expect to get wet and muddy as these caves have no walkways or ladders and often have to be entered through streams.

Surfing

Tasmania has plenty of good surf beaches. Close to Hobart, the best spots are Clifton Beach and the surf beach en route to South Arm. The southern beaches of Bruny Island – particularly at Cloudy Bay – can be good when a southerly swell is rolling. The east coast from Bicheno past St Helens has excellent beaches and fine surf. The greatest spot of all is Marrawah on the west coast, where the waves are often huge as it's the first place they meet since South America. The only downer is that it's a long way from anywhere else in the state.

Windsurfing

Ideal conditions exist for windsurfing, particularly along the east coast. Ocean Sports (☎ 6250 3425) runs windsurfing tours around Eaglehawk Neck, or you can hire a board and do your own thing.

Scuba Diving & Snorkelling

On the east coast and around King and Flinders Islands there are some excellent scuba-diving opportunities. Underwater trails have been marked near Hobart and on Maria Island.

Diving equipment can be rented to licensed divers in Hobart, Launceston or on the east coast. If you want to learn to dive, go on a diving course; they are considerably cheaper than those on the mainland. Courses are run on the Tasman Peninsula, at Bicheno and St Helens; see the relevant chapters for details.

Sailing

Since Tassie is surrounded by so much water, it's not surprising that sailing is very popular. The Derwent River is a popular spot, with many clubs and regular yacht races.

If you really want to get into the swing of things, you can help sail a 50-year-old ketch with Heritage Sailing (☎ 6264 2520 or 018 128 405). Regular trips are conducted on this vessel from Watermans Dock in Hobart. A three hour sail costs $25 per person, or you can spend a full day sailing for $50. If you want to spend a night or two out on the water, join in the two to six-day adventures for $130 per person per day, all meals included. Another option is cruising on a 100-year-old Huon pine boat with the South West Passage Cruising Company (☎ 6298 1197). It runs tours from Dover around the southern end of Bruny Island and to other places by charter. Rates are $43 per person per day for the boat; food is extra but then you might not feel like eating when at sea!

Canoeing & Rafting

With so many rivers and lakes, rafting, rowing and canoeing are all popular pastimes even if the water is a bit cold. The most challenging river to raft is the Franklin (see the Franklin-Gordon Wild Rivers National Park section), although rafting trips are also organised on the Picton, Upper Huon, Weld and Leven rivers. Most rafting trips are now run by commercial groups as it takes a lot of effort to organise your own trip. Major rafting companies are Peregrine Adventures (☎ 6225 0944 or 1800 124 801) and Rafting Tasmania (☎ 6227 9516). One day rafting trips are around $100 (depending on river and group size) while multi-day Franklin River trips are around $1000 per week which includes all camping gear and food.

Sea Kayaking

Another popular activity is sea kayaking. Peregrine Adventures runs three day trips around Freycinet Peninsula for around $400.

Swimming

The north and east coasts have plenty of sheltered, white-sand beaches which are excellent for swimming although the water is rather cold. There are also some pleasant beaches near Hobart, such as Bellerive and Sandy Bay, but these tend to be polluted so it's better to head towards Kingston, Blackmans Bay or Seven Mile Beach for safe swimming. On the west coast there's some pretty ferocious surf and the beaches are unpatrolled.

Fishing

Fishing is another popular activity. Many of the rivers offer superb trout fishing, and the coastal waters are also good. A license is required to fish in Tasmania's inland waters, and there are bag, season and size limits on most fish. Licenses cost $38 for the full season, $20 for 14 days, $12 for 3 days and $7 for one day, and are available from sports stores, post offices and Tasmanian Travel & Information Centres.

In general, inland waters open for fishing on the Saturday closest to 1 August and close on the Sunday nearest 30 April. Different dates apply to some special places and these are all detailed in the *Fishing Code* brochure (see below). The lakes in the centre of the state are some of the best-known spots for both brown and rainbow trout – Arthurs Lake, Great Lake, Little Pine Lagoon (fly fishing only), Western Lakes (including Lake St Clair), Lake Sorell and Lake Pedder.

Tasmanian trout can be difficult to catch as the fish are very fickle about what they eat; the right lures are needed in the right season. If you find you can't hook them then there are experts who can take you around to some good fishing places and teach you the local tricks. The Tasmanian Fly-Fishing School (☎ 6362 3441) at Mole Creek runs guided trips for $150 to $250 per person per day (price varies with group size). There are several individuals who also run fishing tours and this can be a great way to visit the lesser known places. As they vary each year it's best to contact the local information centres for current operators.

Fishing in salt waters is allowed all year without a permit although there are restrictions on size, and bag limits apply. For more information contact the Tasmanian Inland Fisheries Commission (☎ 6233 8305), 127 Davey St, Hobart and ask for a current *Fishing Code* brochure.

Scenic Flights

Scenic flights in four and six seat planes are popular and range from one hour to half a day in length. In fine weather they are a great way to see the wilder regions of the state. The most popular service is that run from Strahan by Wilderness Air (☎ (03) 6471 7280), whose flights land on the Gordon River at the site of the Franklin Blockade. It has also started a service which combines a seaplane flight with a short cruise on a steamboat on the Gordon River.

From Hobart, Par-Avion (☎ 6248 5390) operates from Cambridge Airport (near Hobart Airport) and runs scenic flights as well as some interesting trips into the South-West National Park. You can spend a day in the wilderness with a flight into the south-west and a cruise around Bathurst Harbour for $240 per person including lunch. If you like, you can stay at Par Avion's fully-catered camp beside Bathurst Harbour for $790 for two nights.

There are other scenic flights available from most airports around the state. For example, from Devonport you can fly over the Cradle Mountain region, and flights from Hobart over the South-West National Park and Maria Island are popular. Rates for most flights range from $60 to $90 per hour per person.

Hang-Gliding

Hang-gliding can be difficult to learn and has its dangers. One way to experience the thrill of flying in a controlled situation is to go out with Cable Hang Gliding (☎ 1800 132 788) near Launceston.

Other Activities

If you would like to try a range of activities then there are quite a few commercially organised adventures which are great fun. With Peregrine Adventures (☎ 6225 0944 or 1800 124 801) you can go cycling, walking and hang gliding on a six day trip for $890 or you can spend eight days cycling, sea kayaking, walking and rafting for $995. Tasmanian Outdoor Experience Company (☎ 6334 4442) generally runs shorter trips, including a four day trip combining walking, horse riding and caving for $536. Other deals are offered by Wandering Albatross (☎ 6224 1577) with four days of jet-boating, camel riding, walking and rafting for $480.

Mixed trips are generally dearer per day than single activity trips but that is to be expected, as more equipment and transport are needed.

HIGHLIGHTS

Tasmania has great diversity, even though it is Australia's smallest state. The list of highlights is enormous, although one person's favourite can easily be another's disappointment. There are, however, a number of features which are almost 'compulsory'.

There's the rich heritage of the convict era at places such as Port Arthur, and many beautiful old buildings in places like Salamanca Place and Battery Point in Hobart. The convict-built bridges in Ross and Richmond are historic landmarks, and Tassie is dotted with historic towns and villages, such as Oatlands, Campbell Town, Longford and Bothwell.

Tasmania has some of the most beautiful wilderness areas in Australia. The magnificent Cradle Mountain-Lake St Clair National Park, within the World Heritage Area, is popular with bushwalkers and day visitors from many countries. There is also some spectacular coastal scenery on the Tasman Peninsula and along the south and east coasts.

ACCOMMODATION

Tasmania is very well equipped with youth hostels, backpackers hostels and caravan parks with camp sites. There are plenty of motels and hotels as well as comfortable B&Bs around the state.

Despite the variety of places to stay, Tasmania's major tourist centres are often fully booked in summer, so it's wise to make reservations. If you're in a group, room rates for three or four people are always worth checking. Often there are larger 'family' rooms or units with two bedrooms.

There are a couple of free backpackers newspapers and booklets available at hostels and tourist bureaus. These have fairly up-to-date listings of hostels, although they give neither prices nor details of each hostel.

For more comprehensive accommodation listings, the Royal Automobile Club of Tasmania (RACT) has directories listing caravan parks, hotels, motels, holiday flats and a number of backpackers hostels in almost every town. They're updated every year so the prices are generally fairly current. They're available from the club for a nominal charge if you're a member (or a member of an affiliated club enjoying reciprocal rights). Alternatively, the Tasmanian Tourist Bureau publishes a free bi-monthly guide for visitors called *Travelways* which includes most accommodation places.

Camping & Caravanning

Camping in Tasmania can be really good or very poor! There are a great number of caravan parks and you'll almost always find a camping space. It's also the cheapest form of accommodation, with nightly costs for two being around $8 to $15.

Unlike other states (and probably due to its size), most cities in Tasmania have caravan and camping parks conveniently close to the city centre.

In general, Tasmanian caravan parks are well kept, conveniently located and excel-lent value. Some also have on-site vans which you can rent for the night. On-site cabins are also widely available. These usually have one bedroom, or at least an area which can be screened off from the rest of the unit – just the thing if you have kids. The price difference is not always that great – say $25 to $30 for an on-site van, $30 to $50 for a cabin. If you're travelling in winter, it's worth investing in a small heater of some sort as some vans and cabins are unheated.

YHA Hostels

YHA hostels are part of an international organisation, the International Youth Hostel Federation (IYHF, also known as HI, Hostelling International), so if you're already a member of the YHA in your own country, your membership entitles you to use the hostels in Australia. The annual *YHA Accommodation Guide* booklet, which is available from any YHA office and from some YHA offices overseas, lists all the YHA hostels with useful little maps showing how to find them. Tasmania's YHA office (☎ 6234 9617) is located at 28 Criterion St, Hobart. It provides brochures and informa-tion to travellers as well as an Australia-wide hostel-to-hostel booking service. If you wish to use the hostel at Coles Bay you must book it here.

YHA hostels provide basic accommoda-tion, usually in small dormitories or bunk rooms although more and more of them are providing twin rooms for couples. The nightly charges are very reasonable – usually between $12 and $15 a night per person.

Most YHAs take non-YHA members for an additional nightly fee of $2 per person. When staying at a hostel nonmembers receive an Aussie Starter Card, to be stamped each night by the YHA. Once the card has been stamped 12 times, you are given a year's free membership.

You can become a full YHA member for $26 a year (there's also a $16 joining fee, although if you're an overseas resident you can join without having to pay this). You can join at the main office in Hobart, or at any youth hostel. International visitors joining the YHA at a hostel receive their first night at that hostel for free.

YHA members are also entitled to a number of handy discounts around the country – on things such as car hire, activities, accommodation etc – and these are detailed in the *Discounts* booklet, published each year.

You must have a regulation sheet sleeping bag or bed linen – for hygiene reasons a regular sleeping bag will not do. If you haven't got sheets they can be rented at many hostels (usually for $3), but it is cheaper to have your own. YHA offices and some larger hostels sell the official YHA sheet bag.

All hostels have cooking facilities and 24-hour access, and there's usually a communal area where you can sit and talk. There are usually laundry facilities and most hostels have a maximum-stay period – because some hostels are permanently full it would hardly be fair for people to stay too long when others are being turned away. Most hostels have excellent noticeboards and lots of brochures available.

The YHA defines its hostels as simple, standard or superior. The hostels range from tiny places to big, rambling buildings or historic convict buildings. Most hostels have a manager who checks you in when you arrive and keeps the peace.

Accommodation can usually be booked directly with the manager or through the YHA office in Hobart.

Not all of the hostels listed in the *YHA Handbook* are actually owned by the YHA. Some are 'associate hostels', which generally abide by hostel regulations but are owned by other organisations or individuals. You don't need to be a YHA member to stay at an associated hostel. Others are 'alternative accommodation' and do not totally fit the hostel blueprint.

Backpacker Hostels

Tasmania has plenty of backpacker hostels, and the standard of these varies enormously. Some are run-down, inner-city hotels where the owners have tried to fill empty rooms; others are former motels, so each unit, typically with four to six beds, will have a fridge, TV and bathroom. The drawback with these places is that the communal areas and cooking facilities are often lacking and you may also find yourself sharing a room with someone who wants to watch TV all night – it happens!

Still other hostels are purpose-built as backpackers hostels; these are usually the best places in terms of facilities, although sometimes they are simply too big and therefore lack any personalised service. The best places are often the smaller, more intimate hostels where the owner is also the manager. These are usually the older hostels which were around long before the 'backpacker boom'.

Prices at backpackers hostels are generally in line with YHA hostels – typically $12 to $15 – although some have discount rates for staying several nights.

Guesthouses & B&Bs

This is the fastest growing segment of the accommodation market. New places are opening all the time, and the network of accommodation alternatives includes everything from restored convict-built cottages, renovated and rambling old guesthouses and upmarket country homes to a simple bedroom in a family home. The term guesthouse applies to large buildings, which usually have many rooms. Many of the newer B&Bs are smaller historic buildings which can accommodate from two to 10 people. They are often very cosy, with good facilities.

The breakfast supplied varies tremendously. If you hire a cottage you can expect a light breakfast of cereal, toast and fruit juice to be stored in the kitchen. If you have a room in a family home, you might be offered a full cooked breakfast. Tariffs cover a wide range, but are typically in the $50 to $100 per double bracket.

Hotels & Pubs

The older hotels in Australia are pubs, which were required by the old licensing laws to provide accommodation. Not every pub has rooms to rent, although many still do. A 'private hotel', as opposed to a 'licensed hotel', really is a hotel and does not serve alcohol. A 'guesthouse' is much the same as a 'private hotel'. New hotels being built today are mainly of the Hilton variety; smaller establishments will usually be motels. So, if you're staying in a hotel, it will normally mean an older place; unfortunately these are often a bit drab, but many are colourful places with real character. If the hotel has nothing resembling a reception desk or counter, just ask at the bar.

You'll find most hotels within easy walking distance of the town centre. In some of the older or historic towns, the old hotels can be really magnificent. The rooms themselves may be pretty old-fashioned and unexciting, but the hotel facade and entrance area will often be quite extravagant. They are often the real 'town centre' and you'll meet all the local characters there.

A bright word about hotels (guesthouses and private hotels, too) is that the breakfasts are usually excellent – big and 100% filling. If your hotel is into serving a real breakfast you'll probably feel it could last you all day. Generally, hotels will have rooms for around $40 to $100; the hotels with rooms for $20 are usually of a very low standard. When comparing prices, remember to check if it includes breakfast.

Motels, Holiday Units & Serviced Apartments

If you've got transport and want a more modern place with your own bathroom and other facilities, then you're moving into the motel bracket. Motels are usually located away from the town centres. Prices vary and with the motels, unlike hotels, singles are often not much cheaper than doubles. You'll sometimes find motel rooms for less than $50, but in most places will be looking at least $60 or more. Some motels include continental breakfast as standard; most motels provide at least tea and coffee-making facilities and a small fridge.

Holiday units and serviced apartments are much the same thing: basically, holiday units are found in holiday areas, serviced apartments in cities. A holiday unit is much like a motel room but usually has a kitchen or cooking facilities so you can prepare your own food. Usually holiday units are not serviced like motels – you don't get your bed made up every morning and the cups washed out. In some holiday units you actually have to provide your own sheets and bedding but others are operated just like motel rooms with a kitchen, including cooking utensils, cutlery, crockery and so on.

Holiday units are often rented on a weekly basis but even in these cases it's worth asking if daily rates are available. Paying for a week, even if you stay only for a few days, can sometimes still be cheaper than having those days at a higher daily rate. If there are more than just two of you, another advantage of holiday units is that they often have two or more bedrooms. A two-bedroom holiday unit is typically priced at about 1½ times the cost of a comparable single-bedroom unit. Prices given in this guide are for single night stays and are often in the $60 to $100 range.

Colleges

Although students get first chance at these, non-students can also stay at many university colleges during uni vacations. These places can be relatively cheap and comfortable and provide an opportunity for you to meet people. Costs are typically from about $20 for B&B for students, twice that for non-students.

This type of accommodation is usually available only during the summer vacations (from November to February). Additionally, it must almost always be booked ahead; you can't just turn up.

Other Possibilities

There are lots of less conventional accommodation possibilities. For example, there are plenty of national parks where, providing you have a park pass, you can camp for free. Roadside rest areas provide emergency, short-term camping.

One of the best ways to come to grips with country life is to spend a few days on a farm.

Many farms offer accommodation, often B&B, where you can just sit back and watch how it's done, while others like to get you more actively involved in the day-to-day activities. With commodity prices falling daily, mountainous wool stockpiles and a general rural crisis, tourism offers the hope of at least some income for farmers, at a time when many are being forced off the land. The tourist offices can advise you on what's available; prices are pretty reasonable being about the same as for B&Bs.

Long-Term Accommodation

If you want to spend longer in Tasmania, the first place to look for a shared flat or a room is in the classified advertising section of the daily newspaper. Wednesday and Saturday are the best days for these ads. Noticeboards in universities, hostels and cafes are good places to look for flats/houses to share or rooms to rent.

FOOD

The culinary delights can be one of the real highlights of a visit to Tasmania. There are many fine restaurants offering a wide variety of fresh, local produce. On King Island, for example, are fine quality meat, cheeses and cream from which scrumptious meals are put together to tempt your taste buds. Tasmania is renowned for its superb range of seafood: fish like trevalla and stripey trumpeter are worth trying, as is the Tasmanian salmon. Rock lobster, crayfish and oysters are among the shellfish available.

Food is high in quality and relatively low in cost. A takeaway sandwich or pie and a drink will cost around $4. Counter meals at the local pub will cost between $8 and $15, while restaurants usually charge $12 to $15 for mains.

The cities have a selection of cafes and restaurants serving food which can be termed 'modern Australian'. These are dishes which borrow heavily from a wide range of foreign cuisines, but have a definite local flavour. At some places seemingly anything goes, so you might find Asian-inspired curry-type dishes sharing a menu with Euro-pean or Mediterranean-inspired dishes. It all adds up to exciting dining.

Vegetarians are generally well catered for in most parts of the state. While there are few dedicated vegetarian restaurants, most modern cafes and restaurants have some vegetarian dishes on the menu.

Takeaway Food

Around the state you'll find the well known international fast-food chains – *McDonalds, KFC, Pizza Hut* etc – all typically conspicuous.

On a more local level, you'll find a milk bar on (almost) every corner, and most of them sell pies, pasties, sandwiches and milk-shakes. Then there are the speciality sandwich bars, delicatessens, bakeries and health-food shops, which are all worth seeking out if you want something a little more exotic than a pie.

Most shopping centres have a fish & chip shop and a pizza joint. If the food is cooked for you while you wait it's usually reasonably good. Absolute rockbottom is the kept-lukewarm-for-hours food found at roadside cafes and roadhouses. Give it a miss unless you have absolutely no choice – then you should ask for something which is not in the warmer trays so that they cook a fresh batch.

Restaurants & Cafes

The best Tasmanian eateries serve food as exciting and as innovative as anything you can find anywhere, and it doesn't need to cost a fortune. Best value are the modern and casual cafes, where for less than $20 you can get an excellent feed.

While eating out is a pleasure in the big cities, in many smaller country towns it can be something of an ordeal. The food will be predictable and unexciting, and is usually of the 'meat and three veg' variety. There are of course exceptions, with superb restaurants in many out of the way tourist locations.

All over the state, you'll find restaurants advertising that they're BYO. The initials stand for 'Bring Your Own' and it means that you are permitted to bring your own alcohol with you. This is a real boon to wine-loving but budget-minded travellers because you can bring your own bottle of wine from the local bottle shop or from that winery you visited last week and not pay any mark-up. In fact, most restaurants make a small 'corkage' charge (typically $1 to $1.50 per person) if you bring your own.

Pubs

Most pubs serve two types of meals: bistro meals, which are usually in the $10 to $15 range and are served in the dining room or lounge bar, where there's usually a self-serve salad bar; and bar (or counter) meals which are filling, simple, no-frills meals eaten in the public bar, and which usually cost less than $10, sometimes as little as $4.

The quality of pub food varies enormously, and while it's usually fairly basic and unimaginative, it's generally pretty good value. The usual meal times are from 12 noon to 2 pm and 6 to 8 pm.

DRINKS

Alcohol drinkers should be aware that, in Australia, people who drive under the influence of alcohol and get caught lose their licenses. The maximum permissible blood-alcohol concentration level for drivers is 0.05%.

Beer

Australian beer will be fairly familiar to North Americans; it's similar to what's known as lager in the UK. It may taste like lemonade to the European real ale addict, but it packs quite a punch and is invariably chilled before drinking.

In Tasmania, there's Cascade in the south and Boags in the north, both having their fair share of loyal drinkers. The Cascade Brewery, near Hobart, produces Cascade Premium and Pale Ale. Visitors tend to ask for 'Cascade' expecting to get the one with the distinctive label bearing the Tasmanian tigers, but you are unlikely to get Premium unless you ask specifically for it. Cascade Brewery also conducts an informative tour. When you travel north, you cross an invisible

line where all the hotels serve beer from Boags Brewery. They produce similar style beers such as Boags Export Lager and James Boags Premium.

Standard beer generally contains around 4.9% alcohol, although the trend in recent years has been towards low-alcohol beers, with an alcohol content of between 2% and 3.5%.

Wine

If you don't fancy the beer, then try the wine. The wine industry was started by a few pioneers in the mid-1950s, and the industry is quickly gaining recognition for producing quality wines. Tasmanian wines are characterised by their full, fruity flavour, plus the high acidity expected of cool, temperate wine regions.

Grapes are grown all over the state, with the largest wine-growing region being at Pipers Brook in the north east, and the West Tamar region being the second largest. Notable vineyards, with cellar door tastings, include Pipers Brook, Heemskirk and St Matthias. There are also wineries dotted down the east coast from Bicheno to Dunally including Freycinet and Coombend, and further south to the Huon valley area where you'll find Hartzview Vineyard among others. The Derwent River valley also has major wineries, including Meadowbank and Moorilla Estate. The Moorilla vineyard is the oldest in the southern part of the state, having been established in 1958. In 1995 it faced bankruptcy, but at the time of writing is still trading. If it collapses it will be a setback for the industry.

Tasmania's wines are quite expensive, compared to similar mainland wines. You'll be set back in the vicinity of $20 or more for an acceptable bottle of wine. As the industry is still quite young, hopefully the prices will improve with age!

The best – and most enjoyable – way to get to know Tasmanian wines is to get out to the wineries and sample the wine at the cellar door. Many wineries have tastings: you just zip straight in and say what you'd like to try. However, free wine tastings are no longer common and certainly do not mean open slather drinking. The glasses are generally thimble-sized and it's expected that you will buy something. Many wineries and tasting centres now charge a small 'tasting fee' of a couple of dollars, refundable if you buy any wine.

ENTERTAINMENT
Cinema
In Hobart, only one of the major commercial cinema chains operates. It's the Village 7 Cinema Complex at 181 Collins St and shows mainstream popular films. In Launceston, the Palace Theatre with its pastel, art-deco façade is a work of art in itself. Smaller towns usually have only one cinema, which is often only open on nights at weekends. These theatres are often in grand old buildings. Seeing a new-release mainstream film costs around $15 ($7.50 for children under 15) in Hobart, often less in country areas and on certain nights.

Also in Hobart, you'll find art-house and independent cinemas, and these places generally screen either films that aren't made for mass consumption or specialise purely in re-runs of classic and cult movies. The State AFI Cinema in Elizabeth St, North Hobart is part of the art-house cinema scene.

Discos & Nightclubs
These are confined to the cities. Clubs range from the exclusive 'members only' variety to barn-sized discos where anyone who wants to spend money is welcomed with open arms. Admission charges range from around $6 to $12.

Some places have certain dress standards, but it is generally left to the discretion of the people at the door – if they don't like the look of you, bad luck. The more 'upmarket' nightclubs attract an older, more sophisticated and affluent crowd, and generally have stricter dress codes, smarter decor – and, inevitably, higher prices. Many of these nightclubs double as winebars and cafes earlier in the evening.

Casinos
In Hobart, the Wrest Point Casino is on the shores of Sandy Bay. You can go into the casino dressed neatly; however, strict dress codes operate for the main gaming rooms and private rooms. There are also live shows and discos, and a neat dress code applies to these areas. A similar standard of dress applies to the Country Club Casino at Launceston.

Live Music
Many suburban pubs have live music, and these are often great places for catching live bands, either nationally well-known names or up-and-coming performers trying to make a name for themselves. Most of the famous bands in Australia have played the pub circuit.

The best way to find out about the local scene is to get to know some locals, or travellers who have spent some time in the place. Otherwise there are listings in local newspapers.

Spectator Sports
If you're an armchair – or wooden bench – sports fan Tasmania has much to offer. The football season runs from about March to September and when it ends, it's just about time for the cricket season to begin.

Aussie Rules A very unique form of football is Australian Rules – only Gaelic football is anything like it. It's a team sport on an oval field with an oval ball that can be kicked, caught, hit with the hand or carried and bounced. You get six points for kicking a goal and one point for a 'behind' (kicking it through side posts). There are four quarters of 20 minutes each. Fast, tactical, skilful, rough and athletic, it can produce gripping finishes when even after 80 minutes of play the outcome hangs on the very last kick.

Tasmania has a northern and a southern league, and the two winning teams meet in the Tasmanian Football League Grand Final in late September at North Hobart Football Oval. Match details and tickets to games are available from the Tasmanian Football League (☎ 6234 9177). You'll only need to book for final games.

Cricket This is played during the other (non-football) half of the year. Tasmania held its first international test in Hobart in 1995, though one-day matches had been played at Bellerive Oval in the past. Tasmania takes part in the interstate Sheffield Shield competition and also has district cricket matches. Tasmania has never won the Sheffield Shield, but has produced two outstanding Australian Test side batsmen in David Boon and Ricky Ponting. Contact the Tasmanian Cricket Association (☎ 6244 7099) for tickets and match fixtures.

Horse Racing Major race meetings are the Hobart Cup at Elwick in January and the Launceston Cup at Elphin and the Devonport Cup in January. Regular meetings are held about once every month at the Elphin racecourse in Hobart. You can't book tickets; just go along to the course. Most towns have a horse-racing track or a Totalisator Agency Board (TAB) betting office where you can bet on the races.

Yachting Hobart is the finishing line of the famous Sydney to Hobart yacht race and the lesser-known West Coaster race at New Year. For the three weeks after New Year, regular, short races are held on the Derwent River and spectators can get reasonable views from the hills. In February the Royal Hobart Regatta is worth seeing.

Other good races include the Melbourne to Devonport race in late December and the Three Peaks race in April, which combines sailing with marathon-running.

Tennis The tennis courts at the Domain in Hobart are the venue for the state championships in March and for an international women's tournament in January, the latter being a warm-up tournament for the Australian Open. For bookings, contact the Domain Tennis Centre on ☎ 6234 4805.

THINGS TO BUY

There are lots of things definitely *not* to buy, and a check of where it was actually manufactured should be made! Far too many of the supposedly authentic 'Australiana' items are actually made in Asia.

Australiana

The term 'Australiana' is a euphemism for souvenirs. These are the things you buy as gifts for all the friends, aunts and uncles, nieces and nephews, and other sundry bods back home. They are supposedly representative of Australia and its culture, although many are extremely dubious. A typical example in Tassie is the stuffed toy Tasmanian devil.

Huon Pine

Many woodworkers have taken to producing carvings and wood turnings from the local Huon pine. Some of the work is truly magnificent. Good examples, some of which are available for purchase, can be found at the Esperance Forest & Heritage Centre in Geeveston, the stores in Richmond or the craft shops at the Salamanca Market. Items from other uniquely Tasmanian timbers such as blackwood should also be considered. The timbers have rich colours and are all produced locally.

Killecrankie 'Diamonds'

These 'diamonds' come from Flinders Island. They're beautiful stones, but not actually diamonds. They are really topaz – a semi-precious stone which comes in pale blue, pale pink and white varieties – and can be purchased on Flinders Island. The Gem Shop in Whitemark and the general store in Killecrankie can show you a selection of 'diamonds'. The Gem Shop also conducts fossicking tours where you get to look for your own.

Blundstones

These are heavy-duty boots made in Tasmania. Intended for use on construction sites, they are currently very fashionable footwear. These boots wear well and are reasonably cheap.

Other Gifts

For those last-minute gifts, drop into a deli and buy some Tasmanian leatherwood honey (it is one of a number of powerful local varieties). The local cheeses are often magnificent with King Island Brie being internationally famous. For interesting flavoured cheddars the cheeses produced at

Those well-worn Australian favourites, Blundstone boots, originated in Tasmania

Pyengana and Lactos are well worth finding in the delicatessens.

There are plenty of photographic calendars and coffee table books about Tasmania, many of them displaying the wilderness areas.

Antique stores exist all over the state and there is lots of old furniture to be found. This resulted from the large number of settlers who migrated here from Europe in the 19th century and brought their furniture with them. However, the fact that something is old does not mean it's good quality or worth a high price. Before buying antiques, you really need to know what is good value.

Getting There & Away

For most visitors, getting to Tasmania means flying first to mainland Australia. The only country which has direct air links with Tasmania is New Zealand.

International to Australia

The main problem with getting to Australia is that it's a long way from anywhere. If you're coming from Asia, Europe or North America, you'll find lots of competing airlines and a wide variety of air fares – but there's no way you can avoid those great distances. Australia's current international popularity poses another problem – flights are often heavily booked. If you want to fly to Australia at a particularly popular time of year (the middle of summer, ie Christmas time, is notoriously difficult) or on a particularly popular route (like Hong Kong or Singapore to Sydney or Melbourne) then you need to plan well ahead.

Australia has a large number of international gateways. Sydney and Melbourne are the two busiest international airports. Perth also gets many flights from Asia and Europe and has direct flights to New Zealand and Africa. Other international airports include Hobart in Tasmania (New Zealand only), Adelaide, Port Hedland (Bali only), Darwin, Cairns and Brisbane. One place you can't arrive at directly from overseas is Canberra, the national capital.

Sydney is the busiest gateway and it makes a lot of sense to avoid arriving or departing there. Sydney's airport is stretched way beyond its capacity and flights are frequently delayed on arrival and departure. It's good if you can organise your flights to avoid Sydney, but unfortunately many flights to or from other cities (Melbourne in particular) still go via Sydney. If you're planning to explore Australia seriously, then starting at a quieter entry port like Cairns in far north Queensland or Darwin in the Northern Territory can make a lot of sense. If you're coming specifically to explore Tasmania, avoid the northern ports as it's expensive to get from them to Tasmania because of the distances involved. Instead fly into Melbourne which is the closest major port, or from Christchurch, New Zealand where you can fly directly to Hobart.

DISCOUNT TICKETS

Buying airline tickets these days is like shopping for a car, a stereo or a camera – five different travel agents will quote you five different prices. Rule number one if you're looking for a cheap ticket is to go to an agent, not directly to the airline. The airline can usually only quote you the absolutely by-the-rule-book regular fare. An agent, on the other hand, can offer all sorts of special deals particularly on competitive routes.

Ideally an airline would like to fly all its flights with every seat in use and every passenger paying the highest fare possible. Fortunately life usually isn't like that and airlines would rather have a half-price passenger than an empty seat. When faced with the problem of too many seats, they will either let agents sell them at cut prices, or occasionally make one-off special offers on particular routes – watch the travel ads in the press.

Of course what's available and what it costs depends on what time of year it is, what route you're flying and who you're flying with. If you're flying on a popular route (like from Hong Kong) or one where the choice of flights is very limited (like from South America or, to a lesser extent, from Africa) then the fare is likely to be higher or there may be nothing available but the official fare.

Similarly, the dirt cheap fares are likely to be less conveniently scheduled, will go via a less convenient route or be with a less popular airline. Flying London-Sydney, for example, is most convenient with airlines like Qantas, British Airways, Thai International or Singapore Airlines. They have flights every day, operate the same flight straight through to Australia and are good, reliable, comfortable, safe airlines. At the other extreme you could fly from London to an Eastern European or Middle Eastern city on one flight, switch to another flight from there to Asia, and change to another airline from there to Australia. It takes longer, there are delays and changes of aircraft along the way, the airlines may not be so good and furthermore the connection only works once a week, so you'll be leaving London at 1.30 am on Wednesday. The flip side is it's cheaper.

ROUND-THE-WORLD TICKETS

Round-the-World (RTW) tickets are very popular these days and many of these will take you through Australia. The airline RTW tickets are often real bargains and since Australia is pretty much on the other side of the world from Europe or North America it can work out no more expensive, or even cheaper, to keep going in the same direction right round the world rather than U-turn to return.

The official airline RTW tickets are usually put together by a combination of two airlines, and permit you to fly anywhere you want on their route systems so long as you do not backtrack. Other restrictions are that you (usually) must book the first sector in advance and cancellation penalties then apply. There may be restrictions on how many stops you are permitted and usually the tickets are valid from 90 days up to a year. A typical price for a South Pacific RTW ticket is around £760.

An alternative type of RTW ticket is one put together by a travel agent using a combination of discounted tickets from a number of airlines. A UK agent like Trailfinders can put together interesting London-to-London RTW combinations including Australia stopovers for between £690 and £800.

CIRCLE PACIFIC TICKETS

Circle Pacific fares are similar to RTW tickets, using a combination of airlines to circle the Pacific – combining Australia, New Zealand, North America and Asia. Examples would be Qantas-Northwest Orient, Canadian Airlines International-Cathay Pacific and so on. As with RTW tickets there are advance purchase restrictions and limits to how many stopovers you can take. Typically fares range between US$1760 and US$2240. Possible Circle Pacific routes are Los Angeles-Bangkok-Sydney-Auckland-Honolulu-Los Angeles or Los Angeles-Tokyo-Kuala Lumpur-Sydney-Auckland-Honolulu-Los Angeles.

TO/FROM THE UK

The cheapest tickets in London are from the numerous 'bucket shops' (discount ticket agencies) which advertise in magazines and papers like *Time Out*, *Southern Cross* and *TNT*. Pick up one or two of these publications and ring round a few bucket shops to find the best deal. The magazine *Business Traveller* also has a great deal of good advice on air-fare bargains. Most bucket shops are trustworthy and reliable but the occasional sharp operator appears – *Time Out* and *Business Traveller* provide some useful advice on precautions to take.

Trailfinders (☎ (0171) 938 3366) at 46 Earls Court Rd, London W8, and STA Travel (☎ (0171) 581 4132) at 74 Old Brompton Rd, London SW7 and 117 Euston Rd, London NW1 (☎ (0171) 465 0484), are good, reliable agents for cheap tickets.

The cheapest London to Sydney or Melbourne (not direct) bucket-shop tickets are about £385 one way or £638 return. Cheap fares to Perth are around £330 one way and £550 return. Such prices are usually only available if you leave London in the low season – March to June. In September and mid-December, fares go up by about 30%, while the rest of the year they're somewhere in between. Average direct high-season fares to Sydney, Melbourne or Perth are £468 one way and £875 return.

Many cheap tickets allow stopovers on the

way to or from Australia. Rules regarding how many stopovers you can take, how long you can stay away, how far in advance you have to decide your return date and so on, vary from time to time and ticket to ticket. Most return tickets allow you to stay away for any period between 14 days and one year, with stopovers permitted anywhere along your route. As usual with heavily discounted tickets, the less you pay the less you get.

From Australia you can expect to pay around A$1200 one way, and A$1800 return to London and other European capitals, with stops in Asia on the way. Again, all fares increase by up to 30% in the European summer and at Christmas.

TO/FROM NORTH AMERICA

There is a variety of connections across the Pacific from Los Angeles, San Francisco and Vancouver to Australia, including direct flights, flights via New Zealand, island-hopping routes and more circuitous Pacific-rim routes via Asia. Qantas, Air New Zealand and United all fly USA-Australia; Qantas, Air New Zealand and Canadian Airlines International fly Canada-Australia. An interesting option from North America's east coast is Northwest's flight via Japan.

On the US airlines, if your flight goes via Hawaii, the west coast to Hawaii sector is treated as a domestic flight. This means that you have to pay for drinks and headsets – goodies that are free on international sectors. An advantage of the Qantas and Air New Zealand flights via Hawaii is that they are international flights all the way through.

To find good fares to Australia, check the travel ads in the Sunday travel sections of papers like the *Los Angeles Times*, *San Francisco Chronicle-Examiner*, *New York Times* or *Toronto Globe & Mail*. You can typically get a one-way/return ticket from the west coast for US$830/1000, or US$1000/1400 from the east coast. At peak seasons – particularly the Australian summer/Christmas time – seats will be harder to get and the price will probably be higher. In the USA good agents for discounted tickets are the two student travel operators, Council Travel and

STA Travel, which have lots of offices around the country. Canadian west-coast fares out of Vancouver will be similar to those from the US west coast. From Toronto fares go from around C$2230 return.

If Pacific island-hopping is your aim, check out the airlines of Pacific Island nations, some of which have good deals on indirect routes. Qantas can give you Fiji or Tahiti along the way, while Air New Zealand can offer both these and the Cook Islands as well. See the Circle Pacific section for more details.

One-way/return fares available from Australia include: San Francisco A$1000/1360, New York A$1150/1660 and Vancouver A$1000/1360.

TO/FROM NEW ZEALAND

Air New Zealand and Qantas operate a network of trans-Tasman flights linking Auckland, Wellington and Christchurch in New Zealand with most major Australian gateway cities. You can fly directly between a lot of places in New Zealand and a lot of places in Australia.

Fares vary depending on which cities you fly between and when you fly, but from New Zealand to Sydney you're looking at around NZ$450 one way and NZ$565 return, and to Melbourne NZ$529 one way and NZ$730 return. There is a lot of competition on this route – United, British Airways, Qantas and Air New Zealand all fly it, so there should be some good discounts.

Qantas and Air New Zealand both also fly direct from Christchurch to Hobart in Tasmania and the standard fare is A$521 each way. Return discount fares for each season are peak A$809, shoulder A$613 and low A$576.

Cheap fares to New Zealand from Europe will usually be for flights via the USA. A straightforward London-Auckland return bucket-shop ticket costs around £950. Coming via Australia you can continue right around on a Round-the-World ticket which will cost from around £690-800 for a ticket with a comprehensive choice of stopovers.

TO/FROM ASIA

Ticket discounting is widespread in Asia, particularly in Singapore, Hong Kong, Bangkok and Penang. There are a lot of fly-by-nights in the Asian ticketing scene so a little care is required. Also the Asian routes have been particularly caught up in the capacity shortages on flights to Australia. Flights between Hong Kong and Australia are notoriously heavily booked while flights to or from Bangkok and Singapore are often part of the longer Europe-Australia route so can be very full. Plan ahead. For much more information on South-East Asian travel and on to Australia see Lonely Planet's *South-East Asia on a shoestring*.

Typical one-way fares to Australia from Singapore are S$585 to Darwin or Perth, S$785 to Sydney or Melbourne.

You can also pick up some interesting tickets in Asia to include Australia on the way across the Pacific. Qantas and Air New Zealand offer discounted trans-Pacific tickets.

From Australia return fares from the east coast to Singapore, Kuala Lumpur and Bangkok range from A$700 to A$900, and to Hong Kong from A$900 to A$1300.

The cheapest way out of Australia is to take one of the flights operating between Darwin and Kupang (Timor, Indonesia). Current one-way/return fares are A$198/330.

TO/FROM AFRICA

The flight possibilities between Africa and Australia have increased markedly in the last few years, and there are a number of direct flights each week between Africa and Australia, but only between Perth and Harare (Zimbabwe) or Johannesburg (South Africa). Qantas, South African Airways and Air Zimbabwe all fly this route.

Other airlines which connect southern Africa and Australia include Malaysia Airlines (via Kuala Lumpur) and Air Mauritius (via Mauritius), both of which have special deals from time to time.

From East Africa, the options are to fly via Mauritius, or via the Indian subcontinent and on to South-East Asia, then connect from there to Australia.

TO/FROM SOUTH AMERICA

Two routes operate between South America and Australia. The Chile connection involves Lan Chile's twice-weekly Santiago-Easter Island-Tahiti flight, from where you fly Qantas or another airline to Australia. Alternatively there is the route which skirts the Antarctic circle, flying from Buenos Aires to Auckland and Sydney, operated twice-weekly by Aerolineas Argentinas.

ARRIVING IN AUSTRALIA

Australia's dramatic increase in visitor arrivals has caused some severe bottlenecks at the entry points, particularly at Sydney where the airport is often operating at more than full capacity and delays on arrival or departure are frequent; if possible, make Brisbane, Cairns, Melbourne or another gateway city your arrival point. There is generally an airport bus service at the international airports and there are always taxis available.

LEAVING AUSTRALIA

There is a $27 departure tax when leaving Australia, but this is incorporated into the price of your air ticket and so is not paid as a separate tax.

From Mainland Australia

Because Tasmania is an island, the wide strip of water called Bass Strait has to be crossed by either air or boat.

AIR

The airlines which fly to Tasmania are Ansett (☎ 13 1300), Qantas (☎ 13 1313), Kendell (☎ toll-free 1800 338 894), Phillip Island Air Services (☎ (059) 56 7316), King Island Airlines (☎ (03) 9580 3777), Airlines of Tasmania (☎ toll-free 1800 030 550), Aus-Air (☎ toll-free 1800 338 894) and Hazelton

Air Services (☎ (02) 9235 1411). Some of these are subsidiaries of the big two, Ansett and Qantas.

Ansett and Qantas fly to Tasmania from most Australian state capitals, while the other smaller airlines operate from various airports in Victoria. Most flights are to Hobart, Launceston, Devonport, Wynyard (Burnie), Smithton, Flinders Island or King Island.

Air fares to Tasmania are constantly changing, but because of the number of operators, prices are competitive and you can get some good deals – especially if you book well in advance or if you are planning a trip in the winter months. Discounts are not uniform with advertised 'Rock Bottom' fares ranging from 45% to 55% off depending on the route, day of the week and time – you can often do better. When discount seats are unavailable, students under 26 years can get a 25% discount with the two main airlines.

To/From Hobart

The standard one-way economy fare with Ansett and Qantas from Melbourne is $216, although much cheaper fares are often available. From Sydney the standard fare is $311 and from Brisbane $431.

To/From Launceston

Ansett and Qantas fly from Melbourne for $187 one way, but it's around $220 return if you book well in advance. The smaller airlines flying out of Melbourne generally use the city's second-string airports of Essendon and Moorabbin and have lower base rates but offer fewer discounts. It's worth noting that Airlines of Tasmania runs flights between country Victoria (Sale and Traralgon) and Launceston via Flinders Island and King Island which are only a little more expensive than flying direct; this gives you the option of a stopover on an island, more or less free.

To/From Devonport & Wynyard (Burnie)

There are flights from Melbourne to Devonport and Wynyard (often referred to as Burnie) by Kendell Airlines (both flights are $158) and Aus-Air ($136 and $148). Airlines of Tasmania also flies from Melbourne to Burnie for $154. Phillip Island Air Services flies to Burnie for $105 one way.

To/From the Islands

Aus-Air, Airlines of Tasmania and Kendell Airlines fly to King Island from Melbourne for around $110 to $120. Aus-Air and Airlines of Tasmania also fly to Flinders Island from Melbourne for around $140. Some discounts are available, but as you'll need to book accommodation and hire a car, the best deal is to buy a fly, drive and accommodation package. Packages with two nights' accommodation and car hire to King Island range from $280 per person and similar deals to Flinders Island are from $330.

You can also get package deals to the islands from Launceston and country towns in Victoria. The package price effectively provides the car for free – a good deal as you need a car to fully appreciate the islands.

BOAT

Bass Strait is known as one of the roughest shipping channels in the world, so travellers prone to seasickness should beware.

Ferry

The *Spirit of Tasmania*, which operates between Melbourne and Devonport, is currently the only ferry crossing the Bass Strait. It can accommodate 1300 passengers and over 600 vehicles. It has nine decks and, with its swimming pool, saunas, restaurants, gaming machines and bars, is more like a floating hotel than a ferry. The public areas of the ship have been designed to cater for wheelchair access, and four cabins have been specially designed for this purpose.

It departs from the TT Line terminal (☎ toll-free 1800 030 344) at Melbourne's Station Pier at 6 pm on Monday, Wednesday and Friday and from the terminal on the Esplanade in Devonport at 6 pm on Sunday, Tuesday and Thursday, arriving 14½ hours later, at 8.30 am.

The fares depend on whether you're travelling in the holiday season, which roughly corresponds with school-holidays. One-way fares range from $99 ($120 in the holiday season) in hostel-style accommodation (20-bed cabins) up to suites for $325 ($380). For cabins, discounts of around 35% (called cruise fare) apply to return tickets. For one-way trips discounts of around 25% apply for students for cabins but not for hostel-style accommodation. All fares include an evening buffet dinner and a continental breakfast or you can go to the formal restaurant and pay extra for your meal.

The cost for accompanied vehicles depends on the size of the vehicle. The standard size is a maximum length of five metres long and a maximum height of 2¼ metres. The minimum one-way rate is $125 ($175 holiday season) for cars, while motorcycles cost $70 ($100) and bicycles $20 ($25).

Yacht

An interesting way to get to the state is by yacht. Every year hopeful adventurers head to Sydney to find a berth on a yacht in the Sydney to Hobart Yacht Race, but most have no hope as the yachts use their regular crews. You will have far more luck crewing a boat from Hobart back to its home port after the race has been completed when many of the regular crew fly home. This is far more pleasant as the boats are cruising home, not racing.

PACKAGE DEALS

Tourist agencies often offer various package deals to Tasmania – transport there, accommodation and car hire – which are often considerably cheaper than purchasing each component separately. As you would expect, the biggest discounts apply in the quieter periods of autumn, winter and spring. In summer the package deals rise in price. Most package deals have conditions attached to them, of which the most common is twin share (two people). Sometimes an itinerary is fixed at booking.

Kendell Airlines offers fly, drive, accommodation packages from Melbourne for seven days for $578 per person in winter and $810 in summer. They allow you to alter your itinerary and the accommodation is with the larger motel chains. Autorent Hertz

offers a similar deal from Melbourne for $513 in the off season and $674 over Christmas. Together with Hertz it also offers car and accommodation-only packages from $46 per person per day. Such packages are worthwhile if you prefer motel or B&B accommodation.

When visiting the two major islands in Bass Strait, King or Flinders Island, the package deals should be seriously considered. This is because there are no hostels or super-cheap places to stay, you have to fly there and you really need a car to get around. Booking these separately is considerably more expensive; car hire on both islands is around $60 per day with no discounting (there is only one hire company).

Airlines of Tasmania, Aus-Air and Kendell Airlines all offer packages for two nights including air fares and accommodation from around $250 per person from Launceston, Burnie or Melbourne. Five-night packages start at around $350 per person and are a good deal when you consider that car hire plus accommodation together are around $35 for each extra day.

WARNING

The information in this chapter is particularly vulnerable to change – prices for travel are volatile, routes are introduced and cancelled, schedules change, rules are amended, special deals come and go. Airlines and governments seem to take a perverse pleasure in making price structures and regulations as complicated as possible and you should check directly with the airline or travel agent to make sure you understand how a fare (and the ticket you may buy) works. For non-refundable fares it's often wise to purchase insurance.

In addition, the travel industry is highly competitive and there are many lurks and perks. The upshot of this is that you should get quotes and advice from as many airlines and travel agents as possible before you part with your hard-earned cash. The details given in this chapter should only be regarded as pointers and cannot be any substitute for your own careful, up-to-date research.

Getting Around

AIR

Airlines of Tasmania (☎ 1800 030 550) operates a fairly extensive network of flights around the island which can be booked at most travel agencies and any Tasmanian Travel & Information Centre. Fares from Hobart include Queenstown $113, Launceston $76 and Burnie $115. When you add the cost and time of getting to the airports plus waiting time it's not much faster than the buses, but is much dearer. Most visitors use the small airlines for joy flights for sightseeing rather than for travel between towns.

To get to the islands in Bass Strait, air is the only practical option and several smaller airlines run regular services from Launceston and Wynyard (often shown as Burnie on flight schedules) to both King and Flinders islands. There is also another island you can stay on, Swan Island, and flights

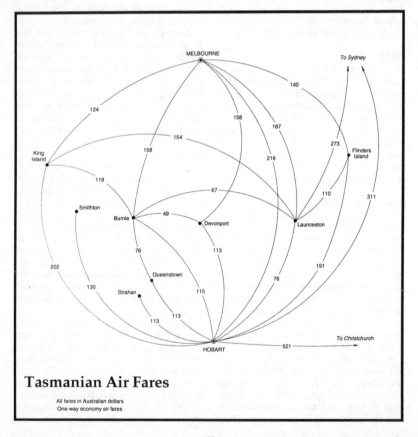

Tasmanian Air Fares

All fares in Australian dollars
One-way economy air fares

there are run by charter and are organised when you make your booking.

BUS

Tasmania has a very good bus network, connecting all major towns and centres and some out-of-the-way places. Weekend services are less frequent, which can be inconvenient for the traveller with only a limited time in the state. There are also more buses in summer than in winter.

The three main bus companies – Tasmanian Redline Coaches, Hobart Coaches (also trading as Inter-City Coaches) and Tasmanian Wilderness Transport – cover most of the state between them. All three have depots in the major centres of Hobart, Launceston and Devonport as well as agents in the stopover towns. Hobart Coaches' fares are sometimes considerably cheaper.

The companies have their own special passes; you can't use your Greyhound Pioneer Aussie Pass in Tasmania. Tasmanian Redline Coaches has the Super Tassie Pass, for seven, 15 or 31 days, which gives you unrestricted travel on all its routes for $98, $138 or $178 respectively, and is also valid for the small east-coast services run by

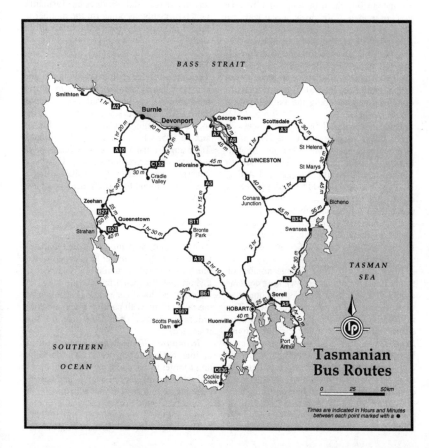

Tasmanian
Bus Routes

Times are indicated in Hours and Minutes
between each point marked with a ●

Peakes. Tasmanian Wilderness Transport and Hobart Coaches have a combined Wilderness & Highway Pass for 7 days ($99), 14 days ($140) or 30 days ($179) which is valid on all of the routes of both companies.

If you are considering buying any of these passes, don't forget to check the weekend timetables. Also, make sure that you buy a pass with a company which has services to the areas you want to visit; *Tasmanian Travelways* has details of timetables and fares for major routes. These passes can also be bought in advance on the mainland from Greyhound Pioneer, but generally it's cheaper to buy them in Tasmania. To give you some idea of the costs, a one-way trip between Hobart and Launceston costs about $18, between Hobart and Queenstown $33 and between Launceston and Burnie $17. The bus passes are often good value if you do lots of short rides between major towns as the total of the individual fares is considerably more than doing the same trip as a single journey.

Buses run along all the major highways all year. These include the Lyell Hwy from Hobart to Queenstown ($33) and Strahan ($38), the Midland Hwy from Hobart to Launceston ($18), the Tasman and Arthur Hwys to Port Arthur ($11) and along the east coast, and the main road along the north coast from Launceston to Smithton ($26). During summer, services along all these routes are daily; during winter there are still regular services but they're not daily on some routes.

Buses also run along a large number of minor roads to popular bushwalking destinations – though they're not as frequent as those which run between main towns. The link road from Devonport past Cradle Mountain to the Lyell Hwy, and the direct route from Devonport past the Great Lake to Derwent Bridge and Cynthia Bay ($45) have daily services in summer and less frequent services in winter. Buses also run on several days of the week from Hobart past Maydena to Scotts Peak ($40), and also from Hobart past Dover to Cockle Creek ($35) in the south.

Some of the youth hostels also run their own bus services which can be very handy. During winter special bus services run to the ski fields (when there is snow!). Details of regional services are described in the relevant Getting There & Away sections of each chapter.

The bus services provided enable visitors to get to most of the interesting places in the state and there is little need or benefit to be gained from hitching around.

TRAIN

For economic reasons there are no longer any passenger rail services in Tasmania, which probably accounts for the number of model railways and train exhibitions in the state!

TAXI

Taxis are available at all the major towns and can be a handy way of getting to places otherwise not easily reached. For example, there are no bus services from Hobart to the top of Mt Wellington and the taxi fare is around $25, which is reasonable if shared. Taxis are also handy for getting back late at night to where you are staying. However, you should not seriously consider using a taxi to get around the state unless you have buckets of money.

CAR & MOTORCYCLE
Rental

Although you can bring cars from the mainland to Tasmania, it might be cheaper to rent one for your visit, particularly if your stay is a short one. Tasmania has a wide range of national and local car-rental agencies, and the rates (along with parking fines) are considerably lower than they are on the mainland.

Tasmanian Travelways lists rental options, but before you decide on a company, don't forget to ask about any km limitations and what the insurance covers – and ensure there are no hidden seasonal adjustments. It is, however, quite normal for smaller rental companies to ask for a bond of around $200.

The large national firms like Budget,

Hertz and Avis have standard rates for cars from $65 to $140 per day. If possible, book in advance and ask first about rates for smaller cars (Corolla, Laser, Pulsar, Barina). Rates can be as low as $44 per day for hires out of holiday season. In summer, rates are generally higher being around $50 to $60 per day for multi-day hire but still considerably cheaper than the full advertised rates. Although this is more expensive than rates offered by many smaller companies, there's no bond and you get unlimited km, comprehensive insurance and reliable cars. The larger companies also have offices at the main airports and the ferry terminal in Devonport.

Small local firms like Advance Car Rentals, which has offices in Hobart, Launceston and Devonport, charge around $44 a day ($264 a week, $37 per day) for the same type of cars, but with varied conditions. Tasmania also has a number of companies renting older cars like VW Beetles for around $20 a day. In this bracket, Rent-a-Bug, with offices in Hobart and Devonport, has a good reputation. To get the cheapest cars you need to book early. The smaller companies don't have desks at arrival points but can usually arrange for your car to be picked up at airports and terminals.

You can take your motorcycle to Tasmania on the *Spirit of Tasmania* ferry. The cost is $70 ($100 during the holiday season).

Campervans Campervans are a popular way to travel around the state. *Tasmanian Travelways* also has a listing of campervan rental companies. All the larger national firms have campervans for around $800 a week, but by far the most popular is Touring Motor Homes (☎ 6334 4424 or 1800 030 106) in Launceston where vans start at $700 per week.

Road Rules

Australia has country-wide road rules. Australians drive on the left-hand side of the road, the same as in the UK, Japan and most countries in Asia and the Pacific. There are a few local variations from the rules of the road which are applied elsewhere in the world.

The main one is the 'give way to the right' rule. This means that if you're driving on a main road and somebody appears on a minor road on you right, you must give way to them – unless they are facing a give-way or stop sign. When you are turning left, you have right of way over any vehicles which are turning right but you must still give way to vehicles on your right which are going straight ahead. Another exception is at T-intersections where the through road has right of way over all traffic on the approaching road. Confused? Some local drivers still are and most major roads are now signposted to indicate the priority road.

In towns and cities, the general speed limit is 60 km/h while on the open road the general limit is 110 km/h. Many of Tasmania's roads are narrow and winding, and signposted limits of 100 km/h are common. For provisional license holders the speed limit is 80 km/h. The police have radar speed traps and like to use their high technology equipment in carefully hidden locations – don't exceed the speed limits as the boys and girls in blue may be waiting for you.

Australia was one of the first countries to make the wearing of seat belts compulsory. If you don't wear a seat belt then fines can be imposed by the police. The other main law applies to drinking and driving, where a strict limit of 0.05 for blood alcohol content applies. For exceeding the limit, heavy fines apply – your licence will be cancelled and jail sentences are imposed on offenders who are convicted several times. Random breath tests are conducted by police without warning. The best policy is to not to combine drinking and driving.

Although overseas licences are acceptable in Australia for genuine overseas visitors, an International Driving Permit is even better. If staying for more than 12 months then you will need to obtain a local licence; apply at any police station.

On The Road

While you're driving around the state, watch

out for the wildlife which, all too often, ends up flattened on the roadside. Many of the animals are nocturnal and often cross roads around dusk. Try to avoid driving in the country just after sunset; if you must drive then, slow down. Hitting a wombat not only kills the animal, but also makes a mess of your car.

Many roads, including some highways, are fairly narrow with many sharp bends not signposted, and there are still some one-lane bridges which are not clearly signposted. Cycling is popular on some roads (particularly on the east coast), and when encountering bicycles you should wait until you can pass safely. It's wise to drive a little more slowly and allow more time to react to these hazards. Distances are short, so there is no need to speed.

Fuel Supplies

Petrol is available in most towns across the state every day of the week. In small towns there'll often just be a pump outside the general store, while the larger towns and cities have conventional service stations and garages. Most are open from 8 am to 6 pm on weekdays. On week nights until midnight and at weekends, a roster system operates between the petrol stations so that at least one place is open in most of the towns.

LPG (gas) is available in some locations. An up-to-date list of stations with LPG is published in each edition of *Treasure Islander* a free tourist magazine which is available from most Tourist Information Centres.

BICYCLE

Tasmania is an ideal size to explore by bicycle and you can hire bikes throughout the state. If you plan to cycle between Hobart and Launceston via either coast, count on it taking around 10 to 14 days. For a full circuit of the island, allow 14 to 28 days. Bear in mind that some roads are rather hilly, and you can expect at least some rainy days in any season, particularly in the western half of the state.

Rent-a-Cycle at the Launceston City Youth Hostel has a good variety of touring and mountain bikes plus all the equipment you'll need for short or long trips. You should be able to hire a bike for between $10 and $15 a day or $60 and $70 a week. If you're planning on an extended ride it's worth considering buying a bike and reselling it at the end.

If you bring a bike over on the *Spirit of Tasmania* it will cost you $20 to $25 each way, depending on the season. By air, Ansett charges $15 to carry a bicycle one way to Hobart or Launceston, while Qantas charges $10. It's easier to get your bike over to Tassie on flights to Hobart or Launceston than on those to smaller airports such as Burnie or Devonport.

While the same road rules that apply to cars also apply to bicycles, riders should also follow another rule; if in doubt either give way or get out of the way. It's no use being in the right, you almost certainly come off second best in any collision. Full notes and lots of practical advice for cycling around the state can be found in *Bicycling Tasmania* by Ian Terry and Rob Beedham, $13.

FERRY

There is a regular car ferry from Kettering to Bruny Island. It operates several times each day and is free for passengers. However, you'll need a car or bicycle to explore this rather long island.

Another useful ferry runs from the east coast near Triabunna to Maria Island. This also operates daily and will carry passengers and bicycles. This island is much smaller and is a national park. Vehicles are not allowed, so you can only explore it on foot or by bicycle.

HITCHING

Travel by thumb in Tassie is generally good, but you'll need to wrap up in winter and keep a raincoat handy. A good number of the state's roads are still unsurfaced and the traffic can be very light, so although these roads sometimes lead to interesting places, you normally have to give them a miss if you're hitching.

Hitching is never entirely safe in any country in the world, and we don't recommend it; Tasmania has excellent bus services to almost all locations. Travellers who decide to hitch should understand that they are taking a small but potentially serious risk. Women should be particularly careful. People who do choose to hitch will be safer if they travel in pairs and let someone know where they are planning to go.

Hobart

- *pop 127,000*

Hobart is Australia's second-oldest capital city and also the smallest and most southerly. Straddling the mouth of the Derwent River and backed by mountains which offer excellent views over the city, Hobart has managed to combine the progress and benefits of a modern city with the rich heritage of its colonial past. The beautiful Georgian buildings, the busy harbour and the easy-going atmosphere, all make Hobart one of the most enjoyable and engaging of Australia's cities.

History

The first inhabitants of the city area were members of the Aboriginal Mouheneer tribe, who lived a semi-nomadic lifestyle. The first European colony in Tasmania was founded in 1803 at Risdon Cove, but a year later Lieutenant-Colonel David Collins, Governor of the new settlement in Van Diemen's Land, sailed down the Derwent River and decided that a cove about 10 km below Risdon and on the opposite shore was a better place to settle. This, the site of Tasmania's future capital city, began as a village of tents and wattle-and-daub huts with a population of 262 Europeans.

Hobart Town, as it was known until 1881, was proclaimed a city in 1842. Very important to its development was the Derwent River estuary, one of the world's finest deep-water harbours, and many merchants made their fortunes from the whaling trade, ship-building and the export of products like corn and merino wool.

Orientation

Hobart is sandwiched between the steep hills of Mt Wellington and the wide Derwent River. With a minimum of flat land, the city has spread along the shores of the Derwent River and is about 20 km long but very narrow. Some development has spread into the hills and you will find many streets extremely steep.

HIGHLIGHTS

- Enjoying the view from Mt Wellington or Mt Nelson
- Browsing in Salamanca market
- Eating chocolate on a Cadbury tour
- Walking around historic Battery Point
- Exploring the botanic gardens

The city centre is fairly small, simply laid out and is easy to find your way around. The streets in the city centre are arranged in a grid pattern around the Elizabeth St Mall. The Tasmanian Travel & Information Centre, Ansett Airlines, Qantas and the GPO are all in Elizabeth St. Hobart has controlled the traffic in its narrow streets by making them one-way and, if driving, you should first study a map.

Salamanca Place, the famous row of Georgian warehouses, is along the waterfront, while just south of this is Battery Point, Hobart's delightful, well-preserved early colonial district. If you follow the river around from Battery Point you'll come to Sandy Bay, the site of the yacht clubs, Hobart's university and the circular tower of

Wrest Point Hotel Casino – one of Hobart's main landmarks.

The northern side of the city centre is bounded by the recreation area known locally as the Domain (short for the Queen's Domain), which includes the Royal Tasmanian Botanical Gardens and the Derwent River. From here the Tasman Bridge crosses the river to the eastern suburbs and the airport. North of the Domain the suburbs continue beside the Derwent River almost all the way to Bridgewater.

There are very few large industries and the ones that exist are well out of the main city area. Electrolytic Zinc, the Cadbury chocolate factory and paper mills at Boyer are beside the Derwent River but well upstream.

Information

Tourist Office The Tasmanian Travel & Information Centre (☎ 6230 8233) on the corner of Davey and Elizabeth Sts opens on weekdays from 8.30 am to 5.15 pm, and on weekends and public holidays from 9 am to 4 pm. You can also get tourist information from the travel section of Mures Fish Centre, Victoria Dock and from many accommodation establishments.

If you have an FM radio, you can pick up a tourist information broadcast on 88 MHz within a six km radius of the city centre.

Post & Communications The GPO is in the centre of the city, on the corner of Elizabeth and Macquarie Sts. Hobart's STD area telephone code is now the same as the rest of south-eastern Australia – 03. All numbers for the Hobart region begin with 62 and calls within the city are classed as local. Calls from Hobart to country regions are usually at STD rates, even when they begin with 62; rates are dependent on the distance involved. If you hear three pips at the start of a call, then STD rates are being charged and you should be ready to insert more coins if you are using a pay phone. Local calls from pay phones are 40c for unlimited time.

Money Banks are open for business from 9 am to 4 pm on Monday to Friday. Automatic Teller Machines can be used at any time and are available at the banks in the city centre and at some of the suburban branches. All the major banks have their offices near the mall in Elizabeth St.

Useful Organisations The Tasmanian YHA (☎ 6234 9617) is at 28 Criterion St and is open Monday to Friday from 10 am to 5 pm. For information about driving around the state, the Royal Auto Club of Tasmania (RACT) (☎ 6238 2200) is on the corner of Murray and Patrick St.

Tasmanian Museum & Art Gallery

The excellent Tasmanian Museum & Art Gallery (☎ 6235 0777), at 5 Argyle St (enter via Macquarie St), incorporates Hobart's oldest building, the Commissariat Store, built in 1808. The museum section features a Tasmanian Aboriginal display and artefacts from the state's colonial heritage, while the gallery has a good collection of Tasmanian colonial art. There are interesting displays of animals, including extinct and prehistoric ones, and a large mineral collection. The bookshop beside the entrance sells a wide range of books, many of which are not available elsewhere. The museum is free and opens daily from 10 am to 5 pm.

Other Museums

The **Allport Museum & Library of Fine Arts** (☎ 6233 7484) is based in the State Library at 91 Murray St. It has a collection of rare books on Australasia and the Pacific region, lots of antique furniture and a large collection of paintings. You can visit the museum on weekdays from 9.30 am to 5 pm; entry is free.

The **Van Diemen's Land Folk Museum** is the oldest folk museum in Australia. It's based in Narryna, a fine Georgian home at 103 Hampden Rd, Battery Point. Dating from the 1830s, it stands in beautiful grounds and has a large and fascinating collection of relics from Tasmania's early pioneering days. It's open on weekdays from 10 am to 5 pm and at weekends from 2 to 5 pm; admission is $5, children $2 or family $10.

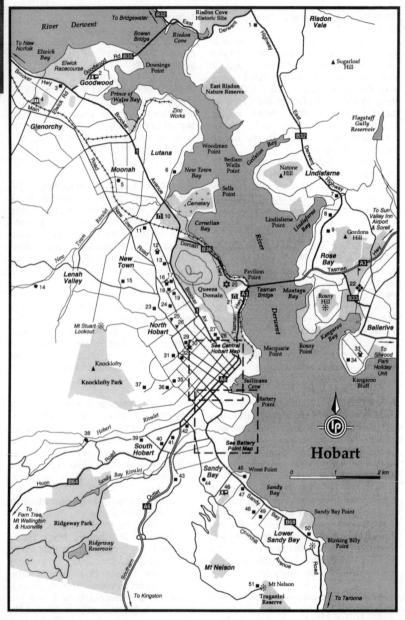

River Derwent
To Bridgewater B32
Risdon Cove Historic Site
Risdon Vale
East
Derwent
1
Highway
Bowen Bridge
Risdon Cove
To New Norfolk
Elwick Bay
Goodwood Rd B35
Dowsings Point
Sugarloaf Hill
Brooker Hwy
3
Elwick Racecourse
Goodwood
2
Prince of Wales Bay
East Risdon Nature Reserve
Flagstaff Gully Reservoir
4
Main
Glenorchy
Zinc Works
Gellibrand Bay
B32
Derwent Highway
Brooker Road
Lutana
Woodman Point
Bedlam Walls Point
Lindisfarne
Natone Hill
New Town Rivulet
Moonah
6
New Town Bay
8
To Sun Valley Inn Airport & Sorell
5
Selfs Point
Lindisfarne Point
9
Gordons Hill
New Town Road
10
Cemetery
Cornelian Bay
Lindisfarne Bay
Rose Bay
A3
New Town Rivulet
11
Domain B36
River
Tasman
22
B33
Lenah Valley
12
13
New Town
Pavilion Point
Montagu Bay
Rosny Hill
Bellerive
14
15
16 17
18
19
Queens Domain
20
21
Tasman Bridge
33
To Silwood Park Holiday Unit
Mt Stuart Lookout
23
24
25
26
North Hobart
27
28
Macquarie Point
Rosny Bay
34
Kangaroo Bluff
Knocklofty
29
30
See Central Hobart Map
Rosny Point
Knocklofty Park
31
32
37
36
35
A6
Sullivans Cove
Kangaroo Bay
Rivulet
Hobart
Battery Point
Hobart
38
39
40
41
42
See Battery Point Map
Huon Road
B64
Sandy Bay Rivulet
43
Sandy Bay
45 Wrest Point
0 1 2 km
To Fern Tree, Mt Wellington & Huonville
44
46
Sandy Bay
Ridgeway Park
A6
47 Sandy
48
49 Bay
B68
Sandy Bay Point
Southern Outlet
Ridgeway Reservoir
Churchill Avenue
Lower Sandy Bay
50
Blinking Billy Point
Mt Nelson
51 Mt Nelson
To Kingston
Truganini Reserve
To Taroona

PLACES TO STAY

1	Bowen Park (Cabins)
2	Elwick Caravan Park
3	Northside Holiday Villas
6	Marina Motel
7	Orana Accommodation
8	Lindisfarne Motor Inn
9	Roseneath Host Accommodation
11	Wendover
12	Woodlands Hostel
13	Hillpark House
15	Jutland House
16	Adelphi Court
17	Hobart Tower Motel
18	Argyle Motor Lodge
19	Northside Manor
23	Elms of Hobart
24	Domain View Apartments
27	Wellington Lodge
28	Corinda Colonial Accommodation

29	Lodge On Elizabeth
31	Warwick Cottages
32	Waratah Hotel
33	Bellerive Hostel
34	Holm Lodge Guest House
35	Marquis of Hastings Hotel
36	Mayfair Hotel
37	Bay View Villas
39	Cascade Hotel
40	Islington Private Hotel
41	Jane Franklin Hall
42	Globe Hotel
43	Andersons
45	Wrest Point Hotel Casino
46	Sandy Bay Caravan Park
47	Sandy Bay Motor Inn
48	Mt Pleasant Mews
49	Red Chapel House
50	Beach House Hotel
51	Signalman's Cottage

PLACES TO EAT

25	Vanidols Restaurant
26	Elizabeth St Restaurants
30	Kaos Cafe

OTHER

4	Tasmania Transport Museum
5	Moonah Arts Centre
10	Runnymede
14	Lady Franklin Gallery
20	Royal Botanical Gardens
21	Government House
22	Eastlands Shopping Centre
38	Cascade Brewery
44	University of Tasmania

The **Maritime Museum of Tasmania** at Secheron House, Secheron Rd in Battery Point, was built in 1831 and is classified by the National Trust. It also contains an extensive collection of photos, paintings, models and relics depicting Tasmania's – and particularly Hobart's – colourful shipping history. Admission is $2 and it's open daily from 10 am to 4.30 pm except Christmas Day and Good Friday.

Close to Constitution Dock, the **Sullivans Cove Whisky Distillery & Museum** at 2 Macquarie St is open every day from 8.30 am to 8.30 pm. It is the only whisky distillery in Australia, it's rather small and you can tour it for $5.

Other museums include the **John Elliott Classics Museum** at the University of Tasmania (free). The **Tasmanian Transport Museum** in Anfield St, Glenorchy is open on weekends from 1 pm to 4.30 pm, entry $3, children $1.50. Australia's first public museum, the **Lady Franklin Gallery**, in Lenah Valley Rd is open on weekends from 1.30 to 4.30 pm; entry is free. The **Moonah Arts Centre** at 65 Hopkins St, Moonah is open from 12.30 to 5 pm on weekdays; entry is free.

Risdon Cove Historic Site

This is the site of the first European settlement in Tasmania and is definitely worth a visit. Very little remains of the original buildings and most sites are simply foundations, but the pyramid-shaped visitor centre has an excellent informative display. A 30 minute nature trail and a bird observatory complete the site. It's open every day from 9.30 am to 4.30 pm and is located on the eastern shore about 10 km from the city. Entry is free. To get there, take a No 68 bus from the Eastlands Shopping Centre.

Settler's hut at historic Risdon Cove

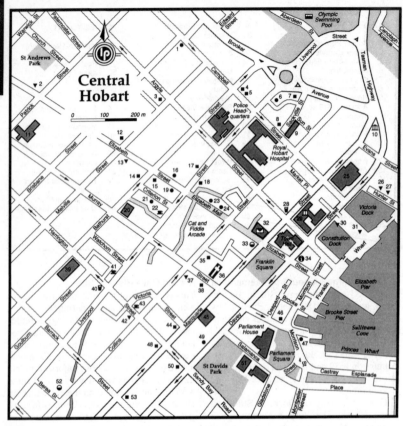

Historic Buildings

One of the things that makes Hobart so unusual among Australian cities is its wealth of old and remarkably well-preserved buildings. More than 90 buildings in Hobart are classified by the National Trust and 60 of them, featuring some of Hobart's best Georgian architecture, are in Macquarie and Davey Sts. The National Trust's office is on the corner of Brisbane and Campbell Sts (☎ 6223 5200) and it has a shop at 33 Salamanca Place.

An excellent booklet on both new and old buildings, *An Architectural Guide to the City of Hobart* (published by the Tasmanian Chapter of the Royal Australian Institute of Architects), is available from the National Trust shop at Salamanca for $3. The shop is open all day Monday to Friday and on Saturday morning.

Close to the city centre is **St Davids Park**, which has some lovely old trees, and some gravestones which date from the earliest days of the colony. In Murray St is **Parliament House**, which was originally used as a customs house. Hobart's prestigious **Theatre Royal**, at 29 Campbell St, was built in 1837 and is the oldest theatre in Australia.

There's a **royal tennis court** in Davey St, one of only three in the southern hemisphere, which you can look into on the National Trust's Saturday-morning tour – see the Organised Tours section for details. (Royal or 'real' tennis is an ancient form of tennis played in a four-walled indoor court.)

The historic **Penitentiary Chapel & Criminal Courts** are at 28 Campbell St; the National Trust runs daily tours of the buildings between 10 am and 2 pm ($4). For groups of more than 10, a tour can be arranged outside these hours; contact ☎ 6231 0911 for details.

Runnymede, at 61 Bay Rd, New Town, is a gracious colonial residence dating from the early 1830s. It was built for Robert Pitcairn, who was the first lawyer to qualify in Tasmania, and named by a later owner, Captain Charles Bayley, after his favourite ship.

Now managed by the National Trust, it is open daily from 10 am to 4.30 pm; admission is $5, children $3 or family $10. It is closed during July and on major public holidays. To get there take bus No 15, 16 or 20 from the corner of Argyle and Macquarie Sts.

Cascade Brewery

Australia's oldest brewery, on Cascade Rd close to the city centre, is still producing some of the finest beer in the country – although no doubt others would argue differently! Two-hour tours take place daily at 9.30 am and 1 pm, and bookings are essential (☎ 6224 1144); entry is $7, children $2. The tour requires climbing many stairs and flat shoes are recommended; thongs and open footwear are not suitable. The brewery is on the south-western edge of the city centre; bus Nos 44, 46, 49 and 50 go right by it – alight at stop 18.

The Waterfront

Hobart's busy waterfront area, centring on **Franklin Wharf**, is close to the city centre and very interesting to walk around. At **Constitution Dock** there are several floating takeaway seafood stalls and it's a treat to sit in the sun munching fresh fish & chips while watching the activity in the harbour. At the finish of the annual Sydney to Hobart Yacht Race around New Year and during the Royal Hobart Regatta in February, Constitution Dock really comes alive. The docks also

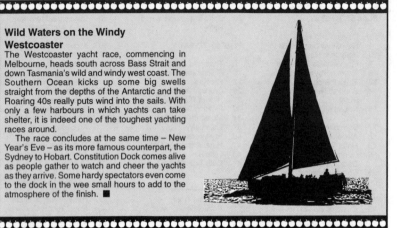

Wild Waters on the Windy Westcoaster

The Westcoaster yacht race, commencing in Melbourne, heads south across Bass Strait and down Tasmania's wild and windy west coast. The Southern Ocean kicks up some big swells straight from the depths of the Antarctic and the Roaring 40s really puts wind into the sails. With only a few harbours in which yachts can take shelter, it is indeed one of the toughest yachting races around.

The race concludes at the same time – New Year's Eve – as its more famous counterpart, the Sydney to Hobart. Constitution Dock comes alive as people gather to watch and cheer the yachts as they arrive. Some hardy spectators even come to the dock in the wee small hours to add to the atmosphere of the finish. ■

have some fine sit-down restaurants if you prefer something more formal.

Nearby **Hunter St** has a row of fine Georgian warehouses. They're similar to those in Salamanca Place, but haven't – yet – been developed as a tourist attraction. They are in a similar condition to that of the Salamanca Place buildings before they were restored.

The whole wharf area is actually reclaimed land. When Hobart was first settled, Davey St ran along the edge of the sea and the Hunter St area was originally an island which was used to safely store food and other goods. Subsequent projects filled in the shallow waters and provided land upon which the warehouses of Hunter St and Salamanca Place were constructed.

Salamanca Place

The row of beautiful sandstone warehouses on the harbourfront at Salamanca Place is a prime example of Australian colonial architecture. Dating back to the whaling days of the 1830s, these warehouses were the centre of Hobart Town's trade and commerce. Only 20 years ago, many of these buildings were in a derelict state and under threat of demolition. Thankfully they were saved and today they have been tastefully developed to house

galleries, restaurants, nightspots and shops selling everything from vegetables to antiques. Every Saturday morning a popular open-air **craft market** is held at Salamanca Place from 8.30 am to 3 pm in summer and 2 pm in the other seasons. There are usually about 300 stalls in the market and the businesses in the warehouses are also open. Goods on sale range from the fresh vegetables grown by the Hmong community (a migrant group from Laos), flowers, clothing and art works made by local artisans.

To reach Battery Point from Salamanca Place you can climb up the **Kelly Steps**, which are wedged between two of the warehouses about halfway along the main block of warehouses.

Battery Point

Behind Princes Wharf and Salamanca Place is the historic core of Hobart, the old port area known as Battery Point. Its name comes from the gun battery that stood on the promontory by the guardhouse. It was built in 1818, and is now the oldest building in the district. The guns were never used in battle and the only damage they did was to shatter the windows of nearby houses when fired during practice.

During colonial times, this area was a colourful maritime village, home to master mariners, shipwrights, sailors, fishers, coopers and merchants. The houses reflect their varying lifestyles, ranging from tiny one and two-room houses such as those around Arthur Circus to large mansions built by the wealthy. While most houses are still lived in by locals, a range of buildings are used for visitor accommodation, so you can stay here and experience the village atmosphere of this unique area. Battery Point's pubs, churches, conjoined houses and narrow winding streets have all been lovingly preserved and are a real delight to wander around, especially when you get glimpses of the harbour between the buildings. There is so much to see here; don't miss out on **Arthur Circus** – a small circle of quaint little cottages built around a village green – or **St George's Anglican Church**.

Anglesea Barracks was built in Battery Point in 1811. Still used by the army, this is the oldest military establishment in Australia. There's no admission fee to the museum, which is usually open on weekdays from 9 am to 3.30 pm, and there are guided tours of the restored buildings and grounds on Tuesday at 11 am. At other times you are free to wander around the buildings and look at the outside, but you cannot enter them as they are still in use.

The only way to see the place properly is to walk around, and the *Battery Point & Sullivans Cove Tourist Trail* brochure is well worth obtaining. It's available from many businesses in Battery Point or from the supplier, Avon Court, at 4 Colville St for $1. Alternatively you can go on an organised walking tour on Saturday – see the Organised Tours section below.

Queens Domain

When Hobart was originally settled, the high hill on the north side of the city was reserved for the use of the Governor. This stopped development of housing across the hill and today the area is known as the Queens Domain and is reserved for public parkland.

This large park contains reserves and playing grounds for cricket and athletics as well as wide areas of native grasslands. There are good views across the river and the city from many areas of the Domain; the best view is from the lookouts on top of the hill on the northern end of the park. If walking across the park, don't try to descend the northern end to New Town as deep road cuttings prevent pedestrian access. There are several pedestrian overpasses on the western side which provide good access to North Hobart.

On the eastern side, near the Tasman Bridge, are the **Royal Tasmanian Botanical Gardens** which are open from 8 am to 4.45 pm daily; admission is free. Established by the early governors, the gardens are very pleasant and definitely worth a visit. The massive brick walls were heated by wood fires to combat the effects of frost. Some of the newer features worth visiting are the Japanese Garden and the French Memorial Fountain.

Next door to the botanic gardens is **Government House**, which is the residence of the Governor of the state. It is not open to the public and not visible from the road – you can get a good view of the turrets and towers on the building from high up on the hill of the Queen's Domain.

Mt Wellington

Hobart is dominated by 1270-metre-high Mt Wellington, and there are many fine views and interesting walking tracks across it. You can walk from the city centre to the summit and back in a day, but this is really for fit, experienced walkers. Like all mountains, the top is sometimes under cloud and in winter it often has a light cover of snow.

There is no public transport to the top of the mountain. However, there are buses to Ferntree, a small suburb of Hobart about halfway up the mountain. Metro buses Nos 48 and 49 leave from Franklin Square for Ferntree. From there you can walk to the summit and back in about five to six hours via Fern Glade Track, Radfords Track then the Zig Zag Track. Buses for Ferntree leave from Franklin Square which is near the Post

HOBART

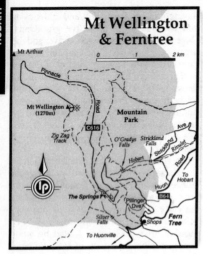

Office in Elizabeth St. Buy a copy of the *Mt Wellington Walks* map for details of all tracks.

You can get to the top by joining a bus tour – see the Organised Tours section below for details. Another enjoyable option is to get a taxi to the top – it costs around $25 for up to five people – and walk downhill back to the city.

Mt Nelson

If Mt Wellington is under cloud, the **Old Signal Station** on Mt Nelson, which is much lower, will still provide excellent views over the city. When Port Arthur was operating as a penal station a series of semaphore stations using flags was positioned on all the high hills. These were used to transmit messages across the colony and Mt Nelson was the major link between Hobart and the rest of the colony.

Beside the signal station is a restaurant. The lookout can be accessed by a steep winding road from Sandy Bay, or via the turn-off at the Southern Outlet on top of the hill. The outlet is the main road from Hobart to Kingston. From Franklin Square, Metro bus Nos 57 and 58 operate to the lookout.

Organised Tours

Cruises Four cruise companies operate from the Brooke St Pier and Franklin Wharf and offer a variety of cruises in and around the harbour. One of the most popular is the four-hour Cadbury's Cruise, run by the Cruise Company (☎ 6234 9294), which costs $33 (children $16). Leaving at 10 am on weekdays you do a slow return cruise to the Cadbury Schweppes factory in Claremont where you disembark and tour the premises.

Cruise timetables are pretty changeable as they depend on tides and seasons so it is best to book. Some cruises have advertised running times, but only operate if there are enough passengers; if you arrive to book just before it leaves you may find the tour that day has already been cancelled. Harbour cruises are also available and vary from one to three hours.

The MV *Cartela* (☎ 6223 1914) runs morning cruises for two hours for $14, one hour lunch cruises for $20, one hour afternoon-tea cruises for $12 and 2½ hour dinner cruises for $20. On Friday, it runs a counter-lunch cruise for a bargain $10.

On Saturdays only, the MV *Southern Contessa* (☎ 6297 1110) operates a five hour cruise from Hobart south to Port Huon and return by bus. Bookings are essential.

Cadbury Chocolate Factory Tour You can go directly to the factory yourself and tour it without taking a cruise. Inspections are run on week days only at 9 am, 9.30 am, 10.30 am, 11.15 am and 1 pm. The factory is closed from the week before Christmas until late January. Admission is $10, children $5 and tickets must be purchased in advance at the Travel & Information Centre (☎ 6230 8233) on the corner of Davey and Elizabeth St. You cannot get tickets at the factory. You can get there by taking Metro bus No 37 to Claremont from the Hobart Bus Station in Elizabeth St.

Walking Tours One of the best ways to get a feel for Hobart's colonial history is to take the Saturday morning walking tour organised by the National Trust. The tour concentrates on the historic Battery Point area and departs at 9.30 am from the wishing well in Franklin Square – you don't have to book, just turn up. The walk costs $5, children $2.50, and takes 2½ hours.

During October to March, twilight walks along the waterfront are run by Sullivans Cove Walking Tours, starting at 6.30 pm. You must book earlier in the day at the Information Centre (☎ 6230 8233) in Elizabeth St; the cost is $8.50.

For a spooky experience the Hobart Ghost Tour (☎ 6273 3361) is a two-hour candlelit tour that runs at 8 pm and 9.30 pm during the warmer months. The tour visits the Penitentiary Chapel and the Criminal Courts on the corner of Brisbane and Campbell St and costs $7, children $4 or a family $19.

Bus Tours Day and half-day bus tours in and around Hobart are operated by Tasmanian Redline Coaches (TRC) (☎ 6231 2200), Hobart Coaches (☎ 6234 4077) and Tasmanian Wilderness Travel (☎ 6234 2226). Bus tours usually run only if there are bookings.

Typical half-day tours with TRC and Hobart Coaches are trips to Bonorong Wildlife Park and Richmond ($22), Richmond only ($17) and the City Sights and Mt Wellington ($20).

Full-day tour destinations with TRC and Hobart Coaches include Port Arthur ($49), the Huon Valley ($55), the Derwent Valley ($47), Ross ($25), Maria Island ($43), Swansea ($30) and Bruny Island ($75).

Tasmanian Wilderness Travel runs one day bus trips to Port Arthur ($33), Mt Field National Park ($60 if guided, $27.50 if self-guided) and to Hastings Caves ($27.50). Entry fees to caves and parks are not included in the bus fare. Most of these tours operate daily in summer and on selected days in winter. As the buses are also used as part of regular bus routes for bushwalkers, the tours will run even with only a single passenger. TWT also runs two-day excursions to places like Mt Field National Park, Cradle Mountain and Strahan.

Motor Cycle Tours For something different, try Harley Tours of Hobart (☎ 6224 1565) for a ride around Hobart in a Harley Davidson sidecar. It operates from the waterfront and rides start from $15.

Scenic Flights Scenic flights are offered by Par Avion (☎ 6248 5390) and Tasair (☎ 6248 5088) from Cambridge Airport, 15 km from the city. Flights start from $60 each for 30 minutes and they operate according to demand. If you have a particular place you want to see, then book in advance. The most common planes used for scenic flights carry three or five passengers.

A popular flight is into the south-west. You can do a 1½ hour flight for $120 each or a longer 2½ hour flight which includes a landing on one of the beaches in the wilderness for $140 each. You cannot always fly over the south-west as the peaks are often covered in cloud. There are some excellent alternatives. The three peaks flight costs $140 each and follows the east coast from Freycinet Peninsula, lands at Maria Island and flies around the Tasman Peninsula. You can also do a shorter flight around the Tasman Peninsula – which has the tallest sea cliffs in the state – for only $90 each.

Both companies also run charter flights where you can fly wherever you like. The rates are based on an hourly rate of around $90 per person. Par-Avion have a camp and a boat in the south-west and offer packages of flights and camping or boating holidays in the Port Davey area. Two night packages are around $500, which includes all food and equipment.

Festivals

From 29 December to 2 January, Hobart's waterfront area is alive with spectators and celebrating yachties at the finish of the annual New Year **Sydney to Hobart Yacht Race** and the **Westcoaster Yacht Race**. The festivities continue for ten days with daily yacht races on the Derwent River and music and other events held around the waterfront.

The **Royal Hobart Regatta**, in early February, is a major four day aquatic carnival with boat races and other activities. The last day of the carnival, a Monday, is a public holiday and almost the entire town closes down.

During January other sporting events like the international **Tasmanian Women's Open** tennis tournament at the Domain, the **Cadbury Marathon** and sailing events for smaller boats are also held.

Places to Stay – bottom end

Hobart has a wide variety of accommodation catering for all tastes and price brackets. The main areas for budget accommodation are the city centre and the older suburbs to the north and west. Middle and upper-end accommodation is spread all over town. The most popular suburb in which to stay is historic Battery Point, just south of the city and very close to the waterfront; prices here are all in the middle to upper range.

Camping & Cabins The handiest camping ground is the *Sandy Bay Caravan Park* (☎ 6225 1264), less than three km from the city, at 1 Peel St, Sandy Bay. It's popular as it's not only close to the city, but the casino at Wrest Point is only a short walk away. It charges $12 a double for a camp site, while on-site vans are $32 a double and cabins $45. To get there, take Metro bus No 54, 55 or 56 from stop D in Elizabeth St near the GPO or walk along Sandy Bay Road for 40 minutes.

The other parks are further out of town and really only useful if you have your own wheels. The *Elwick Caravan Park* (☎ 6272 7115) at 19 Goodwood Road, Elwick is eight km from the city and located next to the road that leads across the Bowen Bridge. There is no camping here with the only accommodation being on-site cabins for $45 a double plus $6 for each extra adult.

Further north, the *Treasure Island Caravan Park* (☎ 6249 2379) is located on a small peninsula at Berriedale, 14 km north of the city. This is very close to the Morilla Estate Winery and provides pleasant camping beside the Derwent River. Camping

costs $11, sites with power $14, on-site vans are $32 and cabins are $42 a double.

If you prefer to stay on the east side of the river then *Bowen Park* (☎ 6243 9879) beside the East Derwent Hwy at Risdon has cabins for $45 a double plus $8 for each extra adult. The other cabin park on the east side is *Mornington Park* (☎ 6244 7070) at 346 Cambridge Road, Mornington. This is located beside the main highway from Hobart airport to the city where you meet the first suburb. It's only five km from town and has cabins which are $45 a double with linen included.

Hostels Right in the centre of town is the *Central City Backpackers* (☎ 6224 2404) at 138 Collins St. It's a huge, rambling place which was previously called the Imperial Private Hotel and has excellent facilities and a friendly couple in charge. There are spacious communal areas, as well as a laundry and individual safe-deposit boxes. The cost is $12 for a bed in a four-bed dorm, or there are twin-share rooms for $17 per person, and singles/doubles for $28/36. Security is good here and it's clean and quiet.

At 87 Bathurst St *Bourkes New Sydney Hotel* (☎ 6234 4516) charges $12 a night for very basic bunks and facilities on the 1st floor of the hotel. The place is very close to the shopping centre; its main fault is that it can be difficult to sleep here when a band is on in the pub, as the main dorm is right above the stage.

For something quieter and less crowded, try the hostel above the Tasmanian Redline Coaches bus depot at 199 Collins St – *Transit Centre Backpackers* (☎ 6231 2400). It has beds for $11 per night and has all the facilities, with security provided by a digitally coded lock. The communal area is very large and for some it lacks atmosphere; the main detraction is that it can be difficult to obtain a room here after hours when the bus depot is closed.

Close by the *Duke Backpackers* (☎ 6223 5206), above the Duke of Wellington Hotel on the corner of Macquarie and Barrack St, has single rooms for $25 and bunks for $12 each. Counter meals are available and on some nights there is live entertainment downstairs.

The cheapest place in town is the *Ocean Child Hotel* (☎ 6234 6730) on the corner of Argyle and Melville Streets. For $10 per person you get an old hotel room on the first floor with basic facilities fairly close to town.

There are three YHA hostels in Hobart. The main one, *Adelphi Court* (☎ 6228 4829), is 2.5 km from the city at 17 Stoke St, New Town. It's an excellent hostel with good facilities and charges $12 for a dorm bed ($14 for nonmembers), or $17 each for a twin room ($19 each for nonmembers). To get there, take Metro bus No 15 or 16 from Argyle St to stop 8A, or any one of bus Nos 25 to 42, 100 and 105 to 128 to stop 13. TRC also provides a drop-off and pick-up service on the airport bus.

The *Woodlands Hostel* (☎ 6228 6720), at 7 Woodlands Ave, New Town, is near Adelphi Court, but is only used as overflow accommodation when the main hostel is full. It is a superb building and one of New Town's original homes. It's best to turn up at nearby Adelphi first, and if there isn't any room you'll be directed here.

The peaceful *Bellerive Hostel* (☎ 6244 2552) is well out of town, on the other side of the Derwent River at 52 King St, Bellerive, and charges $10 a night. The lovely old stone building used to be a schoolhouse and dates from 1869. To get there at the weekends, when the ferry doesn't run, you can catch any of the Bellerive buses (Nos 83 to 87) from stop C or D near the GPO in Elizabeth St.

Colleges During the longer school and university holidays you can stay in the hostels and halls of residence used by the students. The most convenient is *Hollydene House* (☎ 6234 6434) at 55 Campbell St which offers B&B for $25 plus $10 for each extra adult in a room, or $15 for a dormitory bed. Next to the university in College Road, Sandy Bay, *Christ College* (☎ 6221 4567) has dormitory beds for $25 each which includes breakfast. *Jane Franklin Hall*

(☎ 6223 3000) is at 6 Elboden St, South Hobart and is next to Davey St. It has mainly single rooms and with breakfast is $28/42 for singles/doubles.

Places to Stay – middle

Hotels Hobart has a large number of old hotels built from sandstone or brick and usually two to four storeys in height. Most were built last century and are close to the city centre. They generally offer single and double rooms with shared bathroom and vary in standard depending on how long ago the last major renovation was done. Often the hotel area downstairs is very classy while the rooms upstairs are fairly plain.

City At 67 Liverpool St, near the mall, the *Brunswick Hotel* (☎ 6234 4981) is pretty central and has average rooms costing $33/50 with a continental breakfast. Across the road, at 72 Liverpool St, the *Alabama Hotel* (☎ 6234 3737) is a little more comfortable and charges $27/44 for singles/doubles. The *Astor Private Hotel* (☎ 6234 6611), 157 Macquarie St, is centrally located only two blocks from the mall, and the tariff of $40/55 for singles/doubles includes breakfast. Just around the corner the *Freemasons Hotel* (☎ 6223 6655) on the corner of Harrington and Davey St has rooms for $40/50.

Two blocks up from the mall, at 145 Elizabeth St, is the *Black Prince* (☎ 6234 3501), which has large, modern rooms with bathroom and TV for $40/50. Over near the hospital the *Theatre Royal Hotel* (☎ 6234 6925) at 31 Campbell St has rooms for $45 a double. One block away in the same street the *Royal Exchange Hotel* on the corner of Campbell and Bathurst St charges $39/49.

On the corner of Macquarie and Harrington St is the multistorey *Hobart Macquarie Motor Inn* (☎ 6234 4422) where rooms are $85/95. In a similar multistorey building is the *Hobart Mid City Motor Inn* on the corner of Bathurst and Elizabeth Sts, (☎ 6234 6333) with rooms for $80/92.

The best value of the middle to upper range hotels is *Country Comfort Hadleys*

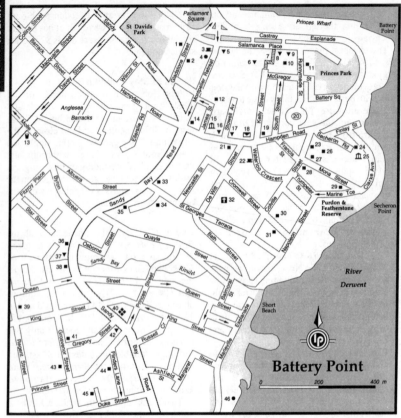

Battery Point

Hotel (☎ 6223 4355), at 34 Murray St. Rated as a four star hotel, the 140-year-old building has a lot more charm than the large new hotels and at $83 a double is a bit cheaper for about the same standard.

Battery Point If you want to stay near the docks, the *Customs House Hotel* (☎ 6234 6645), at 1 Murray St, charges $40/65 with a continental breakfast. The *Prince of Wales Hotel* (☎ 6223 6355) in Hampden Rd, Battery Point is two km from town and provides basic accommodation with private facilities for $50/65 including breakfast.

North Within walking distance but just out of town are several reasonable hotels. *Waratah Hotel* (☎ 6234 3685) at 272 Murray St has singles/doubles for $42/58 and includes breakfast. If you prefer to be well out of the city then the *Claremont Hotel* (☎ 6249 1119), 1 Main Rd, Claremont, is 12 km out and is close to the Cadbury chocolate factory; rooms are $35/50 with breakfast. Beside the Tasman Hwy on the eastern edge of the city, the *Sun Valley Inn* (☎ 6244 3855) at 322 Cambridge Rd has rooms for $36/48.

South There are a couple of moderately

priced hotels in Sandy Bay. The *Dr Syntax Hotel* (☎ 6223 6258), at 138 Sandy Bay Rd, is very close to Battery Point. It has comfortable singles/doubles with TV for $35/49. The *Beach House Hotel* (☎ 6225 1161), at 646 Sandy Bay Rd, is two km south of the casino and has good rooms with TV and continental breakfast for $42/49.

A bit classier is the *Cascade Hotel* (☎ 6223 6385) at 22 Cascade Road, South Hobart where rooms are $60/70. It's three km from town and easily found as Cascade Road is the continuation of Macquarie St.

West High up on the hill, one km west of the city, is the *Marquis of Hastings Hotel* (☎ 6234 3541) on the corner of Brisbane and Hill St. With breakfast, rooms are $50/60 for singles/doubles.

The *Globe Hotel* (☎ 6223 5800) is a bit more basic and also includes breakfast for $30/45.

Motels There are plenty of motels in Hobart, but most are rather a long way out; you'll need your own transport. Some of them are attached to licensed hotels and often have their own restaurants.

City On the northern edge of the city centre is the *Fountainside Motor Inn* (☎ 6234 2911), at 40 Brooker Avenue. It's beside the fountain at the large roundabout where the highways enter town. Rooms in the multi-storey motel are $59 to $89 a double.

Battery Point *Blue Hills* (☎ 6223 1777) at 96A Sandy Bay Rd has rooms for $70 and holiday units for $90. One block away at 86 Sandy Bay Rd is the *St Ives Motel* (☎ 6224 1044) where rooms are an expensive $115 a double.

North As you would expect, the cheapest motels are all well out of town. Way north of the city, the *Highway Village Motor Inn* (☎ 6272 6721) at 897 Brooker Hwy, Berriedale is in a pleasant spot beside the Derwent River and the rooms are only $48/58.

The *Marina Motel* (☎ 6228 4748) at 153 Risdon Rd, Lutana, is four km from town and is beside the Derwent River; singles/doubles are $39/49. Just around the corner from the Adelphi Court YHA is the *Hobart Tower Motel* (☎ 6228 0166) at 300 Park St, New Town. This is in a good location beside the Brooker Hwy, two km from town; rooms are

$46/54. Nearby on the corner of Lewis and Argyle St the *Argyle Motor Lodge* (☎ 6234 2488) has doubles ranging from $69 to $112.

Closer to the city centre is the *Mayfair Motel* (☎ 6231 1188) at 17 Cavell St, West Hobart, which is high up on the hill and has rooms for $65/75.

South Near the casino, at 429 Sandy Bay Rd, is the pink, four-storey *Sandy Bay Motor Inn* (☎ 6225 2511). The rooms have good views of the casino and the Derwent River and are $75/85 for singles/doubles.

East On the eastern side of the Derwent River, the *Shoreline Motor Motel* (☎ 6247 9504) on the corner of Rokeby Rd and Shoreline Drive, Howrah, is seven km from town. It's located beside a major road junction and is not beside the river as the name suggests; rooms are $45/55 with continental breakfast. The other motel on this side is *Lindisfarne Motor Inn* (☎ 6243 8666) at 101 East Derwent Hwy, Lindisfarne. It's beside the main highway one km north of the Tasman Bridge and rooms are $50/60.

Guesthouses & B&B These are often housed in buildings of historical significance. The facilities vary widely but are often of a fairly high standard. Price is usually a good guide to quality, except around Battery Point where you must pay a little bit more to stay in this popular historic area. Most B&B places are fairly small with two to five rooms available for hire.

Battery Point You can stay in some beautiful colonial guesthouses and cottages in Battery Point. While there is a wide selection from which to choose, there are no real bargains during the main tourist periods. During winter some discounts are sometimes available.

At 72 Hampden Rd, *Barton Cottage* (☎ 6224 1606), is a two-storey building which dates back to 1837 and is classified by the National Trust. There are six rooms and B&B accommodation costs $75/95. Another similar place worth considering is *Cromwell*

Cottage (☎ 6223 6734) at 6 Cromwell St. This two-storey townhouse dates from the late 1880s and is in a beautiful position overlooking the Derwent River. Each of the five rooms costs $75/95 and includes a cooked breakfast.

At 32 Mona St, *Colville Cottage* (☎ 6223 6968) has six rooms with B&B for $77/98. Further down the same street at number 8 *Tantallon Lodge* (☎ 6224 1724) has seven rooms at $75/95 for singles/doubles.

Next door to the Maritime Museum, *Secheron Villa* (☎ 6234 2463) at 11 Clarke Avenue is more private, with one suite which has excellent views across the river for $95 a double.

North In addition to its hostel, *Adelphi Court* (☎ 6228 4829), at 17 Stoke St, New Town, also has guesthouse accommodation at $45/55 which includes a cooked breakfast. Just around the corner from the hostel is *Hillpark House* (☎ 6228 7094), 344 Park St, New Town. It is a small place with only two rooms and a cooked breakfast is provided in the $40/$65 tariff.

Close to the city in North Hobart, the *Lodge on Elizabeth* (☎ 6231 3830) on the corner of Elizabeth and Warwick St is an old mansion full of antiques. Large rooms with tiny ensuite bathrooms range from $85 to $120 a double. A bit further up the road, the *Elms of Hobart* (☎ 6231 3277) at 452 Elizabeth St is another old mansion that is even more luxurious and is classified by the National Trust. The rate here with breakfast is from $85/95.

Hidden in the hills of New Town, four km from the city, is *Jutland House* (☎ 6228 4970) at 52 Montagu St, Lenah Valley. It's one block off Augusta Rd and B&B is $35/50; children are welcomed. Close to the city in the small suburb of Glebe, *Wellington Lodge* (☎ 6231 0614) at 7 Scott St is only a 10 minute walk from town. It's in a nice location with good views across the city and is close to the nearby Queen's Domain parkland. Rates for B&B are $55/65.

South The shopping centre of Magnet Court

in Sandy Bay Road is only two km south of the city. Close to the shops is *Merridews* (☎ 6224 2900) at 24 Gregory St which offers colonial accommodation in an 1880s house furnished with antiques. B&B costs $75/95. Two blocks away and close to Sandy Bay Road at 20 Duke St is *Duke House* (☎ 6223 7497) which has two B&B rooms for $60/80.

In Sandy Bay, up on the hill next to the Southern Outlet (the highway from Hobart to Kingston), is *Andersons* (☎ 6225 1005) at 5 Richardsons Avenue. The single room with breakfast is $70 to $75 a double.

One km south of the casino in Sandy Bay, there's *Red Chapel House* (☎ 6225 2273) at 27 Red Chapel Ave. There are eight rooms and singles/doubles in this smoke-free establishment cost $50/70 including a cooked breakfast. The place is family-run and has a friendly atmosphere.

An interesting option is the *Signalman's Cottage* (☎ 6223 1215) on the top of Mt Nelson at 685 Nelson Rd. It's a self-contained, one-bedroom unit and the cost is $55/65. The view over the city is excellent – especially in the evening – and the place is convenient if you have your own transport. Buses do operate to Mt Nelson; take No 57 or 58 from Franklin Square.

East Just across the Tasman Bridge *Roseneath Host Accommodation* (☎ 6243 6530) at 20 Kaoota Rd, Rose Bay has fine views across the river and is actually quite close to the city if you have your own vehicle. Rates for B&B are $65 to $95 a double and they can cater for six people and prefer family or group bookings. In the same area is *Orana Accommodation* (☎ 6243 0404) at 20 Lowelly Road, Lindisfarne. It's just off the East Derwent Hwy and this stately mansion has good-value B&B from $72 a double.

To the south at Bellerive, *Holm Lodge Guest House* (☎ 6244 3656) at 24 Victoria Esplanade is located close to the river near Kangaroo Bluff and has magnificent views across the river. The ferry and shops are about a 10 minute walk away and rooms are $58/75, including breakfast.

Holiday Units Hobart has a number of self-contained holiday flats with fully equipped kitchens. Prices vary and the cheaper units are normally flats in apartment blocks while the dearest are historic cottages. There are only a few of these around Hobart as most such buildings are used as B&Bs.

Battery Point The biggest concentration of units is in the narrow streets of Battery Point. The *Knopwood Apartment* (☎ 6223 2290), at 6 Knopwood St, Battery Point, is a three-bedroom upstairs flat overlooking Salamanca Place. It costs $60 a double and $14 for each extra person, and has a one-night surcharge. Slightly dearer is *Crelin Lodge* (☎ 6223 1777) at 1 Crelin St which runs off St Georges Terrace with units at $70 a double plus $10 for each extra adult. The *Battery Point Holiday Flat* (☎ 6223 6592) at 15 Secheron Rd is $85 a double or $105 for three people.

At 62 Montpelier Retreat, Battery Point, close to Hampden Rd, *Portsea Terrace* (☎ 6234 1616) has nine apartments for $70/90 which includes breakfast. If you prefer a new unit then try *Avon Court Holiday Apartments* (☎ 6223 4837). Recently constructed from sandstone to blend in with the older buildings, the apartments at 2 Colville St include kitchens and are $98 a double.

North The best bargains are well out of the city. *Northside Holiday Villas* (☎ 6272 4472) at 9 McGough St, Glenorchy is eight km from Hobart. It's beside the Brooker Hwy and the units are $58 a double plus $12 for extra adults. About two km from town, the *Domain View Apartments* (☎ 6234 1181) at 352 Argyle St, North Hobart, charges $55 a double and $5 for each extra person, with a one-night surcharge.

South Sandy Bay is a convenient location; it is fairly close to town and has some good shops and units. *Grosvenor Court Holiday Apartments* (☎ 6231 0775) at 42 Grosvenor St is just one block from the main shopping centre at Magnet Court in Sandy Bay Rd.

The apartments are $85 a double, plus $16 for extra adults or $13 for children, and sleep six people. Just around the corner *Flinders Apartments* (☎ 6234 6882) at 4 Flinders Lane have rooms for $60 a double or $70 for three people but a minimum stay of three nights applies. Slightly closer to town at 123 Sandy Bay Rd is *Woolmers Inn* (☎ 6223 7355) where the units are $105 a double plus $12 for extra adults and $8 for children.

West About eight km from town the *Bay View Villas* (☎ 6234 7611) at 34 Poets Rd, West Hobart is located on the slopes of Mt Knocklofty where rooms are $85 a double.

East On the eastern shore of the Derwent River, *Silwood Park Holiday Unit* (☎ 6244 4278) at 7 Silwood Avenue, Howrah is cheap at $48 a double plus $10 for each extra adult. It can sleep five people and is close to the Howrah Beach.

Places to Stay – top end

Compared to other capital cities in Australia, the top end accommodation in Hobart is cheap and basically starts at around $110 a double. Prices are low enough even for the budget traveller to splash out on a luxury night. The four and five star hotels and luxury B&Bs are all fairly close to the city. Outside of the holiday seasons many of these places offer special deals, particularly for weekends when either rates are reduced or romantic dinners are included.

Hotels There are plenty of top-bracket hotels to choose from. Of the following recommendations, one hotel is five-star and the rest are four-star.

City Five star accommodation is available at the *Hotel Grand Chancellor* (☎ 6235 4535), at 1 Davey St. Previously known as the Sheraton Hobart Hotel, this red-brick block dominates the city centre and costs from $180 a suite.

Battery Point Just behind Salamanca Place, the *Salamanca Inn* (☎ 6223 3300) at 10 Gladstone St has rooms from $164 to $188 a double. About half of the 60 suites have kitchens. If none of these appeal, there's always the wonderful *Lenna of Hobart* (☎ 6232 3900), an old mansion at 20 Runnymede St, Battery Point, which is steeped in history and luxury and charges $140 to $200 for a double room.

North *Northside Manor* (☎ 6231 1588) is on the corner of Argyle and Lewis St. It's in a restored building and offers antique-furnished suites as well as modern hotel rooms and costs $128 a double.

South The *Wrest Point Hotel Casino* (☎ 6225 0112) is a fairly well known hotel, located at 410 Sandy Bay Rd, five km south of the city centre. Rooms here start at $145 and range up to $340 a double for the executive suites in the tower. Motel units are also available from $100 a double.

West On the west side of town, *Westside Hotel* (☎ 6232 6225) on the corner of Bathurst and Harrington St is another large hotel with suites from $120 a double.

If you prefer something smaller and more intimate then try the *Islington Private Hotel* (☎ 6223 3900) at 321 Davey St. The hotel has only eight suites and was constructed in 1845; the tariff is $75/120 and includes breakfast.

B&B The very best restorations of Hobart's older mansions provide some fine accommodation. All these places are rated as four to five star and provide quality accommodation.

Battery Point The only five-star-rated B&B is the *Colonial Battery Point Manor* (☎ 6224 0888), 13 Cromwell St, Battery Point. Built in 1834, it has fine views to the south-east over the Derwent River; B&B is $120/145 for singles/doubles. Just around the corner and almost as luxurious is *Ascot of Battery Point* (☎ 6224 2434) at 6 Colville St. The rate includes a cooked breakfast and is $90/115.

Very close to Salamanca Place is the *Battery Point Guest House* (☎ 6224 2111 or 018 124 102) at 7 McGregor St. Hidden down a side lane this was originally the coach house and stables for the nearby Lenna of Hobart. A cooked breakfast is included for $85/110 and families with young children are catered for.

North An unusual area to stay is on the steep hill on the north side of the city where the only place to stay is *Corinda Colonial Accommodation* (☎ 6234 1590) at 17 Glebe St, Glebe. It is conveniently located next to the Queen's Domain, and the botanic gardens and the city are both within walking distance. There are two apartments and rates are $120 a double plus $20 for each extra adult and a continental breakfast is provided.

If you want to stay in one of the oldest houses in Hobart then make your way to *Wendover* (☎ 6278 2066), 10 Wendover Place, Newtown; it's about four km north of the city. The mansion is one of the original houses of the region, being built in 1815, and is much older and more beautiful than the nearby Runnymede. The four spacious apartments contain kitchens and cost $110 to $125 a double plus $28 for each extra adult.

Holiday Units & Cottages There's a fairly small selection of holiday units and cottages in this price bracket.

Battery Point The most centrally located holiday units are the *Salamanca Executive Suites* (☎ 6224 3896 or 018 125 969), 5 Gladstone St, Battery Point where an apartment costs $160 a double plus $20 for each extra adult.

South About three km from the city in Sandy Bay, *Regent Park* (☎ 6223 3200) at 17 Regent St has 27 serviced apartments ranging from $99 to $139 a double. If you prefer a secluded, colonial cottage for two then stay at *Mt Pleasant Mews* (☎ 6225 1467), 32 Maning Ave, Sandy Bay. It's up on the hill about one km south of the casino and is $140 a night.

West Within walking distance of town, *Warwick Cottages* (☎ 6254 1264) is at 119 Warwick St, West Hobart. The two units can each hold four guests and cost $120 a double plus $25 for each extra adult.

East *Pines Resort* (☎ 6248 6222) at Seven Mile Beach is a good place to stay. Complete with its own tavern, it is well out of town (18 km) but very close to the main airport; rooms are $120 a double.

Places to Eat
Cafes & Light Meals Hobart has plenty of street cafes such as the *Kaf Kara*, at 119 Liverpool St, which has good food, real cappuccinos (not too common in Hobart) and great décor.

A good lunch-time cafe is *Cafe Toulouse* at 79 Harrington St. There's a good selection of croissants and quiches and you can get a quick, light meal for around $8. A trendy place that serves excellent light meals and is popular with all age groups is the *Kaos Cafe* at 273 Elizabeth St. It's open daily from noon to midnight, except Sunday when it closes at 10 pm.

Another popular place is the *Retro Cafe* which is on the corner of Salamanca Place and Montpelier Retreat; it's so popular that you often can't get a table. It opens at 8 am and serves great breakfasts, then continues with good food through the day. It closes at 6 pm except on Friday, when the doors stay open until midnight.

If you're looking for a late-night snack, you could also try *Mummy's Coffee Shop* at 38 Waterloo Crescent, just off Hampden Rd, Battery Point. Cakes of various types are the speciality and it's popular for after-theatre snacks. It's open from 10 am to midnight Sunday to Thursday and from 10 am to 2 am Friday and Saturday.

Another good place for quality snacks is *The Cove* buffet in the Hotel Grand Chancellor (formerly the Sheraton). Prices are actually quite reasonable with light meals at $5 to $14. For a late-night treat try the dessert and cheese selection; for a bargain $8.50 you can eat all you like from the buffet.

Constitution Dock has a number of floating takeaway seafood stalls such as *Mako Quality Seafoods* and *Flippers*. Close by is *Mures Fish Centre*, where you can get excellent fish & chips and other fishy fare at the bistro on Lower Deck, or an ice cream. Another good fish & chip shop which the locals frequent is the *Dolphin In The Bay* at 141 Sandy Bay Road.

For more exotic takeaways try the tiny *Little Bali* at 84a Harrington St. The dishes are mainly Indonesian and excellent value for around $5. It's open from 11 am to 3 pm weekdays and every evening from 5 pm to 9.30 pm. If pasta is more to your liking, then *Little Italy* at 152 Collins St serves excellent, cheap pasta and is open from 8.30 am to 8 pm or later on weekdays. Both of these places have some limited tables at which to sit.

A little more difficult to get to, but well worth the effort, is the historic *Mount Nelson Signal Station Tea House*, on the summit of Mt Nelson, which has spectacular panoramic views of Hobart and the surrounding area. Buses Nos 57 and 58 operate to the lookout.

Pub Meals For $8 you can get a very filling meal at the *New Sydney Hotel*, 87 Bathurst St. Many other hotels serve good counter meals and those in the $8 to $14 range include the *Shamrock* on the corner of Harrington and Liverpool St and the *Aberfeldy Hotel* on the corner of Davey and Molle St.

A short distance out of town is the *Globe Hotel* at 178 Davey St which has fine counter meals. A little further away is the extremely popular *Cascade Hotel* at 22 Cascade Rd, South Hobart. It is crowded and it's often hard to find a seat.

Stoppy's Waterfront Tavern, on Salamanca Place, is a little trendier and has good counter meals for around $10 or more, as well as bands from Thursday to Sunday nights.

Restaurants The licensed *Hara Wholefood Cafe* (☎ 6234 1457) at 181 Liverpool St has an extensive range of mouth-watering vegetarian and vegan dishes and is open from 10 am until late evening Monday to Saturday.

Elizabeth St, in North Hobart, has a reputation for good-value, interesting places to eat. At 321 Elizabeth St is *Ali Akbar* (☎ 6231 1770), a popular BYO Lebanese restaurant. For good value pasta and Italian dishes try *Trattoria Casablanca* at 213 Elizabeth St. Open every evening until after midnight, it's popular with taxi drivers.

North Hobart also has plenty of Asian restaurants. *Vanidols* (☎ 6234 9307), at 353 Elizabeth St, is a comfortable BYO restaurant specialising in Thai, Indian and Indonesian cuisine with main courses a reasonable $10 to $14; it's open from Tuesday to Sunday. Just down the street is another BYO Asian restaurant, *Dede* (☎ 31 1068), which has good food, but can feel a bit cramped on a busy night. Chinese food is also available from *Fortuna Restaurant* at 275 Elizabeth St and the *Golden Bamboo*, at 116 Elizabeth St.

At Salamanca Place, *Mr Wooby's* (☎ 6234 3466), tucked away in a side lane, is a pleasant licensed eatery where you can get excellent meals; it's open until quite late. Nearby, at 87 Salamanca Place, is the licensed *Ball & Chain Grill* (☎ 6223 2655), which has a good reputation for grilled steaks; main courses are around $13.

At No 89 there's *Panache* (☎ 6224 2929), a licensed cafe/restaurant which has an outdoor eating area by the adjoining rock walls. For excellent Japanese food, try the licensed *Mikaku* (☎ 6224 0882) at 85 Salamanca Place.

At 31 Campbell St, there's the *Theatre Royal Hotel* (☎ 6234 6925), with a highly acclaimed bistro. It's right next door to the Theatre Royal, Australia's oldest functioning performing-arts theatre.

In Hampden Rd, Battery Point, is the very popular *Brasserie*, which has a reputation for excellent food at moderate prices. Also in Hampden Rd at No 47, is the popular *Da Angelo Ristorante* (☎ 6223 7011) which serves pasta and pizza for $8 to $12 for mains. Come early or book as it's often full.

The *Astor Grill* (☎ 6234 3809), which is inside the Astor Hotel at 157 Macquarie St, is one of the town's better restaurants. Other fine hotel restaurants include *Alexander's*

Restaurant (☎ 6232 3900) at the Lenna of Hobart, 20 Runnymede St, Battery Point and the *Starlight Restaurant* (☎ 6234 6733) at the Hobart Pacific, Kirby Court, Mt Knocklofty.

The large hotels each have several restaurants. The Wrest Point Casino has the *Point Revolving Restaurant* (☎ 6221 1707) on top of the tower, where main courses are reasonably priced, $10 to $20. It also has an *Asian Restaurant* and a coffee shop. The Westside Hotel, at 156 Bathurst St (☎ 6232 6255) has the *Silver Skillet* which serves game and exotic dishes and the *Last Drop* which has more traditional steaks.

On the waterfront, the licensed *Drunken Admiral* (☎ 6234 1903) at 17 Hunter St is open every evening and has good seafood and a great atmosphere. Right next door is the *Riviera Ristorante* (☎ 6234 3230), a popular Italian restaurant. The very popular Mures complex has the *Upper Deck Restaurant* (☎ 6231 2121) which has fine seafood and is justifiably famous. Mains range from $20 to $30 and booking is recommended.

Entertainment

The *Mercury* newspaper which is published daily has details on most of Hobart's entertainment.

The *New Sydney Hotel* at 87 Bathurst St is Hobart's Irish pub and there's live music most nights. For jazz, blues and rock & roll, the *St Ives Hotel* at 86 Sandy Bay Rd and the *Travellers Rest*, 394 Sandy Bay Rd, have bands from Wednesday to Sunday nights.

You're guaranteed a good time at *Maloney's Hotel* on the corner of Macquarie and Argyle St; there are bands on Friday and Saturday nights and a nightclub upstairs. Another recommended nightclub is *Round Midnight* at 39 Salamanca Place, which is open until 4 am Tuesday to Saturday. Round Midnight is on the top floor of the building which houses the bars *Knopwood's Retreat* and *Cutty's Cafe*.

Nickelby's Wine Bar at 217 Sandy Bay Road is a popular late-night venue. In the early evening it is a reasonable restaurant and later the live music starts and lasts until the early hours. A similar place to be seen at is the trendy *Cafe Who*, 251 Liverpool St, which serves meals until 10 pm and has live jazz most nights.

There are 17 bars at the Wrest Point Hotel Casino; and some, like the *Birdcage*, need to be seen to be believed. The casino also has a disco every night with a cover charge on Friday and Saturday only.

At 375 Elizabeth St, North Hobart, you'll find the *State Cinema* (☎ 34 6318), which screens alternative films, while at 181 Collins St there's a large *Village* complex (☎ 34 7288) which shows the mainstream releases.

Things to Buy

Most of the speciality shops and services are in the city centre. The main shopping area extends west from the mall on Elizabeth St and shopping arcades are dotted through the blocks. There are also major shopping centres to the south at Sandy Bay, to the north at Glenorchy and on the eastern side of the river at Bellerive. Shopping hours are 9 am to 5.30 pm from Monday to Friday. Most shops also open on Friday until 9 pm and on Saturday morning from 9 am to 12 noon. Most supermarkets stay open on Thursday until 9 pm and are open until 5.30 pm on Saturday. Most places are closed on Sunday and public holidays.

For bushwalking, lightweight camping and travel goods, Paddy Pallin (☎ 6231 0777) is at 76 Elizabeth St with the Jolly Swagman (☎ 6234 3999) opposite. The Wilderness Society's head office (☎ 6234 9366) is at 130 Davey St and its shop is in the Galleria, 33 Salamanca Place; the National Trust shop is in the same arcade.

For some ideas about what to buy in Tasmania, see Things to Buy in the Facts for the Visitor chapter.

Getting There & Away

Air For information on international and domestic flights to and from Hobart see the Getting There & Away chapter. Ansett (☎ 13 1300) has an office in the Elizabeth St Mall, as does Qantas (☎ 13 1313). The Airlines of

Tasmania (☎ 6248 5030) office is at Hobart Airport.

Bus The main bus companies operating from Hobart are Tasmanian Redline Coaches (TRC) (☎ 6231 3233) at the Transit Centre, 199 Collins St; Hobart Coaches (☎ 6234 4077) at 4 Liverpool St; and Tasmanian Wilderness Transport & Tours (☎ 6334 2226), also operating out of the Hobart Coaches office. Hobart Coaches has additional departure points at St David's Cathedral, on the corner of Macquarie and Murray St, and outside the Treasury Building in Murray St.

Hobart Coaches' destinations include New Norfolk, Woodbridge, Cygnet, Geeveston, Dover, and Port Arthur ($11.50). TRC and Hobart Coaches run to Bicheno ($18.80), Swansea ($15.30), St Marys, St Helens (Hobart Coaches $27.30/TRC $26.60), Oatlands, Ross, Campbell Town, Launceston ($16.80), Deloraine, Devonport ($28.60) and Burnie ($32.60). TRC also runs to Wynyard, Stanley, Smithton, and Queenstown ($29.40).

Tasmanian Wilderness Transport fares are usually more expensive, ranging from $20 to $40, but they provide smaller buses with more personal service to interesting destinations off the main roads such as Cockle Creek and Scotts Peak Dam in the southwest.

If you are using the buses extensively then consider getting a bus pass. The passes allow you unlimited travel for their duration and are really worthwhile if you want to make lots of shorter journeys. TRC has its own pass and Tasmanian Wilderness Travel and Hobart Coaches have a combined pass. Prices are 7 days for $99, 14 days for $140 and 30 days for $179.

Car Rental There are more than 20 car-rental firms in Hobart. Some of the cheaper ones include Rent-a-Bug (☎ 6231 0300) at 105 Murray St; Advance Car Rentals (☎ 6224 0822) at 277 Macquarie St; Bargain Car Rentals (☎ 6234 6959) at 189A Harrington St; and Statewide Rent-a-Car (☎ 6225 1204) at 388 Sandy Bay Rd, Sandy Bay.

Hitching To start hitching north, take a Bridgewater or Brighton bus from opposite the GPO in Elizabeth St. To hitch along the east coast, take a bus to Sorell first. With the regular and reasonably priced bus routes which visit most places we do not recommend hitching. Lifts on some roads are few and far between.

Getting Around

To/From the Airport The airport is in Hobart's eastern suburbs, 16 km from the city centre. TRC (☎ 6231 3900) runs a pickup and drop-off shuttle service between the city centre (via Adelphi YHA and some other accommodation places on request) and the airport for $6.60. They also take bicycles for $6.60.

Bus The local bus service is run by Metro. The main office (☎ 6213 2201) is at 18 Elizabeth St, opposite the GPO. Most buses leave from this area of Elizabeth St, known as the Metro City Bus Station, or from around the edges of the nearby Franklin Square.

If you're planning to bus around Hobart, it's worth buying Metro's user-friendly timetable, which only costs $1.50. For $2.80 ($8 for a family), you can get a Day Rover ticket which can be used all day at weekends and between 9 am and 4.30 pm and after 6 pm on weekdays. It cannot be used at peak hours so you do need to plan carefully. If you are staying in Hobart for a while you can get a Day Rover pass for $19.50 which is valid for 10 consecutive days but has the same restrictions on peak-hour travel. An alternative is to buy a book of 10 tickets which is available for around a 25% discount and can be used at any time of the day.

If you want to go to Mt Wellington without taking a tour, take bus No 48 from Franklin Square in Macquarie St; it will get you to Ferntree halfway up the mountain, and from there it's still a 13-km return walk to the top!

Bicycle The Transit Centre Backpackers has mountain bikes for $15 per day, or for $70 per week. Brake Out (☎ 6234 7632) also hires bicycles from the Wrest Point Casino. If you find Hobart's hills too steep, then Brake Out provides transport to the summit of Mt Wellington ($25) and Mt Nelson ($21) allowing you an easy return ride downhill.

Boat On weekdays the ferry MV *Emmalisa* (☎ 6223 5893) operates between Franklin Wharf and Bellerive Wharf and is a very pleasant way to cross the Derwent River. The ferry departs from Hobart at 7.30 am and 8.15 am and 4.35 pm and 5.15 pm. From Bellerive there are services at 7.57 and 8.35 am and at 4.50 pm. A one-way ticket costs $1.20, children 60c. Extra services run during the warmer months and the crossing takes 15 minutes. There is no weekend service.

Around Hobart

The district around Hobart is dotted with historic villages and there are many reminders of convict history among rolling hills of farms and forests. There are also some rapidly expanding towns, which are really satellite suburbs of Hobart, where many residents live country lifestyles while working in the city. The best known places are the historical town of Richmond and the shot tower at Taroona. However, there are many other lesser known – but just as interesting – places to discover. There are many good minor roads linking places together and following some of these reveals interesting views and hidden features.

HIGHLIGHTS

- Visiting the historic town of Richmond
- The waterfalls and tall trees at Mt Field
- Hop farms in the Derwent Valley
- Taroona's old sandstone Shot Tower

South of Hobart

The Channel Hwy is the continuation of Sandy Bay Road and hugs the coastline as it heads south. The construction of the Southern Outlet from Hobart to Kingston has removed most of the traffic and today it's a pleasant tourist drive. The winding road is benched into the lower slopes of Mt Nelson – drive slowly.

Six km south of Hobart and right beside the highway you will find **Tudor Court** (☎ 6225 1194). This is a model of a village in England that was constructed by John Palotta, a polio victim with very limited mobility. The model took about 20 years to build and has been on display for over 30 years. It is still worth a look as it has much intricate detail including the building interiors. It's open every day from 9 am to 5.30 pm and entry is $3, children $1. To get there by bus take a No 56 or 60 bus from Franklin Square and disembark at stop 30.

TAROONA

Eleven km from Hobart, on the Channel Hwy, is the satellite suburb of Taroona which gained its name from an Aboriginal word meaning 'seashell'. Just past the town is one of the region's most famous landmarks, the **Shot Tower**. It is made from sandstone with every block curved and tapered. It was completed in 1870. From the top of the 48-metre-high tower, there are fine views over the Derwent River estuary. Lead shot for use in guns was once produced in high towers like this by dropping molten lead from the top which, on its way down, formed a perfect sphere.

The tower, small museum, craft shop and beautiful grounds are open daily from 9 am to 5 pm and admission is $3 (children $1.50). There is also a tearoom which advertises 'convictshire' teas. Take bus No 60 from Franklin Square near Elizabeth St and get off at stop 45.

From Taroona Beach, you can walk for five km around to Kingston Beach along the

CHRIS KLEP

TASMANIAN DEPARTMENT OF TOURISM

LINDSAY BROWN

LINDSAY BROWN

CHRIS KLEP

CHRIS KLEP

A	B
C	D
E	F

A: Bennett's wallaby
B: Tasmanian devil
C: Cushion plants

D: Snow gum
E: Pandani
F: Eastern quoll (native cat)

GLENN BEANLAND

CHRIS KLEP

CHRIS KLEP

GLENN BEANLAND

CHRIS KLEP

A	B
C	
D	E

A: Constitution Dock, Hobart
B: Salamanca Market, Hobart
C: Hobart from Mt Nelson

D: Lenna of Hobart, Battery Point
E: Rear Admiral Sir John Franklin, Franklin Square, Hobart

$150 a double plus $15 for extra adults. It can sleep up to six and breakfast is provided.

KINGSTON
• *pop 12,900*

The town of Kingston, 11 km south of Hobart, has expanded rapidly in recent years as the Southern Outlet expressway has provided fast access to the town. Today, it is a large sprawling outer suburb of Hobart which is bypassed by the highways.

The town is the headquarters of the **Australian Antarctic Division** which is located beside the Channel Hwy, two km south of Kingston. This department administers Australia's 42% portion of Antarctica. Australia has had a long history of exploration and scientific study of the frozen continent and is one of the original 12 nations who set up the Antarctic Treaty in 1961. An excellent display (☎ 6229 0209) which features original equipment is open for free inspection on weekdays from 9 am to 5 pm. For a snack or coffee the cafeteria at the centre is open to the public from 9 am to 3 pm.

In Kingston there's a pleasant picnic area beside Browns River at the northern end of Kingston Beach. The picnic area is at the southern end of the Alum Cliffs walk from Taroona. Close by, there are also some pleasant beaches, including **Blackmans Bay**, which has a blowhole; **Tinderbox**, where you can go snorkelling along an underwater trail marked with submerged information plates; and **Howden**. Beaches in the area rarely have surf and provide safe family swimming most of the time.

The Tinderbox Peninsula makes an interesting scenic drive through the settlements of Blackmans Bay, Tinderbox and Howden. Excellent views are obtained along the minor roads with the best being from Piersons Point Lookout. If you are after some interesting artwork then visit the **Hythe Gallery** (☎ 6229 2588) at 248 Summerlea Rd. It's on the northern side of the Southern Outlet near the Welcome Inn and holds a large variety of selected Australian and Tasmanian art works. It is open from 10 am to 5 pm daily,

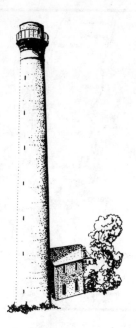

The Shot Tower at Taroona

Alum Cliffs Track; at some points the track runs along the top of cliffs from where you get good views of the Derwent River across to Opossum Bay. Allow two to three hours each way.

Places to Stay

One km north of the Shot Tower, the *Taroona Hotel* (☎ 6227 8748) has basic rooms for $40/65 which includes a continental breakfast. It is beside the highway and easy to find. Opposite the Shot Tower, you can rent the entire ground floor of comfortable *Hillgrove Colonial Accommodation* (☎ 6227 9043). It can hold three adults and rates are $65 for a single plus $20 for each extra adult; full breakfast is provided.

One km south of the Shot Tower, *Pine Banks Cottage* (☎ 6229 7882) is on top of a hill near Taronga Rd. The views from the cottage are rather expensive with rates being

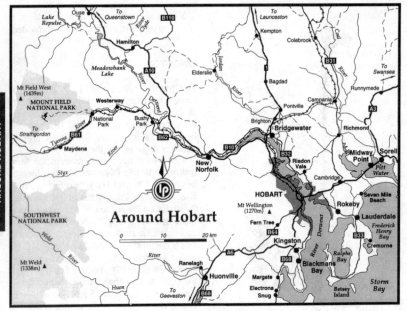

Around Hobart

and is closed on Wednesday and also for the entire month of July.

Places to Stay

The *Beachside Hotel* (☎ 6229 6185) on the corner of Beach Rd and Osborne Esplanade is opposite Kingston Beach. The plain hotel rooms include breakfast for $45 a double. Just one block away at 30 Osborne Esplanade is *Tranquilla Guest House* (☎ 6229 6282) where a room only is $56/72.

Two km west of Kingston, near the Southern Outlet as it heads towards Huonville, is the recently built *Welcome Inn* (☎ 6229 4800) in Kingston View Drive. The complex has an à la carte restaurant, views across the river and sporting facilities next door. Rooms are $60 a double.

Getting There & Away

Hobart Coaches (☎ 6234 4077) runs a regular bus service from Hobart to Kingston and Blackmans Bay at about one hour intervals on weekdays and about every three hours on weekends. Buses leave Hobart from Murray St between Davey and Macquarie Sts.

MARGATE
- *pop 740*

Eight km south of Kingston on the Channel Hwy is the small town of Margate. Train buffs will be interested in taking a look at the last passenger train to be used in Tasmania. It now stands disused on a piece of railway track beside the highway on the north side of town. A weekly market is held in the shed near the train every Sunday from 10 am to 3 pm.

On weekdays, Hobart Coaches (☎ 6234 4077) runs several bus services from Hobart through Margate to Kettering; on weekends there is one service on Saturday and none on Sunday.

Derwent Valley & Mt Field

NEW NORFOLK
• *pop 5800*

Set in the lush, rolling countryside of the Derwent Valley, New Norfolk is an interesting historical town. It was first visited by Europeans in 1793 and was soon settled after Hobart was established. In 1808 an Irish convict became the first police constable and built the first house. By the 1860s the valley became an important hop-growing centre, which is why the area is dotted with old oast houses used for drying hops. Hops are very sensitive to winds and trees were planted for wind protection. The most distinctive are the rows of tall poplars which today mark the boundaries of the former hop fields.

Originally called Elizabeth Town, New Norfolk was renamed after the abandoned Pacific Ocean colony on Norfolk Island. Over 500 people arrived from that colony in 1807 and 1808 to settle in the area. Today the town is a mixture of the old and the new and has some interesting sights that are unique to this area.

Things to See & Do

The **Visitors Historical & Information Centre**, next to the Council Chambers in Circle St, has an interesting photographic and memorabilia display. The key to the centre can be obtained from the Council office during working hours.

The **Oast House** (☎ 6261 1030), just off the highway on the Hobart side of town, is a unique museum devoted to the history of the hop industry. It also has a tearoom and a fine-arts gallery. The timber building dates back to the 1820s. In 1867, the first hop kiln was built and hops were dried here for 102 years until 1969 when the kilns closed. You can go on a self-guided tour of the kilns and follow the story of how hops were processed. It's open daily from 10 am to 5 pm and admission is $3.50, children $1.50. The building itself has been classified by the

National Trust and is worth seeing from the outside, even if you don't go in.

Also interesting to visit is **St Matthew's Church of England**, built in 1823, which is Tasmania's oldest existing church. The building has been extensively altered since it was built and today the best features are the excellent stained glass windows. The church is centrally placed facing the open gardens and lawns of Arthur Square.

In Montagu St, the **Bush Inn**, built in 1815, claims to be the oldest continuously licensed hotel in Australia and is an interesting place in which to have a drink. The **Old Colony Inn**, at 21 Montagu St, is a wonderful museum of colonial furnishings and artefacts; there's also a tearoom where you can get some great home-made snacks and sit in the award-winning garden. The inn is open from 9 am to 5 pm and admission is only $1.50; children 50c.

Behind the Bush Inn, **Devil Jet** (☎ 6261 3460) runs 30-minute jet-boat rides up the river for 19 km. Rides cost $40, children $20 and leave every half hour during summer. Rides are available all year and bookings in advance are advised.

Australian Newsprint Mills (☎ 6261 0433) is one of the area's major industries and tours can be arranged Tuesday to Friday if you give at least 24 hours notice. It's located on the north side of the river, five km out of town.

In 1864, the first rainbow and brown trout in the southern hemisphere were bred in the **Salmon Ponds** (☎ 6261 1076) at Plenty, 11 km west of New Norfolk. You can feed the fish in the six display ponds, visit the hatchery and investigate the museum. The ponds and museum on Lower Bushy Park Rd are open daily, entry $3.50, children $2. You can also sit in the restaurant which serves fine food, at reasonable prices, and watch the fish being fed by others without paying an entry fee.

Next to the Salmon Ponds is **Redlands Historic Site** (☎ 6261 1122) which is a privately owned estate with buildings dating from 1823 made with convict bricks. It is currently under restoration and there is a lot

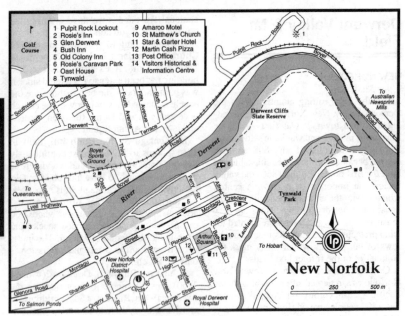

Golf Course

1 Pulpit Rock Lookout
2 Rosie's Inn
3 Glen Derwent
4 Bush Inn
5 Old Colony Inn
6 Rosie's Caravan Park
7 Oast House
8 Tynwald
9 Amaroo Motel
10 St Matthew's Church
11 Star & Garter Hotel
12 Martin Cash Pizza
13 Post Office
14 Visitors Historical &
   Information Centre

Derwent Cliffs State Reserve

To Australian Newsprint Mills

Boyer Sports Ground

To Queenstown

Lyell Highway

Tynwald Park

To Hobart

New Norfolk District Hospital

To Salmon Ponds

Royal Derwent Hospital

New Norfolk

0   250   500 m

of work to do; entry is $4, children $1. Inspection of the larger buildings is limited for safety reasons and as restoration proceeds there will be more to see.

You can get a fine view over New Norfolk by following the road along the northern side of the river eastwards for one km, then up a steep side road to **Pulpit Rock**. This overlooks a sweeping bend of the Derwent River and is the spot from where most photos of the town are taken.

Places to Stay & Eat

Camp sites ($7), on-site vans ($35) and cabins ($40) are available at *Rosie's Caravan Park* (☎ 6261 1268), on the Esplanade, about one km north of town. A great place if you want to fish in the river.

The hotel choices here are pretty limited. The *Bush Inn* (☎ 6261 2011), in Montagu St, was built in 1815 and has plain singles/doubles for $28/48 including a cooked breakfast, but there's a one-night surcharge.

The hotel also has reasonable meals in the restaurant. As you enter town from Hobart, the *Amaroo Motel* (☎ 6261 2000) on the corner of the Lyell Hwy and Pioneer Avenue has rooms for a reasonable $48/56 and also has an à la carte restaurant.

The *Old Colony Inn* (☎ 6261 2731), at 21 Montagu St, has just one double room for short people at $70 for B&B. The upper floor was added in 1835 and has great character with its small doors and low ceilings. If you don't stay here its still worth calling in for the historic display and afternoon teas. On the other side of the river to the main town, *Rosie's Inn* (☎ 6261 1171) at 5 Oast St has plenty of rooms and provides bed and breakfast for $60 to $85 a double. Three km north of town at Magra is *Denmark Hill* (☎ 6261 3313) with a single B&B unit for $60 to $70 a double. At the *Redlands Historic Site* (☎ 6261 1122), 11 km west of town, there is B&B accommodation for $98 a double.

Near the Oast House museum is *Tynwald*

(☎ 6261 2667). It's a three-storey house which dates back to the 1830s and is oozing with character. For many years it was the residence of the operators of the nearby Oast House and was altered in the 1890s with wide verandahs, lace work and bay windows. The rooms are well furnished, and it has a heated swimming pool and a tennis court for the energetic. The cost is $116 a double which includes a light breakfast. For the same price you can stay in the nearby *Old Granary* which was part of the original flour mills and is still part of Tynwald. The main house also has a fine à la carte restaurant which is open to the public every evening.

Beside the Lyell Hwy just west of the bridge over the Derwent River is the luxurious *Glen Derwent* (☎ 6261 3244). Hidden behind a hawthorn hedge in extensive grounds this large mansion has rooms from $88 a double. The rooms range from couples only to ten-person suites.

If you are after something simpler to eat than the meals at the restaurants then the *Martin Cash Pizza* near the corner of Stephen and High Sts serves Italian-style meals and takeaways. As well, the *Star & Garter Hotel* in High St opposite Arthur Square has counter meals on some days.

Getting There & Away
Hobart Coaches (☎ 6234 4077) is the main operator between Hobart and New Norfolk and on weekdays there are eight or nine buses in both directions. At weekends there's a limited service. A one-way/return fare costs $3.40/6.80 In New Norfolk, the buses leave from Stephen St, beside Arthur Square. You can also use the Tasmanian Wilderness Transport bus from Hobart to Mt Field, but unless you are using their bus pass the fare is uneconomical as a flat rate of $25 applies.

BUSHY PARK TO WESTERWAY
As you proceed further west from New Norfolk towards Mt Field you leave the Derwent River and follow the narrow valley of the Tyenna River. The three historic villages of Bushy Park, Glenora and Westerway are small, rural communities where you can see old barns, a working water wheel and extensive hop fields. Many of the buildings are of shingles and still in use allowing you to see how farms of last century were built. Most features are right next to the road and are easily seen, but are on private property.

Hop growing has vanished from most parts of Tasmania but the Bushy Park area has a new kiln and, with new techniques, the industry is being revived. In late summer and autumn you can see the hops growing up the thin leader strings. Bushy Park and Glenora are so close that they are really one town. A new industry to the area is wine making and the **Meadowbank Vineyard** is open daily from 11 am to 5 pm. It's well off the main road being seven km away down a gravel road.

In Bushy Park there is one place to stay; *Hawthorn Lodge* (☎ 6286 1311) is on the Salmon Ponds Rd and provides comfortable B&B accommodation for $70 a double. It was the home of the pioneer hop grower Robert Shoobridge and was built in 1869; today the house is set in beautiful gardens off the road. Afternoon teas are also available to passing visitors.

Westerway is a more substantial town with a general store, petrol station and tea shop. You can also stay here at the *Haven Tea Garden* (☎ 6288 1120) where B&B is provided at $35/50 for singles/doubles. For transport information see getting There & Away in the Mt Field National Park section.

MT FIELD NATIONAL PARK
Mt Field, only 80 km from Hobart, is a favourite place for both locals and visitors. The park is well known for its spectacular mountain scenery, alpine moorlands, dense rainforest, lakes, abundant wildlife and spectacular waterfalls. The area around Russell Falls was first made a reserve in 1885 and by 1916 it became one of the first National Parks in Tasmania. To many locals it is simply known as National Park and indeed this title has been given to the small town at the park entrance.

The major attraction for most people is in the valley close to the park entrance. It is the

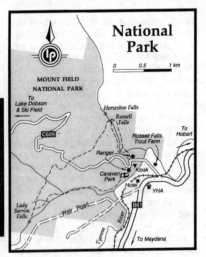

magnificent 40-metre **Russell Falls**; an easy 15-minute walk from the car park along a path which is suitable for wheelchairs. You can continue from Russell Falls along the Tall Trees Circuit to Lady Barron Falls for a two-hour walk.

There are also some magnificent walks on the plateau of top of the range. If you walk there you will need wet weather protective clothing and something warm for the colder weather. Some of many available walks are to the Tarn Shelf (three hours return), Rodway Range and Tarn Shelf (six hours return), Mt Field East (five hours return) and Mt Field West (eight hours return).

In winter snow usually lies on the highest peaks and skiing was first attempted here in 1922 on **Mt Mawson**. A low-key resort of club huts and rope tows has developed and is a refreshing change from the highly commercial developments in the ski fields of mainland Australia. Snow cover is unreliable and often patchy and current reports are available on a recorded message service (☎ 6288 1319).

At peak holiday periods the rangers organise many free activities. The nightly film shows are informative and even better is the after-dark walk to Russell Falls where you get to see glow worms and a different aspect of the rainforest.

Places to Stay

The only camping ground is the *Mt Field Caravan Park* (☎ 6288 1149) which is just inside the national park entrance. Camp sites are $10 and powered sites are $12; it is popular and usually booked out at peak holiday periods. A park entry permit is also needed for your stay. One advantage of camping here is the nightly parade of animals but they present problems too as all food has to be securely locked away. If you prefer to stay on the plateau then consider booking the *Lake Dobson Cabins*. They are 15 km into the park and there are three very basic six-bunk cabins with the cost per cabin being $20 a night, plus $10 each extra adult. Book at the rangers office.

Outside the park the *National Park Youth Hostel* (☎ 6288 1369) is 200 metres past the turn-off to the park and charges $11 a night, YHA members only, and is conveniently located near the only hotel. The YHA office in Criterion St, Hobart sometimes offers a special deal on weekdays only with two nights at this hostel and bus to and from Hobart for $35. The nearby *Russell Falls Holiday Cottages* (☎ 6288 1198) consists of four one or two-bedroom fully equipped cottages, which cost $50 a double, plus $10 for each extra person.

Getting There & Away

On weekdays, Hobart Coaches (☎ 6234 4077) operates one bus at 4 pm that runs from Hobart to New Norfolk then continues on through Bushy Park, Glenora and Westerway to Mt Field. There is a return service to Hobart on weekdays at 7.55 am.

During summer, Tasmanian Wilderness Transport (☎ 6334 4442) runs one daily service which leaves Hobart at 8.30 am then Mt Field at 10.15 am and arrives at Lake St Clair at 12.45 pm. The same bus returns every day along the same route except Sunday when the return bus does not pass near Mt Field. It leaves Lake St Clair at 1.30

pm and Mt Field at 3.50 pm to arrive in Hobart at 5.15 pm. The fare from Hobart is $25. During other seasons the same service operates on Monday and Wednesday plus a one-way service from Hobart to Mt Field on Saturday.

Tasmanian Wilderness Transport also runs buses from Hobart past Mt Field to Scotts Peak in the South West National Park. This service is primarily used by bushwalkers, and during summer buses follow this route in both directions on Tuesday, Thursday, Saturday and Sunday. During autumn and spring a once-a-week service operates on Thursday only, and there are no services in winter.

North of the Derwent

BRIDGEWATER
• *pop 8680*

This town, 19 km north of Hobart, is so named because of the causeway built here by convicts in the 1830s. More than 150 convicts laboured in chains, moving two million tonnes of stone and clay, to build this main crossing of the Derwent River. The old **watch house**, on the other side of the river from the town, was built by convicts in 1838 to guard the causeway and be used as a gaol. It is now a museum housing relics from the convict days. Admission is $1.50.

PONTVILLE & BRIGHTON
• *pop 1125*

Six km north of Bridgewater, on the Midland Hwy, is Brighton and just north of it the historic town of Pontville. At one stage these two towns were considered for the capital of Van Diemen's Land and some interesting buildings dating from the 1830s were erected. Pontville has good examples of sandstone buildings and much of the freestone used in Tasmania's early buildings was supplied from quarries at Pontville.

Beside the river in Pontville, the **Barracks** (☎ 6268 1665) is an impressive Georgian sandstone building that originally housed

soldiers. Today you can stay overnight in one of the three stone barracks for $85/100 which includes breakfast. The Pontville and Brighton area is still used by the military with some large bases nearby.

In Pontville, up on top of the hill, is **St Mark's Anglican Church** from where there is an excellent view of Mt Wellington. The church was built in 1841 and there are also other sandstone buildings in the area. North of the church on Rifle Range Rd is the *Sheiling* (☎ 6268 1951), a cute two-storey house covered in ivy where B&B is $50 a double. This is one of the oldest houses in the state being built in 1819.

Brighton is less interesting, composed mostly of recently built houses to serve the nearby military base. You can stay at the *Brighton Hotel Motel* (☎ 6268 1201) for $35/55 which includes breakfast. Nearby, three km down side roads which are well signposted, you will find the very good **Bonorong Park Wildlife Centre** (☎ 6268 1184) on Briggs Rd. Bonorong comes from an Aboriginal word meaning 'native companion' and you can feed the wombats, koalas and Tasmanian devils. It is open daily from 8 am to 5 pm; admission is $5, children $2.50. You can get to Bonorong by bus; from Hobart take any service to Glenorchy Bus Station from where you take bus No 125 or 126.

RICHMOND
• *pop 750*

Richmond is just 24 km from Hobart and, with more than 50 buildings dating from the 19th century, is Tasmania's premier historic town. Straddling the Coal River, on the old route between Hobart and Port Arthur, Richmond was once a strategic military post and convict station. The much-photographed **Richmond Bridge** is the highlight of the town.

With the completion of the Sorell Causeway in 1872, traffic travelling to the Tasman Peninsula and the east coast bypassed Richmond. The town was not abandoned as it was still the centre for a farming community but it ceased to grow. For over 100 years the

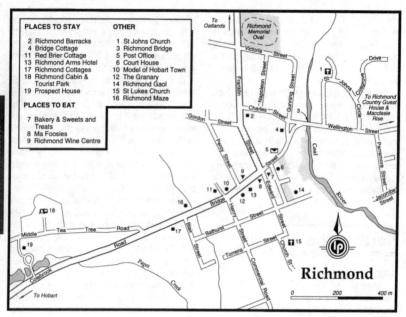

To Oatlands

Richmond

PLACES TO STAY

2 Richmond Barracks
4 Bridge Cottage
11 Red Brier Cottage
13 Richmond Arms Hotel
17 Richmond Cottages
18 Richmond Cabin & Tourist Park
19 Prospect House

PLACES TO EAT

7 Bakery & Sweets and Treats
8 Ma Foosies
9 Richmond Wine Centre

OTHER

1 St Johns Church
3 Richmond Bridge
5 Post Office
6 Court House
10 Model of Hobart Town
12 The Granary
14 Richmond Gaol
15 St Lukes Church
16 Richmond Maze

AROUND HOBART

town was little changed until the recent tourist boom when visitors discovered the well-preserved town.

Things to See & Do

The **Richmond Bridge** is the most famous construction in the town and is still used for road traffic today. You can freely walk around it and under it and there are good views on both sides. Built by convicts in 1823, it is the oldest road bridge in Australia. When it was first built it formed a vital link for the young colony and encouraged construction of the many buildings seen today.

The northern wing of **Richmond Gaol** was built in 1825, five years before the settlement at Port Arthur, and is the best preserved convict jail in Australia. It has not been modified and has original locks, cells and relics. Displays describe the old penal system, and the gaol is open daily from 10 am to 5 pm; admission is $3, children $1.50 or $7.50 for a family.

Other places of historical interest include **St John's Church** (1836), the oldest Catholic church in Australia; **St Luke's Church of England** (1834); the **courthouse** (1825); the **old post office** (1826); the **Bridge Inn** (1817); the **granary** (1829); and the **Richmond Arms Hotel** (1888).

There's also a model village (designed from original plans) of Hobart Town as it was in the 1820s. It's worth a look as the detail is excellent and you can see how much Hobart has changed in 170 years. The waterfront has seen the most dramatic changes with the reclamation of most of the shallow waters. It's open daily from 9.30 am to 5.30 pm and admission is $5, children $3.50 for children). The **Richmond Maze**, on Bridge St, is fun but has wooden walls, not hedges; admission is $3.50, children $2.50.

There are several art and craft places around the town selling paintings, carved timber bowls and trinkets, leather goods, books and furniture. Prices are not particularly cheap but then many items are of good quality and locally made.

Places to Stay & Eat

Accommodation in Richmond is mostly of the 'colonial cottage' type and is not particularly cheap. Cheapest of all is the *Richmond Cabin & Tourist Park* (☎ 6260 2192), on Middle Tea Tree Rd opposite Prospect House. It has camp sites ($12 for two people), on-site vans ($32) and cabins ($48).

The cheapest B&B is the *Richmond Country Guest House* (☎ 6260 4238), on the gravel surfaced Prossers Rd, four km north of town, which charges $45/70 for B&B for singles/doubles. The other reasonably priced B&B is *Macclesie Rise* (☎ 6265 1814) on Brinktop Rd which is also four km out of town.

In the upper price group, the pick of places to stay is *Prospect House* (☎ 6260 2207) which is a superb two-storey Georgian country mansion set in 10 hectares of grounds. It's just outside Richmond, on the Hobart road. Accommodation costs $86/96, or $10 more if breakfast is included. The house also has a well-known restaurant with à la carte menu for lunch and dinner every day.

In the centre of town you can stay in some of the historic cottages. *Richmond Cottages* (☎ 6260 2561) at 12 Bridge St is $115 a double, *Red Brier Cottage* (☎ 6260 2349) at 15 Bridge St is $100 a double, *Bridge Cottage* (☎ 6260 2247) at 47 Bridge St is $115 and the *Richmond Barracks* (☎ 6260 2453) at 16 Franklin St is $105 a double. All these cottages have breakfast provided.

There are more cottages providing similarly-priced accommodation in the side streets around the town. For a hotel room the *Richmond Arms Hotel* (☎ 6260 2109) at 42 Bridge St is $85 a double with breakfast included. The hotel also provides meals every day in its dining room.

If you prefer to be more in the countryside then there are a few places near Cambridge, about 12 km south of Richmond. The *Cambridge Caravan Park* (☎ 6248 5453) is beside the road to Richmond and has camp sites for $10, on-site caravans for $25 to $30 and cabins from $35. The park also serves meals with three-course lunches and buffet dinners at cheap prices. North of the caravan park toward Richmond at the end of a side road is *Barilla House* (☎ 6248 5654) on Denholms Rd. It's two km off the road and overlooks the wide estuary of Pitt Water; B&B rooms are $75/85.

In Richmond you can get something to eat and drink at the *Richmond Wine Centre* in Bridge Road. This new building is set back from the street and is a good place for breakfast and lunch. There are several tearooms with light meals; try *Ma Foosies* in the main street for some good country service. The town also has a bakery which is hidden behind the Saddlery building. If you have a sweet tooth then the old-fashioned lolly shop called *Sweets and Treats* in Bridge St will be tempting. If the lollies don't appeal then try the wide variety of ice cream.

Getting There & Away

If you have your own car or transport, Richmond is an easy day trip from Hobart. If you don't, both Tasmanian Redline Coaches (☎ 6231 3233) and Hobart Coaches (☎ 6234 4077) have bus tours most days to Richmond. Hobart Coaches runs four regular buses a day on weekdays to and from Richmond ($6 return) and most services continue to Campania; there are no scheduled weekend services.

South-East Coast & Tasman Peninsula

The south-east coastal region of Tasmania is best known for the Huon pine and for apple-growing – both of which have suffered declined fortunes in the region in recent years. Spectacular rainbows in the Huon Valley, interesting state reserves, plus the attractions of Bruny Island make the region well worth a visit.

The Tasman Peninsula is popular with visitors, as it is the home of the notorious Port Arthur penal colony and the whole area is rich in convict history.

South-East Coast

South of Hobart are the scenic fruit-growing and timber areas of the Huon Peninsula, D'Entrecasteaux Channel and Esperance, as well as beautiful Bruny Island and Hartz Mountains National Park. The wide Huon River dominates the region, carving the hills into deep valleys and wide waterways. Synonymous with this river is the famous Huon pine, a unique tree that can exceed 2000 years in age. Sadly, those trees were logged out many years ago and only a few young specimens remain. The area is also known for its spectacular rainbows, which are probably due to a combination of southern latitude and abundant waterways.

In the 1960s, it was apple-growing in the Huon Valley that put Tasmania on the international export map. At one stage there were over 2000 orchards exporting eight million boxes of apples, mainly to the United Kingdom. When demand from Europe declined, so did the orchards.

In recent years, farmers have diversified into other fruit crops, along with Atlantic salmon, wines and tourism. Tasmania's reputation for clean air and low pollution has led to these new products finding markets in Asia. The abundance of high-quality local produce has encouraged some of the hotels

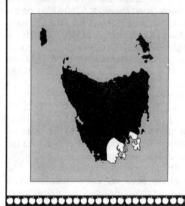

HIGHLIGHTS

- Peaceful, unspoilt Bruny Island
- Exploring the caves at Hastings
- The forestry display at Geeveston
- The convict ruins at Port Arthur
- Sea cliffs on Tasman Peninsula

to compete with restaurants in other regions for providing the state's best meals. Being so close to Hobart, many of the northern towns have become outlying suburbs of the city, with a significant commuter population. While growing in size, they have little of interest for visitors; the smaller places further south have more to offer.

If you are looking for work here, then from around the end of December to March there is fruit-picking, but competition for jobs is stiff. Grape-picking work is sometimes available in late autumn and early winter as most wineries are still hand-picking their crops. Hostels are good sources of information on how to find such jobs. Be warned though, as fruit-picking is a tough way to earn a few dollars and pay is proportional to the quantity and quality picked. Many

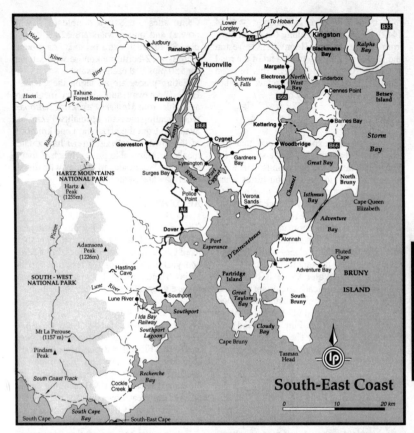

South-East Coast

0   10   20 km

pickers struggle to earn enough to pay for their accommodation.

Getting There & Around

The region south of Hobart has two distinct areas; the peninsula which includes Kettering and Cygnet, and the coastal strip which the Huon Hwy follows from Huonville south to Cockle Creek. Each of the two areas has separate bus services.

For the peninsula, Hobart Coaches (☎ 6234 4077 or 1800 030 620) runs several buses on weekdays from Hobart south through Margate, Snug and Kettering to Woodbridge. The weekend services are poor with a single bus on Saturday from Hobart to Kettering and none on Sunday. One bus each weekday runs from Hobart to Snug and inland across to Cygnet. The YHA at Cygnet runs a bus to the Hobart YHA at Adelphi Court and back; services run according to demand and bookings are essential.

A different set of buses is run by Hobart Coaches from Hobart through Huonville and Geeveston to Dover. There are four services each weekday as far as Geeveston and one bus continues to Dover. On school days extra services run between Dover and Hobart.

Tasmanian Wilderness Transport (☎ 6334 4442) also runs buses along the Huon Hwy from Hobart through Huonville, Geeveston and Dover all the way to the end of the road at Cockle Creek. In summer this runs on Monday, Wednesday and Friday; in other seasons it runs on Friday only.

SNUG
• *pop 760*
Early European explorers found that this area provided a safe, sheltered anchorage for their ships, hence the name Snug. The town became famous in the 1967 bushfires when 80 houses (most of the town) were burnt to the ground. A temporary village was established in caravans beside the oval and this led to the creation of the caravan park.

Since then the town has been rebuilt and is a popular holiday place, with sheltered waters and good boating facilities.

The nearby **Oyster Cove** has little for visitors but is historically important as it was the home of the last of Tasmania's full-blood Aboriginal people. In 1847 the last 40 were transferred here from Flinders Island and remained for 30 years. The quiet cove was a favoured site of the Aboriginal people for its shellfish.

Things to See & Do
The nearby **Snug Falls** are worth a visit and are located 3.5 km off the highway on a minor side road. An easy one-km walk each way, complete with seats and picnic shelters, leads to the foot of the falls.

One km south of the town, beside the highway, the **Channel Historical and Folk Museum** (☎ 6267 9169) illustrates the history of the timber and fishing industries as well as recording the huge 1967 fires. It's open daily in summer, but on Sunday only during the rest of the year; entry is $2.

Just south of Snug, there is a good swimming beach at **Coningham**.

Places to Stay & Eat
The *Snug Beach Caravan Park* (☎ 6267 9138) is one of the best in the state with shady, grassed sites located beside the beach.

Camp sites are $10 a double ($12 with power) and on-site vans are $28 a double plus $5 for each extra person. For groups, there is a 12-berth bunkhouse with kitchen for $50 plus $10 each person.

Eating places are all along the Channel Hwy. Takeaway and sit-down meals are available from *Mothers Favourite Seafoods*, where scallop pie is the speciality. Pizzas are available from the pizza shop one km north of the town. The *Snug Tavern* has counter meals for reasonable prices, lunch is available from Wednesday to Sunday with dinner on Friday and Saturday nights only.

KETTERING
• *pop 295*
The small port of Kettering lies at the head of the scenic Little Oyster Cove. This sheltered bay contains a marina for fishing boats and yachts as well as the terminal for the Bruny Island car ferry. It's a reasonable place to base yourself for exploring the region.

Places to Stay & Eat
Try the excellent food at the *Oyster Cove Inn*. The restaurant meals are reasonably priced at $14 to $17, and cheaper meals are available at the bar. The inn was once the residence of a wealthy grazier and dominates the end of the bay. The B&B accommodation upstairs has great views over the marina, but is in need of renovation and overpriced from $70 a double.

Better value accommodation for around the same price is available at the nearby *Heron Rise Vineyard* (☎ 6267 4339). Luxury B&B accommodation in two self-contained units is available from $80 a double. The vineyard was established in 1984, and wine tastings as well as dinner can be provided to guests upon request. The vineyard is located one km north of the town on Saddle Road.

Getting There & Away
On weekdays, Hobart Coaches (☎ 6234 4077 or 1800 030 620) runs four buses daily from Hobart to Kettering, continuing further south to Woodbridge at 8.15 am, 2.40 pm, 5.10 pm and 6.15 pm. A single service runs

on Saturday morning from Kettering to Hobart at 7.20 am with the return service at 3.20 pm. There are currently no Sunday services.

BRUNY ISLAND
• *pop 440*

Bruny Island is almost two islands, joined by a narrow, sandy isthmus less than 100 metres wide. Locals refer to the two sections as 'North Bruny' and 'South Bruny' as they are also different in character. North Bruny consists of rolling hills which are extensively farmed while South Bruny has higher, steeper hills which are forested.

In between, the narrow isthmus is over five km in length and is the home of mutton birds and other waterfowl. It is a peaceful and beautiful retreat. The sparsely populated island has five state reserves and is renowned for its varied wildlife, including fairy penguins and many species of reptile. It has great natural appeal and is well worth visiting.

The island's coastal scenery is superb and there are plenty of fine swimming and surf beaches, as well as good sea and freshwater fishing. There are a number of signposted walking tracks within the reserves, especially the southern Labillardiere State Reserve and at Fluted Cape.

The island was sighted by Abel Tasman in 1642 and later visited by Furneaux, Cook, Bligh and Cox between 1770 and 1790, but was named after Rear-Admiral Bruni D'Entrecasteaux, who explored and surveyed the area in 1792. Confusion existed about the spelling and in 1918, it was changed from Bruni to Bruny.

The Aboriginal people called the island Lunawanna-Alonnah and this name has been retained in the form of the names of two settlements. However, the Aboriginal people were hopelessly outnumbered and couldn't cope with diseases introduced by the settlers. By the 1840s they had been forced off the island and were transported to Flinders Island. The many landmarks named after them are the only reminder of their tragic clashes with European culture.

The island saw several commercial ventures come and go during its history. Sandstone was mined from one of the rocky points and used in prominent buildings such as the GPO and the Houses of Parliament in Melbourne. Coal was also mined, but these industries declined as transportation costs were high. The only long-term industry came from farming and forestry operations.

Not much else changed on the island until the car ferry started in 1954. Since then roads have been created and today there are over 200 km of roads to explore.

Tourism has now become an important part of the island's economy but it is still fairly low key. There are no massive resorts; instead there are interesting cottages and houses, most of which are self-contained. Unless you're staying at Adventure Bay you should bring food with you. Also it is wise to book accommodation in advance as managers often don't live next door.

Things to See & Do
This island is not an overdeveloped tourist destination; instead it is a peaceful place with an interesting past and many unpopulated and unpolluted beaches. Major activities for visitors include walking in the reserves and along beaches, looking for rare birds and just enjoying the relaxed lifestyle.

The island was one of the first places that European explorers visited and its history is recorded in the **Bligh Museum of Pacific Exploration** (☎ 6293 1117) at Adventure Bay, South Bruny. Constructed of bricks made by convicts, it has a display on European exploration in the South Pacific. The collection includes maps, charts and globes and information on the early Antarctic explorations. Many of the books and manuscripts are originals or first editions and well worth seeing. It's open daily from 10 am to 3 pm except for Wednesday and public holidays; entry fee is $2.50, children $1.50.

Also of historical interest is South Bruny's **lighthouse**, which was built in 1836 and is the second oldest in Australia. Built from local stone, it's located on the stormy southern end of the island. It's worth a visit just to see the rugged coastline. The lighthouse reserve is open to the public.

For something different, camel rides are available at Camel Tracks (☎ 6260 6335) which is located north of the isthmus beside the main road linking North Bruny to South Bruny. Open all year and operating on demand, short rides start at $5, one hour is $22 and all day costs $68. Overnight rides are also available with costs ranging from $70 to $120 per day depending on the accommodation used.

State Reserves There are five major reserves. The **Neck Beach Game Reserve** is the home of mutton birds and fairy penguins which nest in the sand dunes. The best time and place to see these birds is at dusk in the warmer months at Highest Hummock Lookout. Climb the 273 timber steps to the lookout and **Truganini Memorial** which provides sweeping views of both parts of the island. A timber walkway also crosses the Neck to the other beach. You should keep to the boardwalks in this area as the mutton birds dig deep holes into the sand. The holes can be very hard to see and stepping into them can result in a broken ankle.

The popular **Fluted Cape Reserve** is at the southern end of the small township of Adventure Bay. Here you can walk along the shore to **Penguin Island** which is accessible at low tides or complete a more difficult circuit and climb **Fluted Cape** for more extensive views.

On the southern end of the island the lighthouse marks the start of the large **Labillardiere State Reserve** which features rugged coastal scenery. Walks range from beach explorations to a long seven-hour circuit of the entire peninsula. Other reserves feature a waterfall behind Adventure Bay and habitat of the rare 'forty-spotted pardalote' bird. Many birdwatchers come here to catch a glimpse of this endangered species.

For more information on walks around the island get the little booklet *Bruny Island: A Guide for Walkers* which is obtained from shops on the island; the cost is $4.

Places to Stay
This is a popular holiday destination for some Tasmanian families, as shown by the large number of self-contained cottages for hire which offer economical rates for one-week rentals. Many of these are suitable for medium size groups. Rentals for shorter periods are available for most places but pre-booking is essential.

Adventure Bay on the southern part of the island is the main accommodation area, but there are also individual places dotted around the island. **Alonnah** is the other main settlement on South Bruny, with **Dennes Point** being the main area on North Bruny.

If you have a vehicle and a tent then the cheapest place to stay is at any of the free camping areas. To prevent the island's foreshores being damaged by indiscriminate tent sites, camping is restricted to specified locations which have pit toilets, some water and fireplaces. They are: **Neck Beach** which is at the southern end of the sandy isthmus; **Jetty Beach** which is three km north of the lighthouse at Cape Bruny; and **Cloudy Bay** at the southern end of South Bruny. These are all signposted. There are no camping grounds on North Bruny.

Adventure Bay The *Adventure Bay Caravan Park* (☎ 6293 1270) is beside the beach at the end of the road at Adventure Bay. It has camp sites for $10 a double, powered sites for $12 a double, on-site vans for $30 a double or cosy little three-bed cabins for $40. The *Captain James Cook Caravan Park* (☎ 6293 1128) is closer to town and is less interesting being just a large, flat, grassed area. It is cheaper for camping with sites for $6 a double ($8 with power) and on-site vans for $30 a double.

The only hostel on the island is the *Lumeah Hostel* (☎ 6293 1265) in Adventure Bay, which has dormitory beds for $13 for YHA members, or $15 for others.

There are plenty of self-contained cottages or houses. It is best to book ahead as managers and keys are not always easily located. Cottages include: *Rosebud Cottage* (☎ 6293 1325) at $60 a double plus $7 for each extra person; *Mavista Cottage* (☎ 6293 1347) from $68 a double and $15 each extra person; and *Seaside Cottages* (☎ 6293 1403) at $60 for four plus $8 for each extra person.

Some cottages require a minimum stay of two nights; these include *Adventure Bay Holiday Home* at $60 a double and $8 for each extra person, and *Bruny Island Quiet Corner Units* (☎ 6264 2011) which cost $50 a double.

More upmarket is *Morella* (☎ 6293 1131) which has three units and is located beside the entrance road to Adventure Bay. The two larger units cost $75 to $80 a double per night plus $10 for each extra person; the smaller double unit costs $120 to $130 with breakfast provided.

Lunawanna & Alonnah The two main settlements on the eastern side of South Bruny are very small villages which are not as attractive for visitors as the Adventure Bay area. The best value accommodation in the area is *Coolangatta Cottage* (☎ 6293 1164), which is in an uninspiring location in the middle of nowhere beside the Cloudy Bay Road and costs only $60 a night for up to five people. On the same road is *Mill Cottage* (☎ 6293 1156) for $55 a double plus $10 each extra person, and *Inala Country Accommodation* (☎ 6293 1217) for $70 double plus $10 each extra person.

For larger groups, the only choice is the *Whalers Inn Holiday Village* (☎ 6293 1271), located in dry forest beside the Lighthouse Road at Lunawanna. It has six timber cabins that can cater for 36 people. Rates are $65 a double plus $10 for each extra person with discounts for groups and weekly bookings.

In Alonnah the *Bruny Hotel* (☎ 6293 1148) costs only $35/50 for singles/doubles. There are no cooking facilities.

North Bruny On North Bruny the major settlement is around Dennes Point on the very northern tip of the island. Here the *Channel View Guest House* (☎ 6260 6266) has good-value B&B at $30/45 for singles/doubles.

The only place on the island offering full

board is *House Sofia Holiday Accommodation* (☎ 6260 6277) at Dennes Point. It charges $40, children $20. Bring your own sheets as there is an extra charge for linen. Advance bookings are essential.

Barnes Bay was once the ferry terminal but is now a peaceful location. The *Barnes Bay Villas* (☎ 6260 6287) overlooks the bay and has one unit for five adults available for $60 a double plus $5 for each extra person; a minimum stay of two nights applies. Also overlooking the same bay, *Lyndenne Cottage* (☎ 6260 6264) is for couples only and comes with breakfast for $65 a night.

If you want a bit of privacy, rent the large *Christopher Lumsden Cottage* (☎ 6239 6547) which is located beside the main road north of the isthmus. The charge of $55 a double plus $10 for each extra adult is very reasonable for this interesting two-storey house. A minimum stay of two nights applies.

Places To Eat

Most visitors bring their own provisions, as the range of food available on the island is very limited. Standard takeaways are available at the *Lunawanna General Store*, *Alonnah General Store*, *Cafe Bruny* (which is beside the road leading to the ferry terminal) and *Kelly's Village Store* at Dennes Point.

For excellent afternoon teas including Devonshire teas and continental cakes the *Penguin Tea Room and Craft Shop* in Adventure Bay next to the general store is well worth visiting. It's closed from June to August but opens daily the rest of the year.

Counter meals are available at the *Bruny Hotel* at Alonnah on South Bruny. Lunches and dinners are available every day over the summer and holiday periods. In the quieter months, meals are only available from Thursday to Sunday. Prices are reasonable with $9 to $12 for mains. Takeaways are also available.

There is a limited choice of restaurants on the island. The *Lyndenne Restaurant* (☎ 6260 6264) at Barnes Bay offers à la carte meals on Friday, Saturday, Sunday and public holidays; bookings are essential for dinner.

Getting There & Away

Access to the island is by a modern car ferry (☎ 6233 5363) from Kettering to Roberts Point on North Bruny and takes only 15 minutes. There are nine services a day from Monday to Saturday and eight services on Sunday leaving roughly every hour. Ferries start at 7 am and the last ferry departs from the island at 6.50 pm most nights. It's best to check on the day. An extra service is run on Friday nights. The ferry can carry 75 cars and has an interesting propulsion system using the unusual 'Voith Schneider' propellers. These look like vertical paddle wheels and provide excellent manouverablity.

All fares are for return trips and a car costs $18 for standard times and $23 for public holiday weekends. Bicycles are taken across for $3 and this can be a very good way to see the island. The charge for motorcycles is normally $11; $14 for holiday times. There is no charge for passengers.

Most of the buses from Hobart to Kettering stop at the ferry terminal, but the terminal on the island is a long way from anywhere. You'll need a vehicle to get around as there are no buses. Traffic on the island is quiet, except for a mini peak which occurs after each ferry trip. Most roads are gravel and in good condition. With over 200 km of quiet roads leading to many scenic spots, several days can be spent exploring the island.

If you have limited time and no transport, then an organised day tour around the island with Bruny Island Ventures (☎ 6273 2886 or 1800 124 835) might appeal. With a maximum group size of seven this tour visits all major features. The cost from Hobart is $90 each for the day with discounts available to YHA members.

WOODBRIDGE

This tiny village, just five km south of Kettering, contains the School of Marine Studies, established to assist students in marine biology. The main attraction of Woodbridge is the magnificent food at the

Woodbridge Hotel (☎ 6267 4604) which has won state awards for its quality. The dining room has good views over the channel and prices for main courses are a very reasonable $10 to $15. For wine buffs the hotel also provides a tasting service for many of the tiny wineries in the area. A charge applies with $5 for a selection of six different wines.

For more **wine tasting** try the Hartzview Vineyard & Wine Centre (☎ 6295 1623). It is located in the hills behind the town off the road to Gardners Bay and features fruit ports and liqueurs under the Pig & Whistle label as well as wines from the smaller nearby vineyards. It's open every day from October to February from 10 am to 5 pm; in other months it's open only at weekends.

Places to Stay

The cosy *Honeywood Cottage* (☎ 6267 4550), located 1.5 km north of the hotel provides self-contained accommodation for up to four people on a working farm property. It's $50 a double plus $15 for each extra person. *The Melaleucas* (☎ 6267 4877) charges $45/80 for singles/doubles with breakfast provided, and is particularly suitable for people with disabilities and senior citizens. It's advisable to book ahead.

The *Woodbridge Hotel* also has accommodation with B&B at $80 a double – unfortunately the accommodation is not as good as the food. If you are after something really special then stay at the *Hartzview Vineyard Homestead* (☎ 6295 1623) near the wine centre. Complete with antiques, a log fire and complimentary wines the price for B&B is $120 a double plus $24 for each extra adult.

Getting There & Away

See Getting There & Away in the Kettering section of this chapter.

CYGNET

- *pop 925*

This small township was originally named 'Port de Cygne Noir' (Port of the Black Swan) by the Frenchman Rear-Admiral D'Entrecasteaux because of the many swans seen on the bay. Now known as Cygnet, the town and surrounding area have many apple and other fruit orchards and offer excellent fishing, plenty of easy bushwalks, flat-water canoeing and some fine beaches, particularly further south at Randalls Bay and Verona Sands.

The town is the largest on this peninsula and provides a good range of services, including several banks, supermarkets, food shops and sporting facilities. Travellers who are interested in antiques will enjoy browsing in the many stores around the town which sell old furniture. Another attraction is the open-air market which is held in the town centre on the third Sunday of each month.

Things to See

During the summer it is fruit-picking season and the town becomes rather busy. You can pick fruit and vegetables from December to March at Huon Organic Farm at Petchy's Bay, seven km south-west of the town.

There are eight small vineyards in the region but most are not open to the public. The temperate climate encourages slow ripening of the grapes, producing strong fruit flavours that are typical of the wines of this region. The Hartzview Vineyard & Wine Centre is the main place for local tastings; see the note under Woodbridge. Also the Panorama Vineyard (☎ 6223 7481), seven km north of the town, has wine tastings on Sunday during December and January.

The **Talune Wildlife Park & Koala Garden** is in the hills six km south-east of the town. Animals on display include Tasmanian devils, wallabies, koalas and wombats. It's open every day except Christmas Day; entry is $5 for adults and $2 for children. Woodturning and handmade dolls are a speciality produced at The Deepings. It's open every day except Sunday morning and entry is free.

After heavy rain the nearby **Pelverata Falls** are well worth visiting. Located 12 km north of the town, a four-km walk leads to the base of the 81-metre-high waterfall. Allow three to four hours for the return walk.

Places to Stay

Huon Valley YHA & Backpackers (☎ 6295 1551) is on the Channel Hwy, about five km north of the town. It used to be called 'Balfes Hill' and charges $12 a night ($14 for non-members), and can get crowded during the fruit-picking season. From December to April, the manager organises twice-weekly walks to South Cape Bay, the most southern beach in Tasmania; a package including two nights' accommodation costs around $89, children $69 or family $300. You can explore the area on the mountain bikes which the hostel rents for $12 per day. Meals are available at the hostel if required.

The *Cygnet Hotel* (☎ 6295 1267) has basic singles/doubles for $25/50 with a cooked breakfast. There's also the very basic *Cygnet Caravan Park* (☎ 6295 1869) opposite the hotel for a bargain $5 a camp site, $7 with power.

The *Talune Wildlife Park* (☎ 6295 1775) has three self-contained cabins in a grassy paddock near the entrance for $50 a double plus $5 for each extra person. Further south at Deep Bay *Cherry Hill Cottage* (☎ 6297 8155) is located in a commercial cherry orchard. It is suitable for a group of up to five people. The cost is $60 a double plus $10 for each extra adult.

For B&B the *Leumeah Lodge* (☎ 6295 1839) provides a peaceful setting by the water at Crooked Tree Point just south of town. The cost is $70 to $75 for doubles. Further south the *Lower Bagot Farm* (☎ 6295 1615) is another B&B hidden away in the hills above a commercial flower farm. It's located close to the Wildlife Park and is rented to couples or families only for $55 a double plus $35 for each extra adult or $20 for children. Another similar standard B&B is at *The Deepings* (☎ 6295 1398) in the hills east of town; doubles are more expensive at $83 to $88.

Places to Eat

The *Old School House Coffee Shop* in the centre of town has good light lunches and bakehouse produce which are all made at the shop. For delicatessen and breads try the

Mimosa Wholefood and Deli. There are also the usual takeaways. For something more substantial, the *Cygnet Hotel* has cheap counter meals for $7 to $11. Some of the accommodation places provide dinners to order.

Getting There & Away

Hobart Coaches (☎ 6234 4077 or 1800 030 620) has a once-daily, weekday-only service from Hobart at 5.15 pm to Cygnet via Snug. The service to Hobart leaves Snug at 6.55 am. The YHA at Cygnet runs a bus to the Adelphi Court YHA in Hobart.

HUONVILLE
• *pop 1520*

Straddling both banks of the Huon River the major reason for this town's existence is that it is sited beside the first rapid on the river and was an important crossing point. Today a modern bridge crosses the Huon River enabling access to the south. The valuable softwood, Huon pine, was first discovered here.

The Huon and Kermandie Rivers were named after Huon D'Kermandec, the second in command to the European explorer D'Entrecasteaux. Prior to that the Aboriginal people called the area Tahune-Linah. As the region was originally covered in tall forests, timber milling was the first major industry to develop. At first the Huon pine was wasted but once its properties were understood it became the major forestry product. Being very slow-growing, with a typical tree being over 800 years old, it didn't take long for Huon pine to be virtually wiped out, and today only immature trees can be found along the river. Once the forest was cleared, apple trees were planted and this began the orcharding industry which is still the primary agricultural product of the region.

Things to See & Do

For the visitor, one of the main attractions of Huonville is a **jet-boat ride** through the rapids on the river. For $30 for adults and $16 for children you get a thrilling 40-minute ride. It operates daily from 9 am to 5 pm and bookings are essential as it runs according to demand. You can also hire pedal boats and aqua bikes for $20 an hour from the same office (☎ 6264 1838) on the Esplanade.

The other feature in the town is **Model Train World** (☎ 6264 2116), located behind

---

Huon Pine

Huon pine (*Dacrydium franklinii*) is a species endemic to Tasmania and is found primarily in the western half of the state. It is not a true pine, but is a softwood which grows extremely slowly on the banks of streams and nearby slopes. Huon pine enjoys the cool temperatures and high rainfall of this area as well as the company of other rainforest species such as myrtle, sassafras, blackwoods and leatherwoods.

Huon pine is a highly prized timber. It has a very fine texture, light yellow colouring and a distinctive fragrance. It is highly regarded for furniture making, turning and joinery as well as ship-building. It hardly shrinks, is easy to work with and is very durable due to the high proportion of oil contained in the timber.

In the past, 'piners' worked hard in very rough conditions to fell the timber, cart it to a stream, brand the logs and float them downstream during floods. A substantial amount of timber was lost owing to breakages on the way downstream and 'poaching' was also rife. For many years now, Huon pine has been in short supply. The easily accessed areas have all been logged and it is not viable as a commercial crop because of its slow growth, around 12 cm per century.

Two reserves have been set aside to protect mature Huon pine. The Olegas Truchanas Reserve is located on the Denison River and the Gilbert Leitch Reserve on the shores of Lake Gordon. Probably the best and easiest way to see examples of mature Huon pine is to head off to Strahan and join one of the cruises on the Gordon River or take a seaplane flight. On each of these trips you are able to go ashore and get a close-hand view. Many craft shops across the state sell wood turnings made of Huon pine. ■

the Shell service station. Inside the converted apple warehouse, alpine scenes from Germany have been recreated; if you like trains then you will enjoy the display. It's open from Tuesday to Sunday all year except July when it's closed; admission $3, children $1.50.

Grove, a small settlement six km to the north, has become the tourist capital of the apple industry. Beside the highway, the **Huon Valley Apple & Heritage Museum** is crammed with displays about apples and also depicts life in the 1800s; entry is $2.50, children $1.50. Closer to town the *Huon Apple* has displays of local history and crafts along with tearooms; entry is free.

If you like old cars then visit the **Tasman Antique Motor Museum** (☎ 6264 1346) at Ranelagh, two km north-west of Huonville; entry is $3, children $1.50. There are over 40 cars, mostly American and dating back to 1906. If you find it difficult to catch fish then you should visit the **Snowy Range Trout Fishery** (☎ 6266 0243) where your catch is guaranteed! It's in the hills 15 km west of Huonville and the cost is $2 per family plus you pay by weight for the fish you catch.

In the nearby hills are Horseback Wilderness Tours (☎ 018 128 405 or 6264 2540) which follow quiet trails near the Huon River. Rides cost $25 per hour up to a maximum of $90 for the whole day; discounts are given to YHA members. Overnight rides are also available on request.

Places to Stay & Eat

The town itself is the commercial centre of the region but is not a major overnight stop for visitors. The only accommodation in the town is the *Huonville Grand Hotel*, (☎ 6264 1004) near the river. It is an old brick pub with plenty of basic rooms for $25/35 for singles/doubles.

There are the usual takeaways and roadhouses. For light lunches of pastries and cakes try the *Mustard Pot*. Pizza and pasta are available at *Tower Pizza* in the main street. It is open every evening from 5 pm till late. For a more substantial meal the *Huon Manor* (☎ 6264 1311) opposite the hotel

near the river, provides à la carte lunch and dinner, Tuesday to Saturday, at very reasonable prices (from $6). Local wine is sold by the glass.

The *Apple Valley Teahouse* at the Huon Apple near Grove is worth a stop for its excellent egg & bacon pies and cakes.

FRANKLIN
• *pop 460*

The highway follows the Huon River south for a long way passing through the tiny settlements of Franklin, Castle Forbes Bay and Port Huon. These were all once important shipping ports for exporting apples. Today the wharves and packing sheds are rarely used.

Franklin is the oldest town in the Huon area and the peaceful, wide river provides the venue for one of Australia's best rowing courses. The town itself is fairly large for its small population and there has been little change to the buildings in the last 100 years. The main street with its Federation architecture is worth stopping to view. You can meet the locals at the Sunday market which is held inside the Palais Theatre from 10 am to 3 pm. Local produce and crafts are on sale and often accompanied by a local folk band. Local crafts can also be seen daily in Country Collections and Huon Showcase which are signposted off the highway as you travel south.

Places to Stay & Eat

The *Franklin Lodge* (☎ 6266 3506) is a lovely building that started in the 1850s and was extended around 1900 into the grand Federation building seen today. Bed and continental breakfast is provided here for $90 a double plus $25 for each extra person. The nearby *Franklin Grill* restaurant (☎ 6266 3645) is open for dinner from Wednesday to Sunday. A three-course dinner costs $25, and there's a special menu for children.

For counter meals, the *Franklin Tavern* provides lunch and dinner on most days except for Tuesday and Sunday. This two-storey hotel with its wide balconies is unusual and is more like what you would expect to find in Queensland. For lunch you can also try *Holts* restaurant and wine bar in Franklin.

Further south at Castle Forbes Bay the *Castle Forbes Bay House* (☎ 6297 1995) provides bed and cooked breakfast for a reasonable $40/66 for singles/doubles. This is a former schoolhouse and is located off the highway and surrounded by an apple orchard.

PORT HUON

In the heyday of the apple industry this small village was famous as being its biggest export port. The wharf and cool stores remain as a legacy of those busy times and today are a rarely-used facility. For visitors the **Shipwright Reserve** picnic ground beside the river is a good place to stop and enjoy the view.

Huon River Cruises operates from the Port Huon Resort (☎ 6297 1110). A one-hour **river cruise** runs at 10 am and 2.30 pm daily except Saturday. It visits the Atlantic salmon farms, and costs $15, children $7. The resort itself has a swimming pool, golf course and tennis courts; hotel rooms cost $60 and villas are $85 a double. Ignore the signs; there is no backpacker accommodation available here. The hotel at the resort was once called the 'Kermandie Hotel' and serves lunch and dinner. Unfortunately, they serve bar meals at restaurant prices ($12 to $17) and there are better meals elsewhere.

GEEVESTON

• *pop 825*

Located 31 km south of Huonville, this is the administrative centre for Australia's most southerly municipality and the gateway to the Hartz Mountains National Park. While most towns have declined as apple sales dropped, this town has reversed the trend and grown. It has always been an important base for the timber industry and today its economy is based on forestry industries and the tourists who come to see both the forests and nearby wilderness.

This town was founded in the mid 1800s by the Geeves family; their descendants are still prominent in local affairs. In the 1980s the town was the centre of an intense conservation battle over the forests of Farmhouse Creek. At the height of the controversy some conservationists spent weeks living in the tops of the 80-metre-tall eucalypts to prevent them from being cut down. In the end the conservation movement won, Farmhouse Creek is now protected from logging and peace has resumed to this busy little town.

Things to See

The town's main attraction is the **Esperance Forest & Heritage Centre** in the main street. It has comprehensive displays on all aspects of forestry such as logging practices and land management. There is also a wood-turning workshop where you watch the experts or try it yourself. In the foyer there are often exhibitions of crafts. The centre also incorporates the South-West Visitor Centre (☎ 6297 1836) and is open daily from 10 am to 4 pm; admission is $4, children $2. It's interesting and well worth the visit.

The grandiose gateway to the town, with its swamp gum logs, also has an adjacent reserve where a short walking track highlights the range of forest plants. There are also picnic tables and barbecues.

Places to Stay & Eat

The solitary B&B here is *Cambridge House* (☎ 6297 1561) just south of the town. It sleeps six and is rented to families or groups only – rates are $60 a double plus $20 each extra person. For meals there are the usual takeaways and cafes, and a supermarket.

Getting There & Away

Hobart Coaches (☎ 6234 4077 or 1800 030 620) runs four buses a day between Hobart and Geeveston via Huonville for $9 one way. An extra service runs on school days as well as one service on Sunday during school termtime. Tasmanian Wilderness Transport (☎ 6334 4442) also runs a service from Hobart to Cockle Creek three days a week which stops here, but it is considerably more expensive as a flat fare of $35 applies.

ARVE ROAD

From Geeveston this narrow road heads westward through rugged, timbered country to Hartz Mountains and the Huon River. The road was constructed for extracting timber from the extensive forests and although it's a dead-end road, it's an interesting drive. Logging trucks also use the road; drive slowly.

Follow the road to the **Arve River Picnic Area** which has picnic tables and a short forest walk. Just past here you can turn left for the climb to Hartz Mountains. If you keep to the right, the road leads over the next ridge to the Tahune Forest Reserve on the banks of the Huon River.

Along the road to Tahune there are several short tracks (about 10 minutes each) worth walking. **Keogh's Creek Walk** is a short circuit with an all-weather covered bridge for viewing the forest. The **Big Tree Walk** leads to a timber platform beside a giant 87-metre-high swamp gum. The **West Creek Lookout** provides different views with a bridge extending out onto the top of an old tree stump. Presently this has been closed for repairs. The last walk along the road is the **Zig-Zag Walk** which cuts across a steep bend in the road.

HARTZ MOUNTAINS NATIONAL PARK

This national park, classified as part of the World Heritage Area, is very popular with weekend walkers and day-trippers as it's only 84 km from Hobart. The park is renowned for its rugged mountains, glacial lakes, gorges, alpine moorlands and dense rainforest. Being on the edge of the South-West National Park, it is subject to sudden changes in weather, so even on a day walk take waterproof gear and warm clothing. The normal national park entry fees apply ($8 per car per day).

Waratah Lookout is only 24 km from Geeveston and is an easy five-minute walk from the road – look for the jagged peaks of the Snowy Range and the Devils Backbone. Other good walks on well-surfaced tracks are **Arve Falls**, 30 minutes return and **Lake Osborne**, two hours return. For the more

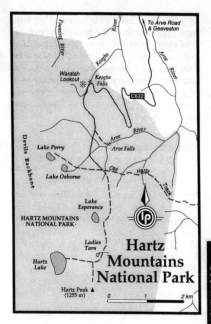

adventurous, a rougher track leads to **Hartz Peak**, five hours return.

TAHUNE FOREST RESERVE

The name of this reserve is derived from Tahune-Linah, which was the Aboriginal name for the Huon River. The picnic ground has tables, toilets and a shelter (it often rains here). There are several signposted walks ranging from 10 minutes to two hours. The longer tracks can be muddy. This is a good place to view Huon pines which grow beside the river. There are plenty of younger trees, recognisable by their feathery foliage and weeping branches.

POLICE POINT

The main road from Geeveston to Dover heads inland at Surges Bay and is an uninteresting but quick route to Dover. The more scenic alternative is to leave the highway at Surges Bay and follow the Esperance Coast Road through Police Point and Surveyors

Bay. Some of this road is unsealed but has a firm, gravel surface. The road provides many fine views over the very wide Huon River and passes many scenic places like **Desolation Bay** and **Roaring Bay**. Along the way you will obtain very close views of the pens of the commercial salmon farms. While you cannot inspect them, you can observe how they are managed.

Places to Stay & Eat

If you want to have an entire valley and bay to yourself, then hire *Huon Charm Waterfront Cottage* (☎ 6297 6314) at Desolation Bay. Suitable for four, this self-contained cottage is $70 a double plus $12 for each extra person. Just around the next point is the more modern brick unit of *Huon Delight Holiday Cottage* (☎ 6297 6336) which has fine views over the river; suitable for couples only at $68.

Further down the road, the friendly people at *Granny Gibbons Jams* (☎ 6297 6309) will let you watch the jam-making process, using local fruit. They also provide excellent Devonshire teas in *Emma's Tearoom* beside the house. Eight varieties of jam are produced here. It is open all year.

DOVER
* *pop 520*

This picturesque fishing port, 21 km south of Geeveston on the Huon Hwy, has some fine beaches and makes an excellent base to explore the area. Originally it was called Port Esperance after one of the ships in Admiral D'Entrecasteaux's fleet but that name is now only used for the bay. The three small islands in the bay are known as Faith, Hope and Charity.

Last century, the processing and exporting of timber was Dover's major industry. Timber was milled and shipped from here and also in the nearby towns of Strathblane and Raminea. While much of it was Huon pine, hardwoods were also harvested and sent to countries like China, India and Germany and used as railway sleepers. If you have your own car and are heading further

south, it's a good idea to buy petrol and food supplies here.

Today the major industries are fruit growing, fishing and the Atlantic salmon fish farms. The three fish factories near the town support 2000 people and produce Atlantic salmon which is exported to many Asian countries. The town centre has reasonable services with supermarkets and some bank agents. An airport is located behind the hotel and pick-ups for flights with Par-Avion over the nearby wilderness can be arranged at the hotel.

Things to See

Casey's Steam and Doll Museum (☎ 6298 1506) in Station St has an interesting mix of antique steam engines and dolls. Children love the display as there is something for every taste; adults $6, children $3.

From December to March, the South West Passage Cruising Company (☎ 6298 3247) runs a one-hour **cruise** three times a day (Sunday to Tuesday only) from the hotel to inspect the salmon farms in the bay. This is a rare chance to see how salmon farms are managed; it costs $15, children $7. During the same months, cruises visit the islands in the bay on a four-hour trip; price $43, children $19. Overnight cruise trips are available to places like Bruny Island from $43 per person per day and bookings are essential for all trips.

The **Esperance Forest Tour** (sometimes called Hastings Forest Tour) is a scenic drive through the southern forests. It starts at Strathblane just south of Dover and winds its way south to the Esperance River, then to Hastings Caves. An audio tape and brochure on this 45-minute drive is available for $8 from local shops and also from the Esperance Forest & Heritage Centre at Geeveston. A $2 refund applies if the tape is returned.

Places to Stay & Eat

This is the major base for the region and has a wide range of accommodation to suit all tastes and budgets. The *Dover Beachside Caravan Park* (☎ 6298 1301) on Kent Beach Rd is situated on flat ground opposite the beach and has camp sites ($9) and on-site vans ($28).

Nearby, *White Cliffs Lodge* (☎ 6298 1180) on Bay View Road has dormitory accommodation for $12. There are also doubles for $35 which includes linen. Mountain bikes and a rowing boat are available for hire. In summer (December to February) staff run a daily bus service between Dover and Hobart. It leaves Dover at 8 am and the return trip leaves the *Adelphi Court YHA* in Hobart at 9.40 am. The fare is $10 one way, and bookings are essential. Transport is also provided to worthwhile local destinations.

The *Dover Hotel* (☎ 6298 1210), on the Huon Hwy just south of the town, has several levels of accommodation. The backpacker dormitory costs $10, hotel B&B is $28 per person, or motel rooms are $55 a double. The hotel also has fairly good meals with mains for a reasonable $10 to $13. Breakfast and lunch is available every day, with dinner available every day except Sunday.

For something more comfortable and homely try *Annes Old Rectory* (☎ 6298 1222), where you share the house with the owners. This is beside the road as you approach the town from the north; it's $55 a double for good, old-fashioned country service. Dinner is available upon request for guests. Light lunches and Devonshire teas are also available in the cosy little tea room adjacent to the rectory.

If you prefer a flat, *3 Island Holiday Apartments* (☎ 6298 1396) near the foreshore has three units with reasonable facilities for $55 a double plus $10 for each extra adult. The more modern *Driftwood Cottages* (☎ 6298 1441) on Bay View Road, has four studio apartments with all facilities for $98 a double plus $25 for each extra adult.

Getting There & Away

Hobart Coaches (☎ 6234 4077 or 1800 030 620) runs one bus a day from Hobart to Dover on weekdays, leaving at 6 pm. The return bus from Dover leaves at 7.05 am. On school days, a second bus operates at similar times in the morning and returns from

Hobart at 4 pm; fare $11 each way. From December to February a daily bus operates from *White Cliffs Lodge* to Hobart and bookings are essential; see the note earlier in Places to Stay & Eat. Tasmanian Wilderness Transport (☎ 6334 4442) also operates a bus three days a week in summer from Hobart to Cockle Creek, but this service, at $35, is considerably more expensive.

SOUTHPORT

Originally, Southport was called 'Baie des Moules' (Bay of Mussels) and has been known by several names during its history. Its current name is fairly descriptive as it's located at the southern end of the sealed highway. In fact, most visitors don't even pass through the town as there is a major road junction two km to the north. It has limited appeal and exists primarily to serve the sparsely populated local area.

The bluff south of the town has a memorial to one of the early shipwrecks in which 35 people perished. The aptly named **Burying Ground Point** on Lady Bay Road is a convict burial ground.

The *Southport Tavern* is the main focal place being the hotel, general store and caravan park. The hotel is open every day providing both lunch and dinner; at the bar, meals are $10 to $11, in the restaurant there is a better range of similar food for $11 to $15. The general store is open daily from 9 am to 6 pm and also sells petrol. Behind the hotel, the caravan park is in a rather ordinary grassed paddock, and costs $10 for a tent; on-site-vans are $28 a double plus $5 for each extra adult.

HASTINGS

Today, it's the spectacular **Hastings Cave & Thermal Pool** which attract visitors to the once-thriving logging and wharf town of Hastings, 21 km south of Dover. The cave is found among the lush vegetation of the **Hastings Caves State Reserve** (☎ 6298 1138), 10 km inland from Hastings and well signposted from the Huon Hwy. Daily tours of the cave (adult $8, children $4, or family $20) leave promptly at 11.15 am and 1.15,

2.15 and 3.15 pm, with up to four extra tours daily from December to April. From the thermal pool allow 10 minutes' drive, then five minutes' walk through rainforest to the cave entrance. For the more energetic a short track continues past the cave to a viewpoint overlooking the forest.

About five km before the cave is a thermal swimming pool ($2.50, children $1.50, or family $6), filled daily with warm water from a thermal spring. Near the pool are a kiosk and restaurant. The 10-minute sensory walk near the pool is well worth doing. This is a feel-and-smell walk, which can also be completed by visually impaired people.

For those interested in a more adventurous exploration of the caves, Exit Cave Adventure Tours (☎ 6243 0546) runs a trip into a nearby locked, undeveloped cave. The trip is suitable for beginners, and bookings are essential as the tour runs a maximum of three times per week. It leaves Hobart at 8 am and the cost is $90 per person.

LUNE RIVER

A few km south-west of Hastings is Lune River, a haven for gem collectors and the site of Australia's most southerly post office and youth hostel. From here you can take a scenic six-km ride on the **Ida Bay Railway** (☎ 6298 3110) to the lovely beach at Deep Hole Bay. The train runs every Sunday at noon, 1.30 pm and 3 pm. In the warmer months extra services run on Saturday and Wednesday. The ride costs $10 ($5 for children).

The most southerly drive you can make in Australia is along the secondary gravel road from Lune River to **Cockle Creek** and beautiful **Recherche Bay**. This is an area of spectacular mountain peaks and endless beaches – ideal for camping and bushwalking. This is also the start (or end) of the challenging **South-Coast Track**, which, with the right preparation and a week or so to spare, will take you all the way to Port Davey and beyond in the south-west. See Lonely Planet's *Bushwalking in Australia* by John & Monica Chapman for track notes.

Cockle Creek provides a good base for several day walks. You can follow the shore-line north-east to the lighthouse at **Fishers Point**, which is three hours return. The South Coast Track can also be followed to **South Cape Bay** and takes five hours return.

Places to Stay

The *Lune River Youth Hostel* (☎ 6298 3163), also known as the 'Doing Place', charges $10 a night, $12 for nonmembers. It's a cosy hostel and there's certainly plenty to do – ask the managers about hiring mountain bikes or kayaks, or about bushwalking, fishing and caving. Don't forget to bring plenty of food with you as the hostel only has basic supplies. The hostel runs a shuttle bus connecting with the Hobart Coaches' Dover service; bookings are essential. For B&B you can hire the *Lune River Cottage* (☎ 6298 3107) for $50 a double. The *Moon Cottage* (☎ 6298 3247) provides B&B for $82 a double and also has packages which include sailing trips in the area.

Getting There & Away

Apart from the hostel bus, the only other service is that run by Tasmanian Wilderness Transport (☎ 6334 4442 or 1800 030 620). The bus runs on Monday, Wednesday and Friday from December to April all the way to the end of the road at Cockle Creek for a flat fee of $35 one way or $65 return. From May to November there is a single service each week on Friday.

Tasman Peninsula

The Arthur Hwy runs from Hobart through Sorell and Copping to Port Arthur, 100 km away. This is the most popular tourist region of the state, but despite the hordes it is definitely worth visiting Port Arthur, the infamous convict settlement of the 1800s. However, there is far more to this peninsula than just its convict past. Much of the coast-line consists of rugged cliffs which, at 300 metres high, are Australia's tallest. In between the headlands are some good

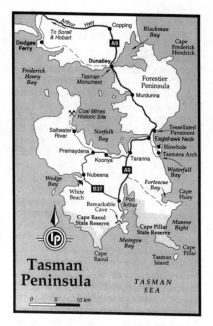

Tasman Peninsula

TASMAN SEA

0   5   10 km

beaches which attract only small numbers of visitors.

The Tasman Peninsula offers many bushwalks, superb scenery, delightful stretches of beach and beautiful bays. Near Eaglehawk Neck are the incredible coastal formations of the Tessellated Pavement, Devils Kitchen, Blowhole, Tasmans Arch and Waterfall Bay. If you have the time it's worth spending a couple of days here and seeing more than just the major tourist destinations.

Getting There & Around

Hobart Coaches (☎ 6434 4077 or 1800 030 620) has a twice-daily Monday-to-Friday service which travels from Hobart and around the main towns on the Tasman Peninsula ($11.50 one way). Convict Country Bus Services (☎ 6265 5397) also runs two services a day on weekdays and visits many of the sights on the Peninsula ($9 one way). There are usually no services on weekends.

Another way is to join a tourist coach. Most coach tours are for one-day trips only but you can sometimes arrange to join a coach and split your journey over two days. This can be a convenient way to visit Port Arthur on weekends. Hobart Coaches (☎ 6234 4077 or 1800 030 620) and Tasmanian Redline Coaches (☎ 6231 2200 or 1800 030 033) run several types of coach trips from $40 to $50 which includes entry fees.

SORELL

- *pop 3,200*

Often known as the gateway to Port Arthur, this town is one of the oldest in Tasmania but few remnants of its history remain today. Europeans started farming here in 1805 and by 1819 the town was established. In those days the journey to Hobart was either by boat or via a long road loop through Richmond. Finally, after eight years of construction, the causeway was completed in 1872, providing a direct link to Hobart. Since then the town has grown to be a satellite of Hobart.

The town itself is at an important road junction of the highways to Hobart, Port Arthur and the east coast. It has good facilities, including banks and supermarkets, and visitors are advised to stock up on food supplies here because shops on the Tasman Peninsula and the east coast are usually more expensive.

Things to See

A few older buildings, located near the centre of town, have survived from the 1800s and are worth a look. Behind the High School, **Scots Uniting Church** was built in 1841 and for many years was abandoned. Recently restored, it is floodlit at night. Also near the school are the Barracks and the Bluebell Inn, historic buildings now used for accommodation.

In the main street is **St George's Anglican Church** and next door is an interesting graveyard with many headstones of the early settlers. Behind this church is the local park, **Pioneer Park**, with a mural about the former railway line.

Just east of the town the **Orani Vineyard**

(☎ 6225 0330 or 6265 1849) is open for cellar-door sales on Saturday, Sunday and public holidays. There are also picnic grounds and a tearooms at the winery. In summer at the **Sorell Fruit Farm**, you can pick your own fresh fruit.

Places to Stay & Eat

For colonial accommodation the *Bluebell Inn* (☎ 6265 2804) is a two-storey sandstone building with B&B for $65 a double plus $20 for extra adults. It also provides à la carte dining for both guests and visitors. Almost next door the *Sorell Barracks* (☎ 6265 1236) is another historic building with B&B for $84 a double plus $25 for each extra adult.

If you want to sample farm life then stay at *Flimby Host Farm* (☎ 6265 1632) on the eastern side of the town. It caters for families or groups of up to five people and B&B is $70 a double plus $25 for extra adults, children $15. For most visitors, Sorell is a stopping place for stocking up on food and this is reflected in a very wide range of reasonable takeaways along the main street.

Getting There & Away

There are plenty of buses passing through this town – any bus from Hobart to the East Coast or to Port Arthur will take you there. Hobart Coaches (☎ 6234 4077), Tasmanian Redline Coaches (☎ 6231 3233) and Convict Country Bus Service (☎ 6265 5397) all run services through the town.

COPPING

This tiny village has only one feature for visitors – the **Copping Colonial and Convict Exhibition** (☎ 6253 5373). Stop here to get into the convict mood; entry $6, children $2.50.

DUNALLEY

The timbered Forestier Peninsula is connected to Tasmania by a narrow isthmus known as Dunalley. A canal complete with an opening bridge cuts across the isthmus providing a short cut for small boats. While the coastal scenery around here is sometimes spectacular, keep going down the highway as the cliffs get higher and the coast more dramatic the further south you travel.

Places to Stay

It's all B&B around this isthmus. *Potters Craft* (☎ 6253 5469) is suitable for up to five guests and is located beside the water. It costs $75 a double, plus $20 each extra adult. On the side road to Fulham the *Fulham Cottage* and *Fulham Shearers Quarters* (☎ 6253 5247) are self-contained units on a working farm; the cost is $80 a double plus $20 each extra person.

EAGLEHAWK NECK

Another narrow isthmus, this connects the Tasman Peninsula to the Forestier Peninsula. In the days of convict occupation, the 100-metre-wide neck had a row of fierce dogs chained across it to prevent escapes. Some dog platforms were also placed into the narrow Eaglehawk Bay to the west to prevent convicts from wading around the barrier. Rumours were circulated that the waters were shark-infested (it's not true) to discourage swimming. Despite the precautions a few did escape.

Things to See

The only remaining structure from convict days is the **Officer's Quarters**, a timber building from 1832 which is now a museum; entry is free. As you approach from the north, turn off east onto Pirates Bay Drive to the lookout. From here you can see the scenic Pirates Bay and the rugged coastline beyond.

At the northern end of Pirates Bay below the hotel is the **Tessellated Pavement** – a rocky terrace which has eroded to look like tiled paving. At low tide it is worth walking further along the foreshore to **Clydes Island** from where there are fine views of the coastline; you can see as far south as Cape Huay.

Follow the side roads to **The Blowhole**, **Tasmans Arch** and **Waterfall Bay** for some close-up views of the spectacular coastal cliffs. Take great care around The Blowhole as several people have died here; at the other features keep behind the fences as the cliff edges are rather crumbly. From Waterfall

Bay there is a good two-hour return walk to Waterfall Bluff where you'll have a fine view along the coast. This walk basically follows the cliff tops south; take care as there are no safety fences.

For a longer walk the **Tasman Trail** starts at Waterfall Bay, climbs over Tatnells Hill then follows the coast to Fortescue Bay. This is a full day's walk and there are some camp sites along the way. Track notes to this walk and many others in this area are available in *Tasman Tracks* by Shirley and Peter Storey.

The road passes through **Doo Town**, a tiny village where almost every house has a name with 'Doo' in its title. This custom was started by a Hobart architect 60 years ago. Some of the titles are quite clever, such as 'This'll Doo Me' and 'Doo-Little'.

Activities

The erosion processes that have formed the impressive cliff faces have also created some amazing caves and canyons which are mainly underwater. The way to see these is to go diving with Eaglehawk Dive Centre (☎ 6250 3566), located on the scenic Pirates Bay Drive, north of the neck. Regular dive sites include caves, kelp forests, a sea lion colony and shipwrecks. A full day's dive with all equipment is $110 per person. Diving tickets are required for diving in Australia and full instruction is provided; a basic course is $195 for three evenings and two days.

Ocean Sports (☎ 6250 3425) runs diving trips in the Eaglehawk Neck area and hires out scuba equipment and sailboards. You can also just go coastal sightseeing by boat from $10 per hour.

Places to Stay & Eat

While there is not a lot of accommodation around the Neck, what is there is varied enough to suit most people's needs. Its advantages are that it's far more scenic than Port Arthur, that it's not crowded, and that it is very close to all major features.

The *Eaglehawk Neck Backpackers* (☎ 6250 3248), on Old Jetty Rd is located on the north side of the isthmus down the side road. It's a small and friendly hostel charging $12 a night (children $6), and a good base from which to explore the Eaglehawk Neck area. The managers hire out bicycles, which are ideal for visiting the remoter parts of the peninsula.

For great views the *Lufra Holiday Hotel* (☎ 6250 3262), perched above the Tessellated Pavement, is hard to beat. B&B is $60 a double plus $20 for each extra person or $90 for families of four. Light snacks are available all day from the lounge, and the restaurant serves breakfast, lunch and dinner seven days a week.

Near the hotel *Wunnamurra Waterfront* (☎ 6250 3145) is perched above Clydes Island providing B&B for $65 to $75 a double. If you prefer a motel, *Pirates Bay Motel* (☎ 6250 3272) on the Blowholes Road provides singles/doubles for $70/92 or a family room for four for $115. For an entire house, *The Neck Beach House* (☎ 6250 3541) near the hotel is suitable for up to five people; rates vary with season, but range from $60 to $110 per night.

For meals the *Officers Mess* and the *Pirates Bay Motel* have licensed restaurants. Takeaway food is available from the *Officers Mess* and the *Eaglehawk Cafe*.

Getting There & Away

See the Port Arthur Getting There & Away for details as most bus services to Port Arthur stop at Eaglehawke Neck.

TARANNA

Taranna is a tiny village spread along the shores of Little Norfolk Bay and its name comes from an Aboriginal word meaning hunting ground. Located 10 km north of Port Arthur this is an historically important village as it was the terminus for a convict-powered tramway which ran from Long Bay, near Port Arthur, to this village. It was Australia's first railway and was powered by convicts; they pushed the carriages uphill, then jumped on for the easy ride down. The line ended at a jetty and the remainder of the route to Hobart was then by sea. In those days Taranna was called 'Old Norfolk'.

Out in the bay, **Dart Island** was used as a semaphore station to relay messages from Port Arthur to Hobart. Today the waters near the island are used for oyster farming.

The major attraction of the village is the **Tasmanian Devil Park and Wildlife Rescue Centre** (☎ 6250 3230). This is not a zoo, but as a refuge for injured and orphaned animals and is linked to the World Wide Fund for Nature. The major feature for most visitors is the feeding of the Tasmanian devils at 10 and 11 am. Other features are a video about the Tasmanian tiger, an arboretum of endemic Tasmanian plants, a kiosk and barbecue facilities. The park is open every day, entry is $8, children $4 or a family $22. A triple pass to this park plus the Bush Mill and Port Arthur is available for $27.50 (children $13.50, family $75) and provides a worthwhile saving if visiting all three places.

Places to Stay & Eat

The *Norfolk Bay Convict Station* (☎ 6250 3487) provides B&B in a historic building from the convict days for $60 a double plus $20 for extra adults or $15 for children. *Taranna House* (☎ 6250 3161) provides similar standard B&B accommodation for $85 a double plus $20 for extra adults.

For light meals, the *Convict Country Bakery* offers freshly baked pastries and cakes. On the other side of the road you can get a more substantial meal at *Mariners Licensed Restaurant* (☎ 6250 3438).

FORTESCUE BAY

Hidden down a gravel road is one of the gems of the peninsula, with a sweeping sandy beach backed by thick forests. Apart from swimming and lazing on the beach, the main activity is walking. Excellent tracks lead to some of the best coastal scenery in the state. The cliffs are taller and more impressive than those around Eaglehawk Neck. For those with their own boats, this is an excellent base for fishing since it has a boat ramp and calm waters.

The sheltered bay was one of the semaphore station sites used during the convict period to relay messages to Eaglehawk Neck. Early this century a timber mill was in operation and the boilers and jetty ruins are still visible near Mill Creek. Timber tramways were used to collect the timber and some of their remains are still visible. The mill closed in 1952. A fish factory was also in operation in the 1940s in Canoe Bay. In 1979 the coastal strip which includes Fortescue Bay was designated a Forest Reserve.

Activities

Several walking tracks start from the bay. The best walk is to **Cape Huay** which takes four hours return. A well-used track leads out to the sensational sea stacks, the **Candlestick** and the **Totem Pole**. To see rainforest, follow the same track towards Cape Huay and then the side track to Mt Fortesque, which takes six to seven hours return. To the north a good track follows the shores of the bay to Canoe Bay (two hours return) and Bivouac Bay (four hours return). The tracks extend all the way to **Cape Pillar**, where the sea cliffs are 300 metres high. This requires at least two days to visit. For track notes see Lonely Planet's *Bushwalking in Australia* by John & Monica Chapman.

Places to Stay

At Fortescue Bay there is a camping ground at Mill Creek – run by the Forestry Commission (☎ 6250 2433). There's no power, but cold showers and firewood are available. The charge is $6 per adult, children $3 or $15 per family group. Bookings are advised at major holiday periods. There are no stores or kiosks so bring all your food with you. There is no public transport to the bay; it is a 12 km walk to the highway where buses run to Port Arthur.

PORT ARTHUR

In 1830 Governor Arthur chose the Tasman Peninsula as the place to confine prisoners who had committed further crimes in the colony. He called the peninsula a 'natural penitentiary' because it was connected to the mainland only by a narrow strip of land, less than 100 metres wide, Eaglehawk Neck.

Between 1830 and 1877 about 12,500 convicts served sentences at Port Arthur, and for some of them it was a living hell. In reality, those who behaved lived in better conditions than where they had come from in Britain and Ireland. The soldiers who guarded them also lived in similar conditions, and they too were often imprisoned for what would be regarded today as minor offences.

The township of Port Arthur became the centre of a network of penal stations on the peninsula, but was much more than just a prison town. It had fine buildings and thriving industries, including timber milling, shipbuilding, coal mining, brick and nail production and shoemaking.

A semaphore telegraph system allowed instant communication between Port Arthur, the penal outstations and Hobart. Convict farms provided fresh vegetables, a boys' prison was built at Point Puer to reform and educate juvenile convicts, and a church, one of the most readily recognised tourist sights in Australia, was erected.

Things to See

Today, the well-presented historic site of Port Arthur is Tasmania's premier tourist attraction. For a fee of $13 ($6.50 for children or $32 for a family) you can visit all the

Convict cuffs and leg fetters

Massacre at Port Arthur

Port Arthur was again the scene of tragedy in April 1996, as this book went to press. A lone gunman opened fire on visitors and staff at the Port Arthur historic site, killing 35 people and injuring several others. He was finally captured after burning down a local guesthouse. As a result of the massacre, some of the information in the Port Arthur section of this chapter is subject to change. ■

---

restored buildings including the lunatic asylum (now a museum) and the model prison. The ticket is valid for 24 hours and entitles you to free admission to the museum, a guided tour of the settlement and a free cruise to the Isle of the Dead. Tickets can be converted to an annual pass at no extra cost at the museum. This is valid all year except during the winter months of June, July and August.

The **museum** contains many displays, but the most popular exhibit is the computerised data base which includes details of all the convicts who were transported to Tasmania. Visitors are encouraged to try to find possible convict ancestors among the many hundred names listed – see if you can spot your great-grandfather's name!

The informative and worthwhile **free tours** of the historic site leave hourly from the car park in front of the information office (☎ 6250 2539) between 9.30 am and 3.30 pm. The site is open daily from 9 am to 5 pm, and there's nothing to stop you from wandering around outside those hours without paying the entry fee, although the museum and tours are closed.

To the north, the **Bush Mill** (☎ 6250 2221) has become a major attraction, with a steam train providing a four-km ride through the bush. The site has recreated much of the pioneer heritage with a sawmill, blacksmith and bush doctor exhibits illustrating what life was like in the Australian bush around 1890. The site is open every day with trains leaving at 10 am, 11 am and 2.30 pm. Entry

TASMAN PENINSULA

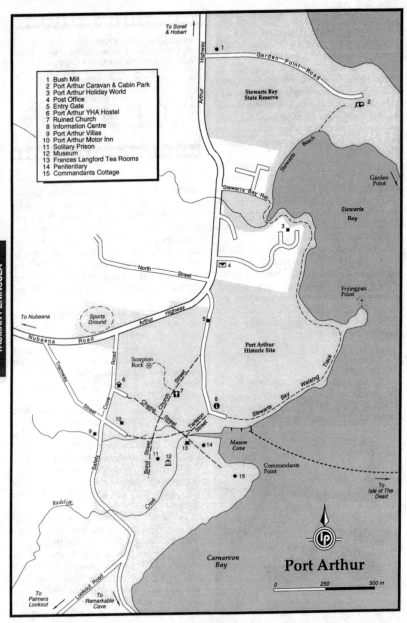

1 Bush Mill
2 Port Arthur Caravan & Cabin Park
3 Port Arthur Holiday World
4 Post Office
5 Entry Gate
6 Port Arthur YHA Hostel
7 Ruined Church
8 Information Centre
9 Port Arthur Villas
10 Port Arthur Motor Inn
11 Solitary Prison
12 Museum
13 Frances Langford Tea Rooms
14 Penitentiary
15 Commandants Cottage

Port Arthur

is $12, children $6 or family $32, including train rides.

Organised Tours

Ghostly apparitions, poltergeists and unexplained happenings have been recorded at Port Arthur since the 1870s, and nightly lantern-lit **ghost tours** of the buildings and ruins are fun, but also pretty spooky. Two-hour tours leave on most days from outside the information office at 8.30 pm, or at 9.30 pm in daylight saving time and are well worth the $8 (children $4, family $20).

Remarkable Tours (☎ 6250 2359) runs one trip a day ($5) to Remarkable Cave as well as twilight tours of the peninsula's other attractions; bookings are essential. Tours leave from the car park in front of the Port Arthur Information Office.

If you want to go on a guided walk, talk to Shirley and Peter Storey at Tasman Trails (☎ 6250 3329); they run guided walks to a variety of locations on the Tasman Peninsula. They take bookings up until the walk starts at 9 am and charge $33 for a days outing including basic gear and lunch.

A really great way to see the sensational coastline is to go on a shark cat with *Tasman Peninsula Advantage Tours* (☎ 6250 3397. The staff run boat trips from Port Arthur around Cape Pillar and Tasman Island; a 1½-hour ride for up to six people costs $180 in total. They also run from Eaglehawk Neck where a shorter ride along the coast for up to six people costs $95.

Places to Stay

The *Port Arthur Garden Point Caravan Park* (☎ 6250 2340) is two km before Port Arthur and is located in picturesque surroundings. It costs $10 to camp, $13 each for the hostel and $45 a double for a cabin. You can follow a track around the shoreline from here to Port Arthur.

The *Port Arthur YHA Hostel* (☎ 6250 2311) is very well positioned on the edge of the historic site and charges $10 a night, $12 for nonmembers. To get there, continue half a km past the Port Arthur turn-off then turn left onto Safety Cove Road at the sign for the hostel and the Port Arthur Motor Inn. You can buy your historic-site entry ticket at the hostel. The hostel often offers package deals such as two nights' accommodation, bus to and from Hobart and Port Arthur entry fee all for $50.

The *Port Arthur Caravan and Cabin Park* (☎ 6250 2340) is located two km north of Port Arthur in lovely bushland surroundings above the quiet Stewarts Bay beach. It has a wide range of facilities with cooking shelters, laundry and games area. The bunkhouse has full cooking facilities, and costs $13 each, children $7. Camp sites are $11 for two people or $13 for powered sites. Cabins are $55 to $65 a double. From the park you can follow a walking track south for 40 minutes to Port Arthur.

The most convenient motel is *Port Arthur Motor Inn* (☎ 6250 2101 or toll-free 1800 030 747) which overlooks the historic site and has rooms from $90 a double. In the same area, but without views of the ruins, are *Port Arthur Villas* (☎ 6250 2239 or toll-free 1800 851 775). The self-contained units sleep four to six people costing $70 per double plus $12 for each extra adult.

Self-contained log cabins are the main feature of *Port Arthur Holiday World* (☎ 6250 2262). Tucked into a quiet area away from the crowds above the swimming beach of Stewarts Bay the 18 units cost $80 a double, plus $10 for each extra person.

Places to Eat

The licensed *Frances Langford Tea Rooms*, in the restored policemen's quarters inside the settlement, is a good place for a cuppa or a light lunch, and is open from 10 am to 5 pm. At the rear of the tearooms is a bakery where the pastries and cakes are baked.

Following the Port Arthur massacre, the cafeteria next to the information centre was closed as this book went to press. Snacks or country style meals are available at the Bush Mill attraction.

For more formal dining, the *Port Arthur Motor Inn*, next to the youth hostel, often has cheap specials on the menu and is worth checking out if you're on a budget. For a

TASMAN PENINSULA

splurge, *Kelley's Seafood Restaurant* (☎ 6250 2666) at Port Arthur Holiday World serves fresh seafood and Tasmanian wines.

Entertainment

There is some unique entertainment at Port Arthur. From November to May inclusive at 7.30 pm every evening, the classic 1926 silent movie *For the Term of His Natural Life* is screened at the Broad Arrow cafeteria (☎ 6250 2242). This film, based on the Marcus Clarke novel about convict life and filmed on location in Port Arthur, costs $5 and finishes just in time for the Port Arthur Ghost Tour.

A special event, **Beating Retreat**, is held on Australia Day every year and is a popular event. Most activities are of a military or convict nature with bands, races, demonstrations and re-enactments forming much of the programme. Tickets for this event are pre-sold and booking early is advised.

The other major event is the **Tasmanian Irish Festival** which is held in spring (usually November) over three weeks. Concerts, workshops on poetry, music and history are just part of this annual event.

Getting There & Away

If you don't have your own transport, the easiest way to Port Arthur is on a day trip from Hobart; there are several from which to choose. Hobart Coaches (☎ 6234 4077 or toll-free 1800 030 620) and Tasmanian Redline Coaches (☎ 6231 2200 or toll-free 1800 030 033) run several types of coach trips from $40 to $50, which includes entry fees.

Hobart Coaches has a twice-daily Monday-to-Friday service which travels via most towns on the Tasman Peninsula for $11.50. Convict Country Bus Services (☎ 6265 5397) also runs two services a day on weekdays and visits many of the sights on the peninsula ($9 one way). It operates from the Transit Centre in Hobart and will pick you up or drop you off at the youth hostel in Port Arthur.

During the summer season on Monday to Friday you can often use the regular bus

services described above for a self-guided day trip. Check timetables first as they regularly alter each season. On weekends it is usually possible to join a coach for a one-way trip but expect to pay a higher price; bookings in advance are essential if doing this.

REMARKABLE CAVE

South of Port Arthur at the end of Safety Cove Road is Remarkable Cave, a series of arches that the sea has eroded. A timber boardwalk provides access and you can walk into the cave when the tide is out. This is the best place to obtain views of the southern coastline where the tall cliffs of the headlands of Cape Pillar and Cape Raoul are seen. From the carpark you can follow the coast east to Maingon Blowhole (two hours return) or further on to Mt Brown (five hours return), from where there are excellent views.

On the return it is worth deviating to **Palmers Lookout** which provides good views of the entire Port Arthur and Safety Cove area.

NUBEENA

• *pop 230*

This is the largest town on the peninsula yet it is a much quieter place than Port Arthur. While it is tucked away and not seen by many visitors it is a popular holiday site for locals. The name Nubeena is the Aboriginal word for 'crayfish'. The town itself is spread along the seashore.

The main activities are swimming and relaxing on the beautiful sand at **White Beach**. Fishing from the jetty or the foreshore is another popular pastime. To the south, down a side road, is some fine walking to **Tunnel Bay** (five hours return), **Raoul Bay Lookout** (two hours return) and **Cape Raoul** (five hours return). *Tasman Tracks* by Shirley & Peter Storey contains detailed notes.

Places to Stay

South of the town, *White Beach Caravan Park* (☎ 6250 2142) has camp sites for $11 ($12 with power), on-site vans for $30 a double and cabins for $45 a double. At the

JOHN CHAPMAN

GLENN BEANLAND

GLENN BEANLAND

MONICA CHAPMAN

GLENN BEANLAND

A	B
C	
D	E

A: St Matthews Church, New Norfolk
B: Russell Falls, Mt Field National Park
C: Late afternoon, Dover, south-east coast
D: The impressive Tasman Arch
E: Richmond Bridge, built 1823

JOHN CHAPMAN

CHRIS KLEP

Top: Hastings Caves, south-east Tasmania
Bottom: The convict church at Port Arthur

other end of the beach *White Beach Holiday Village* (☎ 6250 2152) has self-contained villas in a quiet secluded setting. Units cost $60 a double plus $10 for extra adults and $6 for children.

In the budget range and close to town are *Parker's Holiday Cottages* (☎ 6250 2138), where self-contained units cost $45 a double and $6 for each additional person. There is a B&B at *Parsons Bay Country Accommodation* for $75 a double. For full resort facilities such as golf course, covered pool and sauna the *Fairway Lodge Country Club* (☎ 6250 2171) on the edge of town is the place to stay. Rooms range from $79 to $89 a double.

For takeaways and snacks the *Parsons Bay Bakery* makes cakes and pastries every day. For more substantial meals the *Nubeena Tavern* near the Country Club has good counter meals.

Getting There & Away
Hobart Coaches (☎ 6434 4077 or 1800 030 620) has a twice-daily, Monday-to-Friday service which travels via Nubeena and Koonya for $11.50. Convict Country Bus Services (☎ 6265 5397) also runs two services a day on weekdays along the same route ($9 one way).

SALTWATER RIVER
The ruins of the dreaded **coal mines** are the most powerful and dominant reminders of the past in this section of the peninsula. Started in 1833, the mines were used to punish the worst of the convicts, and they worked in terrible conditions in a poorly managed mining operation. The mining operation was not economic and in 1848 it was sold to private enterprise and within 10 years it was abandoned. Some buildings were demolished and fire and weather took a toll on the rest. Today all that remains are

some sandstone walls, coal near the shoreline and the unexplained circular convict well.

The old mines are interesting to wander around and provide a dramatic contrast to the developments at Port Arthur. Do not enter any of the mine shafts as they have not been stabilised.

Bush camping is allowed near the mine site at **Plunkett Point** and further north along a sandy track at **Lime Bay**. Camping is very basic with pit toilets and fireplaces. Water must be taken in as there is no permanent fresh water. Fees are $3 per person or $7.50 per family.

Apart from the mines, the main attractions are rare birds and butterflies, and easy walks across gentle coastal country. From Lime Bay the two to three-hour return walk to Lagoon Beach is the most popular walk. There is no public transport to Saltwater River.

PREMAYDENA & KOONYA
There is little for visitors at these two tiny settlements apart from the interesting accommodation. The *Seaview Lodge Host Farm* (☎ 6250 2766), provides bunkrooms for $15 each, or $50 a double for B&B. Self-catering is supported with fully equipped kitchens.

The other interesting place to stay is *Cascades* (☎ 6250 3121), originally an out-station of Port Arthur with 400 convicts working there. The historic buildings are all on private property and some of the quarters have been restored in period style and are used for accommodation – B&B is $85 a double. There is also a private museum.

Getting There & Away
See Nubeena Getting There & Away for details.

Midlands & Lake Country

The inland region of Tasmania has a definite English atmosphere, due to the diligent efforts of early settlers who planted English trees and hedgerows. The agricultural potential of the area contributed to Tasmania's rapid settlement, and coach stations, garrison towns, stone villages and pastoral properties soon sprang up.

This mainly agricultural region extends from the Midland Hwy in the east to the Derwent River in the south-west and north to the edges of Launceston. At the centre of this triangle is an elevated, sparsely populated region known as the Lake Country. Three major highways traverse the region: the Lyell Hwy to Queenstown, the Lake Hwy which climbs onto the high Central Plateau and the Midland Hwy which connects Hobart to Launceston.

Midland Highway

In 1804 Hobart was founded and Launceston followed in 1805. By 1807 the need for a land link between the two towns resulted in surveyor Charles Grimes mapping out a route. The road was constructed by convict gangs and by 1821 was suitable for horse and carriage. Two years later a mail cart operated between the two towns; this became the first coach service as it sometimes carried passengers. The main towns along this road were all established in the 1820s as garrisons for prisoners and guards. The Midlands is a fairly dry area and produces fine wool, beef cattle and timber. These products put the Midlands on the map and along with the modern industry, tourism, are still the main sources of income.

The course of the Midland Hwy has changed slightly from its original route and many of the historic towns are now bypassed; actually this is a welcome change

HIGHLIGHTS

- Fishing on the Central Plateau
- The hydroelectric power scheme display at Waddamana
- Detailed carvings on the Ross Bridge
- Climbing to the top of Callington Mill

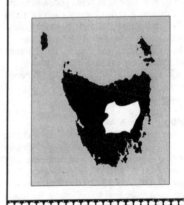

as you can now safely cross the streets without having to dodge the highway traffic. It's definitely worth making a few detours to see these quiet historic towns.

Getting There & Away

Both Tasmanian Redline Coaches (TRC) (☎ 6231 3233 or 1800 030 033) and Hobart Coaches (☎ 6234 4077 or 1800 030 620) have several daily services running in both directions of the Midland Hwy, and you can be dropped off at any of the towns. Fares from Hobart include Oatlands $9.40, Ross $12.60, Campbell Town $14.20 and Launceston $17.80.

OATLANDS

- *pop 520*

With the largest collection of Georgian archi-

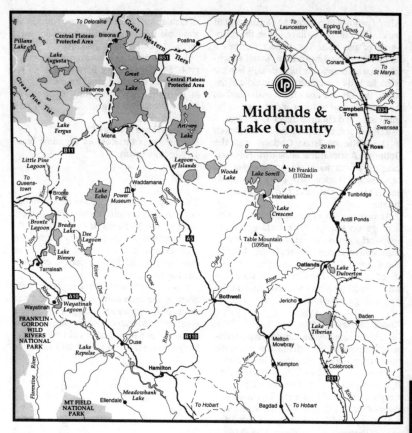

Midlands &
Lake Country

tecture in Australia, and the highest number of buildings dating from before 1837, the town of Oatlands is not to be missed. In the main street alone, there are 87 historic buildings and the oldest is the 1829 convict-built **courthouse**. Much of the sandstone for these early buildings came from the shores of **Lake Dulverton**, now a wildlife sanctuary, which is beside the town.

The town site was chosen in 1821 as one of four military posts on the road from Hobart to George Town, but was very slow to develop. In 1832 a proper survey of the town was made and surveyor Sharland

marked out 50 miles of streets, imagining it would become the capital of the Midlands. Many residents moved in the 1830s and, with the help of the former convicts and soldiers who were skilled carpenters and stonemasons, a large number of solid buildings were erected. The town did not grow into the planned capital, and today is a charming, small town. Some of its historic properties are occupied by residents.

One of Oatlands' main attractions is **Callington Mill**, the restoration of which was Tasmania's main bicentennial project. The mill was built in 1837 and used until 1891.

After a century of neglect the Department of Parks, Wildlife & Heritage began the restoration of the mill. The project features a faithfully restored cap with a fantail attachment that automatically turns its sails into the wind, and you can climb up the middle of the cap to the top. It's just off the main road on the northern end of town and is open daily; entry is $2 and children under 12 are free.

At the other end of town beside the church is the **National Trust Cottage** and the **Oatlands Agricultural Museum**. This contains early farm machinery and horse-drawn vehicles and is open daily; entry is by donation. There are also several old cottages on the site.

An unusual way of seeing Oatlands' sights is to go on one of Peter Fielding's daily historical tours which visit the gaol, courthouse and other convict sites (☎ 6254 1135). The Convict Tour leaves at 5 pm and costs $6 (children $3). The Ghost Tour starts at 8 pm, costs $8 (children $4) and uses candles for lighting on the tour.

Places to Stay & Eat

There's a reasonable amount of accommodation in Oatlands, although much of it is of the more expensive colonial type. The *Oatlands Youth Hostel* (☎ 6254 1320), at 9 Wellington St, is a couple of hundred metres off the main street and charges $10 a night. The *Midlands Hotel* (☎ 6254 1103), at 91 High St, is close to Callington Mill and charges $30/40 for singles/doubles with continental breakfast.

Opposite the hotel at 104 High St, *Amelia Cottage* (☎ 6254 1264) is available for $100 a double plus $20 for each extra person and can sleep 10 people in total; breakfast is provided. The same people also rent out the smaller *Forget-Me-Not Cottage* for the same price. It's located at the back of Amelia Cottage at 17 Dulverton St. Also in the main street is the *Oatlands Lodge* (☎ 6254 1444) at 92 High St; it has four classy rooms with attached bath at $85 a double including breakfast.

Out of town the *Currajong Cottages* (☎ 6255 2150), conveniently located between Oatlands and Ross, are 10 km north

of Oatlands at Antill Ponds. Two cottages are available on farms for $70 a double which includes a continental breakfast.

For à la carte food, *Blossom's of Oatlands* (☎ 6254 1516), on the northern end of the main street, is a good place for meals. There is also the usual shopping centre with takeaways and tearooms.

Getting There & Away

See the notes for Ross as the same buses service both towns.

ROSS
* *pop 280*

This ex-garrison town, 120 km from Hobart, is steeped in colonial history. The realignment of the Midlands Hwy to bypass the town has added to the peaceful charm of this little settlement. The town has strict rules on development and does not have a commercial feel to it at all.

It was established in 1812 to protect travellers on the main north-south road and was strategically important being the crossing point for the Macquarie River. Originally the crossing was a ford, then in 1821 a low-level bridge was made with logs laid on stone

Ross's historic churches are floodlit at night

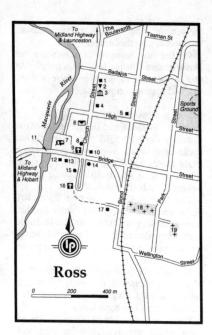

buttresses. In 1836 this rough structure was replaced with the current stone bridge.

In the days of horse and carriage, Ross was also important as a staging post and most of the buildings are from the 1820 to 1870 era and are of sandstone construction. The town then remained a local centre for the wool industry, but ceased to grow in size, remaining a village. In recent years, Ross has realised the historic value of its buildings and refused development along the main street, keeping its village feel.

Things to See

The best way to see this town is to walk around it; it's small and cars seem out of place. The town is famous for the convict-built **Ross Bridge**, the third-oldest bridge in Australia and one of the most beautiful, with its unique, decorative carvings. The graceful proportions of the bridge were designed by John Archer and it was built by two convict stonemasons, Colbeck and Herbert, who were granted their freedom for the work. Herbert has also been credited with the intricate detailed work on the 186 panels which decorate the arches. Each panel is different: Celtic symbols, animals and faces of notable people are carved into the sandstone. At night the bridge is floodlit and worth visiting as the carvings really stand out.

In the heart of town is a crossroads which can lead you in one of four directions – 'temptation' (represented by the Man-o'-Ross Hotel), 'salvation' (the Catholic church), 'recreation' (the town hall) and 'damnation' (the old gaol).

Other interesting historic buildings include the **Scotch Thistle Inn**; the **old barracks**, restored by the National Trust; the **Uniting Church** (1885); **St John's Church of England** (1868); and the still-used **post office** (1896). The three churches are all worth a visit and are floodlit at night.

The **Tasmanian Wool Centre** (☎ 6381 5466), a museum and craft shop in Church St, is open daily from 9.30 am to 5.30 pm. Entry to the museum is $4 ($2 for children) and contains displays of the convict era, including mouldings of some of the carvings from the Ross Bridge, and also of the wool industry in Australia. There are bales of wool you can touch, and an audiovisual about wool. The Wool Centre also runs guided tours around the town for $6 plus; bookings are essential. Tours to farms and other places are also available.

If you just want to wander around the town then collect the *Let's Talk About Ross* brochure which is available from most businesses in the town. This describes virtually every building in the main street (Church St).

On the northern end of Church St is a small **militaria museum**, open 10 am to 5 pm from Saturday to Thursday, featuring uniforms, vehicles and equipment from 1800 to the present period. Entry is $4, children $2.

One place most visitors miss is the **Ross Female Factory** which was actually a prison. This was one of only two female prisons in the convict period, and one of the buildings still stands. It is open every day and entry is free. Although there is little to see inside, a few simple descriptive signs and a model of the prison, will give you sufficient idea of what it was like. Further up the hill is the original **burial ground** where you can see more stone carvings on the headstones;

these were done by the same stonemasons who worked on the bridge.

On the first Saturday in November, the **Ross Rodeo** fills the town with people. As well as the usual rodeo events there is also a wood-chopping competition.

Places to Stay & Eat
Adjacent to the Ross Bridge is the *Ross Caravan Park* (☎ 6381 5462), which has cheap camp sites at $4 per person and rough stone cabins for $20 a double. The stone cabins are small and damp but, at the time of writing were being renovated.

The *Man-o'-Ross Hotel* (☎ 6381 5240), on the corner of Church and Bridge Sts, has reasonable singles/doubles for $30/48. Basic home-cooked counter meals are available for lunch and dinner every day except on Sunday nights.

The only true B&B is *The Elms Inn* (☎ 62 81 5246) in Church St, originally a coaching inn built in 1832. Singles/doubles are $50/79 including a cooked breakfast.

There are quite a few old cottages around town which are available for hire and provide continental breakfast. The following are run by the same people (☎ 6381 5354): *Apple Dumpling Cottage* near the bridge ($90 a double); *Captain Samuel's Cottage* in

The intricate carvings which decorate the arches on Ross Bridge were completed by a convicted highwayman, Daniel Herbert. He was granted his freedom for the work.

Church St ($115 a double); *Hudson Cottage* in Church St ($110 a double) and *Church Mouse Cottage* on the corner of High and Bond Sts ($115 a double).

For lunch you can buy the usual takeaways from the general store or try the bakery and tearooms next to The Elms Inn, which are quite good.

Getting There & Away

TRC (☎ 6231 3233 or 1800 030 033) and Hobart Coaches (☎ 6234 4077 or 1800 030 620) run several buses every day from Hobart to Launceston along the Midland Hwy for $12.

Hobart Coaches also runs bus tours from both Hobart and Launceston to Ross which allow plenty of time to wander around the town. From Hobart the fare is $25, children $12.50, for the day (lunch is not included), and from Launceston the half-day tour is $22, children $12. Tours run from Monday to Friday as needed. Bookings are essential.

CAMPBELL TOWN
* *pop 820*

Twelve km north of Ross is Campbell Town, another former garrison settlement on the Midlands Hwy. Today it is the commercial centre of a cattle and sheep-farming area and has reasonable services with two hotels, a supermarket and general stores.

The town itself has many buildings which are over 100 years old, but they are scattered around the town and display a variety of architectural styles. Most buildings can be seen by travelling along High St (the main highway) and returning along Bridge St. They include the **Grange** (1847), **St Luke's Church of England** (1835), the **Campbell Town Inn** (1840), the building known as the **Fox Hunters Return** (1829), and the **old school** (1878). The main bridge across the Elizabeth River is almost as old as the bridge at Ross, being completed in 1838. While not as beautiful, the 'Red Bridge', as it's known, was constructed by convicts from bricks made on site.

You can visit one of the oldest farms in the area, **Winton** (☎ 6381 1221), which was founded in 1835 as a merino sheep stud and still operates today. Tours of the original buildings and gardens cost $6, children $2, and must be booked in advance.

The showgrounds (behind the high school) stage the annual **Campbell Town Show** in early June. This has been held every year since 1839 and is the oldest continuous show in Australia. The town also runs a country-music festival in November.

Places to Stay & Eat

There are not many accommodation places to choose from. *Powells Hotel* (☎ 6381 1161), in the main street, has basic, old-fashioned motel rooms for $35 a double. The hotel has counter meals for lunch and dinner every day except Sunday evening. There is also a coffee shop in the hotel.

Beside the highway on the north side of town, the *Gables* (☎ 6381 1347) provides B&B for $75 a double but caters only for families or groups. It also hires out cottages for $89 a double with breakfast provided.

If you'd like prefer to stay in a guesthouse on a quiet farm try *Baskerville Hall* (☎ 6381 1116). It's located 10 km north-west of town on Macquarie Rd and rates are $85 a double for B&B. Full catering with all meals is available.

As you head north towards Launceston, just past Conara Junction at Cleveland, you'll find *St Andrews Inn* (☎ 6391 5525). Built in 1845 this old coaching inn is classified by the National Trust and is a good place for Devonshire teas; dinner is available on Friday and Saturday nights.

Getting There & Away

TRC (☎ 6231 3233 or 1800 030 033) and Hobart Coaches (☎ 6234 4077 or 1800 030 620) run buses every day from Hobart to Launceston along the Midland Hwy. Even though there are at least five buses each day bookings are advised.

There's a secondary road from Campbell Town, through the excellent fishing and bushwalking area around **Lake Leake** (32 km), to Swansea (67 km) on the east coast. The weekday TRC bus from Hobart to

MIDLANDS & LAKE COUNTRY

Bicheno travels via this route and can drop you at the Lake Leake turn-off, four km from the lake. Another highway, the A4, runs from Conara Junction, 11 km north of Campbell Town, east to St Marys. Buses running from Launceston to Bicheno follow the A4, as well as buses from Hobart and Launceston to St Helens.

Lake Country

The sparsely populated Lake Country of Tasmania's Central Plateau is a region of breathtaking scenery, comprising steep mountains, hundreds of glacial lakes, crystal-clear streams, waterfalls and a good variety of wildlife. It's also known for its fine trout fishing, and for its ambitious hydro-electric schemes, which have seen the damming of rivers, the creation of artificial lakes, the building of power stations, both above and below ground, as well as the construction of massive pipelines over rough terrain.

Tasmania has the largest hydroelectric power system in Australia. The first dam was constructed on Great Lake in 1911. Subsequently, the Derwent, Mersey, South Esk, Forth, Gordon, King, Anthony and Pieman rivers were also dammed. If you want to inspect the developments, go along to the Tungatinah, Tarraleah and Liapootah power stations on the extensive Derwent scheme between Queenstown and Hobart.

On the eastern edge of the Central Plateau is the Walls of Jerusalem National Park, which is a focal point for mountaineers, bushwalkers and cross-country skiers. There's excellent fishing all over the Central Plateau. Most of the larger lakes have good access and the Great Lake, **Lake Sorell**, **Lake Crescent**, **Arthurs Lake** and **Little Pine Lagoon** are popular spots. The plateau itself actually contains thousands of lakes; many are tiny, but most contain trout. To get to many of the smaller lakes you must walk in. You'll need to be well equipped with

lightweight camping gear, as the region is prone to regular snowfalls.

At Waddamana, on the road which loops off the Lake Hwy between Bothwell and Great Lake, there's the HEC's **Waddamana Power Museum** (☎ 6259 6175). It's a former hydroelectricity power station which was constructed from 1910 to 1916. Originally it was a private venture but financial difficulties resulted in the government taking over and creating the Hydro-Electric Department which today is the Hydro-Electricity Commission. The power station has operational turbines and an interesting display of the state's early hydro history; it's open daily from 10 am to 4 pm and admission is free.

BOTHWELL
• *pop 400*

Bothwell, in the beautiful Clyde River valley, is a charming and historic town, with 53 buildings recognised or classified by the National Trust. Places of particular interest include the beautifully restored **slate cottage** of 1835; a **bootmaker's shop**, fitted out as it would have been in the 1890s; **Thorpe Mill**, a restored flour mill from the 1820s; the delightful **St Luke's Church** (1821); and the **Castle Hotel**, first licensed in 1821.

Although you can walk around the town and read the descriptive plaques, you can learn more by going on a two-hour tour with Fielding's Historic Tours (☎ 6254 1135). The tour includes an inspection of the slate cottage and the bootmaker's shop and costs $8 ($4 for children); advance bookings are necessary.

Although Bothwell is probably best known for its great trout fishing, it also has Australia's oldest golf course. This was built by the Scottish settlers who established the town in the 1820s. The course is still in use today and is open to members of any golf club.

Places to Stay
The *Bothwell Caravan Park* (☎ 6259 5503) in Market Place is centrally located and cheap, with tent sites for $6. All other accom-

modation in Bothwell is in the more expensive B&B category. *Mrs Wood's Farmhouse* (☎ 6259 5612), at Dennistoun, eight km from town, is a working farm and highly recommended, with one basic cabin for $45 a double for B&B ($25 for each extra adult) and the farmhouse for $75 a double ($20 for each extra adult) for B&B. Both places can hold up to six guests.

In town, *Bothwell Grange* (☎ 6259 5556), in Alexander St, provides B&B at $58/70 for singles/doubles. It was originally built in 1836 as a hotel and today provides comfortable accommodation and à la carte meals. If you prefer your own place, then hire a historic cottage. *Whites Cottage* (☎ 6259 5651), in Queen St, is $85 a double including a continental breakfast, or in Elizabeth St there's *Birch Cottage* (☎ 6259 5502) for the same price.

Getting There & Away

Public transport to this area is not good (and neither is hitching). TRC (☎ 6231 2200 or 1800 030 033) runs a daily service on weekdays to Bothwell from Hobart. This leaves Bothwell at 7 am arriving in Hobart at 8.30 am and returns from Hobart at 4 pm to arrive in Bothwell at 5.30 pm. There is no connecting service between Bothwell and Great Lake.

GREAT LAKE

Located 1050 metres above sea level on the Central Plateau this is the largest natural, freshwater lake in Australia. The first European to visit the lake was John Beaumont in 1817; he sent a servant to walk around the lake and this took three days. In 1870, brown trout were released into the lake and it soon became famous as a great trout-fishing area. In 1910, rainbow trout were added to the waters and they thrived. Attempts were also made to introduce salmon but these failed as the fish did not multiply. The trout have now penetrated most of the streams across the plateau and some of the best fishing is now in the smaller streams and lakes west of the Great Lake.

A small dam was constructed on the Great Lake to raise the lake level near Miena for the early power schemes. The lake is linked to the nearby Arthurs Lake by canals and a pumping station, and supplies water to the Poatina Power Station on the north-eastern side of the lake.

While the plateau has interesting plants and excellent fishing, the scenery around the Great Lake is very ordinary as there are no rugged mountains around its shores. For many, it provides an access point for the more interesting lake country further west on the plateau. For well-equipped bushwalkers it is possible to walk across the plateau to the Walls of Jerusalem National Park and also into the Cradle Mountain-Lake St Clair National Park. The Parks, Wildlife and Heritage visitor centre at Liawenee, on the western side of the Great Lake, is worth visiting and a basic camping area is provided.

Fishing

A wide variety of regulations apply to fishing in this area. They are aimed at ensuring there is plenty of fishing for all, and to allow fish to breed future generations. On some parts of the Great Lake you are only allowed to use artificial lures and you are not allowed to fish in any of the streams flowing into the lake. The lake is closed to fishing in June and July each year. On the Central Plateau some waters are reserved for fly-fishing only and bag and size limits apply for all waters. Details of all regulations are provided when you purchase your fishing licence from the Inland Fisheries Commission, 127 Davey St, Hobart. Licences range from $7 for one day up to $38 for the full season. Children under 14 do not need a licence but must still follow all regulations.

The fish can be very difficult to catch, and local knowledge of lures and locations is a considerable advantage. Guided fishing tours are run from both of the hotels at Miena. Ann Moody (☎ 6259 8163) operates from the Greta Lake Hotel and Peter Hayes (☎ 6259 8295) is at the Compleat Angler Lodge. Rates start from $175 per day, which includes transport and all fishing gear.

Tackle the Trout
It should be easy to catch a trout as most of Tasmania's rivers and lakes have been stocked with brown and rainbow trout. However, you need to organise your fishing gear, and be in the right place at the right time. There are restrictions on the types of tackle which can be used in various areas, at different times of the year. A detailed brochure from the Tasmanian Inland Fisheries Commission (☎ 6233 8305) outlines regulations for each area.

Fishing using live bait is probably the oldest form of fishing. It requires a grasshopper, grub or worm to be attached to the hook. However, this form of fishing is banned in most inland waters.

Artificial lures come in many different shapes, sizes, weights and colours. This is probably the easiest way to fish. You cast the lure from a river bank or boat and reel them in. Depending on the season, you might find that a 'Cobra' wobbler or Devon type 'spinner' works well in the lakes, whilst in the streams, the 'Celta' type lures are often effective.

One of the most challenging forms of fishing is fly fishing. Keen anglers make their own artificial

flies, but you can purchase a large variety. There are many areas in Tasmania specifically reserved for this form of fishing, which most often involves wading the shallow rivers and lake shores in the early morning and stalking the wary fish.

Remember to always be prepared for Tasmania's notorious changes of weather, especially in the Lake Country. Take warm and waterproof clothing, even in the middle of summer. ■

Extended trips into remote areas requiring camping are also available.

Places to Stay
At Swan Bay, near Miena, the *Great Lake Hotel* (☎ 6259 8163) has a range of accommodation – camping sites for $8, holiday cabins for $15 per adult and $5 per child, and rooms in the hotel for $55 to $65 a double, including continental breakfast. Also close to Miena is the *Compleat Angler Lodge* (☎ 6259 8197) which is actually a hotel and has singles/doubles for $40/60.

Getting There & Away
Tasmanian Wilderness Transport's services between Lake St Clair and Launceston or Devonport go via Bronte Park, Miena, past the Great Lake to Deloraine. This service runs daily during the summer, and only once a week on Tuesday in autumn and spring. There are no winter services in the months of June, July and August. Booking is essential for this bus service, as its primary purpose is for linking the southern end of the Overland Track to the northern cities; it does not normally operate as a local bus service.

Derwent Valley Highway

This highway follows the rich farmlands and valley of the Derwent River from New Norfolk to the southern edge of the Central Plateau. From there it continues past Derwent Bridge to Queenstown.

HAMILTON
This is another National Trust classified historic town which was originally laid out on a grand scale to be a major centre, yet never became more than a small, sleepy village. Today the few buildings which exist are mostly old, well spread out and closely surrounded by farms, with excellent views of the mountain ranges and peaks further west. There are some good historic buildings from the 1830s and 1840s to visit. It's not somewhere you would spend a lot of time exploring, but makes an interesting overnight stop.

The area was settled in 1807 when New Norfolk was established, and by 1835 had a population of nearly 800, with 11 hotels and two breweries. Many streets were surveyed, but the rich, yet dry, soils near the town defeated many farmers and the town did not grow as expected. As roads and transport improved, the town declined further and many historic buildings were removed. The ones that remain today are a reminder of what was once a boom town during the 1830s and 1840s. The major buildings are floodlit at night and well worth venturing out to see.

You can see a working sheep farm by pre-booking with the **Hamilton Sheep Farm** (☎ 6286 3230) where daily demonstrations of sheep-shearing and mustering are held. It's four km west of Hamilton and lunch is included in the $35 entry fee. The nearby **Stuart Farm** (☎ 6286 3225) is open on Tuesday and Friday. This farm was used as a movie set for the film *Tasmania Story* but while admission is free there is little to see – though there are demonstrations of sheep-shearing and working sheepdogs for pre-booked groups. Light meals are available at this farm.

Places to Stay & Eat

The historic *Hamilton Inn* (☎ 6286 3204), off the highway in Tarleton St, still operates as a hotel and provides good clean rooms from $45 a double for B&B. All the floors slope and the walls lean a little, but then that's the character of the place. It's also the only place in town that serves dinner, with average standard counter meals. The inn has a series of underground cellars which can sometimes be inspected by guests, and they also bottle and export mineral water from an underground spring beneath the hotel.

There are plenty of sandstone cottages for hire. *Emma's*, *George's*, *Victoria's* and *Edward's* are beside the highway and are run by the same people (☎ 6286 3270); they cost $90 a double plus $20 for each extra adult. On the other side of the highway is the larger *McCauley's Cottage* (☎ 018 123 116), which charges $120 a double. One block south, along the main highway, is the *Old School House* (☎ 6286 3292) which was built in 1856 and served as the school until 1935. It

was condemned in 1972, but was saved by being sold and restored and now operates as an unusual B&B for $95 a double. If you prefer to stay on a farm, four km west of the town is *Over the Back Holiday Cottage* (☎ 6286 3230). It's located on the Hamilton Sheep Farm overlooking Lake Meadowbank and at popular periods, like holidays and weekends, must be booked for at least two nights. Rates are $95 a double plus $20 for each extra adult. When there are no bookings, there is often a cheaper stand-by rate of $67 a double.

During the day, light meals are available from the bakery and general store in the main street or from *Glen Clyde House* at the sharp bend at the northern end of town. This former hotel now houses tearooms providing home-cooked food and a well-stocked craft gallery.

Getting There & Away

TRC (☎ 6231 3233 or 1800 030 033) runs a daily service from Hobart to Queenstown and Strahan during the warmer months from September to May. From June to September the buses run on Tuesday, Wednesday, Friday and Sunday.

ELLENDALE

This tiny village is located on a quiet link road that joins the Lyell Hwy to Westerway. The signposted Ellendale Rd leaves the Lyell Hwy about midway between Hamilton and Ouse and is a convenient short cut to Mt Field. The road is narrow, but sealed, for its entire length. Shortly after leaving the Lyell Hwy you cross Lake Meadowbank which is part of the Derwent River hydroelectricity power scheme. It's quite pretty on a calm day and you can see the piers of the original Dunrobin Bridge next to the current bridge crossing. The original bridge was built in 1850 and marked the start of Dawsons Rd which led to Gordon Bend in the south-west. It was intended to continue to Port Davey but was abandoned after settlers decided that the south-west was too rugged to farm.

Ellendale was once a hop-growing area and just north of the town is a huge abandoned hop kiln; next door is a pretty sandstone church and graveyard. Tasmanian Wilderness Transport (☎ 6334 4442) runs regular bus services from Hobart to Mt Field then to Derwent Bridge through Ellendale. In summer these run daily and in other months the service runs on Monday, Wednesday and on weekends. Bookings are essential.

There is little in town apart from a picnic shelter beside the creek, a general store and the *Hopfield Cottages* (☎ 6288 1223) which provide good rooms for $80 a double. Just out of town, three km up a side road is **Old Macdonald's Tourist Farm** (☎ 6288 1199) which is open daily from December to May. Admission is $2 or $10 for a family. The farm also has accommodation with the *Hillcrest Holiday Cabins* being $50 a double plus $12 for extra adults or $7.50 per child.

If you prefer to stay on a dairy farm then *Hamlet Downs* (☎ 6288 1212) at Fentonbury, six km south of Ellendale, has a timber cottage for $65 to $70 a double for B&B. It's a working farm and you can participate in the milking or walk to the lookout at the top of the paddocks. Meals are available by prior arrangement.

OUSE

While this area was also settled early, for a long time there was no town and Ouse was little more than just a river crossing. Most buildings were erected in the 1900s and are weatherboard, so this town does not have any historic charm. The Ouse River was originally called the Big River and the area was home to a tribe of Aboriginal people who were known by the same name. They were forced into other areas following the arrival of European settlers.

The town is a popular stop for food along the highway and has several takeaway shops and cafes. The picnic ground beside the river is the best place at which to eat or rest. If you want to stay here, then the *Lachlan Hotel* (☎ 6287 1215) provides B&B for $25/45 for singles/doubles. Counter meals are also available daily. The only other places to stay are cottages, and *Rosecot* (☎ 6287 1222) is conveniently located opposite the hotel; it

costs $70 a double for B&B. *Sasso-del-Gallo* (☎ 6287 1263) is the same price, but less attractive, being beside the garage. The only other alternative, two km from town, is *Cawood Accommodation* (☎ 6287 1302), which provides a farmhouse for $45 per person for B&B.

Getting There & Away

TRC (☎ 6231 3233 or 1800 030 033) runs a daily service from Hobart to Queenstown and Strahan during the warmer months from September to May. From June to September the buses runs on Tuesday, Wednesday, Friday and Sunday. Tasmanian Wilderness Transport (☎ 6334 4442) also runs daily bus services in summer from Hobart to Mt Field then through Ouse to Derwent Bridge. In the other three seasons, buses are run on Monday and Wednesday in both directions. On Saturday the bus continues to Strahan and on Sunday returns through Ouse to Hobart.

WAYATINAH

This is the permanent village from which the Hydro-Electric Commission runs the six power stations of the Lower Derwent Power Scheme. It is located one km off the Lyell Hwy on a side road; the buses along the highway do not deviate into this town. There is a shop and tavern that is open every day and the only place to stay is the *Wayatinah Camping Ground* (☎ 6272 7966). With water frontage onto the Wayatinah Lagoon this is a very pleasant place to camp and for your camping fee you are allowed to use all the town's facilities such as the tennis courts and heated swimming pool. Site fees are $7 for two, $12 for three and $14 for four people.

TARRALEAH

• *pop 400*

This is the residential village for the Hydro-Electric Commission's staff who work at the nearby power stations and dams. The town has lots of pre-fabricated houses and in recent years much of it has been for sale but there are few buyers. The town advertises itself as Tasmania's best kept secret and will probably stay that way as there is little here for visitors.

The main features of interest are the **power stations** of Tarraleah and Tungatinah which are situated in the bottom of the deep gorge north of the town. These are located next to each other yet receive water from different catchments. The Tarraleah Power Station is the oldest and is open daily for free inspections from 8 am to 5 pm.

The huge pipelines feeding the power sta-tions are also major features and the one that runs past the town has two tall surge tanks that dominate the town. Takeaway food is available daily from the roadhouse and general store in town. The only place to stay is the *Tarraleah Chalet* (☎ 6289 3128) which has singles/doubles for $28/45. Counter meals are available at the tavern in the chalet.

Getting There & Away
See Getting There & Away for Ouse.

East Coast

Tasmania's scenic east coast, with its long sandy beaches, fine fishing and rare peacefulness, is known as the 'sun coast' because of its mild climate. The area boasts more than 2250 hours of sunshine a year; an average of six hours every day.

Settlement of the region, which was found to be suitable for grazing, proceeded rapidly after the establishment of Hobart in 1803. Offshore fishing and whaling became important, as did tin mining and timber cutting. Many of the convicts who served out their terms in the area stayed on to help other settlers establish the fishing, wool, beef and grain industries which are still significant today.

The major towns along the coast are Orford, Triabunna, Swansea and Bicheno. The spectacular scenery of Coles Bay is not to be missed and is worth the deviation.

There are three national parks along the coast. Maria Island National Park has been utilised by several industries and has been reserved as much for its interesting history as its natural beauty. Freycinet National Park is a large peninsula of red granite which provides some fine walking. Further north, Douglas Apsley National Park has waterfalls and remnant rainforest, and also features examples of the dry eucalypt forests that once covered the east coast region.

There is plenty of accommodation along the coast. Expect to pay more during the peak season around December and January when the rates can be up to 50% higher than at other times. As this coast is a holiday destination for many Tasmanians, it is best avoided at Easter, and during the last week of December and most of January when it is crowded. If you must come then, book ahead.

Banking facilities on the east coast are very limited and in some towns the banks are only open one or two days a week. There are agencies for the Commonwealth Bank at all post offices; most have restricted opening

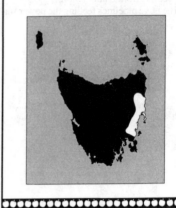

HIGHLIGHTS

- The white sandy beaches at Scamander
- Exploring The Hazards, red granite mountains at Freycinet Peninsula
- Convict ruins on Maria Island

hours. Electronic payment (EFTPOS) is starting to infiltrate the business community and is now available at many country stores and petrol stations. Petrol stations follow a roster system, so you'll find at least one open every day of the week from 9 am to 5 pm in all the major towns.

Getting There & Around

Bus Tasmanian Redline Coaches (TRC; ☎ 6231 2200 or 1800 030 033) and Hobart Coaches (☎ 6234 4077 or 1800 030 620) are the main bus companies operating on the east coast. TRC runs at least one service each weekday from Hobart to Swansea and Bicheno via the Midland Hwy and inland linking roads. There are similar runs from the same towns to Launceston.

The Hobart Coaches service also runs on weekdays and follows the Tasman Hwy along the east coast from Hobart to Bicheno. On Wednesday, Friday and Sunday a special service runs from Hobart along the same route but continues on to St Helens. In the peak summer period there is a Saturday bus.

There are also some smaller companies – Peakes Coach Service (☎ 6372 2390) runs from St Marys to Bicheno and Swansea, and Bicheno Coach Service (☎ 6257 0293) runs from Bicheno to Coles Bay. With all buses you can hail down the bus anywhere and buy your tickets when boarding.

Bus services are limited at weekends, so it might take a little longer to travel between towns than you anticipate. Also, some services do not connect, making overnight stops necessary. In some cases the same buses are used by school children, so most buses run in the early morning or late afternoon. During school terms some extra buses operate.

Bicycle Cycling along the east coast is one of the most enjoyable ways of seeing this part of Tasmania. Traffic is usually light and the hills are not too steep, particularly if you follow the new coastal highway from Chain of Lagoons to Falmouth.

If you are planning to cycle between Swansea and Coles Bay, there's an informal boat service for cyclists and hikers run by *Central Swansea Backpackers* (see Swansea – Getting There & Away) that saves a 65 km ride. Bookings for this service are essential.

BUCKLAND
This tiny township, 63 km from Hobart, was once a staging post for coaches on the way to the east coast. **Ye Olde Buckland Inn**, at 5 Kent St, welcomed coach drivers and travellers a century ago and today offers a good counter lunch every day, and dinner on Friday and Saturday nights. Good, light meals are also available in the roadhouse beside the highway.

The stone church of **St John the Baptist**, dating from 1846, is worth a visit. Built from local sandstone it has many fine stained glass windows, but the best of all is the large, east-facing window behind the altar. How it

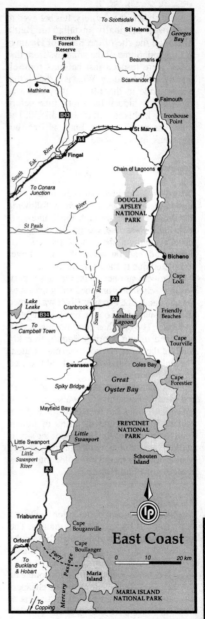

came to be here is a mystery. It is believed to have been originally installed in Battle Abbey on the site of the Battle of Hastings in England. Some of the windows from that abbey were rescued just before Cromwell destroyed the building. What is certain is that it was made in the 14th century and was undoubtedly hidden for a long time before appearing in this church in around 1850. The church is usually open. Entry is free, but donations are welcomed.

ORFORD
• *pop 500*

Orford is a popular, low-key resort. The highway approaches the town by following the Prosser River through the impressive, rock-lined **Paradise Gorge**. In the gorge, close to the town, the remains of a convict-built road can be seen; this was never completed due to the difficult terrain.

The town was once an important sea port, serving the whalers and the local garrison on Maria Island. The **Prosser River** was named after an escaped prisoner who was caught on its banks. The area has good fishing, swimming and diving. **Spring Beach**, four km south of the town, is a good surfing location. The water is cold and wetsuits should be used for water sports.

The beaches close to town are sheltered and ideal for swimming or walking. A two-km walking track has been constructed from Shelley Beach around the cliffs of Luther Point to Spring Beach. This passes the site of an old quarry, which was the primary source of sandstone for many of the older buildings in Melbourne and Hobart.

Places to Stay

There's plenty of accommodation in Orford in the form of flats, cabins and motels. The caravan park is north of the town, beside the beach and has fine views of Maria Island. *Raspins Beach Camping Park* (☎ 6257 1771) has sandy tent sites for $8 a double or powered sites for $9 a double. The cheapest non-camping accommodation in town is at the *Sea Breeze Holiday Cabins* (☎ 6257

1375) on the corner of Rudd Ave and Walpole St; it's $40 a double.

On the Tasman Hwy, the *Blue Waters Motor Hotel* (☎ 6257 1102) has singles/doubles at $35/45. Almost next door, the fancier looking *Island View Motel* (☎ 6257 1114) has similar standard rooms for $42/50.

Conveniently located beside the main road junction in town, is *Prosser Holiday Units* (☎ 6257 1427). Units are $85 for four people with weekly rates of $220 to $330 depending on the season. On the other side of the river, the good-value *Riverside Villas* (☎ 1800 817 533 or 6257 1655) charge only $75 a double for five-star luxury. Hire of a motorised dinghy is included. They also hire out larger motor-boats to guests and visitors from $30 a half-day.

For something more private, *Holkham House* (☎ 6225 0970) is situated in farmland on the edge of town. It sleeps up to 14 people and costs $90 a double plus $25 for extra adults and $12.50 for each child. Next door, *Miranda Cottage* (☎ 6257 1248) is of similar standard but only accommodates four people; it's $90 a double plus $25 for extra adults.

The *Spring Beach Holiday Villas* (☎ 6257 1440) in Rheban Rd, about four km south of town, has units for $85 a double ($100 in peak season). Each of the five villas has magnificent views of Spring Beach and Maria Island.

Rather more lavish and expensive is the *Eastcoaster Resort* (☎ 6257 1172), on Louisville Point Rd, six km north of the post office. This was once a kelp-harvesting factory and now has the usual resort facilities, including swimming pools. Hotel rooms are from $70 a double, self-contained villas range from $80 to $120 ($20 dearer in peak season). The main interest here for most visitors is the *Eastcoaster Express* (☎ 6257 1589), the ferry to Maria Island. This runs three times daily.

Places to Eat

East Coast Seafoods, beside the highway, offers both takeaway and eat-in seafood meals. Diagonally opposite, counter meals are available seven days a week at the *Blue Waters Motor Hotel*. *Josephines Cafe* on the south side of the bridge serves light meals. The *Eastcoaster Resort* does takeaways and bar meals and has a fully licensed seafood restaurant; prices for all three are reasonable.

Getting There & Away

Hobart Coaches (☎ 6234 4077) runs a service in both directions from Hobart through Orford to Bicheno every day except Saturday. During January and February, a single Saturday service travels in both directions along the same route. On Wednesday and Friday there is an extra service along the same route. The same service applies to Triabunna.

WIELANGTA FOREST

There is a direct link from the Tasman Peninsula area to Orford. It leaves the Tasman Hwy at Copping and follows quiet gravel roads north through the Wielangta Forest which is managed for timber harvesting. Significant portions of the forest have been kept in reserves for recreation use and some walking tracks have been marked.

About halfway from Copping to Orford, the **Sandspit River Reserve** has a picnic shelter, a 20-minute nature walk through rainforest, plus a longer walk along the river valley. The other main site of interest, **Thumbs Lookout**, is only six km from Orford. A rough side road leads to a picnic ground and lookout from which there are good views of Maria Island. A two-hour return walk to the open, rocky summit of the highest 'thumb' will reward you with even better panoramic views of the coast.

There are no bus services along this road. It is a pleasant route which is highly recommended for cyclists as there is little traffic.

TRIABUNNA

• *pop 830*

Just eight km north of Orford, Triabunna is a much larger town but not as attractive to visitors. It is located at the head of the very sheltered inlet of Spring Bay which has made it a useful port. The town was originally a whaling station and served as a military base in the penal era. Today it is the commercial centre of the region with woodchip processing and scallop and cray fishing being the major industries.

At one stage there was a ferry from the town to Maria Island but this was destroyed in a fire and never replaced. The town's name comes from an Aboriginal word meaning native hen. It once boasted the largest apple orchard in the southern hemisphere. You can charter boats such as *Crescent* (☎ 6257 1137) and *Crusade* (☎ 6223 6366) for fishing and cruising. Scenic flights over Maria Island are available from *Salmon Air* (☎ 6257 3186).

Places to Stay & Eat

The *Triabunna Caravan Park* (☎ 6257 3575), on the corner of Vicary and Melbourne Sts, is a bargain with camp sites at $8, powered sites $9 and on-site vans at $25 a double. The *Triabunna YHA Hostel* (☎ 6257 3439), an old house located in Spencer St, a 10-minute walk out of town, is a comfortable and quiet place to stay for a night; $10 for YHA members, $12 for nonmembers and $5 for children. It's set in farmland, across the bridge from the main part of town.

Down by the waterfront near the jetty, the *Spring Bay Hotel* (☎ 6257 3115) in Charles St has single/double rooms with continental breakfast at $25/40 and good, cheap counter meals. Beside the highway *Tandara Motor Inn* (☎ 6257 3333) has bed and continental breakfast for $45/60 a single/double. Counter meals are also available here. A bakery and pizza shop provide good takeaway food. In Henry St, near the council offices, *Girraween Gardens & Tearooms* is a relaxing place to go for light meals.

MARIA ISLAND NATIONAL PARK

This peaceful island was declared a national park in 1972. It features some magnificent scenery: fossil-studded sandstone and limestone cliffs, beautiful white, sandy beaches, forests and fern gullies. There are some lovely walks on the island, including the fairly rugged Bishop & Clerk Mountain

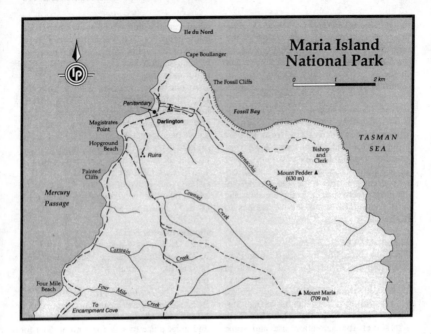

Walk and the historical Fossil Cliffs Nature Walk; brochures are available for both. A visit to the Painted Cliffs is also a must. The marine life around most of the island is diverse and plentiful, and is now protected in a marine reserve.

On a day trip to Maria Island, you can see many of its restored buildings and a variety of wildlife. But if you have time, it's well worth staying here for a few nights. There are no shops on the island, so don't forget to bring your own supplies.

History

Maria Island has had a chequered history, including being used for convicts, industrial factories and farming. The island was originally occupied by Aboriginal people, who called it Toarra Marra Monah. They were members of the Oyster Bay tribe, and lived primarily on shellfish. They crossed to the mainland in frail canoes and rested on the tiny Lachlan Island.

In 1642 Abel Tasman discovered the island for Europeans and named it after Anthony Van Diemen's wife. The Aboriginal people then remained undisturbed until the early 1800s. In 1821 the island was selected as Tasmania's second penal settlement and four years later the first convicts arrived and founded Darlington.

Over the next seven years many major buildings including the Commissariat Store (built in 1825) and the Penitentiary (1830) were constructed from locally made bricks. A water race, mill pond and jetty were also built. In 1832 it was decided that the costs involved in running three penal settlements outside of Hobart were too great and the convicts were moved. For the next 10 years, whalers, farmers and smugglers used the island.

Reopened in 1842, Darlington was once again used by the penal system, this time as a probation station. The existing buildings underwent renovation while new structures were established. During this time, agriculture was the main industry. In 1845 a second settlement was established at **Long Point** and by 1850 a road connecting the two sites had been created. The road gave more ready access to the island and extra land was cleared to allow sheep to graze. At one stage there were more than 600 convicts at Darlington. However, in 1850 the flow of convicts to Tasmania reduced and Darlington was closed in that year, with Long Point closing the following year. The island was then leased for grazing.

In 1884 an enterprising businessman, Signor Bernacchi, leased the island to set up a silk and wine-making industry. The Darlington buildings were renovated and the town of 260 was renamed San Diego. Over the next 40 years various industries existed with the most notable being a cement plant, established in 1922. By 1930 the Great Depression had begun, the cement plant closed down and the island reverted back to farming.

In the 1960s the government gradually bought the properties on the island. Since European occupation none of the larger animals or birds had existed on the island so in the late 1960s, Forester kangaroos, Bennett's wallabies, Cape Barren geese and emus were introduced. These have since prospered and are often seen. In 1971 the island was declared a wildlife sanctuary. It's popular with birdwatchers, being the only national park in Tasmania where you can see 11 of the state's native bird species including the endangered forty-spotted pardalote.

Things to See
The only way to get around is by walking. The old township of **Darlington** is well worth wandering around for a couple of hours. The best short walk of 1½ hours return is to the **Painted Cliffs** at the south end of Hopground Beach. The sandstone has been stained with iron oxide, forming intricate colourful patterns. This walk is a must.

There is a good circuit walk of 1½ hours to **Cape Boullanger**, the **Fossil Cliffs** and return via the old brickworks. If the peaks are clear then you will rewarded with great views by climbing **Bishop & Clerk**. A good track leads to the summit and takes about four hours return from Darlington. An even longer climb of six hours return takes you to **Mt Maria**, the highest point on the island.

The coastline from Return Point to Bishop & Clerk is a marine reserve which means no fishing is allowed, including in the Darlington area. The reserve, together with the giant kelp forests and caves around **Fossil Bay** has created an excellent area for scuba diving and snorkelling. The water is cold and wetsuits are essential.

Places to Stay
The rooms in the Penitentiary at Darlington and some of the other buildings have been converted into bunkhouses. These are called the *Parks, Wildlife & Heritage Penitentiary Units* (☎ 6257 1420) and cost $8 a night, children $4. The cells have only mattresses; bedding is not supplied and there are no cooking facilities or electricity. You must bring your own stove to cook on. The units are very popular and it's essential to book ahead.

There is also a basic camping ground at Darlington with fees of $4 per adult or $10 per family. Fires are only allowed in designated fireplaces and during summer these are often banned. A portable stove is therefore recommended. For those prepared to walk, there are other camping areas three to four hours away. French's Farm, Encampment Cove and Robey's Farm have only small water supplies and are all fire-free areas where only portable stoves are allowed for cooking. There are no camping fees at these grounds.

You'll need to take all your refreshments with you as there are no shops on the island. There is a public telephone close to the centre of Darlington. You'll also need clothing suitable for cool, wet weather, but remember the hat and sunscreen too!

A current national park pass is also required. Day passes cost $2.50 per person, but if you're staying longer and visiting other parks in Tasmania then a $10 backpacker pass provides free entry for two months to all national parks.

Getting There & Away

The only ferry, the *Eastcoaster Express* (☎ 6257 1589), is operated by the Eastcoaster Resort from Louisville Point Rd, six km north of Orford. It has three services daily all year departing from Louisvilla Point at 10.30 am, 1 pm and 3.30 pm. The return service from Darlington leaves 30 minutes later.

In summer (December to April) an extra service departs daily at 9 am. Services will only run if there are passengers. Groups can make charter bookings at other times. The 10 km crossing takes about 20 minutes each way. Fares for day trips are $16 per adult and $10 for children. If staying on the island and returning on a different day then fares are $19 for adults and $12 for children. Bicycles and kayaks are taken over for $3 each.

It is also possible to land on the airstrip near Darlington by light plane. These can be chartered from Triabunna or further away at Hobart or Launceston.

LITTLE SWANPORT

The tiny hamlet of Little Swanport is set around the Little Swanport River, which flows into a large lagoon. Its attractions are its great natural beauty and the fact that although it's undeveloped, it has easy access to the coastline. There are some fine uninhabited beaches in the area, particularly at Mayfield Bay, Kelvedon Beach, Raspins and Cressy Beaches. All these beaches can be accessed by side roads.

The only place to stay is *Gum Leaves* (☎ 6244 8147 or 6244 4167), a new resort set in natural bushland just south of Little Swanport. With an adventure playground, deer park, horse museum and its own lake, it's a pleasant surprise to find that prices are very reasonable. The log-cabin hostel costs $15 each, children $8; self-contained cabins are $49 a double plus $7 for each extra person.

If not staying here, it is still worth calling in to see the **Pioneer Working Horse Museum**. The main feature are the horses

which provide the muscle power to run the various pieces of old equipment that are on display. The horses are very friendly. The museum was recently relocated from Triabunna; entry $4, children $2 or $10 for a family.

SWANSEA
* *pop 420*

On the shores of Great Oyster Bay, with superb views across to the Freycinet Peninsula, Swansea is a popular place for camping, boating, fishing and surfing. It was first settled in the 1820s and was the administrative centre for Glamorgan, Australia's oldest rural municipality. In 1993 it merged with Spring Bay and the administration moved to Triabunna.

Swansea, originally known as Great Swanport, has a number of interesting historic buildings including the original council chambers and the lovely, three-storey, redbrick Morris's General Store, built in 1838. This now serves as the town's information centre.

Because it's a popular holiday destination, prices for accommodation and food are generally higher in Swansea than in other towns along the coast. Several dominating accommodation blocks have been built near the waterfront and the town has lost some of its historic character.

Things to See

The best way to see the town is to walk along Franklin and Noynes Sts passing many of the older buildings in the town, including **Morris's General Store** and the **council chambers**. Most of Swansea's historic buildings are privately owned but the **Glamorgan Community Centre and War Memorial Museum**, dating back to 1860, houses the Museum of Local History and is worth a visit. The major feature here is the only oversized billiard table in Australia. When it was being made, the builders did not want to trim the four pieces of slate and instead made the table larger. You can play a game on the table for $2. The museum also contains Aboriginal artefacts and possessions belonging to early settlers. There is also a war memorial room and an interesting display of old photographs of Swansea. The museum is open from Monday to Saturday and admission is $3, children 50c; ring the bell for entry.

On the northern edge of town at 96 Tasman Hwy, the **Swansea Bark Mill & East Coast Museum**, is worth a look as the display is unique. In the front section, the processing of black-wattle bark is demonstrated on the restored original machinery. This bark produced tannic acid, a basic ingredient used in the tanning of heavy leathers. The mill was made from scavenged materials and what you see today is how it actually operated. During the Depression of the 1930s the bark mill was one of the few industries to operate and kept the town of Swansea alive. Behind the bark mill is a museum featuring displays of Swansea's early history, including some superb old photographs. It's open daily from 9 am to 5 pm and admission is $5, children $2.75 or $12 for a family.

The **Swansea Wool and Wine Centre** at the Bark Mill site sells sheepskin and woollen products. It also sells local wines and wine tastings are available at $2 per person. It's open daily except Christmas Day; entry is free.

Duncombes Lookout, three km south of the town, provides panoramic views of Oyster Bay and the Freycinet Peninsula. Further south, seven km from the town, is the **Spiky Bridge** beside the highway. This was built by convicts in 1843 using thousands of local fieldstones but no mortar. The nearby beach and headland is popular for picnics and rock fishing.

For wine lovers, there are several wineries in the area north of the town. **Springvale Vineyard** is 15 km north of Swansea on the Tasman Hwy. It has cellar door sales on weekends, public and school holidays or by appointment (☎ 6257 8208). Ten km further north along the highway is the **Freycinet Vineyard** (☎ 6257 8574) which has cellar door sales on most days. Next door are the **Coombend Cottages** which have their

The Spiky Bridge was made without mortar

wines made by Freycinet and are open daily for cellar door sales.

Water sports are particularly popular in and around Swansea. You can fish for trout in Lake Leake and for bream in the Swan River and bay, beach and rock fishing are also good in the area. Surfing is good off Waterloo Point. Safe swimming beaches as well as the river provide venues for windsurfing, water-skiing and sailing.

Places to Stay

There is a large amount of accommodation around the town. Because it's a popular holiday resort, advance bookings at the peak times of Easter and Christmas are recommended.

Camping *Swansea Caravan Park* (☎ 6257 8177) in Shaw St on the northern edge of the town is just by the beach. It is very clean and run by friendly staff. Tent sites are $10 a double, $12 with power. Self-contained cabins are $35 to $45 a double. In town the *Swansea-Kenmore Caravan Park* (☎ 6257 8148) is less attractive with caravans packed tightly together. Van sites are $14 with power, on-site-vans are $30 a double and cabins are $45 a double.

Hostels The *Swansea Youth Hostel* (☎ 6257 8367), at 5 Franklin St, is in the centre of town right by the sea. The building, although adequate, is not particularly attractive. It charges $10 a night, $12 for nonmembers. In

Swansea

0   250   500 m

To
Coles Bay
& Bicheno

Jubilee Beach

Waterloo
Beach

Golf
Course

Sports
Ground

Schouten House
Beach

Great Oyster
Bay

Kennedia
Beach

To Orford

Shaw Street
Tasman Highway
Franklin Street
Maria Street
Noyes Street
Wellington Street
Saltwater River
Redcliffe St
Victoria Street
Julia Street
Esplanade
Bridge Street
Waterloo Rd
Esplanade
High Street
Gordon Street
Tewkbury Street
Old Spring Bay Rd
Francis Street

PLACES TO STAY

1 Swansea Caravan Park
2 Swansea Cottages
5 Swansea Ocean Villas
8 Central Swansea Backpackers
12 Canberra Holiday Units
13 Meridith House
14 Scarecrow Cottage
16 Oyster Bay Guest House
18 Swansea Youth Hostel
19 Swan Motor Inn
21 Waterloo Inn
22 Schouten House
23 Swansea Kenmore Caravan Park
24 Lester Cottages Complex
25 Keefers Cottage
26 Wagners Cottage
27 Hollyhock Cottage

PLACES TO EAT

7 Just Maggies
15 Swansea Pier Milk Bar
20 Swansea Cafe/Suevanna's Bistro

OTHER

3 Swansea Bark Mill & East Coast Cottage
4 Swansea Wool & Wine Centre
6 Morris's General Store
9 Glamorgan Community Centre
10 Post Office
11 Council Chambers
17 Swansea Corner Store

the busy summer season, priority is given to members.

More appealing is the nearby *Central Swansea Backpackers* (☎ 6257 8399) at 20 Franklin St. It's in an attractive old house which was built in 1860 and was previously the Swansea Cottage Nursing Home. Its also very conveniently located in Franklin St, and the charge is $12 per person.

B&B The most reasonably priced B&B in town is the *Oyster Bay Guest House* (☎ 6257 8110), almost opposite the youth hostel in Franklin St. It was built in 1836, is a friendly,

colonial-style place, and costs $70 a double. The best value B&B is *Redcliffe House* (☎ 6257 8557) which is located beside the Meridith River, one km north of town. With large rooms, private gardens and a cooked breakfast it is worth $85 a double. They also offer speciality weekends with all meals and organised events for around $300 a double. Meridith House and Kabuki by the Sea participate in some of these weekends.

In town *Meredith House* (☎ 6257 8119), near the top of the hill at 15 Noynes St, is classified by the National Trust. This charming guesthouse offers B&B for $70/95. A home-cooked evening meal featuring local food and wine is available by arrangement. B&B plus dinner costs $140 a double. *Schouten House* (☎ 6257 8564), formerly the Swansea Inn, in the southern part of the town at 1 Waterloo Road, has colonial B&B accommodation for $80/95.

Kabuki by the Sea (☎ 6257 8588), 12 km south of Swansea on the Tasman Hwy, has cabins with great views and continental breakfast for $95/110.

Holiday Units A lot of the accommodation in town is in self-contained units, many of which are for rent at prices you would expect in a major city. Some provide breakfast.

Near the top of the hill, Meridith House manages the *Canberra Holiday Units* (☎ 6257 8119) which are next door. They are fairly basic and cost $60 a double. More upmarket is *Swansea Cottages* (☎ 6257 8328) at 43 Franklin St with self-contained cottages for $95 to $140 a double.

On the southern side of town beside the highway are the restored stone farmhouses of *Keefers Cottage* and *Wagners Cottage* (☎ 6257 8494). Next door is *Hollyhock Cottage*, which has recently been constructed but is furnished in 19th-century style and is run by the same people. For all three, breakfast is provided for around $110 a double. Nearby the *Lester Cottages Complex* (☎ 6257 8105) at 42 Gordon St, provides B&B for $95 a double in either the cottages or units.

Hidden down a laneway on top of the hill, *Scarecrow Cottage* (☎ 6257 8473) at 22 Noynes St is a small cottage built around 1860. It is very close to town but does not have the views you would expect for this price range. Full cooked breakfast is provided for $125 a double.

Hotels & Motels Several apartment-block hotels dominate the foreshore. With good views of the sea, prices are higher than for similar standard accommodation elsewhere. The *Swan Motor Inn* (☎ 6257 8102) in Franklin St is a large two-storey complex charging $50-85 per person plus $10 for each extra person. Next door the *Waterloo Inn* is run by the same people and is more expensive with rooms at $118 a double.

Opposite Morris's General Store, *Swansea Ocean Villas* (☎ 6257 8656) at 3 Maria St, is much better value. The accommodation is of a higher standard and includes breakfast for $79 to $95 a double.

Places to Eat
There are several good places in and around the town for afternoon teas and light meals. *Just Maggies*, at 26 Franklin St, has coffee, cakes and light lunches in a clean modern shop. Just down the road, the *Swansea Pier Milk Bar* is an old shop which serves takeaways.

At the Swansea Bark Mill, *Millers' Pantry* serves light lunches, snacks and Devonshire teas in the old Swansea Roller Flour Mill. Further north the Tea Gardens at *Riversdale*, eight km north of the town are set in delightful gardens alongside the Riversdale Flourmill which was built in 1825. Morning and afternoon teas and light lunches are served from Wednesday to Sunday, 10 am to 4.30 pm.

For main meals, the *Swansea Cafe/ Suevanna's Bistro* at 4 Franklin St, serves breakfast, lunch and dinner and is BYO. It's in the style of a diner and offers below-average pub meals at reasonable prices. Don't have the Friday night pizza.

The *Swan Motor Inn* and *Waterloo Inn* complex in Franklin St, have several restaurants and a bar. All the restaurant meals are expensive ($22 and up). Bar meals are a bit cheaper, but still overpriced.

All the à la carte restaurants in town are expensive compared to those in other towns. The licensed *Shy Albatross Restaurant*, (☎ 6257 8110) in the Oyster Bay Guest House, offers a menu with French and Italian influences and is accompanied by an extensive selection of fine Tasmanian wines in a casual and relaxed atmosphere.

Schouten House also has a licensed restaurant named *Fidler's* (☎ 6257 8564) which specialises in à la carte seafood and game, as well as having a cocktail bar. The décor is extremely formal so don't come dressed casually. It is open daily for dinner, and lunch can be arranged.

For something different at more reasonable prices, *Kabuki by the Sea* (☎ 6257

8588), 12 km south of Swansea, has a unique Japanese-style, fully licensed restaurant open daily for lunch and dinner. Local wine is available by the glass. It also serves morning and afternoon teas.

Getting There & Away

There are good bus services along the east coast and also direct from Swansea to Hobart and Launceston via the inland roads. Hobart Coaches (☎ 6234 4077) has at least one daily service between Hobart and Swansea ($15.30) every day except Saturday. Times alternate between morning and afternoon services. The Wednesday, Friday and Sunday service continues to St Helens. In summer there is also a Saturday afternoon service. Extra buses run between Swansea and Hobart on school days. The Hobart Coaches agent in Swansea is the Shell service station at 6 Franklin St.

Tasmanian Redline Coaches (☎ 6231 2200 or 1800 030 033) has one service on weekdays from Hobart which runs via the Midland Hwy. A separate service also runs from Launceston to Swansea via the Lake Leake Hwy. These services only run along the coast from Swansea to Bicheno. The Redline agent in Swansea is the Swansea Corner Store at 8 Franklin St.

Peakes Coaches (☎ 6372 2390) runs one bus on weekdays between Swansea and St Marys via Bicheno. The bus departs from Morris's General Store in Franklin St.

A handy boat service is run by *Central Swansea Backpackers* (☎ 6257 8399). This operates from Swansea to Coles Bay for $9 one way or $15 return. Children are $5 one way or $8 return. This is an extremely good way to get to Freycinet as the alternative is taking two buses. For bicycle riders it's also a good way to avoid repeating the ride along the road into Coles Bay.

COLES BAY & FREYCINET NATIONAL PARK

The tiny township of Coles Bay is both dominated and sheltered by the spectacular 300-metre-high, red granite mountains known as The Hazards. These mark the start of the beautiful Freycinet National Park which is also noted for its coastal heaths, orchids and other wildflowers. Add its diverse wildlife, which includes Bennetts wallabies, black cockatoos, yellow wattlebirds and yellow-throated honeyeaters, along with the generally fine weather and you'll see why it is such a popular park.

The township of Coles Bay is located 31 km off the Tasman Hwy on a sealed side road and provides reasonable amenities for visitors. It is the gateway to the many white-sand beaches, secluded coves, rocky cliffs and excellent bushwalks on the Freycinet Peninsula.

The town has a post office and a 4 Square Supermarket which is open daily and sells groceries and other basic supplies including petrol. It also has a newsagency and boat hire. The Iluka Holiday Centre has its own mini-supermarket with takeaway food and also sells petrol.

History

The Oyster Bay tribe of Aboriginals lived here as hunters and gatherers. The Freycinet area was important to them, because in winter they could live off the abundant shellfish. The large shell middens along Richardsons Beach are one of the few visible signs of Aboriginal occupation.

The first European to visit this area was Abel Tasman in 1642; he named Schouten Island and mistook Freycinet as an island. Later, in 1802, a French expedition discovered that Freycinet was a peninsula and named it and many other features. Other expeditions noted the number of seals, and greedy sealers arrived from Sydney and quickly wiped out most of them. Some of these sealers stole Aboriginal women as wives and by the time the settlers arrived the Aboriginal population had already decreased severely.

In 1824 a whale station was established at Parsons Cove. This had closed by the 1840s when there were no whales left to hunt; another example of uncontrolled exploitation. The town of Coles Bay was named after Silas Cole, who came here in the 1830s and

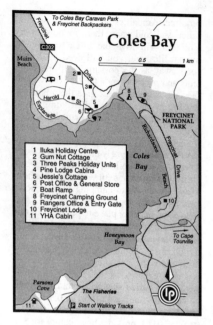

Coles Bay

To Coles Bay Caravan Park
& Freycinet Backpackers

C302

Muirs Beach

0   0.5   1 km

Harold   St

Esplanade

FREYCINET NATIONAL PARK

Coles Bay

Richardsons

Freycinet Drive

Coles Bay Beach

Honeymoon Bay

To Cape Tourville

Parsons Cove

The Fisheries

Start of Walking Tracks

1 Iluka Holiday Centre
2 Gum Nut Cottage
3 Three Peaks Holiday Units
4 Pine Lodge Cabins
5 Jessie's Cottage
6 Post Office & General Store
7 Boat Ramp
8 Freycinet Camping Ground
9 Rangers Office & Entry Gate
10 Freycinet Lodge
11 YHA Cabin

road enters the park (and national park fees apply) and is in reasonable condition, but care must be taken in a few places. The extensive views along the coastline make the trip worthwhile.

Closer to Coles Bay, on a side road, the tiny settlement of **Swanwick** provides good estuary fishing. The shores of Great Oyster Bay offer excellent fishing or you can charter a boat or hire a dinghy and go out to catch your meal. From March to May, Coles Bay is a great base for **big game fishing**, especially when the giant bluefin tuna run. A game-fishing craft run by Freycinet Sea Charters (☎ 6275 1461) will take you to the best spots for $550 per day ($600 on weekends and holidays). The same boat is also available for cruises around the area. The bay is also famous for crayfish but unless you go diving you will find it easier to simply buy one from the local boats.

Coles Bay is located at the head of a large sheltered bay which provides swimming, windsurfing and water-skiing in safe ocean waters. This is a great place to learn these activities.

For a bit more action, try Peregrine Adventures (☎ 6225 0944 or 018 124 801) which conducts three-day sea kayaking trips from November to April leaving every second Wednesday. They start from Honeymoon Bay and you camp on the beach. The per person cost of $490 includes transport from Hobart (if needed), equipment, guides, food and park fees.

The tempting granite peaks of **The Hazards**, as well as other cliffs in the area, attract experienced rock climbers. Rodney Charles (☎ 6257 0141) at 11 Hazards View Road, provides transport, instruction and all gear for abseiling and top rope climbing at White Water Wall. Cost is $40 each with a minimum of two.

The Friendly Beaches are a recent addition to the national park. The signposted turn off is 22 km north of Coles Bay. From the car park at Isaacs Point a five-minute walk leads to a vantage point from which you'll have uninterrupted views of the expanse of white sand and blue water.

burnt some of the midden shells to produce lime. Many of Swansea's older buildings used mortar made from this lime.

Schouten Island was mined for coal from 1840 to 1880 and for tin in the 1870s. Both Freycinet and Schouten Island were also used for farming. In 1906 both areas were declared game reserves to stop the overhunting of animals. In 1916 Freycinet shared honours with Mt Field to become Tasmania's first national park; Schouten Island was added much later in 1977. To complete protection of the coastal regions, the Friendly Beaches were added to the national park in 1992.

Things to See & Do

On the road in to Coles Bay, look out on the right for the **Moulting Lagoon Game Reserve**, which is a breeding ground for black swans and wild ducks.

The best short drive is to follow the six-km road out to **Cape Tourville Lighthouse**. The

Bushwalking Roads only penetrate a small way into the park and the only way to visit the many features is to walk. Well-used tracks lead to the best features.

One of the most beautiful walks in the entire state is to **Wineglass Bay**, which takes from 2½ to three hours return. If that's too far, you can walk along the same track only as far as the **Wineglass Bay Lookout** which has wonderful views and is only one hour return. Another superb walk, if you're fit, is to the summit of **Mt Amos** from which the views are spectacular. It takes about three hours return along a marked track. Instead of driving, you can follow the shore from Coles Bay to Honeymoon Bay to the main walking tracks; this takes about 1½ hours each way.

There are also plenty of shorter walks. **Sleepy Bay**, just off the Cape Tourville Road, is well worth a visit. The lookout on top of the hill in Coles Bay is also good.

For any walk in the national park, remember to sign in (and out) at the registration booth at the car park. A current Tasmanian National Parks permit is also required. For more information contact the rangers office (☎ 6257 0107).

The Freycinet Peninsula also has some excellent overnight walking. Bush camping is allowed south of The Hazards. The scenery at the free camp sites of Wineglass Bay (one to 1½ hours), Hazards Beach (two to three hours) and Cooks Beach (about 4½ hours) is well worth the walk. There's no permanent drinking water at any of these sites and little elsewhere on the peninsula, so you often need to carry your own. To see most of the peninsula, you can follow a 27-km circuit; this is described in Lonely Planet's *Bushwalking in Australia* by John & Monica Chapman.

Places to Stay

Inside the national park, *Freycinet Camping Ground* (☎ 6257 0107) is a series of tent sites in the dunes behind Richardsons Beach. Bookings can be made at the rangers office, and tents are $8 for two ($10.50 for a family) with powered sites $10 a double ($13 a family). A national park permit is also

required. Amenities are very basic with pit toilets and cold water; there are no showers. Children will love the often too-friendly animal life here; you will need to lock all food away as the possums will break into tents and packs to get a feed. If you want to feed the animals, don't give them bread as this brings on a disease called 'lumpy jaw'. Ask the ranger what food is suitable to feed them.

Further north at the Friendly Beaches there are two extremely basic camping areas. These have pit toilets and no fresh water. Bring your own water if you're staying here. While there are no camping fees, national park entry fees apply.

In town the only place to put up your tent is *Iluka Holiday Centre* (☎ 6257 0115) above the eastern end of Muir's Beach. It is the cheapest accommodation in Coles Bay itself and is the YHA key holder. This place is a bit rough around the edges. Camp sites are $10, powered sites $12 and a variety of on-site vans and cabins cost $30. Over the hill close to the shops *Pine Lodge Cabins* (☎ 6257 0113) provides basic cabins for $50 a double.

Coles Bay Caravan Park (☎ 6257 0100) is three km out of town, located on the western end of Muir's Beach. A tent site costs $11 for two and on-site vans are $30. The caravan park also runs the only hostel in town, *Freycinet Backpackers*, at $14 a person. The location is not a real problem as staff provide a free bus service to the walking tracks.

The *YHA* has a hostel at Parsons Cove. This is not a normal YHA hostel, but is more like a cabin and is only available to one group at a time. It must be booked in advance from the YHA state office in Hobart (☎ 6234 9617).

Being a popular holiday destination for families, there are plenty of holiday units and cottages. The closest to the Freycinet National Park is *Three Peaks Holiday Units* (☎ 6257 0333) with relatively modern units for $70 a double. Almost next door, *Gum Nut Cottage* (☎ 6257 0109) can be rented for $65 and holds up to four people. On the Esplanade, *Jessie's Cottage* (☎ 6257 0143) sleeps up to four people and is $60 a double.

There are several other units available at Swanwick, five km from Coles Bay. *Swan River Cottages* (☎ 6257 0216) is good value for groups of up to six people; the self-contained cottages cost $70. Also in Swanwick, *Freycinet Holiday Homes* (☎ 6257 0218) are riverfront homes accommodating up to six people; $75 for two or $85 for up to six.

More upmarket is the recently expanded *Freycinet Lodge* (☎ 6257 0101) at the southern end of Richardsons Beach. There is a variety of cabins, some suitable for wheelchairs, some with spas and others with kitchens. Rates range from $130 to $175 a double for room only; rather high for the standard offered, but then you are paying for the location. Meals are available at the lodge. An in-house naturalist guide is available to guests, as well as a tennis court, games room and boutique. Park fees are paid by the Lodge for guests.

Places to Eat

Opposite the Post Office, *Captains Table Licensed Restaurant & Takeaway* has a variety of reasonably priced meals specialising in seafood and steak. It's open daily for lunch, dinner and snacks.

More expensive is the *Freycinet Licensed Restaurant* at Freycinet Lodge. The views from the restaurant and the à la carte seafood and steak make it an ideal place to eat if you want to splash out a bit. For a cheap, no-frills snack, there's the kiosk at the *Iluka Holiday Centre*. For putting your own food together, the self-serve store is pretty well stocked; the kiosk at Iluka also has some supplies.

Getting There & Away

TRC (☎ 6231 2200 or 1800 030 033) and Hobart Coaches (☎ 6234 4077) can drop you at the Coles Bay turn-off en route from Swansea to Bicheno and you can hitch the 28 km from there, but traffic is often light. Bicheno Coach Services (☎ 6257 0293) runs the school bus service from Coles Bay to Bicheno and this has evolved into a handy bus service. From June to October there are three services on weekdays, two on Saturday and one on Sunday. From November to May extra services are scheduled but only run if needed.

Some services only run if bookings exist and it is wise to book ahead at least the night before. Bus times are mainly from 8 am to 9 am and from 3 pm to 5 pm (school times). The fare each way is $5 plus $2.50 per bicycle. Pick-ups can be made from accommodation if requested. In Bicheno, buses depart from the newsagency in Foster St, and in Coles Bay from the general store.

It is more than five km from the town to the national park walking tracks car park, and Bicheno Coach Services has a weekday shuttle bus running two or three times daily from Monday to Saturday if required. Bookings are advised and the cost is $2 return. Park entry fees apply and can be purchased on the bus.

BICHENO

• *pop 700*

This town has everything a holiday resort needs. The scenery is picturesque, the climate mild and often sunny. The town is known as the sun capital of Tasmania and in summer there is average of 12½ hours of sunshine per day while in winter it is still 7½ hours. There are some unique features worth visiting like the tiny harbour, called the Gulch, which shelters the fishing fleet. Fishing and tourism are the main industries which support the town. With reasonable prices for food and accommodation, it's a great place to stay for a few days.

The main street is Foster St, where you'll find the Information Centre in front of the *Bicheno Cabin & Tourist Park*. It is a good source of information about the town and can book you on any of the organised activities.

History

The town began as a sealers port and was called Waubs Bay Harbour. This was named after an Aboriginal woman, Waubedebar, who was kidnapped by sealers for use as a

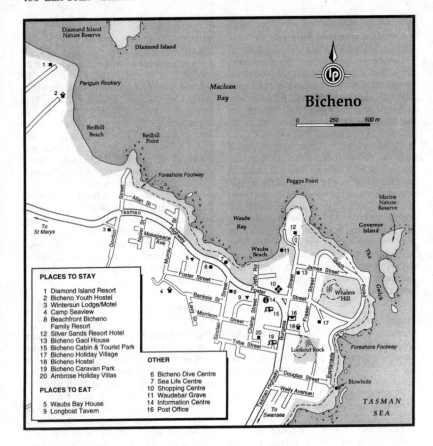

PLACES TO STAY
1 Diamond Island Resort
2 Bicheno Youth Hostel
3 Wintersun Lodge/Motel
4 Camp Seaview
8 Beachfront Bicheno
   Family Resort
12 Silver Sands Resort Hotel
13 Bicheno Gaol House
15 Bicheno Cabin & Tourist Park
17 Bicheno Holiday Village
18 Bicheno Hostel
19 Bicheno Caravan Park
20 Ambrose Holiday Villas

PLACES TO EAT
5 Waubs Bay House
9 Longboat Tavern

OTHER
6 Bicheno Dive Centre
7 Sea Life Centre
10 Shopping Centre
11 Waudebar Grave
14 Information Centre
16 Post Office

wife and slave in the early 1800s. A strong swimmer, she later became famous for rescuing two sealers when their boat was wrecked one km off shore. Years after her death, the town honoured her by constructing a grave which you can still visit.

In 1854 the town became a coal mining port but in 1855 most of the miners left and joined the gold rush in Victoria. The town shrank and almost vanished, explaining why there are very few old buildings. Around the 1940s, the town's fortune changed as it developed into the holiday resort town it is today.

Things to See & Do
The best way to walk around this town is to follow the **Foreshore Footway**. This was constructed as part of the Bicentennial celebrations of 1988. The pathway is three km long and goes from one end of town to the other. The most interesting section is from the Sea Life Centre and eastwards around **Peggys Point**. This takes you through The Gulch and along to the **Blowhole**. Here there is a large rocking granite boulder which the sea moves. You can then return to town by following footpaths then a ladder to the top of **Lookout Rock** for a panoramic view over

the town. The other hill, **Whalers Hill**, is also worth climbing for a view. In the days of whaling these hills were used to sight passing whales.

The Gulch is an interesting place. It's simply a channel behind a low rocky island and provides the sheltered anchorage for the fishing fleet. When the boats return you can often buy fresh crayfish, abalone, oysters or anything else caught. If you want to go out on a boat, then two hours' fishing costs $45 per person; book at the Information Centre.

Near Bicheno is an **Oyster Farm** and guided tours are run on demand around 4 pm daily. Tours include a barge trip to the cages. Book with Bicheno Coach Services (☎ 6257 0293) or at the Information Centre; the cost is $13 each and includes oyster tastings.

At low tide, there is a very short walk from near the Youth Hostel across the sand bar to **Diamond Island**. This is a penguin rookery, and around sunset you might be lucky enough to see them. Watch the tide and make sure you return before it rises. Fairy penguins can also be seen at the northern end of Redbill Beach at nightfall. Guided tours to the rookeries are run every evening by Bicheno Penguin & Adventure Tours (☎ 6375 1333). The penguins can be seen from September to February and April to July; the cost is $7.50, children $3.75.

Water sports are popular. **Waubs Beach** and **Rice Beach** are fairly safe ocean beaches for swimming. For warmer water, the sheltered and shallow Denison River beside the highway eight km north of the town is a popular swimming place. When the surf's up, then **Redbill Point** provides a good break for surfers. Body boards can be hired at the Information Centre for $12 a day. Water-skiing is also popular and all gear, instruction and boats can be hired through the Information Centre.

The **Sea Life Centre** is open daily from 9 am to 5 pm and features Tasmanian marine life swimming behind glass windows. There's also a restored trading ketch, but at $4.50 for admission, the centre is rather overpriced and a bit depressing with all those fish behind glass. Seven km north of town is

The noisy rainbow lorikeet is among the many native birds on display at the East Coast Birdlife & Animal Park

the 32-hectare **East Coast Birdlife & Animal Park**, which is open daily from 9 am to 5.30 pm; admission is $6.50, children $4.

The **Bicheno Dive Centre** (☎ 6375 1138), opposite the Sea Life Centre on the foreshore, runs courses which are more reasonably priced than those run in warmer waters on the mainland, and you can also hire or buy diving equipment from its shop. Scuba tank fills are $6 per tank and diving charges are $24 per boat dive. Diving trips leave twice daily during summer.

For something more active you can hire a mountain bike for $15 for the day or, even better, get transported to **Elephant Pass** – on the highway to St Marys and north of Bicheno – and ride back downhill. This costs $25 and even includes a pancake morning tea; it is certainly not the way to keep fit but is lots of fun.

Places to Stay

The *Bicheno Caravan Park* (☎ 6375 1280), on the corner of the main highway and Tribe St, has lots of grass but little shade. Camp sites are $8, powered sites $10 and on-site vans are $28 a double. More centrally located and more attractive is *Bicheno Cabin & Tourist Park* (☎ 6375 1117), in Champ St. Prices are a little dearer with camp sites $10, powered sites $12.50 and on-site vans $40 a double. Cabins are also available for $60 a double.

Three km north of town, beside the beach opposite Diamond Island, is the *Bicheno Youth Hostel* (☎ 6375 1293). It's a pretty spot but the hostel itself is looking its age and provides only basic accommodation. It charges $9.50 a night for YHA members ($11.50 nonmembers) and is often booked out in summer. In a bushland setting on the edge of town, *Camp Seaview* (☎ 6375 1247) in Banksia St, has hostel accommodation for $10 per person. With bunks for 80 people, a bed is often available here when the smaller hostels are filled.

The handiest hostel in town is *Bicheno Hostel* (☎ 6375 1651 in Morrison St. Located in a short but steep street, this custom-built hostel has good services with some lock-up storage. Rates are $13 per person.

Around town there are plenty of holiday units. The *Bicheno Gaol House* (☎ 6375 1430) in Burgess St is the town's oldest building (1845) and provides the only genuine colonial cottage in town. For this unique experience, it's $90 for two plus $20 for extra people. Most units are modern like *Ambrose Holiday Villas* (☎ 6375 1288) on the corner of Tribe and Champ Sts. This is tucked in behind the caravan parks and doubles are $88 with $12 for each extra adult.

In town and set in bushland between the two lookout hills is *Bicheno Holiday Village* (☎ 6375 1171). It is surprisingly hidden for such a large development. The A-frame holiday units are about the same standard as most other places in town and at $110 a double are a bit pricey.

Better value is found out of town. *Bicheno Berries* (☎ 6375 1481) is four km north of town beside the highway and provides B&B for $45 to $60 a double. It has great views of

the coast and is great value. Three km south of town and down a side road, *Bicheno Hideaway* (☎ 6375 1312) has three arch-shaped holiday units with great ocean views. The units are hidden in a quiet location well away from the crowds, and the hosts speak six European languages. Rates are $75 a double plus $15 for each extra adult.

There are also several hotels and motels. The *Silver Sands Resort Hotel* (☎ 6375 1266) in Burgess St has the best location, right beside the water. Rooms are reasonable and range from $30 to $70 in winter and $50 to $85 in summer. *Beachfront Bicheno Family Resort* (☎ 6375 1111), beside the highway in town, is poorly named. It's a motel, not really a resort, and it's not on the beachfront. It still has good views of the ocean and rooms are $70 a double.

Out near the Youth Hostel, *Diamond Island Resort* (☎ 6375 1161 or 1800 030 299) is a series of two-storey, Tudor style units. It has the usual resort facilities such as a pool, a tennis court and a playground. Each self-contained unit even has its own washing machine. Rates are $80 to $120 a double and children stay free.

Places to Eat

The main shopping centre has a bakery and two coffee shops. *Rose's Coffee Shop* opens at 8.30 am daily and is the place to grab breakfast. It also serves light meals later in the day. Next door, the *Galleon Coffee Shop* has the usual takeaways plus pizza on Thursday, Friday and Saturday nights.

For lunch you can try the *Sea Life Centre* on the foreshore in town. Nearby *Waubs Bay House* has fresh seafood meals. They have a bargain speciality on Wednesday nights with a roast and soup for $10.

For bistro meals the *Longboat Tavern* beside the highway in the centre of town has good counter meals and seafood. The *Silver Sands Resort Hotel* at the north end of Burgess St, also has counter meals at reasonable prices. For a char grill visit the *Bicheno Holiday Village*. For à la carte you can try *Cyrano Restaurant* in the main shopping centre. The best à la carte is out of town at the *Diamond Island Resort*.

Getting There & Away

For information on the Bicheno services run by TRC, Hobart Coaches and Peakes Coach Service, see the Getting There & Away section for Swansea. Basically there are good services from Monday to Friday with limited services on weekends. Peakes Coaches runs a weekday service from Swansea through Bicheno to St Marys. For services to Coles Bay see the Getting There & Away section for Coles Bay & Freycinet.

DOUGLAS APSLEY NATIONAL PARK

One of the newest national parks in Tasmania, this contains a large area of undisturbed dry forest which was typical of much of the original land cover of the east coast. The park was declared in 1989 after much public concern over wood chipping and the large-scale clearing of the remaining original forests. In addition to the forests, major features include rocky peaks, river gorges and beautiful waterfalls. As it has only been a park for a short while, there has been little development and this is one of its appealing features.

Access to the park is by quiet gravel roads. To reach the southern end, the **Apsley Waterhole**, turn left off the highway five km north of Bicheno and follow the signposted road for seven km to the car park. A basic camping ground with a pit toilet is provided. The nearby waterhole provides excellent swimming. To access the northern end, at **Thompsons Marches**, turn left off the highway 24 km north of Bicheno onto E Road. This is a private road, so obey any signs as you follow it to the car park and boom gate beside the park border. There are no suitable places to camp near the car park. As with all other parks, entry fees apply. Open fires are not permitted in this park from October to April, when cooking is only allowed on fuel stoves.

Bushwalking As with most national parks the only way to see anything is to walk. At

Apsley Waterhole a wheelchair-standard track of only five minutes leads to the lookout which provides a great view over the river. A longer walk of two to three hours return leads into the **Apsley Gorge**.

At the northern end, the best walk is to **Heritage Falls** which takes four to six hours return. There is a good bush camping ground near the falls.

The major walk in the park is the **Leeaberra Track** which takes three days; you are requested to walk from north to south to prevent further spreading of a plant disease. Full track notes are available in the third edition of Lonely Planet's *Bushwalking in Australia* by John & Monica Chapman.

ST MARYS

• *pop 630*

St Marys is a charming little town 10 km inland from the coast, near the Mt Nicholas range. There's not much to do there except enjoy the peacefulness of the countryside, visit a number of waterfalls, and take walks in the state forest.

There are some rocky hills surrounding the town which provide fine views and are well worth climbing. The **South Sister** towers over the road leading to the hostel. It's only a 10-minute walk from the car park to the top. East of the town, **St Patricks Head** is a longer climb of three hours return. Cables and a ladder add some excitement to the climb.

Places to Stay & Eat

The superbly positioned *St Marys Youth Hostel* (☎ 6372 2341), on a working sheep farm called Seaview, is surrounded by state forest. It's five km from St Marys on German Town Rd, and commands magnificent views of the coast, ocean and mountains. It costs $10 a night to stay in the hostel and the warden will pick you up from the post office between 10 and 11 am any day except Sunday if you phone.

Accommodation is also available in the *St Marys Hotel* (☎ 6372 2181), where you'll find singles/doubles are $28/52 for B&B. The pub also has counter meals, or there's the *Coach House Restaurant* in the main street, which has pizzas and takeaways. To the south, beside the highway in Elephant Pass, is the famous *Mt Elephant Pancake Barn* which serves delicious pancakes and other light meals and is well worth a visit.

Getting There & Away

TRC (☎ 6231 2200 or 1800 030 033) has one service at around 8.30 am to Launceston on Sunday to Friday. An afternoon service leaves at 5.10 pm on Sunday on the same route. On Monday to Friday another service also leaves at the same time for Hobart. These services start from or finish at St Helens. Peakes Coaches (☎ 6372 2390) runs buses from St Marys to Bicheno ($4) and Swansea ($8). They run once per day each way on weekdays only.

FINGAL
• *pop 430*

Located 21 km west of St Marys, this inland town is near the site of the state's first worthwhile gold strike in 1852. It has seen boom and bust times and today is a peaceful country town serving the local rural community. For visitors its main attraction is the annual **Coal Shovelling Championships** held in early March. This one day event attracts many spectators.

The surrounding valley contains several abandoned towns from the mining era. Mangana, Rossarden and Storys Creek display piles of tailings, mine machinery and tiny cottages that are rarely used. If these sights are too depressing then visit the **Evercreech Forest Reserve** to the north near Mathinna. A 20-minute circuit walk takes you to the White Knights, the highest white gums in the world which reach 89 m. Evercreech Falls are also worth walking to, taking about one hour return.

The *Fingal Hotel* (☎ 6374 2121) provides the only accommodation in town with B&B provided for singles/doubles at $25/35. You can also buy counter meals here. The hotel is rather more famous for its large collection of Scotch whisky bottles; someone's had fun!

Top Left: Stained glass windows, Ross Uniting Church
Top Right: Ross Bridge carvings at sunset
Bottom: Moonlit church, Oatlands

CHRIS KLEP

CHRIS KLEP

CHRIS KLEP

Top: Wineglass Bay and The Hazards, Freycinet National Park
Bottom Left: Worker's cottage, Maria Island National Park
Bottom Right: Painted cliffs, Maria Island National Park

The North-East

The north-east of Tasmania is worth exploring as it is off the normal tourist route. It is very scenic and quiet, with lovely beaches and bushwalks around St Helens and in the Mt William National Park. There are also some other attractions like the Tin Mine Centre in Derby and the Lavender Farm in Nabowla. It is also known to have the 'Worst Little Pub in Tassie' and the lovely coast town of St Helens is a good place to go.

The very scenic coast road from Chain of Lagoons to Falmouth provides a fast, scenic drive to Scamander and St Helens. From St Helens you can either follow the unsealed roads around the coast and visit extensive, untouched beaches or follow the winding Tasman Hwy across the mountain passes to Weldborough, Scottsdale and on to Launceston. Both routes are interesting with little traffic and a lot to see.

Getting There & Around

Bus Tasmanian Redline Coaches (TRC) (☎ 6331 3233 or 1800 030 033) runs a service twice each weekday from Derby to Launceston for $11. Buses leave Derby at 8.30 am and 2.15 pm and Launceston at 9 am and 4 pm. On Sunday evening there is a single service each way. On school days an extra bus runs. From Scottsdale, Stan's Coach Service connects with the TRC buses from Launceston and runs north to Bridport. In the other direction, Suncoast (☎ 6376 1753) runs one service each weekday from St Helens to Derby for $5. The same bus does a circular loop down to St Marys.

TRC also runs two services a day (except Saturday) from Launceston to St Helens via the Midland Hwy and St Marys ($16.60). Hobart Coaches (☎ 6234 4077 or 1800 030 620) runs one bus each way on Wednesday, Friday and Sunday from Hobart along the east coast to St Helens. During January and February it provides an extra Saturday service along the same route.

HIGHLIGHTS

- Coastal scenery at Bay of Fires
- St Columba Falls
- Trying to sink rival rafts in the Derby River Derby
- The lavender farm at Bridestowe

Bicycle The Tasman Hwy is a winding narrow road which crosses two major passes as it heads west through Weldborough and Scottsdale. Cyclists need to be vigilant on this road. A very pleasant alternative is to follow the unsealed roads around the coast. There is very little traffic and you have fewer hills to climb. However, you'll need to carry a tent as there is no accommodation around the coast between St Helens and Bridport; camping areas exist at both ends of Mt William National Park and at Tomahawk on the route from St Helens to Bridport.

IRONHOUSE POINT

The new road which follows the coast from Chain of Lagoons (north of Bicheno) to Falmouth then Scamander passes through some excellent coastal scenery. It also avoids

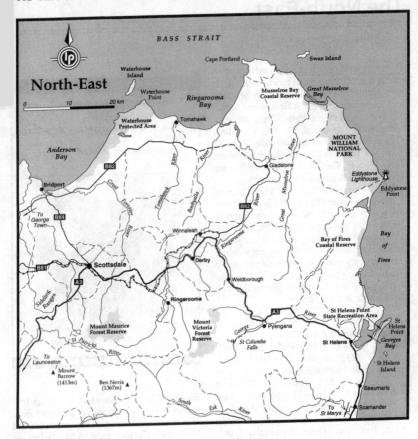

the slow climb over the two passes to St Marys. Much of the coastline is rocky and the best place to stop along it is at Ironhouse Point and **Four Mile Creek** where the beaches begin. Ironhouse Point is named after the first house in the region to have an iron roof.

The *Cray Drop-In Village* (☎ 6372 2228) is near the Point and has holiday units for a very reasonable $40 a double. There are 27 units in all so it caters for large groups. The village is not new and for many years was at the end of a dirt road. There is a restaurant and bar in the village.

SCAMANDER & BEAUMARIS
• *pop 410*

Scamander and Beaumaris townships are stretched along some of the loveliest white-sand beaches on the east coast, and are protected in a coastal reserve. The two towns are really a collection of buildings near the beach and they almost merge together. There is no fishing port and no industry other than tourism.

You can take long walks along the beach, hire a dinghy (☎ 6372 5297), go fishing for bream from the old bridge over the river or try your luck at catching trout further upstream. The wide ocean beach in front of both towns is excellent for swimming. The lagoons north of Beaumaris provide good water-skiing.

For a fine view of the St Helens area and the coast around Scamander a five-km drive from Beaumaris leads to the **Skyline Tier Scenic Lookout**.

Places to Stay & Eat

The *Kookaburra Caravan and Camping Ground* (☎ 6372 5121), 1½ km north of the river has camp sites for $9 for two and on-site vans at $25. It's only a short walk to the beach.

If you don't mind being 500 metres away from the ocean, then *Carramar Holiday Units* (☎ 6372 5160) in Pringle St are a real bargain at $38 a double plus $10 for each extra adult. Up on the hill on the north side of the river, *Blue Seas* (☎ 6272 5211) has fine views and offers self-contained units for $55 a double. On the other side of the highway beside the river, *Pelican Sands* (☎ 6372 5231 or 1800 816 561) has older units for the same price. There are bicycles and fishing rods for hire.

Dominating the river foreshore is the *Scamander Beach Resort Hotel* (☎ 6372 5255). This three-storey building is a bit of an eyesore, but has marvellous views. Rooms are $75 a double and there are bar meals available.

For something more upmarket try *Bensons* (☎ 6372 5587), located on top of a hill at Beaumaris. The imposing two-storey house has sweeping views and elegant décor. For this standard, it's reasonably priced at $86 to $98 a double. There is also an à la carte restaurant here. For light meals the *Home for Tea* tearoom beside the highway has fine afternoon teas and snacks.

ST HELENS
• *pop 1150*

St Helens, on Georges Bay, was first settled in 1830 by sealers and whalers. By the 1850s, farmers had arrived to create a permanent settlement. In 1874 it was discovered that the inland hills were rich with tin and

many arrived to try their luck at mining. St Helens, with its sheltered bay, was the port used for shipping tin. When the mines stopped operating, St Helens continued to grow while the mining towns died. Today it is the largest town in the area.

St Helens is Tasmania's largest fishing port, with a big fleet based in the bay. The main street is Cecilia St, where you'll find the post office. There are three banks in town (ANZ, Trust and Westpac) and EFTPOS facilities are available at the petrol stations and supermarkets.

Things to See & Do

St Helens' interesting and varied history is recorded in the **History Room** (☎ 6376 1744), at 59 Cecilia St, adjacent to the town library. It's open weekdays from 9 am to 4 pm and admission is $3 (children $1).

Both sides of the wide entrance to Georges Bay have been designated state recreation areas and provide some easy walking. A good track circles around St Helens Point, and takes about one hour return. On the north side, **Skeleton Bay** and **Dora Point** are good places from which to explore the coastline.

While the beaches in town are not particularly good for swimming, there are excellent scenic beaches at **Binalong Bay** (10 km north of St Helens) and **Cosy Corner** (12 km north of St Helens) and at **Stieglitz** (seven km east of St Helens), as well as at St Helens and Humbug points.

Georges Bay, with its flat waters, is excellent for canoeing and windsurfing. Its clear waters are also good for diving. Boats can be chartered from Professional Charters (☎ 6343 2070 or 6376 3083) which provides all gear for reef or game fishing. Rates for fishing from a Shark Cat are $60 for a half day, with a minimum of four people. Scuba diving from their boats is also available at $35 a dive, with a minimum of five divers.

For overnight fishing, hire the *Norseman III* (☎ 6424 6900) which is a 53-foot cruiser. It can take a maximum of 12 passengers and costs $900 per day. You need to take your own food.

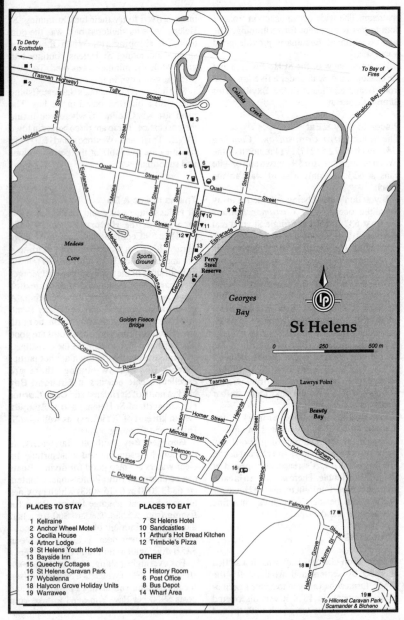

Tasman Highway

Tully   Street

Colchis Creek

Binalong Bay Road

Medea

Anne Street

Cove Esplanade

Street

Quail

Medea

Cove

Circassion

Street

Grant Street

Bowen Street

Groom Street

Cecilia Street

Cameron Street

Quail   Street

Street

Esplanade

Bay

Esplanade

Georges

Medeas
Cove

Sports
Ground

Percy Steel
Reserve

Medeas Cove Road

Georges
Bay

St Helens

0   250   500 m

Golden Fleece
Bridge

Tasman

Lawrys Point

Street

Jason   Street

Homer Street

Heights

Levy   Street

Allen Drive

Highway

Beauty
Bay

Mimosa Street

Grove

Telemon St

Penelopa

Erythos

Douglas Ct

Falmouth

Halcyon Grove

Murray St

Street

To Hillcrest Caravan Park,
Scamander & Bicheno

PLACES TO STAY

1 Kellraine
2 Anchor Wheel Motel
3 Cecilia House
4 Artnor Lodge
9 St Helens Youth Hostel
13 Bayside Inn
15 Queechy Cottages
16 St Helens Caravan Park
17 Wybalenna
18 Halcyon Grove Holiday Units
19 Warrawee

PLACES TO EAT

7 St Helens Hotel
10 Sandcastles
11 Arthur's Hot Bread Kitchen
12 Trimbole's Pizza

OTHER

5 History Room
6 Post Office
8 Bus Depot
14 Wharf Area

Places to Stay

The *St Helens Caravan Park* (☎ 6376 1290), in Penelope St, is just out of town, south of the bridge. Despite being on a hill, it offers no views. Camp sites are $12, on-site vans $30 and cabins $45 for two persons. The other caravan park, *Hillcrest Caravan Park* (☎ 6376 3298), is cheaper with tent sites for $8 and holiday cabins for $40. It's seven km out of town at Stieglitz on the side road to St Helens Point.

The only hostel in town is *St Helens Youth Hostel* (☎ 6376 1661) at 5 Cameron St. It's in a lovely, quiet spot by the beach and is close to town. The cost is $11 a night and $13 for nonmembers.

The *Artnor Lodge* (☎ 6376 1234) is a comfortable guesthouse in the main street. The cost is $35/45 which includes a continental breakfast. Almost opposite is *Cecilia House* (☎ 6376 1723), which provides B&B for $40/60.

Out of town, and south of the bridge beside the highway, is *Wybalenna* (☎ 6376 1611) with B&B for $35/50. Around the next corner, *Warawee* (☎ 6376 1987) is a colonial house set in spacious grounds. Doubles are $55 to $80 for B&B. It also has a self-contained cottage for $55 a double.

For self-contained units with kitchen try the fairly new *Kellraine Units* (☎ 6376 1169) beside the highway on the western side of town. At $35 a double they are a real bargain although they are away from the town and the water.

Just south of the bridge, *Queechy Cottages* (☎ 6376 1321) has self-contained units for $50 with fine views of Georges Bay. High-quality self-contained units with views can be found at *Halcyon Grove Holiday Units* (☎ 6376 1424) at 16 Halcyon Grove, and cost $55 a double.

The best deal for motel units is *Anchor Wheel Motel* (☎ 6376 1358) which is beside the highway on the western side of town. Singles/doubles are $40/50. In the main street at 2 Cecilia St, *Bayside Inn* (☎ 6376 1466) is conveniently located, opposite the wharf, and charges a reasonable $58 a double.

Places To Eat

Arthur's Hot Bread Kitchen, in the main street, has pies and cakes which you can eat on the premises or take away. The staff are very friendly and the food is cheap – the cooked breakfast at $4 is a real bargain. It's open every day. There is another bakery around the corner in Quail St.

Also in the main street, *Sandcastles* is open seven days a week for coffee and cakes. *Trimbole's Pizza*, on the corner of Cecilia and Circassion Sts, has good pizza and pasta. Chinese takeaways and fish & chips are often available from vans in the wharf area.

The *Bayside Inn* serves counter meals seven days a week. For à la carte, try the seafood restaurant at *Queechy* and the *Anchor Wheel Motel*.

Getting There & Away

Hobart Coaches (☎ 6234 4077 or 1800 030 620) runs one service a day from Hobart along the east coast to St Helens on Wednesday, Friday and Sunday. During January and February it runs an extra service along the same route on Saturday.

TRC (☎ 6331 3233 or 1800 030 033) runs two services every day (except Saturday) from Launceston to St Helens via St Marys and the Midland Hwy. It is possible to get to Hobart on some of these services by changing buses at Conara Junction.

Suncoast (☎ 6376 1753) runs a Monday to Friday service from St Helens down to St Marys, back to St Helens then across to Derby and back again. This is a very handy service if you want to travel across the hilly but interesting Tasman Hwy towards Launceston.

St Helens' bus depot is at 30 Cecilia St.

BAY OF FIRES

From St Helens a minor road heads northeast to meet the coast at the start of the Bay of Fires. It was named by early explorers to describe the number of Aboriginal fires they had seen along the shore. The Bay is a series of sweeping beaches, rocky headlands, heathlands and lagoons. As well as being popular with today's tourists it was also popular with the Aboriginal people, who left behind high piles of shells we call middens. The foreshore, lagoons and heathlands are all part of a coastal reserve. If you are after something very cheap, as well as extremely scenic, then this is a great place to camp for a few days.

The ocean beaches provide some good surfing. The lagoons provide safe swimming; it is not advised to swim in the ocean due to the many rips along the beaches. There are many places along the Bay where free camping is allowed. It's pretty basic with no toilets or fresh water.

PYENGANA

This small settlement lies in an isolated valley in the hills. It's worth a detour to see the cheese factory, an interesting hotel and one of the state's best waterfalls. The name Pyengana derives from an Aboriginal word describing the meeting of two rivers in the valley.

Over a hundred years ago, the pioneers of the region recognised that this beautiful green valley was ideal dairy country. However, transporting milk from the isolated valley was impractical. When converted into cheese and butter, the produce survived the slow journey to the markets. Today, cheddar cheese is still produced using the old methods at **Healey's Pyengana Cheese Factory**. It's open daily for tastings and sales.

Further down the road is the **St Columba Falls Hotel** (☎ 6373 6121) which is more generally known as the 'Pub in the Paddock', an apt description. Originally a house, it has been a hotel for over a century and has backpackers beds for $10 a night. A camping ground is also available. Counter lunches and teas are available every day.

The best known feature of the valley is **St Columba Falls**, six km past the hotel. At around 90 metres high they are believed to be the state's highest falls. A short walk of 20 minutes return along a well-made track leads to the foot of the falls. The rivers in the valley provide good trout fishing.

WELDBOROUGH

The **Weldborough Pass** on the Tasman Hwy is spectacular. The road approaching the pass follows a high ridge with wonderful views of the surrounding mountains. As you descend to the north, make sure you stop at the **Weldborough Pass Rainforest Walk**. It is marked with interpretive signs describing the rainforest through the eyes of 'Grandma Myrtle' on a 10-minute circuit.

The town itself is now almost deserted. Last century, tin was discovered here and the town boomed. Many of the miners were Chinese, and at one stage there were 800 Chinese here; they brought along their own culture which included a very ornate joss house, now on display in Launceston's Queen Victoria Museum & Art Gallery. Eventually the tin ran out and by the 1940s the miners had left. There were other mining towns in the area and the cemetery at Moorina to the north has an interesting Chinese section.

The only commercial building still used is the *Weldborough Hotel*, the town's only pub, which also calls itself the 'Worst Little Pub in Tassie'. It serves lunch and dinner, and is worth calling into for a meal and a drink. Don't be put off by the Irish menu which advertises delicacies like 'blow fly sponge', 'gum leaf soup' and 'maggot mornay'. The hotel also provides accommodation for $35 a double. You can also camp at *Weldborough Camping Ground* (☎ 6354 2223) where tent sites are $6 and powered sites are $8; cheap, but then there's not much there.

GLADSTONE

About 25 km to the north, off the Tasman Hwy between St Helens and Scottsdale, is the tiny town of Gladstone. It was one of the last tin-mining centres in north-eastern Tasmania, until the mine closed in 1982. The surrounding area also had a number of mining communities and a large Chinese population. Today, many old mining settlements are just ghost towns, and Gladstone shows signs of heading in the same direction. If you decide to spend the night here then the

Gladstone Hotel (☎ 6357 2143) provides B&B for $25/35.

MT WILLIAM NATIONAL PARK

This little-known park in Tasmania's north-east corner consists of sweeping sandy beaches, low ridges and coastal heathlands. The highest point, Mt William, is only 216 metres high yet provides some breathtaking views. The area was declared a national park in 1973 for the prime purpose of protecting the Forester kangaroo. This animal prefers open, grassy areas, the very lands preferred by farmers and there are now only a few places where it is found. Thankfully the kangaroos have flourished here and are seen throughout the park.

Mt William provides good views of the Furneaux group of islands, including Flinders Island. When sea levels were lower, these formed part of a land bridge to mainland Australia, which the Aboriginal people used to migrate to Tasmania. They lived mainly on shellfish and the discarded shells were tossed together to form heaps called middens. **Musselroe Point** has a very large midden, which illustrates how long Aboriginal people occupied the region.

The main activities here include birdwatching, animal watching, swimming, surfing at Picnic Rocks and diving around Stumpys Bay and Cape Naturaliste. Horse riding is allowed only under permit, so contact the ranger first on ☎ 6357 2108.

The easy climb to the rocky summit of **Mt William** takes 1½ hours return. The view extends from St Marys in the south to Flinders Island in the north. For something less strenuous, the drive south to the **Eddystone lighthouse** is also popular.

Camping in the park is very basic with only pit toilets, bore water for washing and fireplaces provided. There is no power and no fresh water; you need to bring in drinking water. Camping is allowed at four areas in Stumpys Bay, and also at Musselroe Top Camp and in the south at Deep Creek. Fires are only allowed in fireplaces and it is advisable to bring in your own wood or preferably

bring a portable stove for cooking on. In warm weather open fires are often banned.

The best seasons here are spring and early summer when the wildflowers in the heathlands are at their peak. The park is well off the main roads; the northern end is 12 km from Gladstone, the southern end 50 km from St Helens. Try to avoid driving here at night as that's the time the animals are most active. National park entry fees apply; there is a ranger station on the access road from which you can obtain a park pass.

DERBY

In 1874 tin was discovered in Derby and this little township flourished throughout the late 19th century. Several mines operated around the town and, like many other mining regions, these eventually amalgamated into one large mining company which supported a town of 3000 people. Operations continued smoothly until 1929 when the local dam burst, flooding the town and drowning many residents. The mine closed for five years, reopened, then closed again in 1940. Since then, most of the population has moved away. Instead of becoming a ghost town, Derby put the remnants of its past on display and ensured the town's future as a tourist destination.

Derby is a classified historic town and some of the old mine buildings now form part of the excellent **Derby Tin Mine Centre** (☎ 6354 2262), which is a museum and shanty town. The museum is in the old school and displays old photographs and mining implements. The re-created shanty town is very interesting with shops, mine office, cottages and a gaol. You can pan for tin in the river and walk through a reconstructed mine site. The centre is open daily from 9 am to 5 pm and is worth seeing. Admission is $4 (children $1.50, family $10). In winter, opening times are shortened to 10 am to 4 pm. The nearby mural beside the road is worth a look.

The region is famous for its minerals and gemstones. Sapphire Safaris (☎ 6354 6303) runs gem-fossicking excursions on weekends and public holidays from the nearby town of Branxholm. Tours include lunch and are \$40 to \$45 each.

Derby comes alive in late October when approximately 10,000 people arrive for the annual **Derby River Derby**. In 1995, 500 people competed in the 20th derby in rafts of every description on an eight-km course. It's like a battle with no rules and the art is simply to stay afloat; it's all immense fun with the main aim being to sink everyone else rather than to win.

At the nearby town of **Branxholm**, the Imperial Hotel has an impressive facade worth looking at and it's also a good place for a drink – but there is no accommodation. The hop fields behind the hotel can be visited by prior arrangement (☎ 6354 6127). For unique souvenirs, *Two-Headed Treasures* sells a range of two-headed items.

Places to Stay & Eat

The *Dorset Hotel* (☎ 6354 2360) has singles/doubles for \$28/45 including breakfast, and also supplies good counter meals. The *Crib Shed Tea Rooms* (part of the mine museum) specialises in country cooking and serves delicious scones. There are two other tearooms in town.

Six km from Derby, near Winnaleah, is the peaceful *Merlinkie Home Hostel* (☎ 6354 2152), which charges \$10 a night for YHA members and \$12 for others. You can ring from Winnaleah and the manager will pick you up. Being a dairy farm, it has an unlimited supply of fresh milk, and hostellers can help around the farm; you might even get to milk a cow!

Getting There & Away

On weekdays, TRC (☎ 6331 3233 or 1800 030 033) has two services daily between Launceston and Derby via Scottsdale for \$11; one goes in the morning and the other in the afternoon. There's only one service on Sunday, and none on Saturday. The TRC agent is the general store in Derby's main street. On weekdays, you can get to Winnaleah and St Helens (\$5) on the single daily service run by Suncoast (☎ 6376 1753).

SCOTTSDALE

• *pop 2000*

Scottsdale, the largest town in the north-east was named after surveyor Scott who opened the area for European settlement. The rich, fertile valleys supported farming and Scottsdale grew into the business centre of the region. Farming still has a very important role in the town.

In January and February, poppies provide a blaze of colour and there are extensive hop fields which are used to produce beer. In the town, the frozen vegetable factory produces mountains of frozen peas and French fried potatoes. The Department of Defence also keeps its food laboratories here; they produce food for the armed services.

Recently a major industry has developed, with huge pine plantations supplying future timber needs. These look like a sea of uniform dark green trees and should be thought of as tree farms as that's really what they are. Just outside town a large sawmill processes this timber and some of the remaining hardwoods.

At Nabowla, 21 km west of Scottsdale, is the **Bridestowe Lavender Farm** (☎ 6352 8182), the biggest lavender farm in Australia and the only source of perfumed lavender outside Europe. It's open daily during the spectacular flowering season from mid-December to late January when there are guided tours. At other times it's open weekdays only. Admission in flowering season is \$3 (children free); at other times, all admission is free.

The road from Scottsdale to Launceston crosses a pass called **The Sideling**. It's a good place to stop for a rest from the winding road. There are toilets, a shelter and good views. For even better views, take the road on the other side of the pass to **Mt Barrow**. A walk of about one hour return provides panoramic views over one third of Tasmania.

Places to Stay & Eat

A camp site at the *North-East Park Camping Ground* (☎ 6352 2176) costs \$5 and \$7.50 with power. Located beside the river, the camping ground is pretty but has only very basic facilities. At least it's only a short walk to the hotels. *Lords Hotel* (☎ 6352 2319), on the main highway junction in town has basic rooms for $20/30 a single/double. Nearby, the *Scottsdale Hotel/Motel* (☎ 6352 2510) is old, but has a friendly atmosphere. The huge log fire is quite an attraction on cold nights; rooms are $49 a double. Both hotels serve lunch and dinner every day.

For something à la carte try *Clarissa's Restaurant* (☎ 6352 2044) at 6 Elenor St, diagonally opposite the Scottsdale Hotel. It's open from Wednesday to Saturday for lunch and dinner. The other restaurant is *Annabel's of Scottsdale* (☎ 6352 3277). This National Trust classified building is worth a visit; a room here costs $70 a double.

Getting There & Away

For bus services from Launceston to Scottsdale, see the Getting There & Away section for Derby. To get to Bridport, take a local bus from Scottsdale; buses depart twice daily on weekdays from Roses Newsagency, which is the TRC stop in Scottsdale. You'll need your own transport to visit Tomahawk.

TOMAHAWK

Hidden halfway along the north-east coast is this low-key beach resort. With magnificent beaches and large sand dunes, it is very attractive but relatively unknown. For most of the year the beaches are completely deserted, so it's a great place to get away from other people. Located beside the Tomahawk River with a series of lagoons and lakes, it provides some excellent fishing for keen anglers. The only place to stay is the *Wanyeke Caravan Park* (☎ 6355 2268) which has camp sites for $7.50, powered sites for $9 and on-site vans for $30. Petrol is available, but bring your own food supplies.

BRIDPORT
* *pop 1160*

This well-developed holiday resort lies on the shore of Anderson Bay on the northern coast. Just 85 km from Launceston it is very popular with Tasmanians, and there are many holiday houses in town. There is a large resident population, many of whom work inland at other towns and prefer to live beside the coast where the climate is milder.

Bridport has safe swimming beaches and the sheltered waters are ideal for water-skiing. Sea, lake and river fishing are also popular activities. The town has a trout hatchery and a large commercial fishing fleet. The area is renowned for its native orchids, which flower from September through to December.

Places to Stay & Eat

The *Bridport Caravan Park* (☎ 6356 1227) is right beside the beach and has camp sites for $8 and powered sites for $11. The only hostel is the *Bridport Backpackers* (☎ 6356 1585) in Main St. It is close to the town centre and bunks are $12 each or $30 for the double rooms. Basic rooms are available at the *Bridport Hotel* (☎ 6356 1114) with B&B for $25/35.

For a higher standard B&B try the *Bridairre Modern B&B Accommodation* (☎ 6356 1438) on the hill in Frances St. There are great views of the bay, and singles/doubles are $39/59. Rooms at the *Bridport Motor Inn* (☎ 6356 1238) cost $59 to $64 a double and self-contained units with kitchen are $75 to $80 a double. For something different, try the *Platypus Park Farm Chalets* (☎ 6331 5650 or 6356 1873) just out of town beside the Brid River. Set amongst the trees, the units are $80 a double.

The Motor Inn has a bistro and the hotel serves counter meals. There are two restaurants, a bakery and the usual takeaways. The fish & chips from *Bridport Seafoods* at the jetty are good.

Getting There & Away

On weekdays, Stan's Coach Service runs from Scottsdale to Bridport twice daily. It connects with the TRC (☎ 6331 3233 or 1800 030 033) bus service from Launceston. See the Scottsdale Getting There & Away section for details.

Launceston

• *pop 66,750*

Officially founded in 1805, Launceston is Australia's third oldest city and Tasmania's second oldest city. It is the commercial centre of northern Tasmania and is today a charming blend of the old and new.

The region was originally occupied by the Tasmanian Aboriginal people who first arrived about 40,000 years ago. They lived primarily by hunting animals and the open plains of the region were highly regarded hunting grounds. The first Europeans to visit the Tamar River were Bass and Flinders in 1798, who were attempting to circumnavigate Van Diemen's Land to show that it was not joined to the rest of Australia. A large swell south of Point Hicks in Victoria had long encouraged the belief that Tasmania was an island. If this was in fact true it would result in a quicker passage to Sydney than the longer more hazardous journey around the southern Tasmanian coast.

Around the same time French explorers were also exploring the coast. Out of fear that they would also establish a colony, Colonel William Paterson set up a camp near the mouth of the Tamar River in 1804. Unfortunately, a poor site was chosen.

Launceston was the third attempt at a permanent settlement on the river and was originally called Patersonia, after its founder. In 1907, the city was renamed in honour of Governor King, who was born in Launceston, England, a town settled 1000 years before on the Tamar River in the county of Cornwall. The Aboriginal people's name for the area was Ponrabbel, and the fertile plains which the Europeans had occupied were also important Aboriginal hunting grounds. For several years there were skirmishes between the the settlers and the Aboriginals, and many Aboriginal women and children were kidnapped by sealers and whalers.

A notable event in the city's history occurred in 1835 when John Batman sailed

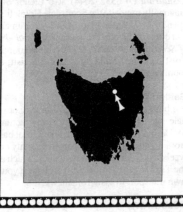

HIGHLIGHTS

- Cataract Gorge walking tracks
- Beautiful parks and gardens
- Queen Victoria Museum & Art Gallery
- The huge blue gum at Ritchies Mill

from Launceston to Victoria and founded Melbourne.

Launceston is situated at the end of the deep water channel of the Tamar River where the South Esk and North Esk Rivers join. This is 64 km inland from Bass Strait and the inland location and steep hills provide a sheltered location for the city.

Orientation

The city centre is arranged in a grid pattern centred around the Brisbane St Mall, between Charles and St John Sts. The main shopping centre is based around the mall and the nearby Quadrant Mall which is a semi-circular side street. Two blocks north, in Cameron St, there's another pedestrian mall in the centre of a block called the Civic Square, around which many of the public buildings such as the library, town hall and

LAUNCESTON

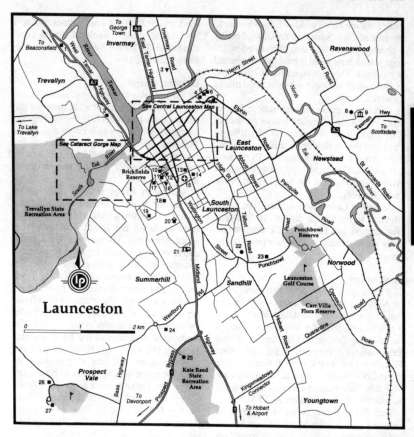

PLACES TO STAY

1. Tamar River Villa
2. Turret House
4. Cottage on the Park
5. Thyme Cottage
6. Cottage on Cimitiere
7. Bifrons Apartments
10. Brickfields Terrace
11. Parkside Backpackers
13. Sportsmans Hall Hotel
14. The Edwardian
17. Mews Motel
18. Edenholme Grange

19. Clark Holiday House
20. Launceston City Youth Hostel
21. Treasure Island Caravan Park
23. Aberdeen Court
24. Olde Tudor Motor Inn
26. Bass Villas
27. Launceston Federal Country Club Casino

PLACES TO EAT

3. Me Wah Restaurant

12. Golden Sea Dragon
16. Quigleys

OTHER

8. Waverley Woollen Mills
9. National Automobile Museum
15. Launceston General Hospital
22. Tamar Knitting Mills
25. Silverdome

police station are to be found. Two blocks to the east of Civic Square is Yorktown Square, a charming and lively area of restored buildings which have been turned into shops and restaurants. The open space is not square and is fairly small but there are some good places in which to eat.

Parks and gardens are important to the city and close to the centre are formal gardens at City Park, wide sweeping lawns of Royal Park and the smaller open spaces of Princes Square and Brickfields Reserve. To the west of the city is Cataract Gorge, a rugged natural river gorge which is the best known of the city's features.

Although Launceston suffers from a lack of street signs, it's not difficult to find your way around and Launceston's main attractions are all within walking distance of the centre.

Information

The Tasmanian Travel & Information Centre (☎ 6336 3119), on the corner of St John and Paterson Sts, is open weekdays from 9 am to 5 pm, and on Saturday and public holidays (and Sunday during the Christmas and New Year holidays) between 9 am and noon. There's a TASMAP Centre at Henty House in the Civic Square where detailed maps are available. Information can also be obtained by listening to radio station 99.3 FM.

The Post Office is on the corner of Cameron and St John Sts near Civic Square and is open from 9 am to 5 pm on weekdays and Saturday morning from 9 am to 12 noon.

Banks are open for business from 9 am to 4 pm Monday to Friday. Automatic Teller Machines (ATMs) can be used at any time and are available at most banks in the city area. Most banks have branches in St John St or Brisbane St near the mall.

The Royal Automobile Club of Tasmania (RACT) (☎ 6331 3166) has its office on the corner of George and York Sts. It provides services for members of automobile clubs from other states of Australia as well.

For bushwalking or camping gear, Paddy Pallin (☎ 6331 4240), at 110 George St, and Allgoods (☎ 6331 3644) on the corner of York and St John Sts – are both excellent. If you're in town at the weekend, there's a craft market in Yorktown Square every Sunday from 9 am to 2 pm.

Cataract Gorge

At the entrance to the magnificent Cataract Gorge, only a 10-minute walk from the city centre, almost vertical cliffs line the banks of the South Esk River as it enters the Tamar. The area around the gorge has been made a reserve for native wildlife and is one of Launceston's most popular tourist attractions.

Starting at Kings Bridge, two walking tracks, one on either side of the gorge, lead up to **First Basin**, which is filled with water from the South Esk River. The walk takes about 30 minutes. The northern trail is easier and it took eight years for local residents to construct the track through the cliffs. The southern trail is known as the Zig Zag Track and has some steep climbs as it passes along the top of the cliffs. The waters of First Basin are very cold and deep, so you may feel safer swimming in the nearby concrete pool. The landscaped area around the basin features picnic spots, the Gorge Restaurant, a cafe, rhododendrons and lots of peacocks. At night the gorge is lit up and is worth a visit.

You don't have to walk to the First Basin – there is car parking at the entrance. From the city follow York St, Hillside Crescent, Brougham St then Basin Rd. Parking fees apply so buy a ticket at the machine.

Upstream of the First Basin, the **Alexandra Suspension Bridge** crosses the river and provides a fine view of another section of the gorge. Downstream of the basin there is a concrete causeway crossing the river. At times of flood the causeway is closed.

There's also a **chair lift**, which crosses the basin to the reserve on the other side; the six-minute ride costs $4 one way or return, children $2.80. Good walking tracks lead further up the gorge to the **Second Basin** and Duck Reach, 45 minutes each way. Duck Reach is the site of the first municipal hydroelectric power station in Australia which provided power from 1895 until 1955.

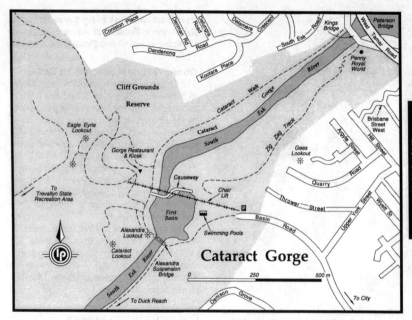

Cataract Gorge

Tracks also lead from the northern side of the First Basin to several lookouts including Cataract and Eagle Eyrie from where there are fine views.

Penny Royal World

The Penny Royal entertainment complex, which claims to take you back to a 'world of yesteryear', has exhibits including working 19th-century water mills and windmills, gunpowder mills and model boats. You can take part in mock battles firing cannons on the man-o-war sloop on the lake in the complex. You can also take a ride on a barge or on the restored city tram which provides transport between the different features. There is also a 45-minute cruise part-way up the gorge on the *Lady Stelfox* paddle-steamer. The main complex is set into an old quarry beside the entrance to Cataract Gorge and is an imaginative use of the area.

Although some parts of the Penny Royal complex are interesting, overall it's not worth the $19.50 ($9.50 for children) admission, unless you plan to spend all day here. You can, however, just pay for one of the attractions; the cruise, for instance, only costs $6.50 ($3.50 for children) or visit the Windmill and Cornmill for just $4, children $2.

Ritchies Mill Art Centre

Near Penny Royal, beside the entrance to Cataract Gorge is this 1834 flour mill and miller's cottage (see the Central Launceston map). It was originally powered by water which was delivered by a pipeline from Cataract Gorge. Beside the mill is a huge 41-metre-tall blue gum; it's 160 years old and dominates the area. With the pleasant leafy grounds and a good restaurant and the art gallery in the mill, it's a nice place to spend an hour or two.

Trevallyn Recreation Reserve

Further upstream from Duck Reach is the

A majestic specimen of the Tasmanian blue gum can be found outside Ritchies Mill

Trevallyn Dam which holds back the waters of Lake Trevallyn. A reserve of 450 hectares beside the lake provides some natural forest and bushlands for recreational use. There are picnic grounds and a motorcycle track, and archery, horse riding and bushwalking are the main activities catered for. Water-skiing is allowed on the lake as well as general boating, windsurfing and canoeing.

At the Trevallyn Dam quarry in the reserve you can do simulated hang-gliding for $7. From December to April you can glide every day from 10 am to 5 pm, in other months it's open on weekends and public holidays. The hang-glider is suspended on a 200-metre-long cable and is much safer than the real thing.

To get to the reserve follow the West Tamar Hwy past the entrance to Cataract Gorge, turn left onto Gorge Rd, then follow Bald Hill Rd, Veulalee Avenue and then Reatta Rd to the reserve. The reserve is open from 8 am until dusk every day except when the river is in flood when access is restricted. Camping is not allowed within the reserve.

Queen Victoria Museum & Art Gallery

The Queen Victoria Museum & Art Gallery in Wellington St was built late last century and displays the splendour of the period both inside and out. It has a unique collection of Tasmanian fauna, Aboriginal artefacts and colonial paintings. A major attraction is the splendid joss house, donated by the descendants of Chinese settlers. The centre is open Monday to Saturday from 10 am to 5 pm, and from 2 to 5 pm on Sunday. The gallery and museum are free. There is a coffee shop inside the museum.

The museum has a planetarium, which is one of only four in Australia. It costs $3, children $2 or family $7, and is open for showings at 2 pm and 3 pm Tuesday to Saturday plus the same times on Monday during school holidays.

Community History Museum

The historic Johnstone & Wilmot warehouse, on the corner of Cimitiere and St John Sts, dates from 1842 and holds the Community History Museum. It houses the city's local-history archives and is open from 10 am to 4 pm Monday to Saturday and from 2 to 4 pm on Sunday; admission is $1.

Historic Buildings

There is less of an architectural heritage left in Launceston than in Hobart and other towns in Tasmania. The older buildings that still exist however, are more varied than those seen elsewhere because they are from several architectural periods. In response to the local availability of materials, less sandstone has been used than elsewhere in Tasmania, and there has been a greater use of bricks.

In the Civic Square is **Macquarie House**, built in 1830 as a warehouse but later used as a military barracks and office building. It now houses part of the Queen Victoria Museum & Art Gallery and is open from 10 am to 4 pm Monday to Saturday, and on Sunday afternoon.

The **Town Hall**, also on Civic Square, is an imposing building from 1864 in a Victorian Italianate style. Directly opposite the Town Hall in Cameron St, the **Post Office** is an interesting building with its unique round clock tower.

One block away at 35 Cameron St, the **Batman Fawkner Inn** was originally built as a hotel in 1848. Before the hotel was built, this was the site of the historic meeting to plan the founding of Melbourne and there are many mementos of that meeting on display. The Inn is still used as a modern hotel/motel.

One corner of City Park contains **Albert Hall**, which was erected in 1891 for a trade fair. The hall has been in constant use as a public venue ever since and features an unusual water organ.

The **Old Umbrella Shop**, at 60 George St, was built in the 1860s and still houses a selection of umbrellas. Classified by the National Trust, it is the last genuine period shop in the state. The interior is lined with Tasmanian blackwood timber, and the shop sells a good range of National Trust items. It's open from 9 am to 5 pm on weekdays and from 9 am to noon on Saturday.

You can pick up a copy of the *Historic Walks* brochure and view the city's architectural heritage at your own pace or join a tour (see Organised Tours below). Many of Launceston's churches were constructed between 1830 and 1860. The wide range of religions and denominations represented reflect the influence of the 1837 Church Act which, in addition to acknowledging the existence of all religions, exempted places of worship from many taxes. By 1860 there were 12 churches. On the Civic Square block are the Pilgrim Uniting and St Andrews churches, and in St John St opposite Princes Square is St Johns Church. The Launceston Historical Society produces a free brochure about the churches which is available from the Community History Museum.

On the Midland Hwy six km south-west of the city is **Franklin House**, one of Launceston's most attractive two-storey

Georgian homes. It was built in 1838 and has been beautifully restored and furnished by the National Trust. An outstanding feature of its interior is the woodwork, which has been carved from New South Wales red cedar. The house is open daily from 9 am to 5 pm (4 pm in June, July and August) and admission is $5, children $3 or $10 for a family. To get there by bus, take Metro bus Nos 20, 22 or 25 from St John St near the mall.

Parks & Gardens

Launceston is sometimes referred to as 'the garden city', and with so many beautiful public squares, parks and reserves, it's easy to understand why.

The 13-hectare **City Park** is a pleasant example of a Victorian garden and features an elegant fountain, a bandstand, a monkey enclosure, a wallaby enclosure and a conservatory. **Princes Square**, between Charles and St John Sts, features a bronze fountain bought at the 1858 Paris Exhibition.

Other public parks and gardens include **Royal Park**, near the junction of the North Esk and Tamar rivers; the **Punchbowl Reserve**, with its magnificent rhododendron garden; **Windmill Hill Reserve**; the **Trevallyn Recreation Area** and the magnificent **Cataract Gorge**.

Other Attractions

The **Design Centre of Tasmania**, on the corner of Brisbane and Tamar Sts, is a retail outlet displaying work by Tasmania's top artists and craftspeople.

The **Waverley Woollen Mills** and **National Automobile Museum** are on Waverley Rd, five km to the east of the city centre. The mills were established in 1874 and are the oldest operating woollen mills in Australia. In 1889 the mill installed a hydro-electricity generating station and it is believed to be the first hydro plant in the southern hemisphere. Both places are open daily from 9 am to 5 pm; admission to each is $4.

The **Tamar Knitting Mills**, founded in 1926, are at 21 Hobart Rd near the corner of Wellington St and Talbot Rd. Socks and

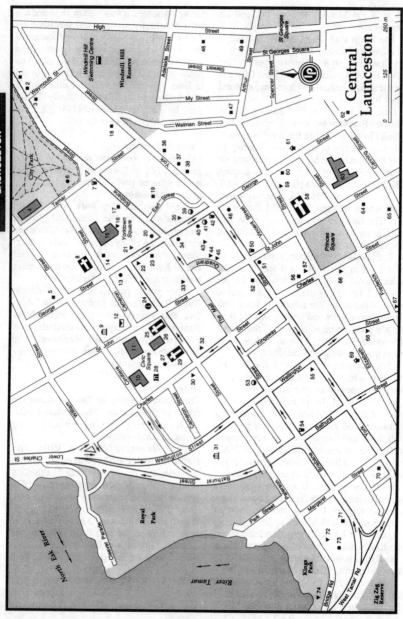

PLACES TO STAY		PLACES TO EAT			
1	Sandors On The Park	7	Royal Oak Hotel	6	Design Centre of Tasmania
2	North Lodge Motel	16	Tairyo Japanese	8	Holy Trinity Church
3	Parklane Motel		Restaurant & Sushi	9	Community History
5	Lloyds Hotel		Bar		Museum
14	Batman Fawkner Inn	21	La Cantina	10	Police Station
15	Novotel Launceston	22	Shrimps	11	Town Hall
	Hotel	30	Arpar's Thai Restaurant	12	Post Office
17	Maldon	32	Star Bar	13	Old Umbrella Shop
18	Adina Place	33	Banjo's	20	Ansett Airlines
19	Great Northern Hotel	35	Konditorei Cafe	24	Travel & Information
23	Royal Hotel		Manfred		Centre
36	York Mansions	42	O'Keefes Hotel	25	St Andrews Church
37	Ivy Cottage	43	Muffin Kitchen	26	Library
38	Balmoral Motor Inn	44	Crows Nest Coffee	27	Tasmap Centre
47	Highfield House		Shoppe	28	Macquarie House
48	Windmill Hill Tourist	45	Pasta Resistance Too	29	Pilgrim Uniting Church
	Lodge	50	St George Hotel	31	Queen Victoria
49	Ashton Gate Guest	54	Victoria Hotel &		Museum & Art
	House		Alfresco's		Gallery
52	St James Hotel	55	Barnaby's Hotel	34	Qantas Airlines
56	Hotel Tasmania &	57	Canton	39	Tasmanian Wilderness
	Saloon	59	Three Steps On George		Travel
60	Colonial Motor Inn	66	Elm Cottage	40	Paddy Pallin
61	Launceston City	67	Pizza Pub	41	Tasmanian Redline
	Backpackers	68	Calabrisella Pizza		Coaches
62	Hilview House	72	Owl's Nest	46	Royal Automobile Club
64	Airlee Dorset Terrace	74	Ripples Restaurant		of Tasmania
65	Canning Cottage			51	Allgoods
69	YHA summer hostel	**OTHER**		53	Hobart Coaches
70	Old Bakery Inn			58	St Johns Church
71	Rose Lodge	4	Albert Hall	63	St Andrews Hospital
73	Penny Royal Village			74	Ritchies Mil Art Centre

LAUNCESTON

embroidery are the specialities produced here and the mill is open daily from 9 am to 4 pm; admission is $1, children free.

Organised Tours

The Coach Tram Tour Company (☎ 6336 3122) runs three-hour trips around the sights of Launceston for $19. Tours leave at 10 am and 2 pm daily. A Country History Dinner, which leaves at 6 pm and includes dinner for $35, operates on Tuesday, Thursday and Saturday.

For something unusual, try the tour of private country homes and gardens that is organised by Behind The Colonial Gate, (☎ 6334 4065). Tours run during winter from May to September and are $55 each.

If you just want a guided walk around the city centre, then Launceston Historic Walks (☎ 6331 3679) departs daily at the Tasma-

nian Travel and Information Centre on the corner of St John and Paterson Sts at 9.45 am. The tour finishes at 11 am and costs $10.

Tasmanian Redline Coaches (☎ 6331 3233) in George St has half and full-day tours of the Tamar Valley ($33), the north-west coast ($32), the north-east ($40) and Cradle Mountain ($39). During summer they also run trips to Deloraine ($40) and to the lavender farm at Brindelstowe ($24).

Tasmanian Wilderness Transport (☎ 6334 4442) has tours to Evandale Market on Sunday ($20), Tamar Valley ($35), Cradle Mountain ($40) and the Mole Creek caves ($42). It also runs two-day trips to Strahan and the Gordon River (from $99) and three-day trips to Cradle Mountain ($439).

Festivals

Cataract Gorge forms the backdrop for many

of Launceston's events. In February there is the **Basin Concert**, a rock concert held at the First Basin. In March the same place is used for a more cultural concert called **A Night in the Gorge** with the Tasmanian Symphony Orchestra. Both of these events are popular with the local residents.

In February, race horses compete for the Launceston Cup and during Easter the trotting track comes alive for the Easter Cup Pacing Championship. Once winter is over there is a whole series of small festivals and art shows. The Launceston Spring Festival in September and the Royal Launceston Show in October are the major events.

Places to Stay

Camping & Cabins The only caravan park in the city is the *Treasure Island Caravan Park* (☎ 6344 2600) in Glen Dhu St, two km south of the city beside the Midland Hwy. It has camp sites ($11) and cabins ($42). As this is the only caravan park in Launceston, it can get crowded at times, and being right next to the highway is quite noisy.

Hostels Conveniently located on the edge of the city centre is the smoke-free *Launceston City Backpackers* (☎ 6334 2327) at 173 George St. It's an old house which has been thoughtfully renovated, and the cost is $14 per person in four-bed rooms or $15 each for a double room.

The *Launceston City Youth Hostel* (☎ 6344 9779), which is not a YHA hostel, is at 36 Thistle St, two km from the centre of town. It is just off Glen Dhu St and close to the caravan park. Dormitory beds and family rooms are $12 per adult and $5 for children. The building dates from the 1940s and used to be the canteen for the Coats Patons Woollen Mill. The hostel has mountain and touring bikes for hire as well as a comprehensive selection of bushwalking gear.

During school holidays the *Parkside Backpackers* (☎ 6331 4615) at 103 Canning St provides good basic smoke-free accommodation for $14 per person. Other hostels regularly appear and vanish the next season; some former backpackers are now upmarket

B&Bs. At present the YHA runs a summer-only hostel at 132 Elizabeth St (☎ 6334 4505) for $14 a night; advance bookings can be made through the Hobart YHA office (☎ 6234 9617).

Guesthouses & B&Bs The *Rose Lodge* (☎ 6334 0120) provides friendly service and small, but comfortable rooms with a cooked breakfast for $50/65 a single/double at 270 Brisbane St. This is beside the windmill at Penny Royal, on the west side of the city. Just around the corner, heading south down Margaret St, the *Mews Motel* (☎ 6331 2861), at No 89, is closer to a guesthouse than a motel and is also reasonably priced at $55 a double including a continental breakfast.

On the same side of town, but further out, is the more expensive *Edenholme Grange* (☎ 6334 6666) at 14 St Andrews St. It's in a side street off Hillside Crescent (the road to First Basin) and rates are $60 to $70 for singles and $106 to $130 a double. It does not cater for children.

South of the city centre, and only a 10-minute walk away near Princes Square, is *Airlee Dorset Terrace* (☎ 6334 2162) at 138 St John St. Located in a set of terrace houses, a cooked breakfast is included in the tariff of $61/80. One block away at 193 George St is *Hillview House* (☎ 6331 7388) where B&B is $50/65. Even closer to town at 32 Brisbane St, the *Maldon* (☎ 6331 3211) provides good rooms in a grand Victorian building for $60/70 for singles/doubles.

The east side of the city is bounded by a steep hill on which some of the earlier mansions were constructed. Today some of these provide good B&B accommodation. While you can walk into town, the hill is very steep. The *Windmill Hill Tourist Lodge* (☎ 6331 9337) at 22 High St, charges $47/57 without breakfast. The lodge also has self-contained holiday flats at $65 a double.

If you can afford the extra cost, there are some great guesthouses offering rather luxurious colonial accommodation, such as the cosy *Ashton Gate Guest House* (☎ 6331 6180) on top of the hill on the corner of High and Arthur Sts. With a cooked breakfast, the cost is $60/80 for singles/doubles or $100 for the best rooms. A short way down the hill, and with better views, is *Highfield House* (☎ 6334 3485) on the corner of Welman and Arthur Sts where B&B is $70/100.

If you prefer to be out of town, then head for *Turret House* (☎ 6334 7033) at 41 West Tamar Road on the west side of the Tamar River. Cataract Gorge is reasonably close and there are excellent views across the river. A cooked breakfast is included for $50/90.

Hotels Launceston has a good selection of hotels for a town of its size and they vary from old one-star buildings to modern four-star hotels. One of the cheapest and quietest places is the *Sportsman's Hall Hotel* (☎ 6331 3968) which is at 252 Charles St. Here, singles/doubles are $28/40, including breakfast. Closer to town, at 191 Charles St, is the *Hotel Tasmania* (☎ 6331 7355), which is better known as the *Saloon*. The rooms have a fridge and telephone for $50/60, including breakfast.

In the town centre, there are several older hotels that are all very similar and all include breakfast in the tariffs. *Royal Hotel* (☎ 6331 2526) at 90 George St is $44 a double, *St George Hotel* (☎ 6331 7277) at 119 St John St is $35/50, *Lloyds Hotel* (☎ 6331 4966) at 23 George St is $30/48 and *St James Hotel* (☎ 6331 6122) at 122 York St is $35/45 for singles/doubles.

Further out of town, *Sandors On The Park* (☎ 6331 2055), at 3 Brisbane St, provides good standard rooms for $60/72. Similar standard rooms are also available at *Penny Royal Village* (☎ 6331 6699), 145 Paterson St. The rooms are more expensive at $120, a double but then it's right beside the entrance to Cataract Gorge. They also have motel rooms for the same price.

For four-star hotels close to town, the *Great Northern Hotel* (☎ 1800 030 567) at 3 Earl St is very close to Yorktown Square. Rooms in the multistorey building start at $112 a double. Of the same standard is the *Novotel Launceston* (☎ 6334 3434) at 29 Cameron St, where rooms start at $140 a double.

If you really want to be pampered then try the *Country Club Casino* (☎ 6444 8855) at Prospect Vale, five km south of the city. At $198 a double, you will need some extra cash for those gaming tables!

Motels There are a large number of motels, most are of a similar standard. Those around the city centre are either refurbished old hotels or multistorey motels, while the motels in the suburbs are the more familiar two-storey modern style.

Most motels are located east of the city centre in either York or Brisbane Sts and are about one km from town. The cheapest in this area is *North Lodge* (☎ 6331 9966) at 7 Brisbane St where rooms are $55 a double. Next door at 9 Brisbane St is *Parklane Motel* (☎ 6331 4233) where rooms are $75 a double and self-contained rooms are $80.

Much closer to town is the *Batman Fawkner Inn* (☎ 6331 7222) at 35 Cameron St next door to Yorktown Square. Rooms at this historic site are $42/62 which includes breakfast.

There are plenty of rooms of various sizes and styles at *Adina Place* (☎ 6331 6866) at 55 York St. The rooms on the upper floors have excellent views across the city and start from $65 a double. Closer to town at 19 York St *Balmoral Motor Inn* (☎ 6331 8000 or 1800 805 090) is another multistorey motel with rooms at $88/95 for singles/doubles.

On the west side of the city the *Old Bakery Inn* (☎ 6331 7900) on the corner of York and Margaret Sts has some real history to it. It was established as a bakery in 1870 and many of the architectural features have been retained. Motel-style rooms are $62/79.

An attractive, but pricey, motel in town is the *Colonial Motor Inn* (☎ 6331 6588) on the corner of George and Elizabeth Sts where rooms are $120 a double.

Five km out of the city beside the Tamar River, the *Riverside Motel* (☎ 6327 2522) at 407 West Tamar Road charges $55/60 for rooms with breakfast supplied. Nearby, the *Tamar River Villa* (☎ 6327 1022), at 23 Elouera St, is beside the same highway and has rooms for $65 or apartments for $85. If you prefer to be south of the city then the *Olde Tudor Motor Inn* (☎ 6344 5044), on Westbury Road, is beside the old highway to Devonport. It's four km from town and rooms are $70/82.

Holiday Flats & Apartments.

Holiday units and flats are aimed more at longer stays, and usually much better rates are offered for stays of one week or longer. Rates for single nights only have been given here. The closest unit to town is at 17 York St where the *Ivy Cottage* (☎ 6334 2231) will set you back $120 for two.

Nearby, the *York Mansions* (☎ 6334 2933) at 9 York St, have five apartments in an 1840 National Trust-classified building. The luxury and opulence is reflected in the $140 a double rate, which includes breakfast. Also near town, *The Edwardian* (☎ 6331 4089) at 227 Charles St has three suites which are $65/85 for singles/doubles.

About one km east of town, *Bifrons Apartments* (☎ 6331 2428) at 1 Bifrons Crt is beside the junction of Brisbane and High Sts. The three apartments are rather ordinary but the price is attractive being only $48/53 plus $5 for each extra adult and $3 for children.

Although a little difficult to find, *Clarke Holiday House* (☎ 6334 2237) at 19 Neika Ave, is about one km out of town and is good value at $35 to $40 a double. To find it, follow the main road of Hillside Crescent then Brougham Street towards the First Basin at Cataract Gorge. Neika Avenue runs left off Brougham Street just past where Basin Road starts.

Most other units are well away from the city centre. *Aberdeen Court* (☎ 6344 5811 or 1800 006 042) at 35 Punchbowl Rd in the suburb of Sandhill has units which are really motel rooms with kitchens. They are a reasonable $48/62 for singles/doubles. To stay near the Casino at a reasonable price consider the two units at *Bass Villas* (☎ 6244 7259). Located at 1 Casino Rise, close to the casino entrance, the rate is $70 per double plus $6 for each extra adult. Each unit can sleep up to eight people.

Cottages For something really different, you could try renting your own fully furnished colonial cottage. The *Canning Cottage* (☎ 6331 4876) is two separate two-storey cottages at 26-28 Canning St. They are both very cosy and there are lots of steep steps and narrow doorways; these are original cottages. The cost is very reasonable at $75 double including breakfast plus $15 for each extra person.

North-east of the city centre, near City Park, *Cottage on the Park*, 29 Lawrence St and *Cottage on Cimitiere*, 33 Cimitiere St, are both two-bedroom cottages that sleep up to five people. With breakfast provided, rates are $130 a double plus $30 for each extra person. For both cottages enquire at 27 Lawrence St (☎ 6334 2238).

Next door at 31 Cimitiere St, *Thyme Cottage* (☎ 6398 5129) can be exclusively yours for $100 a double plus $10 for extra adults.

On the opposite side of town is *Brickfields Terrace* (☎ 6330 1753) at 64 and 68 Margaret St. This is actually two separate townhouses and each can be rented for $135 a double plus $32 for extra adults. They overlook the Brickfields Reserve where bricks were made last century. Enquiries must be made by telephone (☎ 6330 1753) as the owners live elsewhere in town.

Places to Eat

Cafes & Light Meals *Banjo's* bakes all its own breads, pizzas and cakes, and has two shops in town, one in Yorktown Square and one at 98 Brisbane St; both are open daily from 6 am to 6 pm. At Yorktown Square, *Molly York's Coffee Shoppe* is another fine place for breakfast and lunch.

For lunches there are some good-value places around the city's Quadrant, a series of arcades and lanes worth exploring. The best bargain has to be *Pasta Resistance Too* with serves at $4 to $7. It's a tiny place that is always packed with customers. In a side lane off the Quadrant, the *Muffin Kitchen* is worth finding as it provides some interesting light meals.

If you would prefer somewhere more

peaceful, then try the *Crows Nest Coffee Shoppe* which is upstairs on the corner of the Quadrant and the side lane to the Muffin Kitchen. Meals range from $7 to $10.

The *Konditorei Cafe Manfred* has delicious, inexpensive home-made German rolls and pastries. It's at 95 George St, near the Redline depot, and a good place to sit while waiting for a bus. *Ripples Restaurant*, in the Ritchies Mill Art Centre, opposite Penny Royal, specialises in light meals such as crêpes and pancakes, and there's a lovely view of the boats on the Tamar River from the outdoor tables.

Pub Meals Most of Launceston's many hotels have filling, reasonably priced counter meals and most are open seven days a week, but there is usually a surcharge on Sunday. The most popular pub for meals is *Barnaby's* on the corner of Wellington and York Sts. There are over 30 main courses many of which are the same fare offered in different sizes, prices range from $7 to $14. *O'Keefes Hotel* at 124 George St is another popular pub for meals with prices in the $8 to $15 range.

If you don't get put off by the Wild West decor at the *Saloon*, 191 Charles St, then you will find some pretty cheap meals as nothing is over $10 on the menu. If you like seafood then try the *Royal Oak Hotel* at 14 Brisbane St where mains range from $8 to $12.

Some of the larger hotels also have bistros which offer similar menus to the pubs. At the Great Northern Hotel at 3 Earl St, *Oscars Bistro* serves family fare in the $12 to $18 price range. At the back of the Batman Fawkner Inn, at 35 Cameron St, is *Pascoes* which has grills and seafood for $9 to $13. Bistro meals are also available at the *Star Bar* at 113 Charles St.

Just out of town at 111 Wellington St, the *Pizza Pub* offers an unusual range of meals with pizzas (what a surprise), pasta and crêpes on offer. While the prices are reasonable you will get better pizzas at the takeaway pizza shop near the hotel on the other side of Wellington St. In the same area, the *Sportmans Hall Hotel* on the corner of Balfour and Charles Sts offers better value with the normal range of good cheap pub meals.

Restaurants There are also some good restaurants in Launceston charging $10 to $16 for a main course. One of the most popular is *Calabrisella Pizza* (☎ 6331 1958), at 56 Wellington St, which serves excellent Italian food and is often packed, so bookings are advisable. It opens at 5 pm every day except Tuesday and usually closes at midnight. You can also get takeaway pizza.

The *La Cantina* (☎ 6331 7835), at 63 George St beside Yorktown Square, is a popular licensed restaurant with pasta and other Italian dishes for $10 to $18. *Arpar's Thai Restaurant* (☎ 6331 2786), on the corner of Charles and Paterson Sts, is well worth a visit, and main courses cost around $12.

The larger hotels and motels have some fine restaurants which are often overlooked when you are staying elsewhere. In the Colonial Motor Inn in George St, *Three Steps on George* (☎ 6334 2084) has a wide range of à la carte dishes. *Snappers* (☎ 6331 9999) in the Great Northern Hotel at 3 Earl St, serves mainly seafood either in a buffet or à la carte.

If you prefer Chinese food, try the *Canton* (☎ 6331 9448) at 201 Charles St; it's one of the best moderately priced Chinese restaurants in town. The *Golden Sea Dragon* (☎ 6331 7728) at 97 Canning St, on the edge of town, has a rather elaborate interior, but reasonable prices. The *Me Wah Restaurant* (☎ 6331 1308) at 39 Invermay Rd, two km out of town just north of Cataract Gorge, provides a range of regional styles of Chinese food.

For good Tasmanian wines and excellent food, try the *Owl's Nest* (☎ 6331 6699) at 147 Paterson St, next to the Penny Royal complex. The *Gorge Restaurant* (☎ 6331 3330), at Cataract Gorge, has fairly good food and undoubtedly the best setting in Launceston with main courses for $15 to $20. It's open every evening except Sunday.

For upmarket eating try *Shrimps* (☎ 6334 0584), at 72 George St for seafood and an

LAUNCESTON

intimate atmosphere. For French dining in style try the rather expensive *Elm Cottage* (☎ 6331 8468) at 168 Charles St. It's open from Tuesday to Saturday. Launceston's Japanese restaurant and sushi bar is the *Tairyo* (☎ 6334 2620) at Yorktown Square. It is open every evening and mains are \$14 to \$22.

South of the city centre, *Quigleys* (☎ 6331 6971), at 96 Balfour St, is in an 1860s terrace house and provides some of the city's best meals. Main are just under \$20 and they specialise in game, with venison, duckling and crocodile on the menu.

As you would expect the Country Club Casino has several places to eat. The *Terrace Restaurant* (☎ 6335 5777) is open from Tuesday to Saturday providing 1st-class food. If you are hungry then an interesting choice here is 'Temptations of the Terrace' which includes a three-course meal plus a bottle of fine wine for \$40 per person.

Entertainment

There's quite a good choice of evening entertainment in Launceston, most of which is advertised in the daily newspaper *The Examiner* and some are also announced in the free *Launceston Week* newspaper or in the free *This Week in Tasmania*.

The *Pavilion Tavern* in Yorktown Square has music Tuesday to Saturday nights and a cabaret-style nightclub. The *Saloon* at 191 Charles St provides dancing in a trendy western setting while the *Royal Hotel*, in George St, is another popular venue for live bands from Wednesday to Saturday nights. *O'Keefes Hotel* at 124 George St has live bands on Friday, Saturday and Sunday after 10 pm. *Alfresco's* is a popular wine bar in the Victoria Hotel, 211 Brisbane St. Major events are held in the *Silverdome* at Prospect, south of the junction of the Bass Hwy to Devonport and the Midland Hwy to Hobart. You can inspect the Silverdome on Tuesday, Wednesday and Thursday at 10.30 to 11 am and 2.30 to 3 pm for \$1.50, children \$0.50.

If you want to risk a few dollars, or just observe how the rich play, check out the *Launceston Federal Country Club Casino* at Prospect, 10 km from the city centre. Most big-name bands touring from the mainland usually perform here. You don't have to pay to get in and dress standards have been relaxed. As long as you are tidy and clean you will be let in, although after 7.30 pm if you are wearing shorts, sports shoes and tee shirts you won't. The disco at the casino, *Regines*, is also free, and the drinks are not as expensive as you might expect.

Getting There & Away

Air Daily flights operate from Launceston to Melbourne and connect to the other capital cities of Australia. For information on domestic flights to and from Launceston, see the Getting There & Away chapter at the beginning of this book. Ansett Airlines is at 54 Brisbane St, Qantas is on the corner of Brisbane and George Sts and Airlines of Tasmania has an office at the airport.

Regular flights also operate from Launceston to Flinders Island (see The Islands chapter for details) as well as to the other major towns in Tasmania. Charter flights with the small airlines can also be arranged to most destinations.

Bus The main bus companies operating out of Launceston are Tasmanian Redline Coaches (TRC) (☎ 6331 3233), 112 George St; Hobart Coaches (☎ 6334 3600), 174-180 Brisbane St; Tasmanian Wilderness Transport (☎ 6334 4442), 101 George St; and Tamar Valley Coaches (☎ 6334 0828), 26 Wellington St.

Both TRC and Hobart Coaches run several buses every day from Hobart to Launceston (\$17.80), then along the north coast to Deloraine (\$7), Devonport (\$12.50) and Burnie (\$16.70). The TRC service along the north coast also extends to Wynyard, Stanley and Smithton (\$26.40).

TRC also runs buses from Launceston to Conara Junction, then through St Marys to St Helens (\$16.60) on the east coast. It also runs a bus into the north-east as far as Derby (\$11), and Suncoast (☎ 6376 1753) runs a connecting service from there to St Helens.

Along the Tamar Valley, Tamar Valley

Coaches runs a weekday only service along the west side of the river. TRC runs services along the west side of the Tamar to George Town ($6).

Tasmanian Wilderness Transport has services to Ben Lomond during the ski season ($25), as well as Cradle Mountain ($35) and across the central plateau to Cynthia Bay ($45) during summer. For details of services to other destinations see the relevant sections in this book.

Car There are plenty of car-rental firms in Launceston. Some of the cheaper ones are Apple Car Rentals (☎ 6343 3780), 192 Wellington St; Advance Car Rentals (☎ 6344 2164), 32 Cameron St; and Aberdeen Car Rentals (☎ 6344 5811), 35 Punchbowl Rd. Prices range from $30 to over $100 for a single day. Most firms give discounts for multi-day hire except for the really cheap prices where a surcharge is applied for single-day hire. Ask before hiring if insurance is included in the rates as insurance is compulsory and can double the cheaper rental prices.

Getting Around
To/From the Airport The airport is 16 km south of the city. Tasmanian Redline Coaches (☎ 6331 3233) operates an airport shuttle service which meets all incoming flights and leaves about an hour or so before all departures. You can board the bus at the terminal at 112 George St or you can arrange for the bus to collect you from any of the major hotels in the city. The fare is $6.60. By taxi it costs about $20 to get to/from the city.

Bus The local bus service is run by Metro, and the main departure points are the two blocks in St John St, between Paterson and York Sts. For $2.50 you can buy a Day Rover ticket which can be used for unlimited travel all day at weekends and between 9 am and 4.30 pm and after 6 pm on weekdays. Most routes, however, do not operate in the evenings, and Sunday services are limited. If you are staying in Launceston for some time you can buy books of 10 tickets for about a 25% discount; these tickets do not have to be used consecutively and have no expiry date.

Bicycle Rent-a-Cycle, at the Launceston City Youth Hostel (☎ 6344 9779), has a good range of 10-speed tourers and mountain bikes. The tourers cost $10 a day or $65 a week, including helmet and panniers; and the mountain bikes cost $90 a week. There's a reducing rate for each additional week, and a bond of $50 applies to all rentals.

Around Launceston

HADSPEN

• *pop 1330*

Fifteen km south-west of Launceston is the popular residential area of Hadspen. Some attractive Georgian buildings from last century still survive and the **Red Feather Inn**, **Hadspen Gaol** and the **Church of the Good Shepherd** are definitely worth looking at.

Two km past Hadspen on the western side of the South Esk River is **Entally House**, one of Tasmania's best known historic homes. It was built in 1819 by Thomas Haydock Reibey but is now owned by the National Trust. Located in beautiful grounds, it creates a vivid picture of what life must have been like for the well-to-do on an early farming property. The home, its stables, church, coach house and grounds are open daily from 10.30 am to 12.30 pm and 1 pm to 5 pm. Admission is $5, children $3 or a family $10. The Reibeys have quite an interesting family history; for example, Thomas Haydock Reibey's mother was a convict. You can read more in a brochure which is on sale at the property ($1.50).

Places to Stay & Eat

In Hadspen, on the corner of the Bass Hwy and Main Rd, is the *Launceston Cabin & Tourist Park* (☎ 6393 6391). The park has good facilities and charges $9 for a camp site, $30 for an on-site van and $45 for well-equipped cabins.

On the other side of the South Esk River near Entally House is the resort complex of *Rutherglen Holiday Village* (☎ 6393 6307). Motel rooms are $69 a double or holiday units are $79 a double. This is a fully self-contained resort, complete with bars and its own Chinese restaurant.

For international à la carte meals try the *Red Feather Inn* (☎ 6393 6331) at 42 Main St. It was built in 1844 and is open every night from 6.30 pm to 8.30 pm.

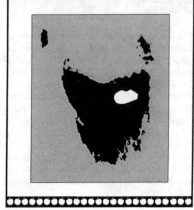

HIGHLIGHTS

• Penny Farthing Race at Evandale
• Clarendon, a grand Georgian mansion
• Ben Lomond views and walks

CARRICK

• *pop 325*

Located 19 km south-west of Launceston on the old highway to Deloraine this small village was a major grain-growing area in the 19th century. Today it is home to several artists, and its most prominent feature is the large four-storey mill beside the old Bass Hwy. It has been restored and now operates as a restaurant (see below). Behind the mill, in Bishopsbourne Rd, is the grand and dramatic ruin known as **Archers Folly**. It's been burnt down twice but the owners are determined to restore it; in the meantime they run the **Copper Art Gallery** (☎ 6393 6440), next door to the ruin. It's open daily and well worth a visit as the art is innovative and unusual, there are no entry fees and all works are for sale.

For food, the *Mill Restaurant* (☎ 6393 6922) is open every day from November to

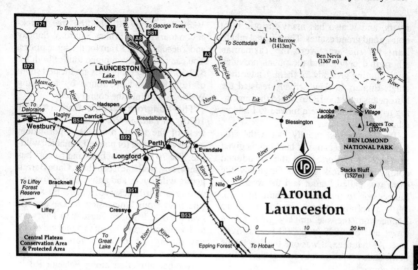

April for lunch and every day except Sunday for dinner. In the other months it's open from Thursday to Sunday for lunch and Thursday to Saturday for dinner.

Nearby is *Stables Restaurant* (☎ 6393 6416). It's set back off the highway next to the Prince of Wales Hotel (now a private house) and is open on Thursday, Friday and Saturday for dinner. For hotel counter meals the *Carrick Inn* beside the highway offers lunch and dinner every day.

Just off Bishopsbourne Rd is *Hawthorn Villa Guest House* (☎ 6393 6150) where B&B is available for $65/99, or you can hire a cottage for the same price.

LIFFEY VALLEY

The Liffey Valley is a small farming community at the foot of the Great Western Tiers and is well known to most Tasmanians. What has made the valley famous is that it is the home of Dr Bob Brown, the conservationist who turned to politics and is leader of the Green Party. It is no coincidence that the Western Tasmania World Heritage Area starts at the back fence of Dr Brown's property.

Of major interest to most visitors is the **Liffey Forest Reserve**, which features the impressive Liffey Valley Falls. There are two approaches to the falls, which are actually three separate waterfalls. From the upstream car park it's a one-hour return walk on marked tracks. You can also follow the river upstream through forest; allow two to three hours return.

The valley is also a popular destination for fishing, and day-trippers are also attracted by an amazing fernery. The fernery, tearooms and gallery were built from pine, tea tree and melaleuca timbers. You can sit in the tearooms, enjoy freshly made scones and take in the view of Drys Bluff, which, at 1297 metres, is the highest peak in the Great Western Tiers. The fernery and tearooms are open from Wednesday to Sunday between 11 am and 5 pm but are closed during July. Liffey is 34 km south of Carrick, via Bracknell, and is a good day trip from Launceston.

LONGFORD

• *pop 2600*

Longford, is 27 km south of Launceston, and is classified as an historic town. The surrounding region is a rich pastoral area watered by the South Esk and Macquarie rivers, and it also has many historic farm houses and grand estates. The original inhabitants of the area were the Tasmanian Aboriginal people and the plains provided good hunting grounds for them. Under their chief, Eumarrah, they actively resisted the Europeans until the 1830s, when the remaining tribal members were moved to Flinders Island.

The Europeans initially called the area Norfolk Plains because of land grants given in 1812 to settlers from the abandoned colony on Norfolk Island. Originally the town was called Latour and the road from Launceston to the town was built in 1813. With a reliable transportation route to Launceston, the site quickly grew into a town, and by 1823 over 500 people lived here. At that time, it was one the few towns in the state established by free settlers rather than convicts.

Based around a village green, called **Memorial Park**, the town is best known for its Georgian architecture. Buildings worth seeing are the Baptist Church, Christ Church, a large warehouse in Union St, the town hall, library and the Queens Arms Hotel.

One of the best ways to explore this historic town is to follow the National Trust's *The Path of History* brochure, which will take you past many colonial buildings. Along with other information, it is available from the Information Centre near the corner of Wellington and Marlborough Sts in the centre of town.

In the early 1960s Longford's streets were used for motor car races and several Grand Prix races were held here. While there are no longer any races, the Country Club Hotel in Wellington St has a large collection of photos and relics of that period. Today the town is much quieter: the **Longford Garden Festival** in November is the highlight of the year.

The rich farming lands near the town supported many estates and two of the earliest are **Woolmers** and **Brickendon**. These farms were established by William Thomas Archer and you can go on guided tours of the estates. Tours to Woolmers operate daily at

10.30 am for $7.50, children free. Brickendon tours run on Friday, Saturday, Sunday and Tuesday at 10.30 am for the same prices. You can also do a combined tour of both for $12.50. The two properties are located south of Longford and are found by following Wellington St into the countryside.

The **Longford Wildlife Park** (☎ 6391 1630), on Pateena Rd, about 14 km northwest of the town, provides a permanent conservation area for native Tasmanian wildlife. The 70 hectares of bush and pasture has kangaroos, wallabies, echidnas, Cape Barren geese, wild ducks and native birds. You can also approach the reserve from the Bass Hwy (the road from Launceston to Devonport) near Carrick. It's open Tuesday to Thursday and weekends from 10 am to 5 pm and every day during school and public holidays. Admission is $4, children $2.

Another attraction along Pateena Rd is **Bowthorpe** (☎ 6391 1253), a country farm and gardens started in 1825. You can walk through the extensive gardens and lanes of the farm and have afternoon tea in one of the cottages. It's open every day from 10 am to 5 pm and entry is $4 each or $10 for a family.

Places to Stay & Eat

The *Riverside Caravan Park* (☎ 6391 1470), on the banks of the Macquarie River, has quiet shady camping and is very close to the centre of town. Tent sites are $9 and on-site vans are $30 a double.

The remainder of the accommodation is of colonial style. The cheapest is *Kingsley House* (☎ 6391 2318) in Wellington St on the north side of town beside the railway line. It provides B&B for $80 a double plus $25 for each extra adult.

In Marlborough St, on the south side of town, is the private hotel, *Racecourse Inn* (☎ 6391 2352) where B&B is $80/110. Other places are out of town; to the south on Wellington St are the *Brickendon Historic Cottages* (☎ 6391 1251) where B&B in a self-contained cottage is $120 a double.

West of the town, on the other side of Back Creek, is the *Old Rosary* (☎ 6391 1662) at Longford Hall. It's found by following

Malcombe St to where a private road leads to the hall which has had an interesting history being a school, monastery and currently a residence. There is one cottage for hire at $110 a double.

For light meals *JJ's Bakery* in Wellington St has won several state awards for its bread and pies. The nearby Memorial Park is a good place to eat takeaways. For hotel meals the *Country Club Hotel* in Wellington St has a bistro with meals available every day. For à la carte food try the *Longford Inn* (☎ 6391 2006) in Wellington St. It also serves afternoon teas.

PERTH
• *pop 1570*

On the Midland Hwy, 19 km south of Launceston, is the quiet town of Perth. Buses pass through the town several times every day on the Hobart to Launceston service.

Governor Macquarie selected the site and the town was established in 1821. By 1834 there were two hotels, two flour mills and a punt across the South Esk River. In 1839 the punt was replaced by the first bridge across the river and it rivalled the bridge at Ross until it was swept away by heavy floods in 1929.

Many of the early buildings have survived; there are 29 places classified by the National Trust. The first two hotels, the **Leather Bottle Inn** and **Jolly Farmer Inn** are still in use. Perhaps the most interesting building is the **Baptist Tabernacle** in Clarence St. Built in 1889, it has an octagonal floor plan and the design was a mixture of Indian and European architecture.

On the corner of Main and Scone Sts is the Information Centre. From there you can get a free brochure called *The Path of History* which describes a three-km walk around Perth.

If you want to stay here, then try the *Queens Head Inn* (☎ 6398 2218) at 88 Main St where basic hotel rooms on the first floor are $40/50. Behind the hotel are motel rooms for the same price. The hotel has counter meals every day for lunch and dinner. The only B&B in town is at the *Old Perth Jail*

(☎ 6398 2100), 20 Scone St, which charges $95/$115.

The only other place for meals is the *Leather Bottle Inn* (☎ 6398 2248) at 55 Main Rd. It is open for light meals every day and on Thursday, Friday and Saturday nights it has an à la carte restaurant.

EVANDALE
• *pop 770*

Evandale, 22 km south of Launceston in the South Esk Valley, is near Launceston's airport and is another town classified by the National Trust. Many of its 19th-century buildings are in excellent condition and its narrow streets give it the atmosphere of an English country village.

In keeping with its olde-worlde feel, Evandale hosts the Evandale Village Fair and the National Penny Farthing Championships in February each year, which attract national and international competitors. In March is another special event – the Evandale Picnic Races, featuring local horses. On a more frequent basis, a popular market is held every Sunday morning on Logan Rd.

Places worth seeing around the town are the brick **water tower**, the two **churches**, and historic houses such as **Solomon House**, **Ingleside** and **Fallgrove**. The Tourism and History Centre in High St is

Evandale stages the annual National Penny Farthing Championships

AROUND LAUNCESTON

open every day from 11 am to 3 pm and provides some excellent information.

The **Clarendon Arms Hotel** has been licensed since 1847 and has some interesting murals in the hall depicting the area's history. The locals may encourage you to see if you can spot the well-concealed rabbit in the stagecoach mural; have a go – it really is there!

Eight km south of Evandale, on Nile Rd, is the National Trust property of **Clarendon** (☎ 6398 6220) which was completed in 1838 and is one of the grandest Georgian mansions in Australia. The house and its formal gardens are open daily from 10 am to 5 pm (closing an hour earlier in winter) and admission is $5, children $3 or $10 for a family.

Places to Stay & Eat

Most places to stay are in Russell St. The *Clarendon Arms Hotel* (☎ 6391 8181) at 11 Russell St has basic rooms from $25/35 for singles/doubles. Counter meals from $7 to $11 are available daily except Sunday. Counter meals are also available at the *Prince of Wales Hotel* on the corner of High and Collins Sts.

Also in Russell St, the *Bees Nees Cottage* (☎ 6391 8223) at No 26 is $90 a double with breakfast, and, just two doors away at No 30 is *Arendon Cottage* (☎ 6391 8806) for $85 a double with breakfast. The newest place to stay in Russell street is the *Stables* (☎ 6391 8048) at 5 Russell St. In the three units doubles are $95 which includes breakfast.

An interesting and quiet place to stay at is *Greg and Gill's Place* (☎ 6391 8248) at 35 Collins St. It is located on the edge of town yet is only a short walk from all the attractions and has a lovely garden setting. The cost is $65 for a double and includes a light breakfast.

You can stay in the old bakehouse – now called *Solomon Cottage* (☎ 6391 8331) – for $70/85 for B&B. It's located on the corner of High and Russell Sts and also serves afternoon teas and light meals from 10 am to 5 pm every day.

Light meals are also available at the *Dalmeny Cafe & Gallery* at 14 Russell St.

The only true restaurant in town is *Russells Restaurant* (☎ 91 8622) at 3 Russell St where main meals are around $10 to $14. It's open from Wednesday to Sunday for lunch and Wednesday to Saturday for dinner.

Getting There & Away

Tasmanian Redline Coaches (☎ 6331 3233) operates buses on weekdays only between the town and Launceston. The bus takes only 15 minutes to travel between the two towns and one service runs on Monday to Friday around 8 am and another around 6 pm in both directions. Some extra services run mid-morning and mid-afternoon on Thursday and Friday. There are no buses on public holidays or weekends. There is no agent in Evandale, the bus travels via Barclay, Macquarie and Russell Sts in Evandale.

BEN LOMOND NATIONAL PARK

This 165-sq-km park, 50 km south-east of Launceston, includes the entire Ben Lomond Range and is best known for its skiing. The range does not have any dramatic peaks; instead it is an elevated plateau about 14 km long by six km wide. The plateau is around 1300 metres high, with the gentle hills on the plateau being 1500 metres in height. The highest point is Legges Tor (1573 metres), which is the second highest peak in Tasmania and well worth climbing in good weather for its panoramic views.

The scenery at Ben Lomond is magnificent all year round. The park is particularly noted for its alpine wildflowers which run riot in spring and summer.

Ben Lomond was named after its Scottish namesake by the founder of Launceston, Colonel Patterson, in 1804. In 1805-06, Colonel Legge explored the plateau and named most of the major features after explorers of the Nile River in Africa and members of the fledgling Van Diemen's Land colony.

From Launceston, a good road leads to the foothills of the park where the road changes to gravel. The now rough road is easily followed to **Carr Villa**, from where a walking track leads to the plateau above. You can also drive to the top via the unsealed and very steep Jacobs Ladder. This is a set of six sharp hairpin bends; once above the ladder it's an easy drive to the ski village. In winter, chains are essential for the final climb.

Things to See & Do

In summer, the plateau provides some easy walking. The most popular place to visit is the highest point, **Legges Tor**. It can be reached via a good walking track from Carr Villa, about halfway up the mountain and takes about two hours each way. You can also climb to the top from the ski village on the plateau, which takes about 30 minutes each way on marked tracks.

You can easily walk across the plateau in almost any direction but there are no marked tracks and navigation is difficult in mist. Unless you are well equipped, walking south of the ski village is not advised.

During the ski season, a kiosk, tavern and restaurant are open in the alpine village at *Creek Inn* (☎ 6372 2444 in ski season, 6344 5674 in other seasons). Bistro meals are available every day for both lunch and dinner. The same place also has accommo-

dation all year from $85 and upwards per person for B&B (bookings are essential).

There are eight tows for skiers and a day-visitors shelter with heating is provided. To check conditions for downhill or cross-country skiing, phone ☎ (190) 229 0530. Lift tickets and ski equipment hire cost about half what they do on the mainland. There are three T-bars and five Poma lifts.

Getting There & Away

During the ski season, which runs from July to September, Tasmanian Wilderness Transport (☎ 6343 4442) has a daily return service between the ski fields and Launceston. It leaves from 101 George St at 7 am and a second service leaves at 8.30 am if there are enough bookings. The fare from Launceston to Ben Lomond is $25 for same-day return or $20 for one way. Booking is advised; if there are no booked passengers, services for that day are usually cancelled. The service is also cancelled when there is no snow on the mountain.

The same buses are also used to run a shuttle service from the bottom of Jacobs Ladder to the alpine village, $6 each for a one-way or same-day return.

AROUND LAUNCESTON

The North

NORTH

The northern plains are actually rolling farm-lands and hill country, which extend from the Tamar River valley north of Launceston west to the Great Western Tiers. There are some interesting towns and scenic spots, and the best way to explore this area is to leave the highways and follow the quiet, minor roads through the small towns.

The Tamar River separates the east and west Tamar districts and links Launceston with its ocean port of Bell Bay. Crossing the river near Deviot is Batman Bridge, the only bridge on the lower reaches of the Tamar. The river is tidal for all of the 64 km to Launceston and wends its way through some lovely orchards, pastures, forests and vine-yards, as well as providing a habitat for black swans.

The Tamar Valley and nearby Pipers River are among Tasmania's main wine-producing areas and the dry premium wines produced here are starting to achieve national recogni-tion.

Heading west from Launceston, the main highway skirts the foot of the Great Western Tiers then heads north to Devonport, the state's third-largest city. The terminal for the car ferry from Melbourne is here and the town is the gateway to the well-known Cradle Mountain-Lake St Clair National Park. Between Devonport and that park are a series of small towns hidden in the hills, some of which are well worth passing through.

For thousands of years Tasmanian Aborig-inal people lived in this area, but the only permanent reminders of their long occupa-tion are the many middens of shells and the rock carvings around Devonport. With the coming of Europeans, who turned the Aboriginal people's traditional hunting grounds into farms, the Aboriginal popula-tion quickly declined. By the time the Aboriginal people were rounded up and sent to Flinders Island only a couple of family units remained.

HIGHLIGHTS

- Sampling wine in the Tamar Valley
- Views of Batman Bridge
- The water tower at George Town
- The murals at Sheffield
- The parks and military monuments at Ulverstone

European history in the region dates from 1798, when Bass and Flinders discovered the Tamar estuary. Settlement commenced in 1804. Slowly the valley developed, first as a port of call for sailors and sealers from the Bass Strait islands and then as a sanctuary for some of the desperate characters who took to the bush during the convict days. By the 1830s the Aboriginal people had van-ished from their former hunting grounds, and Europeans slowly spread across the plains turning the forested land into farming country.

In the late 1870s, gold was discovered by William and John Dally at Cabbage Tree Hill, just west of present-day Beaconsfield, and the fortunes of the north took a new turn. The region boomed and for a time this was the third-largest town in Tasmania, before the mines closed in 1914.

Getting There & Around

Bus On weekdays, Tamar Valley Coaches (☎ 6334 0828) has at least one bus a day running up and down the West Tamar Valley, but there are no weekend services.

During the week, Tasmanian Redline Coaches (TRC; ☎ 6331 3233 or 1800 030 033) has three buses each day which run up the East Tamar Valley between Launceston and George Town. The service extends to Low Head only if bookings have been made in advance. On Sunday, there is a single service each way in the evenings. There are no Saturday services.

On weekdays both TRC and Hobart Coaches (☎ 6234 4077 or 008 030 620) have several services daily from Launceston to Devonport, Ulverstone and on to Burnie. These services also call at the ferry terminal in Devonport. On Saturday and Sunday, TRC has three services along this route while Hobart Coaches has only one.

Buses also run from both Launceston and Devonport to Cradle Mountain. From November to April Tasmanian Wilderness Travel (☎ 6334 4442) runs daily buses from Launceston, Deloraine and Devonport to Cradle Mountain, costing $35 one way or $65 return. From May to October the same service operates on Tuesday, Thursday and Saturday. From December to April, Tasmanian Wilderness Travel runs another service from Devonport and Launceston to Lake St Clair, the southern end of the Cradle Mountain-Lake St Clair National Park. The fare is $45 one way or $80 return. For those walking the Overland Track, a special circuit fare of $70 applies.

Bicycle The ride north along the Tamar River is a gem. On the west bank, it is possible to avoid most of the highway and follow quiet roads with very few hills through the small settlements. On the eastern shore, follow the minor roads inland to Lilydale. There are plenty of hills but the different landscapes more than compensate for the hard work!

From Launceston to Deloraine, the construction of the new highway is a real plus for riders: most vehicles follow the new road, and riders can now enjoy the old highway which the new one has replaced. The old highway is slower, with more hills but it's far more interesting, passing through all the small towns. From Deloraine the rebuilt highway which heads directly to Devonport is best avoided by travelling through the quieter towns of Sheffield or Railton.

Tamar Valley

Running north from Launceston the Tamar Valley is off the normal tourist circuit and has some interesting sights. Tourism is just starting here but so far is very minor and you usually get good service and value in the region. You can drive up either side of the river and cross over on the unusual single-tower Batman Bridge.

There is no public transport along the western side of the Tamar. To visit Exeter and Beaconsfield you need your own transport. There are regular weekday services down the east side of the Tamar from George Town to Launceston.

LEGANA
* *pop 1400*

Just 12 km north of Launceston, this is fast becoming a satellite suburb of the nearby city. It originally consisted of orchards, but these days new houses are growing faster than anything else. There are some vineyards here, but the wineries are not open to the public.

The main tourist feature in the area is **Grindelwald**, a reproduction Swiss village sitting in a shallow valley on top of the nearby hills. It started as a residential village but has evolved into a convention and conference centre. It's really a bit out of place and not that special.

More interesting is a visit to **Notley Fern**

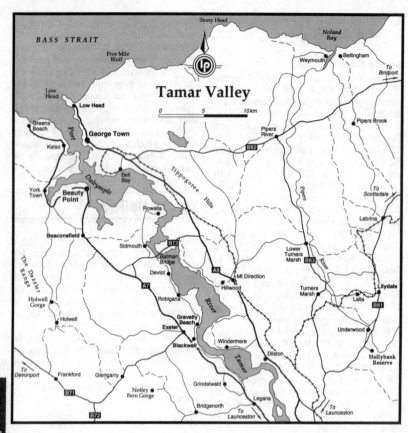

Gorge. This is hidden in the hills 14 km west of Legana and while only small it is the last remnant of the original forest that once covered the region. The big hollow tree in the park is reputed to have been the hiding place of Matthew Brady, a famous bushranger from last century; who knows if it's true but it makes a good story. It's a nice cool place on a warm day and the marked circuit walk takes about 45 minutes.

Places to Stay & Eat

The *Legana Caravan Park* (☎ 6330 1714), beside the highway, is a bit ordinary. Tent sites are $10, on-site vans are $29 and cabins are $35. In Legana, well off the highway overlooking the river, is *Freshwater Point* (☎ 6330 2200). It's an original homestead with sweeping views and is impressive but then so is the price: B&B is $120 to $135 a double.

Just as expensive is the *Grindelwald Holiday Village* (☎ 6330 1799 or 1800 817 595) with rooms for $125 and units at $140 a double. At least you can eat at *Alpenrose Restaurant*, where main meals are $18 to $41.

In the Village Square the bakery sells

GLENN BEANLAND

JOHN CHAPMAN

CHARLOTTE HINDLE

ADRIENNE COSTANZO

JOHN CHAPMAN

CHRIS KLEP

A	B
C	D
E	F

A: Dilapidated jetty, St Helens
B: Culinary delights at the Weldborough Hotel, north-east Tasmania
C: Yorktown Square market, Launceston

D: Kings Bridge, Launceston
E: Cataract Gorge, Launceston
F: Clarendon, near Evandale

CHRIS KLEP

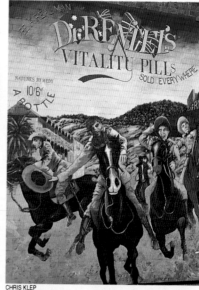
CHRIS KLEP

CHARLOTTE HINDLE

GLENN BEANLAND

Top Left: "Old Grocer's Shop", mural by John Lendis (Sheffield)
Top Right: "Spirited Horseman", mural by John Lendis (Sheffield)
Bottom Left: Penguin, Penguin
Bottom Right: The majestic Furners Hotel, Ulverstone

German cakes and is an excellent place for morning tea.

ROSEVEARS

On the west side of the Tamar, it is worth leaving the highway and following the narrow sealed road that winds along the river banks, passing through the tiny town of Rosevears. This was the place where the *Rebecca*, John Batman's ship, was constructed; he sailed across in it Bass Strait to settle Melbourne. The *Rosevears Tavern* was opened in 1831 and you can still get a beer and counter meal there seven days a week.

Within walking distance of the hotel, the **Waterbird Haven Trust** (☎ 6394 4087) is a sanctuary for marine birds. Entry is $4 (children $1). B&B is available beside the Haven at $30/50 for a single/double.

Local wines can be tasted free of charge at the **Strathblynn Wine Centre** (☎ 6330 2388), which is open every day except Christmas Day. This is an outlet for Pipers Brook and Ninth Island. Light lunches are also available at the centre. The nearby **St Matthias Vineyard** (☎ 6330 1700) is also open daily for free tastings of their products.

Next door to the vineyards *Conmel Cottage* (☎ 6330 1466) can be rented for $85 a double, which includes breakfast. A little further north, *Tamar House* (☎ 6340 1744) offers similar B&B for $65 to $75 a double.

When you again meet the highway, it is worth following the signs to the nearby **Bradys Lookout State Reserve**. Brady was a well-known bushranger who used this rocky outcrop to spy on travellers on the road below. You can do the same today and also enjoy the fine views over the Tamar River.

EXETER
- *pop 400*

This quiet town serves as the centre for an orchard region. In recent years, grapes have become a popular crop and the **West Tamar Wine Centre** offers tastings of wines produced by many of the smaller vineyards. A fee of $5 applies to tastings, but this is refunded if wine is purchased. Light meals and a range of Tasmanian cheeses are also available; it's open from 11 am to 3 pm most days.

The Tamar Visitor Centre (☎ 6394 4454), in the main street, is well stocked with information on the region.

If you are hungry then visit the *Exeter Bakery* which is open daily and bakes its own creations in a wood-fired oven – real country cooking. On the second Sunday of every month the **market** is held in the show hall from 11 am till 3 pm.

There is nowhere to stay in town. The closest accommodation is at **Gravelly Beach**, four km north-east of town where *Aviemore Orchard Retreat* (☎ 6394 4631) provides B&B for $80 a double. This is a blueberry and cherry farm and, from late December to early February, is open every day for fresh-fruit sales.

ROBIGANA & DEVIOT

Instead of following the main highway from Exeter to Beaconsfield it is far more scenic to follow the minor roads beside the Tamar River. Turn off just south of Exeter and pass through Gravelly Beach, Robigana and Deviot.

Robigana – named after an Aboriginal word for 'swans' – is the spot where the road crosses the Supply River. From here there is a marked walking track beside the Tamar River to **Paper Beach**, which takes one hour return. If you prefer a shorter walk then it's only 400 metres along the Supply River to the ruins of a **flour mill**. This was the site of the first water-driven flour mill in Australia. It's a pleasant walk under the trees, although there is not a lot to see at the ruins.

Further upstream on the Supply River is *Norfolk Reach* (☎ 6394 7681 or 018 138 248), which provides B&B for $80 a double. This is well hidden in quiet bushland and is great place for birdwatching. Access is via Motor Rd.

At Deviot, Marions Vineyard (☎ 6394 7434) is open daily with a $2 fee for wine tastings. The fee is refunded if you make a purchase from its range of four wines. The vineyard provides good free facilities, with a sheltered barbecue area, timber tables and sink.

BATMAN BRIDGE

This is an important link between the two sides of the Tamar River. Its eye-catching design resulted from foundation problems. The east bank has poor foundations for a large bridge so it just supports a minor part of the span. Most of the bridge is supported by the 100-metre-tall west tower which leans out over the river. Opened in 1968, it was one the world's first cable-stayed truss bridges. There are good views and toilets on the eastern bank of the river.

Passing underneath the bridge on the western bank, a gravel road leads to **Sidmouth**. About all there is to see here is the Auld Kirk and graveyard and the nearby views of the Batman Bridge. Close by, in the forest, *Kirk Tea House and Gardens* is open every day except Tuesday for light lunches and teas. If booked, dinner is available on Friday and Saturday nights.

BEACONSFIELD

• *pop 1090*

The once-thriving gold-mining town of Beaconsfield is still dominated by the ruins of its three original mine buildings. Two of these house the **Grubb Shaft Museum** complex, which is open daily from 10 am to 4 pm; entry is $3, students $1.50 and children free. This was Tasmania's largest gold mine, as seen in the size of the equipment and depth of the mine. It is staffed by volunteers and has some working machinery demonstrating how the mine operated. It's worth a visit. Opposite the mine buildings, a miner's cottage and old school are on display. The old Hart Shaft next to the museum has been opened up and, using today's technology, the miners hope to strike some of the town's still plentiful gold reserves.

The *Club Hotel* (☎ 6383 1191), north of the gold mine in Weld St, offers basic rooms and serves counter meals every day. *Garwoods Bakery* produces some tasty breads from a wood-fired oven. There is also another bakery in town. The supermarket has an unusual takeaway counter hidden in the back corner. You can buy groceries while you wait for your fish & chips. For a sit-down Chinese meal there is *Red Ruby Chinese* (☎ 6383 4153), which also does takeaways.

HOLWELL GORGE

In the hills, nine km south of Beaconsfield, the small reserve of Holwell Gorge contains some original forest. There are some giant trees reaching 60 metres, many ferns and three waterfalls. A reasonable one-way track runs through the gorge and it takes about two hours return.

BEAUTY POINT

• *pop 1140*

Initially the port for the nearby Beaconsfield gold mines, this town still has a wharf and ship-loading facilities. The name did not originate from the landscape; rather it was named after a bullock called Beauty. In spite of that, however, the name is definitely appropriate!

Beauty Point is home to the **Australian Maritime College** which conducts training in fisheries, navigation and other maritime skills. With its many live-in students and three training vessels, the college is a significant supporter of the town's economy, as is shipping.

For visitors there is a marina and swimming and boating in sheltered waters. The *Tassie Teddy Bear Fantasy Gardens* feature a huge fibreglass bear and tearooms. It's a bit out of place but children love it as there is a well-equipped playground.

Just west of the town, *Redbill Point Van Park* (☎ 6383 4536) provides tent sites for $8 and on-site vans for $25. A room for two at the *Beauty Point Motor Hotel* (☎ 6383 4363) near the college is $50 and the *Riviera Hotel* (6383 4153) on the north side of town charges $48 a double. Both hotels have counter meals daily.

If you prefer somewhere more peaceful, then the nearby holiday settlements of Kelso and Greens Beach might appeal. *Kelso Sands Caravan Park* (☎ 6383 9130) has tent sites for $10 and on-site-vans for $35. The more basic *Greens Beach Caravan Park* (☎ 6383 9222) has tent sites for $7. The basic *Holiday Lodge Hotel* (☎ 6383 4188), just south of Kelso, has B&B for $35 a double. It is a licensed hotel and serves counter meals daily.

Most of the accommodation is fairly basic with a two or three-star rating. If you prefer something more luxurious then try the *Yorktown Manor* (☎ 6283 4647) where B&B is $85 a double. If you're staying several nights it offers a 'three nights for the price of two' deal that is good value.

ASBESTOS RANGE NATIONAL PARK
This little-known park is located roughly midway between the Tamar River and Devonport. The scenery is not as sensational or rugged as in many other parks; instead it's a gentle landscape. Part of the park was once farmland, and the cleared land provides grasslands. The prime purpose of the park is to provide some habitat for Tasmania's larger animals, particularly the Forester kangaroo. Around dusk you will also see wombats, wallabies and pademelons grazing.

Park entry fees apply and permits are available from the ranger (☎ 6428 6277). The rangers provide guided walks, talks and activities during the summer months. Horse riding is allowed and corrals and a 26-km trail are also provided. Permits are needed for horse riding and bookings should be made with the ranger as facilities are limited. **Bakers Beach** provides the safest swimming area. Water-skiing is allowed at Bakers Beach in summer.

The park can be reached from the Beaconsfield area or from Port Sorell near Devonport. Bush camping is allowed at three places in the western half of the park, with pit toilets and bore water supplied.

There are some interesting walking trails in the park. Badger Head provides a four-hour circuit walk. Archers Knob has good views of Bakers Beach and takes four hours return. The **Springlawn Nature Trail** is short

and has an interesting boardwalk across a swamp. The beach from Griffiths Point to Bakers Point is a good place for beachcombing and is also a great place to watch the sunset.

LOW HEAD
• *pop 450*
Located on the eastern side of the Tamar River where it enters Bass Strait, this scattered settlement contains the historic **Pilot Station**. The station was established in 1805 and the current buildings were convict-built in 1835. Today the building contains the interesting **Pilot Station Maritime Museum**. With 10 rooms of displays it is good value; entry is $2 (children $1) and it's open every day. In the same building there is a good cafe.

At Low Head itself, the **lighthouse**, built in 1888, is worth a visit. Despite what the signs tell you, there is no display, but it provides great views over the river mouth and surrounding area. There is good surf at **East Beach** on Bass Strait and safe swimming in calm water at **Lagoon Bay** on the river.

The town itself does not have a centre, but there are shops at George Town which is only five km away. Around the town are navigation lights which look like mini-lighthouses and are very striking with their painted red stripes. From September to February at dusk you can watch the fairy penguins return to their nests near the lighthouse.

The *Beach Pines Holiday Village* (☎ 6382 2602) is right by the sea, facing Bass Strait, and is a great place to stay. It has a kiosk and a family restaurant which is open every day. Tent sites are $8, sites with power $12 and cabins $45/50. Less attractive is *Low Head Caravan Park* (☎ 6382 1573) which is about midway between George Town and Low Head. All camp sites have power and cost $12, on-site-vans are $35 and cabins $45 a double. The other alternative is in the town next to one of the navigation lights. *Belfont Cottages* (☎ 6382 1841) provides B&B for $90 a double. If phoned in advance they can provide a courtesy car from George Town.

NORTH

GEORGE TOWN
• *pop 5025*

George Town is located on the eastern shore of the Tamar River close to the heads. As a town it has a mixed history, with short boom periods followed by years as a quiet, backwater town.

It is best known as the site where Colonel Paterson landed in 1804, leading to the settlement of northern Tasmania. In 1811 the town was named after King George. It might have become the northern capital but for its lack of water and in 1825 Paterson moved south to establish Launceston. In the 1830s and 1840s the town prospered when it became the port which linked Tasmania to Victoria. Some of its older buildings date from this period. After many years of little activity, the opening of the aluminium smelter at Bell Bay in 1949 revived the town.

Today George Town is growing steadily, with guaranteed employment in the nearby large industries at Bell Bay. The town gets relatively few visitors, yet it has some interesting attractions, as does the surrounding region.

Things to See
In Cimitiere St, **The Grove** is a lovely Georgian stone residence, dating from the 1830s, which has been classified by the National Trust. It's open daily from 10 am to 5 pm and admission is $4, children $1.50, family $10. Refreshments are available and lunch is served by staff in period costume. You can also stay here (see Places to Stay).

The **old watch house** in Macquarie St dates from 1843 and has been turned into a museum; it's open on weekdays from 8 am to 5 pm and it costs nothing to look around. Also of interest is the **St Mary Magdalene Anglican Church** in Anne St. On the east side of town you will find a distinctive **water tower**. The mural is an innovative way of disguising what might otherwise be a dominant eyesore. For great panoramic views visit **Mt George**, which has a restored semaphore mast on it.

The nearby industrial area of **Bell Bay** has Tasmania's only thermal power station, along with several other unattractive heavy industries; it can be clearly seen from the highway. In recent years these factories have been reducing their output of pollutants and improving their image. Temco (☎ 6382 1411) has a tour of its furnaces on the first Wednesday of every month at 11 am and Comalco (☎ 6382 5111) has site tours of the aluminium smelter every Monday, Wednesday and Friday at 2 pm. Make sure you wear enclosed shoes, long sleeves and pants for protection.

Places to Stay & Eat
For caravan parks, see the section on Low Head, which is only five km north. The YHA in town is *Travellers Hostel* (☎ 6382 1399) at 4 Elizabeth St. It is in a restored house close to the waterfront and has beds for $12 ($14 for nonmembers) and family rooms for $40.

The *George Town Hotel/Motel* (☎ 6382 1057) has units on the edge of town for a reasonable $35/45 and also has a family bistro. A little closer to the town centre, in Friend St, are more motel units at *Central Court Apartments* (☎ 6382 2155).

If you prefer a hotel room, then try *Gray's Hotel* (☎ 6382 2655), in the main street, which has rooms for $55/65. The family bistro serves meals every day and has Tasmanian wines. The classiest hotel in town is the *Pier Hotel Motel* (☎ 6382 1300), at 3 Elizabeth St. It is an old building, but the motel rooms are new and right beside the waterfront. Rates are a reasonable $75 a double. The pub is open for breakfast and its bistro has counter meals every day.

The only B&B in town is at the historic house *The Grove* (☎ 6382 1336). There is space for three in the on-site cottage and it costs $55 for one person plus $10 for each extra adult.

Apart from the hotels, there are takeaways, including pizza and chicken, and a Chinese restaurant. The only other option is *Mario's* (☎ 6382 1479), at 20 Macquarie St, which is cheap ($6 to $10 for mains) and open from Monday to Saturday for lunch and dinner.

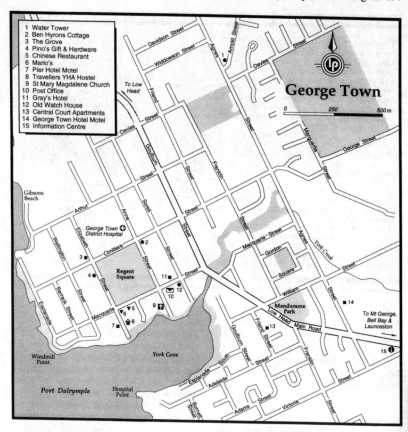

1 Water Tower
2 Ben Hyrons Cottage
3 The Grove
4 Pino's Gift & Hardware
5 Chinese Restaurant
6 Mario's
7 Pier Hotel Motel
8 Travellers YHA Hostel
9 St Mary Magdalene Church
10 Post Office
11 Gray's Hotel
12 Old Watch House
13 Central Court Apartments
14 George Town Hotel Motel
15 Information Centre

George Town

To Low
Head

Gibsons
Beach

George Town ✚
District Hospital

Regent
Square

Mandurama
Park

To Mt George,
Bell Bay &
Launceston

Windmill
Point

York Cove

Hospital
Point

Port Dalrymple

NORTH

Getting There & Away

TRC (☎ 6331 3233 or 1800 030 033) runs three buses every weekday along the east side of the Tamar River from George Town through Hillwood and Dilston to Launceston. There are no services on Saturday. On Sunday evenings one bus leaves Launceston at 5.15 pm for George Town then returns immediately to Launceston at 6.15 pm. On some services the bus will continue to Low Head for pick-ups, but only if it's-pre-booked.

The George Town agent is at Pino's Gift & Hardware, 21 Elizabeth St.

PIPERS RIVER REGION

This rural region is central to the Tasmanian wine industry. It started in 1974 with Pipers Brook and today the area produces about half of the state's wines. There are 10 vineyards and six have wine-tastings. There is little else here, but some of the vineyards serve light meals and provide playgrounds for children while you tantalise your taste buds.

The most famous vineyard is **Pipers Brook**, which was started in the wake of an academic exercise by Dr Andrew Pirie comparing the famous wine regions of France with Australian regions. The winery is open

How do you like your grapes?

I prefer my grapes ... squeezed. It doesn't really matter what colour they are so long as they have been lovingly processed and matured.

The Tasmanian wine industry is relatively young, with commercial crops first planted in the mid-1970s. Rapid expansion in the 1980s saw many new vineyards being developed and this has continued through the 1990s. There are now more than 90 grape growers in the state with about 330 hectares under vines.

Most of the vineyards in the state are very small. A couple of years ago, the ten largest vineyards produced nearly 70% of the total grapes and most of them came from the Tamar Valley and Pipers Brook regions. Just over half the total annual wine was produced by the three largest wineries.

While Tasmania's wine production is not yet on a grand scale, it has great potential owing to its cool-climate location. Tasmania's vineyards are at latitudes which, in the northern hemisphere, correspond to the French wine regions of Bordeaux and Burgundy. However, just as these cool climates offer potential, so too do they bring their share of difficulties as grape growers combat severe frost and high winds.

For the visitor, there is a good selection of wine tasting and cellar-door sale venues all around the state. ■

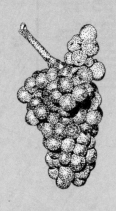

every day during summer and only on weekdays in winter. Light meals are available during summer. Other vineyards worth visiting include **Delamere**, **Heemskerk** and **Dalrymple** at Pipers Brook and **Rochecombe** at Pipers River.

HILLWOOD

South of George Town, beside the Tamar River, is the attractive, rural area of Hillwood, where you can pick strawberries, raspberries and apples and sample Tasmanian fruit wines and cheese at the **Hillwood Strawberry Farm** (☎ 6394 8180). It's open all year, but of course you can only pick fruit in season, which is mainly from December to March. The fruit wine is unusual and a real novelty – try it!

Next door to the farm is the Tasmanian Gourmet Cheese factory. The nearby airstrip provides ultralight aeroplane flights over the hills with Ultralight Aviation (☎ 018 120 199). The village is also noted for its fishing and lovely river views.

LILYDALE & LALLA

The tiny towns of Lilydale and Lalla, 25 km north of Launceston, form the centre of an interesting region that is popular with visitors. There is something here for everybody, ranging from wine to flowers, and easy strolls to strenuous walks.

At Lalla, the **WAG Walker Rhododendron Reserve** has superb floral displays from September to December. In other months it is less colourful but still worth a visit. Exotic and rare trees are a feature of the reserve. It's free and open every day for much of the year, except in summer when it's only open on weekends. If you prefer small plants then visit the nearby **Brown Mtn Nursery & Gardens** and have a look at their bonsai plants.

Opposite the rhododendron reserve is **La Provence** (☎ 6395 1290), which was first planted in 1956, making it Tasmania's oldest vineyard. It is open for cellar-door sales on weekends during summer.

Three km from Lilydale is the **Lilydale Falls Reserve**, which has camping facilities and an easy 20-minute walk to two waterfalls. To the south of Lilydale is **Hollybank Forest** which has fine picnic areas, numerous short tracks and an information centre. In its short history the reserve has been a sawmill, an ash forest producing wood for tennis racquets and cricket bats, and today it showcases the way forests are managed. While the displays are interesting, in our experience real forests are not as neatly managed as the reserve!

For a more energetic walk, climb **Mt Arthur** which towers above Lilydale. A five to seven-hour return walk leads to the summit from which there are lovely views if you ignore the towers on top.

Places to Stay & Eat

For something different, stay near Lilydale at *Plovers Ridge Host Farm* (☎ 6395 1102). With B&B, the self-contained units are $55/90. Vegetarian meals are available for guests. Closer to Lalla, *Hawkspur* (☎ 6395 1268) offers similar farm B&B accommodation for $70 a double. There are several tearooms including the *Lilydale Bakery*, which is famous for its old-fashioned breads. The landmark of the town is *Bardenhagen's General Store* which is one of the few stores of its type still operating in Australia.

Western Tiers & the North Coast

Between the northern coastal strip and the Great Western Tiers (which rise up to Tasmania's central plateau), there are some interesting towns and scenic places. Through the centre of this region, the Bass Hwy runs from Launceston to Deloraine then to Devonport. The best way to see the region is to leave the recently built highways from Launceston to Deloraine and follow the older roads through the small towns. Once you reach Deloraine, the most interesting route is through the hill country to the west of the Bass Hwy, through Sheffield.

WESTBURY

- *pop 1290*

The historic town of Westbury, 32 km west of Launceston, is best known for its **White House**, a property built in 1841 as a general store. It is now managed by the National Trust and features several collections, such as period furniture and old vehicles, including an 1888 Penny Farthing. The house is open from 10 am to 4 pm on Tuesday, Thursday and weekends; admission is $5 ,children $3, family $10.

In front of the White House is the **village green** – the only one in Tasmania. It's a long narrow grassy park which includes a maypole and war memorial. Around town there are several commercial displays which may keep you amused for a few hours.

The **Westbury Gemstone, Mineral & Mural Display**, on the Bass Hwy, has a huge collection and is open daily; admission is $2.50 ($1 children). If you find minerals a bit boring, then at least walk down the side of the shed for a free look at the mural. Next door is **Pearn's Steam World**, which is also open daily. It costs $3 to inspect a wide range of working steam engines; you might even get to ride on one.

On the other side of the old highway is the **Westbury Maze**. This hedge maze is open daily from October to June and is entry $3 (children $2, family $10). See the Deloraine Getting There and Away section for information on bus services to the town.

Places to Stay & Eat

The *Westbury Hotel* (☎ 6393 1151), at 107 Bass Hwy, provides basic rooms for $30/45. For B&B, *Fitzpatricks Inn* (☎ 6393 1153), an old building beside the highway at No 56, is good value at $40/60. Slightly further out of town, *Westbury Inn* (☎ 6393 1627), at 1 Bass Hwy, is of a similar standard at $55/70. In town, the *Old Bake House* (☎ 6393 1140), at 52 William St, is expensive at $95 a double plus $20 for each extra person.

There are various tearooms such as *Henny Penny* at 44 William St. The *Hot Bread* shop beside the main road is quite unusual in Tasmania, being open 24 hours a day.

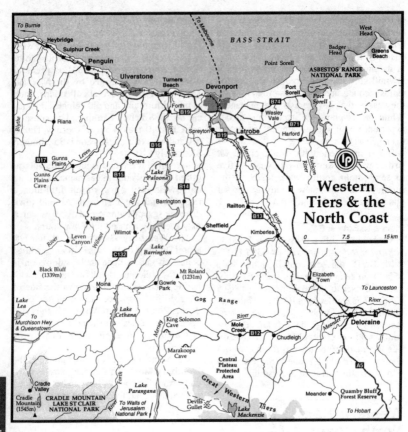

DELORAINE

• *pop 2250*

Deloraine is Tasmania's largest inland town and with its lovely riverside picnic area, superb setting at the foot of the Great Western Tiers and good amenities it makes a great base from which to explore the surrounding area. Being so close to the Cradle Mountain area, and even closer to a number of impressive waterfalls and shorter walking tracks, Deloraine is fast becoming a major bushwalking centre. You'll find the visitor centre by the roundabout at the top of the main street, Emu Bay Rd.

The town itself has a lot of charm, as many of its Georgian and Victorian buildings have been faithfully restored. It was first settled by Europeans in the 1820s and the older buildings date mainly from the 1830s and 1840s. Initially cattle grazing and wheat growing were the mainstays of the region but competition and disease closed the wheat mills. The farms have since diversified and now cultivate a wide variety of crops as well as raising livestock.

Things to See & Do

In town, just downstream from the main

bridge, is a pleasant **park** with good views of the river's rapids and the old power station opposite. Complete with an old railway steam engine, it's a great place for a picnic lunch. A walking track runs through town along the river bank. For something more historic, you can muse over the exhibits at the **folk museum** in the Family and Commercial Inn, opposite the visitor centre; admission is $1.

Two km to the east of Deloraine is the **Bowerbank Mill**, which is classified by the National Trust; these days it has accommodation and an art gallery. Also nearby is the **Christmas Hills Raspberry Farm** where you can pick fruit in December and January.

Dominating the southern skyline are the Great Western Tiers which provide some excellent walking. There are lots of waterfalls, forest and some long climbs to the top of the Tiers. The **Meander Forest Reserve** is the most popular starting point. From here Split Rock Falls can be visited in two to three

hours, or you can walk further to Meander Falls, which are four to five hours return. Overnight camping is allowed in the area.

Other good walks on the Great Western Tiers are to Projection Bluff (two hours); Quamby Bluff (five hours) and Mother Cummings Peak (three hours). There are many other walks described in various walking guides; these can be purchased at the visitor centre, and at newsagents and bookshops in Devonport and Launceston.

If walking is too energetic then go fishing. Tasmanian trout can be difficult to catch and the Tasmanian Fly-Fishing School (☎ 6362 3441) will show how it's done. It is located beside the road to Mole Creek at the western end of town and training and guided trips range from $150 to $250 per person per day.

Places to Stay

A basic tent site at the *Apex Caravan Park* (☎ 6362 2345) costs $6 and powered sites for two people are $9. It is actually on the

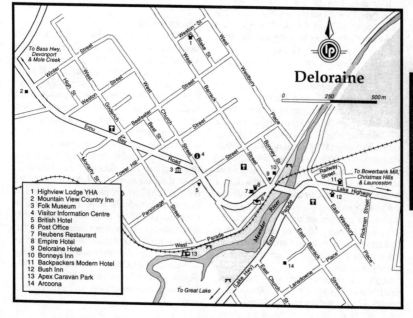

Deloraine

0   250   500 m

1 Highview Lodge YHA
2 Mountain View Country Inn
3 Folk Museum
4 Visitor Information Centre
5 British Hotel
6 Post Office
7 Reubens Restaurant
8 Empire Hotel
9 Deloraine Hotel
10 Bonneys Inn
11 Backpackers Modern Hotel
12 Bush Inn
13 Apex Caravan Park
14 Arcoona

To Bass Hwy, Devonport & Mole Creek

To Bowerbank Mill, Christmas Hills & Launceston

To Great Lake

NORTH

other side of the river, but is only a short walk into town across a handy footbridge.

The *Backpackers Modern Hotel* (☎ 6362 3408), also called Kevs Kumphy Korner, is a hostel at 24 Bass Hwy, across the river from the main part of town. The pink-painted hostel is cheap, with beds for $10. Almost opposite is the *Bush Inn* (☎ 6362 2365), at 7 Bass Hwy, which offers good backpackers accommodation for $13 a night with breakfast. This old hotel also serves lunch and dinner every day.

The YHA hostel is the *Highview Lodge Youth Hostel* (☎ 6362 2996), perched on the hillside at 8 Blake St. This is further from town than Kevs and is reached after a steep, uphill walk – but you are compensated for this with magnificent views of the Great Western Tiers. It charges $12 ($14 for non-members). The managers organise reasonably priced and well-equipped trips to Cradle Mountain, the Walls of Jerusalem and other destinations. The hostel rents mountain or touring bikes to guests.

If you're looking for a motel, try the *Mountain View Country Inn* (☎ 6362 2633) on the road to Mole Creek. The price is a reasonable $55 a double and good discounts are given for multiple nights. Breakfast is available if needed and the motel has a restaurant.

For farm accommodation try *Bonneys Farm* (☎ 6362 2122), four km from town on the north side of the expressway. It has three units and a guesthouse for a very reasonable $60 a double, plus $12 for each extra person. It runs half-day ($20) and day tours ($40 to $45) from the farm in conjunction with the YHA hostel and can pick up guests from town. *Ashgrove Farmhouse Accommodation* (☎ 6368 1137) at Elizabeth Town, 10 km north of Deloraine, has an old, comfortable farmhouse suitable for up to six people for $60 a double, plus $10 for each extra person. This farm produces award-winning cheeses and anyone can call in to see the cheese-making process.

Right in town, next door to the Deloraine Hotel, is *Bonneys Inn* (☎ 6362 2974), which charges $25 per person for B&B in colonial accommodation; one room even has a water bed! There is also a self-contained cottage hidden around the back. This was the first brick building in Deloraine and for years operated as a hotel. In recent years it has fluctuated between being a B&B and a restaurant.

Another notable historic place to stay is *Bowerbank Mill* (☎ 6362 2628), two km east of the town. The corn mill is classified by the National Trust and was built in 1853. You can stay in the old machinery rooms for $95 a double for B&B.

If you want to spoil yourself, then stay at the luxuriously appointed *Arcoona* (☎ 6362 3443 or 018 463 347). Located on top of the hill on the eastern side of the river, the driveway is accessed from East Barrack St. This historic building was originally the town doctor's residence and then became the district hospital. A feature is the billiard room with its original table. To stay here it costs $120 a double, which is what you would expect for such a high standard.

Places to Eat

The shopping centre is good for a small town and there are several takeaways and coffee shops. One of the best places to eat is *Reuben's Restaurant*, under the Empire Hotel in the main street. It is open daily from 8 am onwards for breakfast, through lunch to dinner and late into the evening. It's more of a fancy coffee shop than a restaurant and the atmosphere is relaxed. The range of food is excellent and prices are reasonable; the 'Door Stop' sandwich is very filling and worth trying. The cakes are home-baked.

At the *Deloraine Hotel*, main meals are only $8 to $12 but are pretty average. Similar fare is also available at the *British Hotel* at the other end of the shopping centre and at the *Bush Inn* on the other side of the river. Ten km north, the *Elizabeth Town Hotel* is open every day for lunch and from Monday to Saturday for dinner. The best à la carte dining is at *Arcoona* in East Barrack St. Prices are quite reasonable given the elegant surrounds.

Getting There & Away

From Monday to Friday TRC (☎ 6331 3233 or 1800 030 033) runs five buses per day from Launceston through Deloraine to Devonport and return. On weekends there are three services daily along the same route. Bookings are essential for all services and the buses will do pick-ups and drop-offs any where along the route.

Hobart Coaches (☎ 6234 4077 or 1800 030 620) runs buses along the same route from Launceston to Devonport, and operates three services on weekdays and two services on weekends.

Tasmanian Wilderness Transport (☎ 6334 4442) runs buses through Deloraine from Launceston, Devonport and also from Cynthia Bay at the southern end of the Overland Track. From December to April these services are daily. From May to November there are three services a week (Tuesday, Thursday and Saturday) from Cradle Mountain to Launceston, through Deloraine and one service a week (Tuesday) from Cynthia Bay to Launceston and Devonport passing through Deloraine.

MOLE CREEK

• *pop 250*

About 25 km west of Deloraine is Mole Creek, in the vicinity of which you'll find spectacular limestone caves, leatherwood honey and one of Tasmania's best wildlife parks. The town is tiny with very few services but has excellent views of the Western Tiers and is a handy access point for caving and bushwalking.

Things to See & Do

Most visitors come here to explore the caves. **Marakoopa Cave** – from the Aboriginal word meaning 'handsome' – is a wet cave, 15 km from Mole Creek, which features two underground streams and an incredible glow-worm display. **King Solomon Cave** is a dry cave with amazing calcite crystals which reflect light. This cave contains very few steps, making it the better cave for the less energetic. There are at least five tours daily in each cave, except on Christmas Day

when they are closed. A tour of one cave costs $8 (children $4), or you can visit both for $12 (children $6). Current tour times are prominently displayed on access roads or you can ring the ranger (☎ 6363 5182).

If you want to explore a wild cave (one without steps or ladders) then you will need to take a guided tour. All wild caves are locked and only caving-club members can enter them without a guide. Wild Cave Tours (☎ 6367 8142) provides caving gear and guides for $60 a half-day or $120 a full day per person. Take spare clothing and a towel as you will get wet.

The leatherwood tree only grows in the damp western part of Tasmania, so honey made by bees visiting its flower is unique to this state. From January to April, when the honey is being extracted, you can visit the **Stephens Leatherwood Honey Factory** in Mole Creek and learn all about this fascinating industry. The factory is open on weekdays and admission is free.

Two km from Chudleigh, east of Mole Creek, is the **Tasmanian Wildlife Park & Koala Village**, which is worth a visit. Pre-booked nocturnal tours (most of the animals are active at night) take place from January to April and cost $7.50. It's open daily from 9 am to 5 pm and admission is $7.50,(children $3.50.

In fine weather, those with transport should head for the Western Tiers. The only road which actually reaches the top of the plateau is the one to Lake McKenzie. Follow this road to the **Devils Gullet**. The 30-minute return walk leads to a platform bolted to the top of a dramatic gorge overlooking the Devils Gullet. Looking over the edge is not for the faint hearted.

Bushwalking Popular short walks in the area are **Alum Cliffs Gorge** (one hour return) and **Westmoreland Falls** (two hours return). The most popular full-day walk is to the Walls of Jerusalem National Park. This park comprises a series of glacial valleys and lakes on top of the plateau. If you have the time and equipment, it's worth camping in the park. Camping is not allowed inside the main valleys of the Walls, but there are plenty of good sites nearby for a base to explore the area. The park is exposed so you must be prepared for strong winds and snowfalls even in summer. Walks across the park are described in *Cradle Mountain Lake St Clair and Walls of Jerusalem National Parks* by John Chapman and John Siseman.

If you prefer a guided walk, then Taswalks (☎ 6363 6112) at Chudleigh will help you to explore the bush. Rather than running set tours, the company varies the places it visits, so you are able to see the real bush.

Places to Stay & Eat

Three km west of town beside Sassafras Creek, at the turn-off to the caves and Cradle Mountain, is the *Mole Creek Camping Ground* (☎ 6363 1150). It has basic facilities with coin-operated showers and charges $5. There are no hostels, so the basic rooms at the *Mole Creek Hotel* (☎ 6363 1102) in the main street (Pioneer Drive) are the cheapest in town. Singles/doubles are $20/35 and there are counter meals every day with mains for around $9. Nearby, the small *Mole Creek Guest House* (☎ 6363 1313) has B&B for $50 to $60 a double. The tearoom and restaurant downstairs provide meals and snacks.

To the east of town, *Mole Creek Holiday Village* (☎ 6363 6124) provides units for $59 a double, and has a restaurant and tearooms. *Bentley Cottage* (☎ 6363 6131) and *Alum Cliffs Homestead* (☎ 6363 6149) are in the same area and offer units for around the same price. Closer to Mole Creek, *Blackwood Park* (☎ 6363 1208) offers the highest-standard units around town for $74 a double.

Getting There & Away

TRC (☎ 6331 3233 or 1800 030 033) runs one service daily from Monday to Friday, which leaves Mole Creek at 7 am for Deloraine and returns at 5.50 pm. These buses connect with services to Launceston.

During summer, Tasmanian Wilderness Transport (☎ 6334 4442) runs three buses a week from Launceston, through Deloraine and Mole Creek, to the Walls of Jerusalem National Park. This comes through from Deloraine in mid-morning and returns in mid-afternoon; bookings are essential.

SHEFFIELD
• *pop 990*

For a town that really has little going for it in the way of unusual or significant natural features, Sheffield manages to attract a good number of tourists. For most of its history this town was a quiet farming backwater which struggled to exist. In the 1980s the shopkeepers decided to take positive steps and copied the idea of painting **murals** from the Canadian town Chemainus. The first mural was completed in 1986; it was a success with tourists and a craze started. There are now 25 murals around the town with a further 10 in the surrounding district. There are so many paintings that it's reaching the stage where new sites are becoming hard to find. Today the town is often referred to as 'the town of murals' or 'the outdoor art gallery'.

The scenery around Sheffield is also impressive, with **Mt Roland** (1231 metres) dominating the peaceful farmlands, thick forests, and rivers. Nearby is beautiful **Lake Barrington**, part of the Mersey-Forth hydroelectric scheme and a major rowing venue and state recreation reserve.

Things to See

At the **Diversity Murals Theatrette**, at the western end of the main street, you can see an interesting 18-minute documentary about the paintings. The theatrette is open all day from Monday to Saturday, and on Sunday afternoons; admission is free with an optional donation. A map with a brief description of the murals and how to find them is available from the theatrette and costs 60c.

The **Kentish Museum**, next to the high school in Main St, has a display on the Mersey-Forth hydroelectricity scheme. There is also a display about Gustav Weindorfer, the founder of Waldheim near Cradle Mountain, plus artefacts from the area. It is open from 10 am until 3 pm every day except Saturday. During school holidays it's open from 1 pm till 4 pm and admission is by donation.

At the eastern end of town is **Redwater Creek Steam Rail** which has locomotives running on a narrow track. It's open on the first weekend of each month; admission is $2, children $1.

Gowrie Park, 16 km south-west of Sheffield, provides a great base to climb Mt Roland and is the site of a huge 94-metre-long mural on the hydro maintenance shed. The walks to the summits of Mt Roland or Mt Vandyke take about four to six hours return, as does the day walk to Minnow Falls. There are shorter walks in the cool, shady forests of the lower slopes.

Places to Stay & Eat

In town, the *Sheffield Caravan Park* (☎ 6491 1386) is tucked in behind the town hall. It's basic and costs $8 to pitch your tent.

The cheapest non-camping accommodation in the area is 16 km out of town in Gowrie Park, at the base of Mt Roland. *Black Stumps Backpacker Accommodation* (☎ 6491 1385) charges only $8.50 a night for bunk beds. The owners also run *Weindorfers Restaurant*, which some travellers think is marvellous while others have been very disappointed. If you stay here, try it but bring some of your own supplies just in case. This is an excellent base for walks to Mt Roland.

The *Sheffield Hotel* (☎ 6491 1130), near the Diversity Murals Theatrette, has very basic rooms for $30/40 including a light breakfast. It also has counter meals every day for around $9. On the other side of Main St the *Sheffield Aria Motel* (☎ 6491 1821), hidden behind the Saddlery Tea Room, has hostel bunks for $15 and motel rooms for $45 a double. Almost next door, the *Sheffield Country Motor Inn* (☎ 6491 1800) has motel rooms for $59 and units for $69 a double.

Holiday units are available at *Sheffield Holiday Pioneer Units* (☎ 6491 1149) in Pioneer Crescent, just a few metres off Main St. There is a range of units costing from $75 to $85 a double, plus $30 to $35 for each extra person.

Sheffield

0   125   250 m

✕ *Mural Locations*

1	Acacia
2	Sheffield Caravan Park
3	Sheffield Aria Motel
4	Saddlery Tea Room
5	Sheffield Country Motor Inn
6	Diversity Murals Theatrette
7	Sheffield Hotel
8	Flo's Country Kitchen
9	Jekyll & Hyde
10	Information Centre
11	Tanglewood
12	Sheffield Holiday Pioneer Units
13	Kentish Museum
14	Redwater Creek Steam Rail

NORTH

The B&B in town is *Tanglewood* (☎ 6491 1854), at 25 High St, which provides some luxury in an old timber home for $85 to $95 a double. Meals are an optional extra. Further away from the town centre, at 113 High St, *Acacia* (☎ 6491 2482) provides B&B for $60/75, and has wheelchair access.

Most other accommodation is out of town on farming properties. *Paradise Cottage*

Magical Murals

Once upon a time, in a small, sleepy town called Sheffield in north-western Tasmania, the townsfolk called a special meeting to try to find some magical way of awakening the town and stop it slipping into eternal economic slumber. The Kentish Association for Tourism Inc (KAT) was formed at the meeting and named after the municipality. One member had heard of a Canadian town being transformed by a magical mural momentum and thought that the same might work for Sheffield.

In December 1986 the first mural was unveiled to the public. This was the start of a continuing commitment by KAT to retell the history of the town through these colourful murals. Some murals, such as 'The Smithy at Work' and 'Early Trading' depict the early settlers. Others, such as 'Cradle Mountain Beauty' and 'The Forth Falls' highlight the beauty which surrounds the town, while 'Kentish Nocturnal', 'Kentish Birds' and 'Tassie Tigers and Devils' illustrate some of the wildlife to be found in the area. Murals also depict events, such as the 'Cradle Mountain Rescue' which shows the rugged, snow-covered scenery, and bushwalkers – as well as Snr Constable Harry Clark who was in charge of this first helicopter rescue in the park.

In the beginning, there was no shortage of stories to tell nor walls to paint. Today, however, while there are still many tales to tell, there are so many marvellous murals that it's getting harder to find space for more. Some artists have even ventured further into the Kentish countryside: to Railton, Gowrie Park, Roland and Moina, to use sides of shops and sheds to present their work.

Hopefully for Sheffield, they will live happily ever after, thanks to the mural magic which has created substantial growth for the town. A look at this outdoor art gallery is a must for every visitor. ■

(☎ 6491 1613 or 6491 1626) has two units at $45 to $60 a double. Hidden down a side road near Gowrie Park, *Gnome Home* (☎ 6491 1560) provides good-value B&B for $30/55. If you prefer to be on a working farm, then stay at *Carinya Farm Accommodation* (☎ 6491 1953 or 018 144 877) for $60/70, plus $15 for extra adults.

For curiosity value alone, *Flo's Country Kitchen* in Main St is worth a look. This is run by former Queensland senator Flo Bjelke-Petersen, whose husband, Sir Joh, was Australia's most notorious state premier. Today, Flo's speciality is pumpkin scones. Afternoon teas are also available at the *Diversity Murals Theatrette* where the mural films are shown. The offer of a hot drink and a biscuit for $1 is a real bargain and the service is very friendly. Directly opposite is a similar place called the *Saddlery Tea Room*. The *Jekyll and Hyde* family bistro at 60 Main St provides more substantial meals, including pasta, with mains for $10.

Getting There & Away

All buses follow the Devonport, Spreyton, Sheffield, Gowrie Park route on the way to Cradle Mountain. TRC (☎ 6424 5100 or 1800 030 033) runs a daily service from mid-September to May from Devonport through Sheffield to Queenstown and Strahan. In the other direction, only the Saturday and Sunday service from Queenstown passes through Sheffield on the way to Devonport. From June to mid-September, services run along the route on Tuesday, Thursday and Sunday from Devonport to Queenstown and Strahan, but in the other direction only the Sunday service comes this way.

Tasmanian Wilderness Travel (☎ 6334 4442) runs daily services from November to April from Devonport through Sheffield to Cradle Mountain Lodge and return. From May to October buses operate on Tuesday, Thursday and Saturday along the same route. There is also an all-year service from Devonport to Strahan via Sheffield on Saturday and returning the same way on Sunday.

LATROBE

• *pop 2550*

Located just 10 km from Devonport, this historic town is often overlooked in favour of its larger neighbour, yet is far more interesting. Founded in the 1830s it was originally the region's port, with ships sailing up the Mersey River to its docks. It was also the location of the first ford across the river, and the discovery of coal nearby assured its development. It was named after Charles La Trobe, the first Lt Governor of the state of Victoria. By 1889 a railway line was established and the first hospital opened. At this stage it was one of the state's largest towns.

The extension of the railway line and construction of a deep-water port at the river mouth at Devonport moved shipping business away from Latrobe. The town remained the business centre for the farming community. Today it's becoming an outer suburb of Devonport and is known as the town of restaurants.

The town's history is depicted through the 600 prints on display in the **Court House Museum** next to the post office in the centre of town. It's open on Friday and Sunday from 2 to 5 pm; admission is $1, children 50c.

At Christmas, the town stages an annual bicycle race, the **Latrobe Wheel Race**, which attracts professional riders from all over Australia. It is held on December 25 and 26. Latrobe also hosts the **Henley-on-the-Mersey carnival** which is held in March at Bells Parade, the site of the town's former docks.

Places to Stay & Eat

Out of town, opposite the hospital, the *Old Latrobe Motel* (☎ 6426 2030) has rooms for $43/55. In town the *Lucas Hotel* (☎ 6426 1101), at the western end of Gilbert St, provides B&B for $65 a double. The restored hotel also has a moderately priced grill which is open every day for lunch and dinner.

On the edge of town at 35 Gilbert St, *Erica Cottage* (☎ 6426 2717 or 018 133 895) can be rented for $95 a double. It's a quaint little self-contained cottage with a pretty garden. Alternatively, stay at the higher class *Lucinda* (☎ 6426 2285) where B&B is $75 to $110 a double. Hidden halfway up the hill in Forth St, it also has a good à la carte restaurant.

For such a small town, Latrobe has plenty of eating places. There's the usual pizza shop and *D'Oylies* is quite a good coffee shop. For Indian and Thai food, try *Navi's Indian Delights* (☎ 6426 1236), which is set back from the shopfronts in Gilbert St. It's open from Wednesday to Saturday.

The most famous restaurant in town is *Gillies* (☎ 6426 1082 or 018 140 789) at 20 Gilbert St. The à la carte menu contains unusual, innovative dishes and is recommended for those who like experimenting with new tastes. It's also very reasonably priced, with mains for $12. For traditional à la carte go to *Glo Glos* (☎ 6426 2120) at 78 Gilbert St. It's a little more expensive than Gillies, with mains at $17.

PORT SORELL
* *pop 1500*

Located just east of Devonport, Port Sorell and Hawley Beach are well-established holiday retreats and retirement villages on the shallow estuary of the Rubicon River. Originally named the First Western River in 1805, this was the first area to be settled on the north-west coast. In 1822, it was renamed Port Sorell after the Governor of the day. In the 1840s, it was the largest town on the coast and home to the region's police headquarters. With the development of Latrobe, then later Devonport, this port declined and bush grew over much of the town. Modern transport has helped it gain favour as a holiday resort and as a place to retire.

The town is split into two sections by the flats of Poyston Creek. At Port Sorell there are several islands in the estuary which can be reached at low tide. The flats are rather muddy so you must return before the tide rises. An alternative walk is to follow the track along the shoreline north to Point Sorell, which takes three hours return. Hawley Beach has sandy and sheltered swimming beaches and coves.

Places to Stay

The *Moomba Holiday Park* (☎ 6428 6140) at the corner of Kermode and Meredith Sts has tent sites for $9 and holiday cabins for $27. Closer to the foreshore, *Port Sorell Caravan Park & Camping Ground* (☎ 6428 6261) charges $10 a camp site. *Heron on*

Earth (☎ 6428 6144) is a small organic farm on River Rd at the southern edge of town. This is close to town and good value, with backpacker beds for $15 each including breakfast, or B&B for $45 a double.

Most other accommodation is four km west of the town, in the hills. *Tudor Cabins* (☎ 6428 6390), in Appleby's Rd, has good-value cabins for $43 a double. Nearby *Appleby Creek Lodge* (☎ 6428 7222) provides high-standard B&B for $56 a double.

DEVONPORT
• *pop 22,660*

Located on both sides of the Mersey River estuary, Devonport is Tasmania's third-largest city. Originally there were two separate towns on each side of the Mersey River; Formby on the west side and Torquay on the east side. In 1890, they merged into Devonport although the old town of Torquay is still referred to by locals as East Devonport.

Following the name change and the extension of the railway to the town, Devonport took over from Latrobe as port for the region. The flat land, a rarity in Tasmania, aided the town's growth. The most dominant feature of the town is the lighthouse-topped Mersey Bluff, from where there are fine views of the coastline. The lighthouse was built in 1889 to aid navigation for the expanding port. Today, the port remains important, handling much of the produce from the agricultural areas of northern Tasmania.

For many visitors the city is the site of the terminal for the *Spirit of Tasmania*, the vehicular ferry between Victoria and Tasmania. Devonport tries hard to attract tourists but its visitors are usually arriving or departing rather than actually staying. Indeed, the city is often referred to as the 'gateway to Tasmania'.

Information

For any information about Devonport and Tasmania in general, head for the Backpackers Barn (☎ 6424 3628) at 12 Edward St. The Barn is open daily from 8 am to 6 pm and the friendly staff can arrange transport and car rental, help organise itineraries or look after your backpack. It has a cafe, an excellent bushwalking shop, and a rest room with showers which travellers can use for $3. If you would like to go bushwalking but did not bring all your gear, you can hire major items like sleeping bags, backpacks, stoves and tents.

The Devonport Showcase (☎ 6424 8176), at 5 Best St, also has a complete range of tourist information with displays and workshop demonstrations of arts & crafts. The centre is currently the official information centre and is open daily from 9 am to 5 pm. You can also listen to the tourist radio on 99.3 FM. This runs 24 hours a day and repeats a one-hour tape about the city.

The post office is one block away from the mall, on the corner of Stewart St and Formby Rd. It's open on weekdays from 9 am to 5 pm and on Saturday morning from 9 am to noon.

Tiagarra

The Tasmanian Aboriginal Culture & Art Centre is at Mersey Bluff, on the road to the lighthouse. It's known as Tiagarra, which is the Tasmanian Aboriginal word for 'keep', and was set up to preserve the art and culture of the Tasmanian Aborigines. The centre has a rare collection of more than 250 rock engravings, and is open daily from 9 am to 4 pm (4.30 in summer); it's well worth the $2.50 admission fee (children $1). From the centre a walking track leads to Aboriginal rock carvings on Mersey Bluff.

Museums

The **Tasmanian Maritime & Folk Museum** is located halfway to Mersey Bluff from the town centre, and has models of sailing ships, both old and new, which have visited Tasmania. The Bass Strait ferries are a major feature and there are lots of marine items. It's open Tuesday to Sunday from 1 to 4 pm and admission is $1, children 40c.

Taswegia, in a lovely old building at 55-57 Formby Rd, is a commercial printing house with a historic printing museum as well as a craft studio and gift shop. It's open

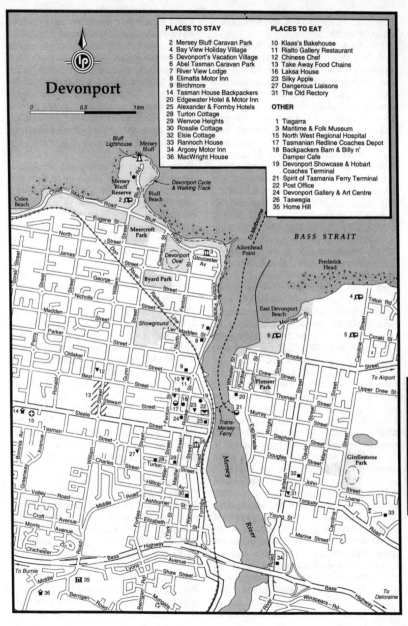

Devonport

0   0.5   1 km

PLACES TO STAY

2 Mersey Bluff Caravan Park
4 Bay View Holiday Village
5 Devonport's Vacation Village
6 Abel Tasman Caravan Park
7 River View Lodge
8 Elimatta Motor Inn
9 Birchmore
14 Tasman House Backpackers
20 Edgewater Hotel & Motor Inn
25 Alexander & Formby Hotels
28 Turton Cottage
29 Wenvoe Heights
30 Rosalie Cottage
32 Elsie Cottage
33 Rannoch House
34 Argosy Motor Inn
36 MacWright House

PLACES TO EAT

10 Klaas's Bakehouse
11 Rialto Gallery Restaurant
12 Chinese Chef
13 Take Away Food Chains
16 Laksa House
23 Silky Apple
27 Dangerous Liaisons
31 The Old Rectory

OTHER

1 Tiagarra
3 Maritime & Folk Museum
15 North West Regional Hospital
17 Tasmanian Redline Coaches Depot
18 Backpackers Barn & Billy n'
   Damper Cafe
19 Devonport Showcase & Hobart
   Coaches Terminal
21 Spirit of Tasmania Ferry Terminal
22 Post Office
24 Devonport Gallery & Art Centre
26 Taswegia
35 Home Hill

NORTH

daily from 10 am to 5 pm, and admission is $2, children 50c.

The **Don River Railway & Museum** (☎ 6424 6335), four km out of town on the Bass Hwy towards Ulverstone, has a collection of steam locomotives and passenger carriages, and you can take a ride on a vintage train along the banks of the Don River. It is owned and run by volunteers. Trains leave on the hour for 30-minute journeys along the Don River. It's open most days from 11 am to 4 pm and a ride costs $6, children $3. Occasionally there are special services from Don to Devonport, and also to Spreyton on horse-racing days. The fare is $10 return (children $5), which includes entry to the racecourse.

Other Attractions

The **Devonport Gallery & Art Centre**, at 45-47 Stewart St, is open Monday to Friday from 10 am to 5 pm and on Sunday afternoons from 2 pm to 5 pm; there is no entry fee. As well as its own permanent collection there are regular special exhibitions.

At 77 Middle Rd, not far from the youth hostel, is **Home Hill**, which used to be the residence of Joseph and Dame Enid Lyons and is now administered by the National Trust. Joseph Lyons is the only Australian to have been both a state premier and the prime minister of Australia, and Dame Enid Lyons was the first woman to become a member of the House of Representatives and a cabinet minister. Home Hill is open from Tuesday to Thursday and at weekends from 2 to 4 pm; admission is $5, children $3, family $10.

Every Sunday from 9 am to 4 pm the **Don Village Market**, opposite the railway museum, has locals selling their arts & crafts. Further south, beside the Don River at Eugenana (10 km from Devonport), is the **Tasmanian Arboretum**. This park contains native and exotic trees, and entry is free.

Most of the shoreline around the city is lined with parks and reserves which provide good walking. You can walk from the city centre along the Mersey River shore to Mersey Bluff. Walking tracks continue to Coles Beach then upstream along the Don River to the Don River Railway.

Organised Tours

Tours of Devonport are run every day by Top Centa Tours (☎ 6424 4466) and the half-day tours range from a budget $28, which takes you to all sites, up to $35 including entry to all sites. They also run full-day tours for $72 which travel through the surrounding rural district.

Many of the full-day tours from Devonport are to Tasmania's wilderness areas. Tarkine Tours (☎ 6428 2089 or 018 143 057) goes to places like Cradle Mountain ($55), Pieman River ($70), Gordon River ($85), Arthur River ($65) and Leven Canyon ($50). In December and January, tours are daily and in other months they're on Friday, Saturday and Sunday.

You can also visit Cradle Mountain with the Tasmanian Wilderness Transport (☎ 6334 4442) service. In summer this runs every day and in winter it runs on Tuesday, Thursday and Saturday. The return fare is $40; if you want to stay overnight then the return fare is $45. There are many other tours which can be taken and the Backpackers Barn or Devonport Showcase are the places to visit to find out what's available.

A great way to see most of the wilderness areas is by light plane. Bass Flight Services (☎ 6427 9777) flies from Devonport over Cradle Mountain and the surrounding areas. Prices vary according to flight time and the number of passengers, but work out roughly at $60 to $90 per hour per person. Flights run on demand.

Places to Stay

Camping East Devonport has three caravan parks, all close to the beach and with good reputations. The *Abel Tasman Caravan Park* (☎ 6427 8794), at 6 Wright St, has camp sites for $7, bunkhouse accommodation for $11, on-site vans for $30 and cabins from $46. *Devonport's Vacation Village* (☎ 6427 8886), in Caroline St, has camp sites for $15 and cabins from $42. Further north on Caroline St, *Bay View Holiday Village* (☎ 6427

0499) is very close to the beach but further from town. Camp sites are $12 and cabins range from $40 to $55.

On the west side of the river, the *Mersey Bluff Caravan Park* (☎ 6424 8655) is 2.5 km north of town, near Tiagarra and the lighthouse. It's a pleasant place with some good beaches nearby. It has camp sites for $12, vans for $34 and cabins for $44.

Hostels *MacWright House* (☎ 6424 5696), 400 metres past Home Hill at 155 Middle Rd, is Devonport's YHA hostel; it charges $9 a night ($11 for nonmembers). It's three km from the town centre, about a 40-minute walk. A Tasmanian Wilderness Transport bus can take you from the ferry terminal or airport to the hostel.

The other budget accommodation option is *Tasman House Backpackers*, (☎ 6423 2335 or 018 139 207), at 169 Steele St. Rooms vary from bunk house to motel-style and prices range from $8 to $12 per person. It is a 15-minute walk from town and transport can be arranged when booking.

B&B The friendly *River View Lodge* (☎ 6424 7357), at 18 Victoria Parade on the foreshore, charges $45/55 for singles/doubles, which includes an excellent cooked breakfast. It's deservedly popular with travellers.

Very close to the city centre is *Wenvoe Heights* (☎ 6424 1719), at 44 Macfie St. A completely renovated, two-storey Federation brick building, it charges $54/68 for singles/doubles with shared facilities and $15 extra for rooms with private facilities. Even closer to town is *Birchmore* (☎ 6423 1336), at 10 Oldaker St, which caters particularly for business people. Rates for doubles are $85 to $95. Singles start at $75.

In East Devonport, *Rannoch House* (☎ 6427 9818), at 5 Cedar Court, is a bit out of town but has orchards and a large garden. Rates are $60/78. Great views can be had at the *Ochill Manor* (☎ 6428 2660) at Forth, 10 km west of Devonport. Located on a hill and with extensive gardens, it's a good place to get away from the city. À la carte meals are available. Rates are $75/110.

Hotels & Motels Two good hotels close to the centre of town are the *Alexander Hotel* (☎ 6424 2252), at 78 Formby Rd, which charges $35/50 for a single/double room with breakfast; and the *Formby Hotel* (☎ 6424 1601), at 82 Formby Rd, where rooms cost $35/55 with breakfast.

There are quite a number of motels in the city centre and East Devonport. The *Edgewater Hotel & Motor Inn* (☎ 6427 8441), at 2 Thomas St in East Devonport, is not very attractive from the outside, but is close to the ferry terminal and charges $44/49 for singles/doubles. The *Argosy Motor Inn* (☎ 6427 8872), in Tarleton St, East Devonport, charges $72 a double. North of the city centre at 15 Victoria Pde, the *Elimatta Motor Inn* (☎ 6424 6555) charges $55/60.

Cottages *Rosalie Cottage*, at 66 Wenvoe St, and *Turton Cottage* (☎ 6424 1560 or 018 142 295), at 28 Turton St, are managed by the same people, and can be hired for $90/110 for a single/double, which includes a light breakfast. Both cottages can sleep four and extra adults are charged $20 each. Over in East Devonport, *Elsie Cottage* (☎ 018 123 500), at 150 David St, is another restored house which sleeps four. It is reasonably close to the ferry and costs $110 a double plus $25 for each extra person.

Places to Eat

There are plenty of coffee lounges and takeaways in the mall, but for a good atmosphere and great snacks try *Billy N Damper*, the cafe at the front of the Backpackers Barn, 12 Edward St. The 'eat all you can' pancake deal for $6 is great value. It's open daily from 8 am to 6 pm, and will take party bookings in the evenings. The *Old Devonport Town Coffee Shop* in the Devonport Showcase is also open daily and is good for a drink or a snack. *Klaas's Bakehouse*, 11 Oldaker St, is only open on weekdays but has excellent cakes and pastries.

Most hotels have good counter meals for around $8 to $15; try the *Tamahere* at 34 Best St, the *Alexander* at 78 Formby Rd, or the

NORTH

Formby nearby at 82 Formby Rd. In East Devonport, the *Edgewater Hotel*, at 2 Thomas St, has cheap counter meals.

Devonport has a good selection of moderately priced restaurants. A bargain lunch for $4.50 a dish can be found at *Dangerous Liaisons* at 28 Forbes St, open Tuesday to Friday for lunch and dinner and on Saturday for dinner only. If pasta's your choice, try the *Rialto Gallery Restaurant*, 159 Rooke St. While the pasta is not fancy, service is prompt. It's open Monday to Friday for lunch and every evening for dinner until late with main courses for $10.

For Asian food, try the *Silky Apple* at 33 King St, the *Chinese Chef* at 4b Kempling St, or *Laksa House* at 1/5b Edward St. All are open every evening and also serve takeaways. Prices for mains range from $8 to $10.

If you're looking for something special, then try the à la carte restaurant at the *Old Rectory* (☎ 6427 8037) at 71 Wright St, East Devonport. It's open Wednesday to Monday and for Sunday lunches and serves French/Italian cuisine, with mains costing around $18. It also sells home-made breads and chocolates.

There are several takeaways in William St between Best and Steele Sts. Here you'll find well-known places such as KFC, Burger Hut and Pizza Hut as well as fish & chips and Chinese restaurants.

Entertainment

Check the *Advocate* newspaper for Devonport's entertainment listings. The *Warehouse Nightclub* and *Spurs Saloon* are in King St. The *Elimatta Motor Inn*, at 15 Victoria Pde, occasionally has bands on weekends. On Wednesday, Friday and Saturday nights, you can step out at a nightclub called *Steps*. At the Tamahere Hotel, there's a nightclub called *Club One*, while *City Limits*, at 18 King St, is also a popular nightspot.

Getting There & Away

Air For information on domestic flights to and from Devonport, see the Getting There & Away section for the whole state. There are several daily flights to Melbourne with Qantas and Ansett, plus regular flights with smaller airlines to major regional towns in Victoria.

Airlines of Tasmania also runs small planes between the major cities and towns of Tasmania and this can be a scenic way to see some of the state. It's more expensive and sometimes not much faster than the bus if there are intermediate stops on the route.

Bus TRC's agent is the Backpackers Barn (☎ 6424 3628) at 12 Edward St, although the depot (☎ 6424 5100) is right across the road at No 9. All buses also stop at the ferry terminal when the ferry is in town. TRC has daily buses from Devonport to Hobart ($30.30), Queenstown ($31.70), Strahan ($36.90), Launceston ($12.50) and Burnie ($6.60). It runs at least three services every day from Hobart to Launceston, on to Devonport and Burnie, and return. On weekdays most services continue to Smithton. At weekends, only one Saturday service operates to Smithton and there are no services on Sunday.

The other main route TRC operates on is to Queenstown and Strahan on the west coast. Most services run from Devonport through Sheffield to Cradle Mountain Lodge, then down the Murchison Hwy to Queenstown then Strahan. The return route is different, being from Strahan to Queenstown then following the highway north directly to Burnie and along the northern coast back to Devonport. Just to confuse everyone, the weekend services follow the Cradle Mountain Lodge-Sheffield route in both directions. From September to May, TRC runs daily services to Queenstown and Strahan and during the remainder of the year there are three services a week.

The Hobart Coaches office (☎ 6424 6599 or 1800 030 620) is at the Devonport Central shopping centre in King St. Hobart Coaches has daily buses to Launceston, Hobart and Burnie, and stopping at all towns along the way.

During the summer many of the Tasmanian Wilderness Transport (☎ 6334 4442) buses depart daily from Devonport. They can take you to Sheffield ($30), Cradle Mountain ($30) or Lake St Clair ($45). A once-a-week service runs on Saturday to Strahan ($40) and Zeehan ($40) and returns on Sunday. A bus runs three times a week to the Walls of Jerusalem National Park ($40); this actually starts from Launceston and uses a Hobart Coaches bus to Deloraine. The departure point is at the Devonport Showcase at 5 Best St. You can also be picked up from Devonport airport for $5 extra per person. Some services do run in winter to Cradle Mountain, Lake St Clair and Strahan.

Similar services are also provided by Maxwells (☎ 6492 1431), who run buses on demand to Cradle Mountain, Lake St Clair, Walls of Jerusalem, Frenchmans Cap and other walking destinations. For a group of four or more, the fares are about the same as Tasmanian Wilderness Travel.

Outside the summer period, or if none of the scheduled wilderness services suit your particular needs, you can charter a minibus from either Tasmanian Wilderness Transport, Maxwells or the Backpackers Barn. For example, a bus from Devonport to Cradle Mountain costs $120 or, if there are five people or more, $30 each.

Car Rental There are plenty of cheap car-rental firms such as Range/Rent-a-Bug (☎ 6427 9034), at 5 Murray St, East Devonport where rates start from $20 per day (insurance is extra). You might also try Discount Auto Rentals (☎ 6424 8222), on the Esplanade opposite the ferry terminal in East Devonport, where rates start at $25 per day (insurance is extra). Major companies like Avis, Thrifty and Budget are in the ferry terminal. In all, there are seven companies with desks at the *Spirit of Tasmania* terminal –or just opposite to it – which hire out everything from new cars to old petrol guzzlers.

Around the main shopping centre, parking meters operate during business hours. Rates are very cheap at 20c per hour; they take 10c and 20c coins.

Boat See the Getting There & Away section at the beginning of this book for details on the *Spirit of Tasmania* ferry service between Melbourne and Devonport. It operates three times every week each way across Bass Strait. The TT Line terminal (☎ toll-free 1800 030 344) is on the Esplanade, East Devonport. You can't miss seeing the ferry as it dominates the town when it's in port.

Getting Around

There's no shuttle bus to the airport but you can save a $10 taxi fare if you have arranged for a bus service to meet you. Most buses do call at the airport. Around town, south of Best St, local buses are run by Tasmanian Wilderness Transport, while East Devonport and the area north of Best St are covered by Hobart & Inter-City Coaches. The local buses run from Monday to Friday. If this is confusing don't worry; most places in Devonport are within reasonable walking distance.

Local Ferry There's a bridge across the Mersey River two km south of town and it's a long walk from Devonport to the ferry terminal at East Devonport. It's much quicker to use the small ferry, the MV *Torquay*, which crosses the river just north of the Devonport railway station. On the east side it docks next to the giant ferry, the *Spirit of Tasmania*. On weekdays it runs from 8 am to 6 pm and on Saturday it starts at 8.30 am and stops at 5.30 pm. There is a return trip roughly every 30 minutes except in peak hours when it runs more frequently. There are no Sunday services. One-way fares are $1.20, children 70c. Bicycles cost 40c.

ULVERSTONE

• *pop 14,460*

Ulverstone, at the mouth of the River Leven, is a pleasant town with some fine beaches and good amenities; it's a good base from which to explore the surrounding area. The town's main features are its war memorials and spacious parklands.

The major memorial is the **Shrine of**

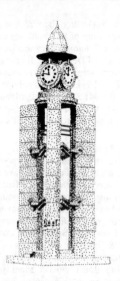

The columns on Ulverstone's war memorial represent the three services

Remembrance, located at one end of the main street and dominating the town. It's actually two memorials in one, with three large columns built above the original small memorial. Beside the River Leven is a series of spacious parks, many of them containing memorials. For children there are some excellent playgrounds. There are many barbecue facilities, shelters and huge stretches of grass which make this a great place for a picnic.

In West Ulverstone there is a **lookout tower** in Upper Maud St. This provides a good view over the town and river. The **local history museum**, at 50 Main St, is open on Saturday and Sunday afternoons from 1.30 to 4 pm. The display focuses on the lives of the Europeans who cleared the forests and created farms in the area; admission is $2, (children $1).

If you're driving from Ulverstone to Penguin, consider taking the old Bass Hwy. This narrow, winding road follows the coast and offers attractive views of the shores around Penguin Point. The three small islands known as the **Three Sisters** are particularly scenic.

Places to Stay

There are plenty of camping grounds in Ulverstone, including the *Apex Caravan Park* (☎ 6425 2935) in Queen St, West Ulverstone, where camp sites are $8. The *Ulverstone Caravan Park* (☎ 6425 2624) in Water St, is somewhat closer to town and has camp sites for $8.20, on-site vans for $30 a double, cabins for $41 and units for $51.

The redecorated *Lighthouse Hotel* (☎ 6425 1197), on the corner of Victoria and Reibey Sts, has good rooms for $65/75. Nearby, the *Furners Hotel* (☎ 6425 1488), at 42 Reibey St, has simpler rooms for $40/60 for singles/doubles.

For a great location try the *Ocean View Guest House* (☎ 6425 5401) at 1 Victoria St, 100 metres from the beach. It's a lovely old house where singles/doubles with a continental breakfast cost $40/65. If you prefer a motel, there's the *Bass and Flinders Motor Inn* (☎ 6425 3011) just across the river from the town, with rooms for $55 a double. Older, and closer to the beach, is *Beachway Motel* (☎ 6425 2342) in Heathcote St. It's opposite the Ulverstone Caravan Park and has doubles for $50.

Holiday units can be hired at *Willaway Apartments* (☎ 6425 2018) at 2 Tucker St. This is next door to the Beachway Motel and very close to the beach; it's $55 a double plus $10 for each extra adult.

Places to Eat

Pedro the Fisherman (☎ 6425 5181), down by the wharf, has extremely cheap but filling takeaway fish & chips – if you can't finish the packet there are plenty of obliging seagulls around!

Furners Hotel (☎ 6425 1488), in Reibey St, has a family bistro with the usual steaks and seafood dishes for around $12 to $14. Similar fare at similar prices is available at the unusually decorated *Lighthouse Hotel* (☎ 6425 1197) on the corner of Reibey and

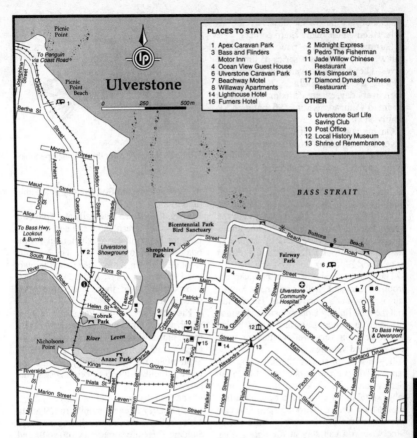

PLACES TO STAY

1 Apex Caravan Park
3 Bass and Flinders
  Motor Inn
4 Ocean View Guest House
6 Ulverstone Caravan Park
7 Beachway Motel
8 Willaway Apartments
14 Lighthouse Hotel
16 Furners Hotel

PLACES TO EAT

2 Midnight Express
9 Pedro The Fisherman
11 Jade Willow Chinese
   Restaurant
15 Mrs Simpson's
17 Diamond Dynasty Chinese
   Restaurant

OTHER

5 Ulverstone Surf Life
  Saving Club
10 Post Office
12 Local History Museum
13 Shrine of Remembrance

Victoria Sts. This has a special menu for children.

There are a number of restaurants which offer a multiplicity of cuisines. In West Ulverstone, the *Midnight Express* restaurant in Queen St combines Chinese, Indian and Australian food for around $9 for mains. In Ulverstone itself, the *Diamond Dynasty Chinese Restaurant*, at 48 King Edward St, serves Malaysian as well as Chinese food and is open every day.

A little more upmarket is the *Bass and Flinders Restaurant*, at 49 Eastlands Drive, which has mains for $13 and occasionally

has entertainment. Another similarly priced restaurant is *Mrs Simpson's*, at 31 King Edward St, where everything is home-made.

Getting There & Away

See the Burnie Getting There & Away section for details of transport to and from Ulverstone; the same buses continue to Burnie.

AROUND ULVERSTONE

The hills south of this city are well worth exploring, with the major sites easily reached by car or motorcycle. The roads are mostly sealed but very narrow. Go slowly as care has to be taken on the many sharp corners.

Gunns Plains is a peaceful farming valley which contains a series of limestone caves. They were discovered by farmers out hunting the local wildlife. The caves are open every day, except Christmas Day, from 10 am to 4 pm; admission is $6 (children $3, family $15).

On the south side of Gunns Plains, the River Leven emerges from a deep gorge. To view the gorge, follow roads through Nietta to the **Leven Canyon Lookout**, 41 km from Ulverstone. The car park is a good picnic site and a well-graded track leads, after 10 minutes walk, to the sensational lookout on top of the gorge. You can walk through the gorge, but this takes at least 10 hours and is not recommended. Better nearby day walks lead to Winterbrook Falls (four hours return) or to Black Bluff (six hours return).

There are several other smaller waterfalls around Castra and Nietta, and Cradle Mountain is only a short drive away. Be warned that the road linking Upper Castra to Wilmot crosses a deep river gorge and is very steep; don't use it in very wet weather or with low-powered vehicles.

If you wish to stay in the hills, you can camp at *Wings Farm Park* (☎ 6429 1335) at Gunns Plains, for $3 per person or stay in a cabin suitable for up to 10 people for a flat rate of $40. On this working farm you can ride horses for $15 an hour or milk cows. Otherwise you can stay at *Kaydale Lodge* (☎ 6429 1293) in Nietta with B&B for $95 a double or *Mountain Valley Log Cabins* (☎ 6429 1394) in Loongana for $100 a double.

PENGUIN
• *pop 2900*

Named after the fairy penguins which nest along the coast, the town today has an ugly concrete penguin on the foreshore in the main street. The nearby mural depicting 19th century Penguin is also rather ordinary. Fortunately the real penguins still appear around dusk each day during the warmer months of

Penguin is named after the little fairy penguin

the year at **Penguin Point**; entry is $5, children $2.

Overall, the town is actually quite pleasant to visit as it's a residential site and does not have the large industries which many of the other northern towns possess. The beach in front of the town is very clean and there are good sporting facilities. In the **Dials Range**, behind the town, there are some good walking tracks.

Hiscutt Park, beside Penguin Creek, is worth a visit. It has good playground equipment, plus a working windmill which was a present from Holland to the town in 1988. In September, the tulip display around the windmill adds a touch of brightness to the park.

The town has a market on the second and fourth Sunday of every month from 9 am to 4 pm. In December, the market opens every Sunday. There are sometimes 140 stalls and all goods on sale have to be new.

Places to Stay & Eat
Located below the highway and perched on a small cliff beside the ocean, *Penguin Caravan Park* (☎ 6432 2785) provides small cabins with good views for $35 a double.

The best place to stay in town is the pretty *Beachfront Lodge* (☎ 6437 2672) at 64 Main St. As the name implies, it is opposite the beach and B&B is a very reasonable $40/55 for singles/doubles. Further along Main St the *Neptune Grand Hotel* (☎ 6437 2406) offers more basic B&B for $25/45.

If you want to hire a cottage on a farm then

Watercress Cottage (☎ 6437 1145) near Riana should suit. It's three km inland from the coast, hidden at the end of a steep road, and charges $60/70 for singles/doubles. It is only large enough for two people and breakfast is included.

The other nearby farm accommodation is not so private. *Pindari Deer Farm* near Riana can sleep up to 16 guests in motel-style units for $90 to $135 a double for B&B. The farm is open to all resident guests. It has many birds and animals, including alpacas and deer. Non-residents can also visit the farm; admission is $6, children $4, family $15. Lunch and dinner are served in the restaurant.

Counter meals are available at the *Penguin Hotel* in Main St. Next door to the hotel is *Sereenah's Tea House* which is only open on weekends and public holidays. The alternative is the *Penguin Pizza & Coffee Lounge* which is fine as long as they cook fresh food while you wait. The lukewarm pizza in the warmer is not very inviting. The town has a bakery, but not much else.

À la carte meals are only available at *Monty's* (☎ 6437 2080) near the caravan park. It is open from Tuesday to Sunday for lunch and Tuesday to Saturday for dinner.

Getting There & Away

See the Burnie Getting There & Away section for details of transport to and from Penguin as the same buses run from Devonport through to Burnie.

The North-West

Tasmania's magnificent north-west coast is a land as rich in history as it is diverse in scenery. Its story goes back 37,000 years to a time when giant kangaroos and giant wombats roamed the area, and Aboriginal tribes took shelter in the caves along the coast. All that remains of their long occupation is a series of rock engravings, and middens containing the leftovers of their meals.

Europeans realised the potential of the region and the settlers moved further and further west, building towns along the coast and inland on the many rivers. The Aboriginal people were very quickly subdued, with the last group being captured near the Arthur River in 1842. Originally heavily forested, the area was cleared and soon transformed into a vital part of the young colony's developing economy. Today it's a major producer of frozen vegetables and potatoes for Australia. To most locals, the coastal region is known as Cape Country and indeed there are some impressive headlands which provide spectacular views of the coast.

Inland, the region is still quite wild with very few settlements and extensive unlogged forests. Conservation battles have raged for years over the Arthur River area with little success and slowly the roads are creeping into it for timber and mining exploration. From the northern coast across to the Queenstown region there are few towns and little to see apart from the impressive scenery as you pass through.

The most important of the new roads has been the link road CI32 from the Murchison Hwy through to Cradle Mountain Lodge. This has enabled drivers and bus companies to go direct from Devonport to Queenstown without visiting the north-west coast. If you have the time, it is far better to follow the older, slower roads as there is a lot to see along the north-west coast.

The other new road that is under construction is near the west coast from Balfour to

HIGHLIGHTS

- Climbing the Nut at Stanley
- Admiring the tulips at Table Cape
- The patchwork farming landscape
- Surfing at Marrawah

Corinna. At present it is only suitable for 4WDs with good drivers but eventually this may be upgraded into an interesting tourist drive.

Getting There & Around

Tasmanian Redline Coaches (TRC; ☎ 6431 3233 or 1800 030 033) runs at least four buses every day from Hobart to Devonport and Burnie. On weekdays four buses run from Burnie along the coast to Smithton, on Saturday there is a single service and on Sunday none at all.

Hobart Coaches (☎ 6431 1971 or 1800 030 620) runs buses every day from Hobart to Devonport and Burnie. From Monday to Friday local buses operate around Burnie suburbs and the outlying towns and these are handy for getting to places like Somerset, Penguin and Wynyard.

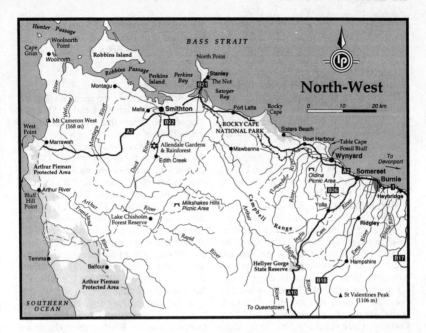

North-West

BURNIE

- *pop 20,500*

Although Burnie sits on the shores of Emu Bay and has a backdrop of rich farming land, it's factory smoke, not the views, which usually welcomes the visitor to Tasmania's fourth largest city. One of Burnie's main assets is its deep-water port, which makes cargo shipping an important industry. Another major employer, Amcor, owns Associated Pulp & Paper Mills (APPM), which began producing paper in 1938.

The town (named after William Burnie, who was a director of the Van Diemen's Land Company) started life quietly as a potato-growing centre for the first forty years, until the discovery of tin at Mt Bischoff in Waratah. In 1878 the Van Diemen's Land Company opened a wooden tramway between the mine at Waratah and the port of Burnie. This was the humble beginning of the important Emu Bay Railway, which, in the 1900s, linked the port of Burnie to the

rich silver fields of Zeehan and Rosebery. The Emu Bay Railway, which travels through some wild and impressive country, still operates today but does not carry passengers.

The coastal plain around Burnie is very narrow and the lack of flat land has resulted in the town spreading along the coast. From Wivenhoe on the east side to Somerset on the west, buildings stretch for 10 km. This strip includes Parkdale, Cooee and Camdale, all included into the greater town of Burnie.

The largest industry is the APPM, which employs 1400 people. Other large industries in Burnie produce titanium pigments and, along with milk production for chocolate and cheese, these form the core of the town's prosperity.

The Tasmanian Travel & Information Centre, 48 Cattley St, is a good source of information on Tasmania's north-west. Pick up a copy of the *Walk Through Burnie* brochure for a self-guided walking tour of the

NORTH-WEST

town centre and the nearby Burnie Park. The town is trying hard to attract tourists, and provides lots of information on the area.

Things to See & Do

The **Pioneer Village Museum** (☎ 6430 5746), in High St, next to the Civic Plaza, has recreated an original village dated around 1900. It includes an authentic blacksmith's shop, printer, wash house, stage coach depot and boot shop. This impressive museum with 30,000 items on display is open from 9 am to 5 pm Monday to Friday, and from 1.30 to 4.30 pm at weekends; admission is $4, children $1.

Burnie Park is quite pleasant and features an animal sanctuary and the oldest building in town, the Burnie Inn. The Inn was built in 1847 and moved from its original site to the park in 1973. It's classified by the National Trust and is open from 1 pm to 5 pm on weekends from November to April. Afternoon teas are available at the inn when it is open. The oval on the north side of the park is the site of the annual **Burnie Athletics Carnival** which is held on New Year's Day. The carnival has been held for over one hundred years and, with substantial cash prizes, attracts many professional athletes. Nearby, in Crown St, there is a lookout which provides a good view over the city centre.

From Monday to Thursday, at 2 pm, you can take a free tour of the Amcor complex (☎ 6430 7777). On weekdays you can also visit the Lactos cheese factory, on Old Surrey Rd, where you can taste and purchase the products. The **Burnie Regional Art Gallery**, in Wilmot St, is open daily and is also worth a look; admission is free.

The lovely **Emu Valley Rhododendron Gardens**, eight km south of Burnie, are open daily between September and March from 10 am to 5 pm with a small entry fee of $2. They are managed by a branch of the Australian Rhododendron Society. Nearby are the **Annsleigh Gardens & Tea Rooms** which are also open daily from September to May; admission $3, children free.

In the Burnie area, there are a number of waterfalls and viewpoints, including **Roundhill Lookout** and **Fern Glade**, just three km from the town centre, and the impressive **Guide Falls** at Ridgley, 16 km away.

Places to Stay

For such a large town, the centre is small and restricted by the highway location. This, plus the pollution, means that many places to stay are well out of town.

In town most accommodation is in hotels. The cheapest is the *Regent* (☎ 6431 1933) at 26 North Terrace overlooking West Beach. It charges $20/30 for singles/doubles for basic rooms. Also overlooking West Beach, the *Beach Hotel* (☎ 6431 2533) at 1 Wilson St has rooms for $60 to $66 a double. On the opposite corner, *Voyager Motor Inn* (☎ 6431 4866) is more upmarket in style with rooms for $99 a double. At the southern end of the town centre, beside the highway, the *Burnie Town House* (☎ 6431 4455) at 139 Wilson St has rooms for $75/85.

Within easy walking distance of the town centre, *The Duck House* (☎ 31 1712) at 26 Queen St provides B&B accommodation for four guests; $65/85 for singles/doubles. Further up the hill at 36 Queen St, *Weller's Inn* (☎ 6431 1088) is a large motel complex with high-priced rooms at $97/106, and units for $110 a double.

In the hills south of the town, *Glen Osborne House* (☎ 6431 9866) at 9 Aileen Crescent provides high standard B&B with ensuite rooms in a National Trust registered house for $70/90. The *Hillside Motor Inn* (☎ 6431 3222) at the corner of Edwardes and Menai Sts has basic rooms for a bargain $35/50.

To get away from the industrial areas, head west out of town to Cooee and Somerset. The *Treasure Island Caravan Park* (☎ 6431 1925) at Cooee, four km from town, has camp sites for $10, on-site vans for $35 and cabins for $50 a double. On the same site is a backpackers hostel for $12 and the *Ocean View Motel* (☎ 6431 1925) has rooms for $50/58.

Further west, *Somerset Caravan Park* (☎ 6435 2322) is six km from Burnie and has

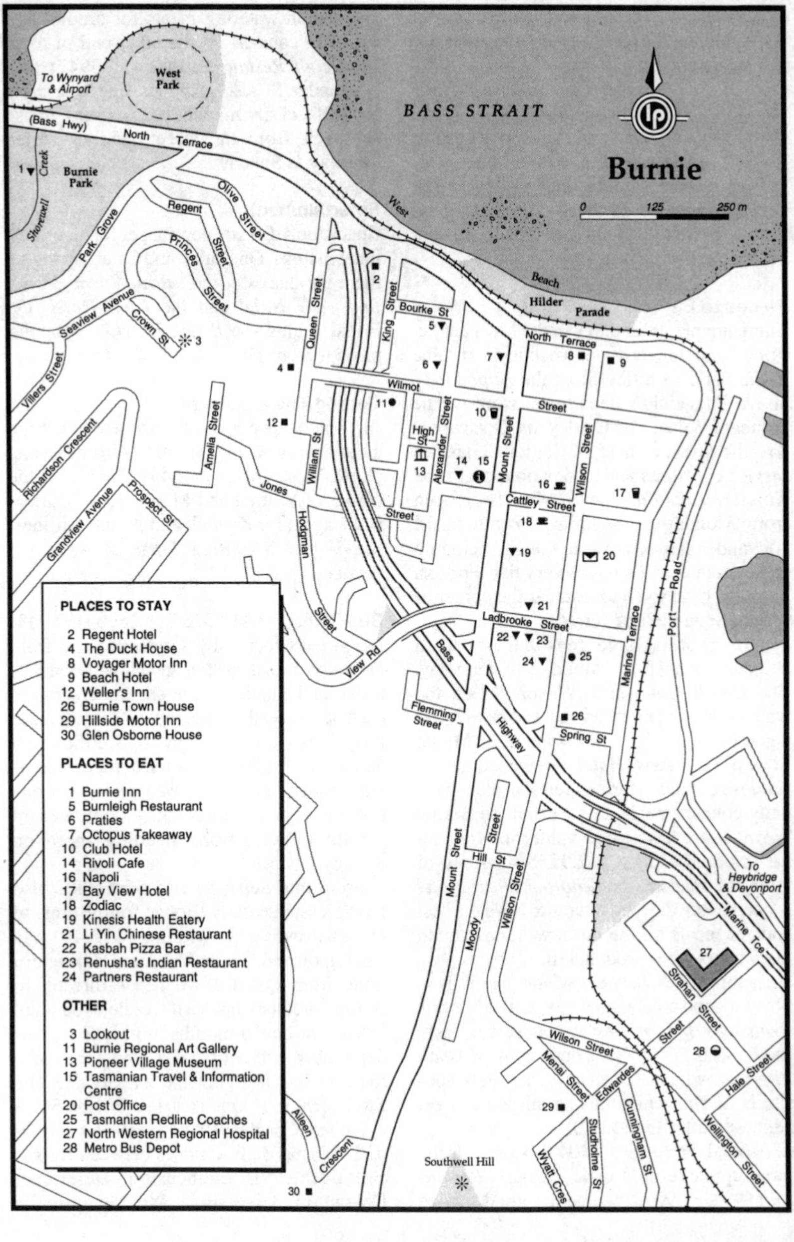

BASS STRAIT
Burnie
0
125
250 m
To Wynyard & Airport
West Park
(Bass Hwy)
North Terrace
Burnie Park
Shorewell Creek
Regent Street
Olive Street
Park Grove
Princes Street
Seaview Avenue
Crown St
Villers Street
Queen Street
King Street
Bourke St
West Beach
Hilder Parade
North Terrace
Wilmot Street
High St
Alexander Street
Mount Street
Wilson Street
Amelia Street
Richardson Crescent
William St
Jones Street
Hodgman Street
Grandview Avenue
Prospect St
Cattley Street
Ladbrooke Street
Port Road
Marine Terrace
View Rd
Bass Highway
Flemming Street
Spring St
Moody Street
Hill St
To Heybridge & Devonport
Marine Tce
Strahan Street
Wilson Street
Menai Street
Edwardes Street
Hale Street
Cunningham St
Studholme St
Wyatt Cres
Wellington Street
Aileen Crescent
Southwell Hill
PLACES TO STAY
2 Regent Hotel
4 The Duck House
8 Voyager Motor Inn
9 Beach Hotel
12 Weller's Inn
26 Burnie Town House
29 Hillside Motor Inn
30 Glen Osborne House
PLACES TO EAT
1 Burnie Inn
5 Burnleigh Restaurant
6 Praties
7 Octopus Takeaway
10 Club Hotel
14 Rivoli Cafe
16 Napoli
17 Bay View Hotel
18 Zodiac
19 Kinesis Health Eatery
21 Li Yin Chinese Restaurant
22 Kasbah Pizza Bar
23 Renusha's Indian Restaurant
24 Partners Restaurant
OTHER
3 Lookout
11 Burnie Regional Art Gallery
13 Pioneer Village Museum
15 Tasmanian Travel & Information Centre
20 Post Office
25 Tasmanian Redline Coaches
27 North Western Regional Hospital
28 Metro Bus Depot

camp sites for $10 and good value cabins for $36 a double. It's part of a nursery which also has a cafe and art gallery.

Also in Somerset, the *Somerset Hotel* (☎ 6435 2346) and *Seabrook Hotel Motel* (☎ 6435 1209) have good value hotel rooms for $40 to $45 a double. Around the corner in Somerset at 9 Murchison Hwy, *Murchison Lodge Motor Inn* (☎ 6435 1106) has good rooms for $65/70. This is in a peaceful spot beside the Cam River.

Places to Eat

There are plenty of cafes in the town centre. For cheap lunches on weekdays, try the *Zodiac* at 29 Cattley St or the *Napoli* cafe above Fitzgerald's department store on the corner of Wilson and Cattley Sts. Open every day, the *Rivoli Cafe* at 54 Cattley St has fast service and light meals. For wholesome food *Kinesis Health Eatery* at 63 Mount St is open from Monday to Saturday. *Praties* at 18 Alexander St specialises in snacks, including jacket potatoes; it's open every day. For fish & chips, head to *Octopus* near the corner of Mount St and North Terrace.

Most hotels have reasonably priced counter meals from Monday to Saturday. The *Beach Hotel* at 1 Wilson St, on the waterfront, is open every day and always has a good spread. The *Club Hotel* at 22 Mount St and *Bay View Hotel* on the corner of Cattley St and Marine Terrace also have daily counter meals. *Glo-Pots* at the Burnie Town House has a good-value, all-you-can-eat smorgasbord for $12.95. Six km out of town at Somerset, the *Seabrook Hotel Motel* is open every day and claims to have the best counter meals on the north-west coast with main courses for around $10.

Ladbrooke St, between Mount and Wilson Sts, is a good area to go when you're hungry. *Renusha's Indian Restaurant* serves tasty food and is BYO. Next door is the *Kasbah Pizza Bar* which is open until late, and opposite is *Li Yin*, which has an all-you-can-eat Chinese buffet for $12.80.

Around the corner, at 104 Wilson St, is the more upmarket à la carte *Partners Restaurant* (☎ 6431 9393) which has good service

and mouth-watering meals for around $19 for main courses. At the other end of town *Burnleigh Restaurant* (☎ 6431 3947) at 8 Alexander St also provides fine à la carte food. It's easily missed, being a pink house set back from the street, and it's open Tuesday to Sunday.

Entertainment

Check the *Advocate* newspaper for entertainment listings. On Friday and Saturday nights there are discos at the *Burnie Town House*, *Bay View Hotel* and the *Club Hotel*. On Friday nights, the *Beach Hotel* is a popular place for a drink.

Getting There & Away

Air The nearest airport – known as Burnie airport – is at Wynyard, 20 km from Burnie. North West Travel (☎ 6431 2166), on the corner of Wilmot and Mount Sts in Burnie, is the agent for Kendell and Ansett Airlines. See Wynyard Getting There & Away for details.

Bus TRC (☎ 6431 3233 or 1800 030 033) has at least four daily services to and from Devonport, Launceston and Hobart. On Saturday and Sunday there are three services each day along the same route. Many of these buses also continue on to Smithton on Monday to Friday with some of them detouring through Stanley. On weekends, only one service – in the evening – continues to Smithton, with none heading there on Sunday.

From mid-September to May, TRC also has at least one daily service from Burnie to Queenstown and Strahan ($30.40) via Devonport and Cradle Mountain. The return route from Queenstown heads directly to Burnie and does not visit Cradle Mountain. During the cooler months from June to mid-September, a bus operates along the same route on Tuesday, Thursday and Sunday. The TRC agent in Burnie is at 117 Wilson St.

Hobart Coaches (☎ 6431 1971 or 1800 030 620) has daily services between Hobart and Burnie via Launceston, Deloraine, Devonport, Ulverstone and Penguin. Its buses leave from outside the Tasmanian Travel & Information Centre in Cattley St.

During the week, Metro Burnie (☎ 6431 3822), at 30 Strahan St, has regular local buses to Ulverstone, Penguin and Wynyard which depart from the bus stops in Cattley St. There are no weekend services.

WYNYARD
• *pop 4680*

Sheltered by the impressive Table Cape and geologically fascinating Fossil Bluff, Wynyard sits both on the seafront and on the banks of the Inglis River. The town is surrounded by beautiful patchwork farmland, which is best appreciated by flying into Wynyard airport.

The area was first settled by Europeans in 1841 and, for most of the 19th century, Wynyard was the principal port on this section of coast. While Burnie eventually took over the shipping trade, Wynyard remained as the centre of a rich agricultural region. Butter, cheese, milk, vegetables and speciality crops such as tulips support the town's economy.

Although there's not much to see in the town itself, Wynyard is a good base from which to explore the many attractions in the area. A good source of tourist information is the Information Centre in Goldie St.

Organised Tours
The information centre has details on the latest tours. Holiday Coast Tours (☎ 6442 2891) runs day and half-day tours to Circular Head and Stanley for $30, Marakoopa Caves for $30 and places south of Devonport like Cradle Mountain for $30. Scenic flights over the town and the west coast can be arranged with Western Aviation (☎ 6442 1111) at the airport.

Places to Stay
Close to town, on the Esplanade right beside the beach, is the *Wynyard Caravan Park* (☎ 6442 1998) which has camp sites for $10, on-site vans for $30 and cabins for $50 a double. It also has hostel beds for $12 each or $20 a double. Further out of town, at 145

Old Bass Hwy, the *Rod Walker Leisure Ville* (☎ 6442 2291) has on-site vans for $34, cabins for $46 and holiday units for $68 for doubles.

The *Wynyard Youth Hostel* (☎ 6442 2013) is at 36 Dodgin St, one block south of the main street and has rooms for $11, $13 for nonmembers and $7 for children. If you've arrived by air, it's only a five-minute walk from the airport.

The *Federal Hotel* (☎ 6442 2056) at 82 Goldie St, in the middle of town, has singles/doubles for $30/50 for B&B. The *Inglis River Hotel Motel* (☎ 6442 2344) at 4 Goldie St is next door to the Wynyard Theatre and has rooms for $42/50. Out-of-season rates are as low as $25/35 and they can provide breakfast.

On the other side of Goldie St beside the river, the *Wynyard Motor Lodge* (☎ 6442 2351) has motel rooms for $54/62. For upmarket B&B, *Blackwell Lodge* (☎ 6442 2430) at 96 Jackson St charges $70/80 for singles/doubles. It's in an excellent setting, being the last house in the street beside the river. A five-minute walk along the river bank leads you into town. The other quality B&B is *Alexandria* (☎ 6442 4411) which is on the north side of town at the start of the road to Table Cape. Singles/doubles are $65/85.

Places to Eat
Fish & chips is the speciality at *YT's Fish Place* which is at the wharf opposite the Inglis River Hotel and is open daily. In the main shopping centre in Goldie St are several coffee shops and a hot bread shop.

Good-value counter meals for around $10 are available every day at *Inglis River Hotel* at 4 Goldie St, the *Federal Hotel* at 82 Goldie St and the *Wynyard Hotel* on the corner of Inglis and Goldie Sts. The Wynyard Motor Lodge complex contains *Blackbeards Bistro* which is open daily and serves meals for around $11 and *Romeos Pizza* which is open every day from 11 am to 10 pm.

For Chinese food, *Toysun Chinese Restaurant* (☎ 6442 1101) at 25 Goldie St provides takeaways as well as table service. And for international food, go to *Peppers Restaurant* (☎ 6442 1177) at 43 Jackson St which is just off Goldie St.

Getting There & Away

Air The airport is just one block from Wynyard's main street; about a five-minute walk away. This is also the airport for Burnie (which is 20 km away) and it is often listed on many of the schedules as Burnie, not Wynyard. Qantas (☎ 13 1313) and Ansett Airlines (☎ 13 1300) run two daily services plus an extra flight on Friday to Melbourne and return. These services link with flights to most other major cities on mainland Australia. Aus-Air (☎ 1800 331 256) also runs regular flights to Wynyard from Moorabbin in Victoria, and Albury and Merimbula in New South Wales.

For flights around Tasmania, Airlines of Tasmania (☎ 1800 030 550) runs regular services between all the major airports in the state including King Island. It also flies to Sale and Traralgon in Victoria.

Bus TRC (☎ 6431 3233 or 1800 030 033) runs four buses on weekdays from Burnie to Wynyard and on to Smithton and return. On Saturday morning they run one bus from Smithton through Wynyard to Burnie and the return bus from Burnie operates on Saturday evening. There are no Sunday services. The TRC agent is the BP service station next to the post office.

On weekdays Metro Burnie runs regular local buses from Burnie to Wynyard. They depart from outside the St Vincent de Paul shop in Jackson St.

AROUND WYNYARD
Fossil Bluff

Three km from the town centre is Fossil Bluff, where the oldest marsupial fossil found in Australia was unearthed. Some of the fossils which have been collected here are on display in the Tasmanian Museum & Art Gallery in Hobart. The soft sandstone here also features numerous shell fossils deposited when the level of Bass Strait was much higher. At low tide you can walk along

the foot of the bluff, observe the different layers in the rocks, and find fossils. It's also worth walking east along the rocks to the mouth of the Inglis River where there is a seagull rookery. If the tide is high, it is still worth climbing to the top of the bluff for the good views.

The Bluff is quite close to the town on the northern side of the river. By using the tracks from town beside the river you can take a pleasant two-hour return walk to the Bluff.

Table Cape

If you have transport, then ignore the highway and follow the minor roads towards Table Cape which is four km north of Wynyard. The narrow, sealed roads lead to the car park and lookout on top of the cape, 177 m above the ocean. It's often windy here and the view over Wynyard and the coast is excellent. You can also visit the nearby lighthouse which was built in 1885, although the views are not as good.

In September and October the **Table Cape Tulip Farm** is in full flower and is worth visiting. It's located beside the road to the lighthouse, where the fields are stripes of bright colours which contrast with the rich red soils of the cape. Do not enter the paddocks as the farm is on private land. From late September to mid-October, the farm is open to the public from 10 am to 4 pm daily. Admission is $10 per car, for which you get a tour of the paddocks as well as entry to a large display of tulips in the greenhouses.

The best route from the cape to Boat Harbour is to follow Tollymore Rd north-west. There are some great views of the cliffs and rocky coast along this road. Some of the best views are obtained from *Skyscape* (☎ 6442 1876) on Tollymore Rd. This new two-storey building has great ocean views and does B&B for $120 a double. Next door the older *Cape Cedars* (☎ 6442 4144) has the same views and does B&B for $75 a double.

Flowerdale

Located inland from Table Cape near the Bass Hwy, there is little to see here except

MONICA CHAPMAN

CHARLOTTE HINDLE

CHRIS KLEP

CHRIS KLEP

Top: The Nut, Stanley
Middle Left: Van Diemen's Land Company store, Stanley
Middle Right: Coastline near Arthur River, north-west Tasmania
Bottom: Highfield House, Stanley

CHRIS KLEP

CHRIS KLEP

RAY STAMP

   Top: Cradle Mountain with Lake Dove in the foreground
Middle: The picturesque port of Strahan
Bottom: Eerie landscape around Queenstown

for the **Flowerdale Valley Emu Farm** (☎ 6442 3911) where you can feed the birds and go on a guided tour of the farm. It's open from Tuesday to Saturday; admission is $2.50, children $1.50 or family $8.

Oldina State Forest

Most of the hills south of Wynyard are used for timber production and form part of the Oldina State Forest. Pines were first planted here in 1920 and willows, Douglas firs and poplars, as well as native trees, are a feature of the forest.

Some sections have been reserved for recreation, with separate zones for walking, horse riding and trail-bike riding, and with each forest zone having its own parking and picnic site. The walking reserve features the **Noel Jago Walk** which is a short nature walk beside Blackfish Creek. Passing under manferns and eucalypt trees it takes about 30 minutes to complete.

Lapoinya Rhodo Garden

Located in the hills 20 km west of Wynyard, this 8½ hectare garden is well worth seeking out. Stocked with a wide variety of rhododendrons, azaleas and begonias, there is something in flower every month of the year. It is open every day except major holidays; entry is $1, children 50c.

BOAT HARBOUR BEACH

Just 14 km from Wynyard, this holiday resort has a beautiful bay with white sand and crystal-blue water – a lovely spot for exploring rock pools, and snorkelling. It was originally used in the 19th century as a port, but because the harbour is not sheltered from easterly winds it very quickly lost favour as a port. In the 1920s holiday-makers discovered the firm white sand and clear waters. Most buildings in the small village are holiday shacks.

Located three km off the Bass Hwy, the town consists of a single street, The Esplanade, which is the continuation of the steep access road. As you descend towards the town, a short path on the left leads to a timber platform and panoramic view over **Boat Harbour**.

The *Boat Harbour Camel Farm* (☎ 6445 1489), beside the Bass Hwy near the Boat Harbour Beach turn off, is worth a visit. Camel rides range from $4 for a short ride to $90 for the whole day. It's open every day from 10 am to 4 pm. Also away from the beach, is the **Boat Harbour Strawberry Farm** where fresh fruit can be picked in summer.

In town, close to the ocean, is the Seaside Garden Motel whose award-winning garden is open to the public from September to June.

Places to Stay & Eat

The *Boat Harbour Beach Caravan Park* (☎ 6445 1253) is on an open, sunny site halfway up the hill on the top edge of town. It has a general store with takeaways and tent sites are $8. On-site vans are available for $26 and cabins for $30 a double.

On the hill above the town, is the *Backpackers Hostel* (☎ 6445 1273) in Strawberry Lane. From here it is a two-km walk down to the beach. Bunks are $12 per person and some double rooms are available for $24 to $35.

In town, the *Seaside Garden Motel* (☎ 6445 1111) provides B&B for $48 to $53 a double or newer holiday units with breakfast for $75 to $90 a double. The French restaurant is open every day, with main meals around $16.

Next door, *Boat Harbour Beach Resort* (☎ 6445 1107) has rooms for $70/85 for singles/doubles and contains *Jacobs Restaurant*. The restaurant has won state awards for its à la carte menu and is open every day; mains are around $16. Right beside the beach is the family style *Harbour Restaurant* (☎ 6445 1371) which is open Tuesday to Sunday. The same building also has a kiosk with takeaways.

If you cannot find a bed in the village, then try *Country Garden Cottages* (☎ 6445 1233) back near the highway. Doubles are from $60. Also nearby is the overpriced *Killynaught Cottages* (☎ 6445 1041) where B&B is $110 a double.

Getting There & Away

Unless you have your own transport, you will have to hitch to get to most of these places. The TRC (☎ 6431 3233 or 1800 030 033) service to Smithton will drop you at the turn-off to Boat Harbour (three km) and Sisters Beach (eight km). Boat Harbour Beach Backpackers also does pick-ups from the highway.

ROCKY CAPE NATIONAL PARK

This small area was declared a national park in 1967. Its major features are the rocky headlands, heath-covered hills, and caves which were once occupied by Aboriginal people. Excavations have shown the caves were first used 8000 years ago and were still used up until European occupation in the 19th century. There are a couple of beaches within the park and the best known is **Sisters Beach**. This is reached by following the side road from nearby Boat Harbour. It is a popular beach resort, surrounded by the national park.

The western end of the park has a more rugged coastline. On Rocky Cape, there is a lighthouse with road access. There are many good walking tracks in the park and because of the open heathlands, views are excellent. Overnight camping is not allowed. It is best to visit in spring and summer when the wildflowers are at their best. As with all parks, entry fees apply.

Sisters Beach is an eight-km expanse of glistening white sand providing safe swimming and good fishing. On the east side of the creek there are picnic tables and a shelter beside the beach and a walking bridge crosses the creek.

In the Sisters Beach village is the 10-hectare **Birdland Native Gardens** (☎ 6445 1471 or 6445 1270), which contains aviaries, and also attracts native birds from the national park. It's open daily and entry is $2, children 50c. Holiday cottages are available at Birdland for $40 to $50 a double. The other place to stay is *Tasman Buray Holiday Units* (☎ 6445 1147) for $65 a double plus $10 for extra adults. There are also holiday shacks which are sometimes available for hire; enquire at the general store.

Bushwalking

From Sisters Beach, the walk to **Wet Cave** and **Banksia Grove** takes 45 minutes. You can continue further along the coast to Anniversary Point which is three hours return. It's also possible to follow the coast to Rocky Point and return along the Inland Track (eight hours return).

From the western end of the park at Rocky Cape Rd you can visit the two large Aboriginal caves; both are a 20-minute return walk away. There is also a good circuit of the Cape itself; allow 2½ hours.

Around Rocky Cape

In the hills south of the national park, you can visit a number of waterfalls including **Detention Falls**, three km south of Myalla, and **Dip Falls**, near Mawbanna. The area also contains some giant eucalypts.

PORT LATTA

This part of the coastline is a series of pretty, little beaches and rocky coves which is marred by the ugly smoke and pollution from the industrial complex at Port Latta. This is the terminus for the 85-km iron ore pipeline from Savage River. Fortunately, there is only one factory here and, once away from the smokestack, it's a pleasant part of the coast.

At Crayfish Creek, two km east from Port Latta, *Caradale Caravan Park* (☎ 6443 4228) has on-site vans for $20/26 and cabins for $35/45 for singles/doubles. Located beside the wide creek and a pretty beach, this is a cheap place to stay, but you need to bring your own supplies.

STANLEY

• *pop 580*

Nestled at the foot of the extraordinary Circular Head (better known as The Nut), Stanley is a very appealing historic village which has changed very little since its early days. In 1826 it became the headquarters of the London-based Van Diemen's Land

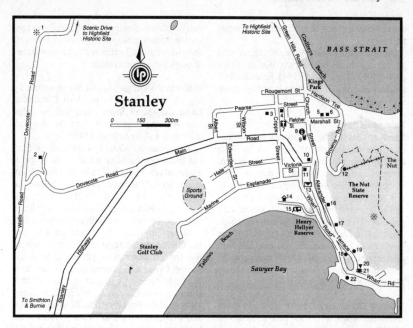

PLACES TO STAY

2 Stanley Motel
3 Ride Cottage
4 Pol and Pen
5 Bleak House
6 Hanlon House
10 Union Hotel
11 Wistaria Cottage
14 Stanley Youth Hostel
15 Stanley Caravan Park
16 Harbour Masters
   Cottage

17 Captains Cottage

PLACES TO EAT

20 Julie & Patrick's,
   Kermie's Cafe
21 Hursey Seafoods

OTHER

1 Jimmy Lane Memorial
   Lookout
7 Presbyterian Church

8 Stanley Discovery
   Centre
9 Plough Inn
12 The Nut Chairlift
13 Post Office
18 Van Diemen's Land
   Company Store
19 Lyons Cottage
22 Grain Store

Company, which was granted a charter to settle and cultivate Circular Head and the north-west tip of Tasmania. The company built its headquarters at Highfield, to the north of Stanley and the town started at the same time serving as the port.

For 30 years the company struggled with its vast land-holding and by 1858 had sold most of it. The area then prospered when it began shipping large quantities of mutton,

beef and potatoes to Victoria's goldfields in the 1850s and 1860s, and continued to prosper when settlers discovered rich dairying land behind Sisters Hills and tin reserves at Mt Bischoff.

Today Stanley is a charming fishing village with many historic buildings and great seascapes. The **Circular Head Arts Festival** is held here every March and this has become one of the major events in the

NORTH-WEST

state, featuring arts & crafts and live entertainment.

An interesting way to see the region is to go for a ride with Morgans Harley Tours (☎ 6458 1379 or 018 142 144). Rates are $45 an hour and you'll be given information on scenic tours.

Things to See

The Nut This striking 152-metre-high volcanic rock formation, thought to be 12.5 million years old, can be seen for many km around Stanley. It's a steep, 15 minute climb to the top, but the view is definitely worth it. For the less energetic, a chairlift (☎ 6458 1286) operates daily from 9.30 am to 4.30 pm; rides cost $6, children $2 or family $15. The best lookout is a five-minute walk to the south from the chairlift. You can follow a path around the top; this is a 40-minute walk. Take care in windy weather as there are no fences on top of the sheer cliffs.

Stanley Discovery Centre To learn more about the town, visit this folk museum in Church St. For most of the year, it is open every day, but it's closed during June and July; entry is $2.

Scenic Drive Follow Dovecote Rd past the Stanley Motel to the **Jimmy Lane Memorial Lookout**. This is a timber platform which provides a reasonable view over the cape area. Continue to follow the scenic road passing Highfield then past more scenic views as you approach Stanley.

Highfield The Van Diemen's Land Company headquarters were located on the high land north of Stanley. The company was formed in 1824 to establish a wool-growing venture and was granted 250,000 acres of unexplored territory. In 1835 Highfield was built, but the company had great difficulty developing its land and in 1856 Highfield was leased, then eventually sold some years later.

In 1982 the state government purchased Highfield, undertook extensive restorations and made it into an historic site. It's open

daily with a site entry fee of $2 and you can see the stables, grain stores, workers cottages and chapel. For $3 extra you can also wander through the historic house.

Historic Buildings The old bluestone building on the seafront is the **Van Diemen's Land Company Store**, designed by John Lee Archer, Tasmania's famous colonial architect, and dates from 1844.

Also near the wharf is a particularly fine old bluestone building which used to be a **grain store** and was built in 1843 from stones brought to Stanley as ship's ballast. In Church St, next door to the Discovery Centre, the **Plough Inn** (1840) has been fully restored and decorated with period furniture.

Other buildings of historical interest include **Lyons Cottage**, in Church St, which was the birthplace of former Prime Minister Joseph Lyons and is open from 10 am to 4 pm, admission by donation; the **Union Hotel**, also in Church St, which dates from 1849; and the **Presbyterian Church**, which was probably Australia's first prefabricated building, bought in England and transported to Stanley in 1853.

Places to Stay

Beside the sea at Sawyer Bay, *Stanley Caravan Park* (☎ 6458 1266) is very close to town; tent sites are $9, on-site vans $30 and cabins $40. Next door, the small *Stanley Youth Hostel* (☎ 6458 1266) is part of the caravan park and charges $12 a night for YHA members.

Most of the town's businesses are in Church St. The *Union Hotel* (☎ 6458 1161) on the corner of Church and Victoria Sts has basic hotel rooms for $25/35.

Around the town there are some cute historic cottages for rent. *Captains Cottage* (☎ 6458 1109) at 30 Alexander Terrace was built in 1838 and *Harbour Masters Cottage* (☎ 6458 1209) at 42 Alexander Terrace built around 1860. Both have good views to the south and provide B&B at $90 a double plus $20 for extra adults. Close to the hotel *Wisteria Cottage* (☎ 6458 1186) costs $90 a double for B&B.

With views to the north, *Pol & Pen* (☎ 6458 1334) at 8 Pearse St are a pair of two-bedroom self-contained cottages, which are good value at $55 to $65 a double. Close by, at 12 Pearse St, *Ride Cottage* (☎ 6458 1315) is available for $60/70. In the same area of town, *Bleak House* (☎ 6458 1428) at 4 Marshall St provides B&B for $88 a double. Next door *Hanlon House* (☎ 6458 1149) also offers B&B for $80 a double.

Not far from town on the scenic Dovecote Rd, *Stanley Motel* (☎ 6458 1300) has great views of the town and the Nut. Rooms are $65 a double or two-bedroom holiday cottages are $70 a double plus $10 for extra adults. Just north of the town you can stay at *Anthonys At Highfield* (☎ 6458 1245 which was built for the Van Diemen's Land Company in 1828 with B&B for $80 a double.

Places to Eat
Hursey Seafoods, at 2 Alexander Terrace, sells live fish from the tanks in the shop as well as serving takeaways, including fish & chips. Next door is *Kermie's Cafe* where they serve basically the same food, but it's on plates and you get to sit down for a higher price. Upstairs is *Julie & Patrick's Seafood Restaurant* where the best of the fish and crayfish are served in the evenings. All three businesses are run by the same people and the cafe and seafood shop close at 6 pm when the restaurant opens.

Counter meals for around $8 are available every day at the *Union Hotel* on the corner of Church and Victoria Sts. The other family restaurant is *Dovecote Restaurant* at the Stanley Motel in Dovecote Rd which has standard fare for around $12. In town, *Sullivans*, a licensed restaurant at 25 Church St, is open daily and serves light lunches, teas and dinner with main courses costing around $16.

Getting There & Away
TRC (☎ 6431 3233 or 1800 030 033) has several services on weekdays from Burnie to Smithton and at least one service a day does the side trip to the town of Stanley. Bookings are recommended to ensure the coach does come into town. The TRC agent is the BP service station on the corner of Wharf Rd and Marine Esplanade.

SMITHTON
- *pop 3,500*

Twenty-two km from Stanley, Smithton serves one of Tasmania's largest forestry areas and is also the administrative centre for Circular Head. There's not much to see or do in the town itself, but the town's airport makes it an arrival point for some chartered light aircraft flights from the mainland.

The town is located on the Duck River, named after the wild ducks that frequent the estuary. The town started to develop in the 1850s after the Van Diemen's Land Company sold off most of its holdings. At first, clearing of the giant forests was the primary activity and then the land was used for potato farming. Little happened until the 1890s when the first sawmill opened; soon afterwards dairy farming began, and the Duck River Butter Factory began production. In the 1940s vegetable dehydration and fish processing added to the town's economy.

Things to See
Woolnorth On the north-western tip of Tasmania, near Cape Grim, is this 220-sq-km cattle and sheep property which is the only remaining holding of the Van Diemen's Land Company. This is the only surviving Royal Charter Company in the world and today is a diversified business with sheep, cattle, crops and tree plantations. The 80-bail rotary dairy milks 1800 cows a day. Tours of the property are only available to groups on bus tours (☎ 6452 1252 or 6452 2577). Tours leave from the Bridge Hotel in Smithton. A day-tour from Smithton includes lunch and snacks and also visits Cape Grim and Woolnorth Point as well as touring the working farm. Cost is $52.50 per adult, $27.50 for children or you can do a shorter tour which just includes lunch and is $42.50, children $21.

Montagu The road heading north-west towards Woolnorth passes through farmlands, with views over the narrow waterways that separate Perkins and Robbins Islands. The only place of interest is **Montagu Blueberries** (☎ 6456 6187) where you can pick fruit from Christmas to mid-February.

Lacrum A rich dairy (☎ 6452 2322) just six km west of Smithton, this farm and factory produces cheese. During milking season, it's open daily from 3.30 pm to 5 pm when you can see the turnstile dairy in operation, taste the cheese, and enjoy afternoon tea. Entry is $5, children $2.50 or family $10. It's usually open from November through to June.

Allendale Gardens South of Smithton on the road to Edith Creek, these gardens (☎ 6456 4216) are a good place to walk around or relax. The two-hectare property includes impressive botanical gardens, a rainforest walk, a wildflower section and a cafe serving Devonshire teas. The centre is open daily from 10 am to 6 pm (closed June to August) and admission is $5, children $2.50 or family $13.50. Colonial style B&B is also available.

Milkshakes Hills Forest Reserve Temperate rainforest and button-grass moorland can be found at this reserve, 45 km south of Smithton. There are several very short walking tracks around the picnic grounds and a longer one of one hour return to the top of Milkshakes Hills.

Lake Chisholm Located even further south of Smithton on gravel roads, which are closed after heavy rain, is this tranquil lake. Located in beautiful rainforest, the lake is actually a sinkhole in the limestone. From the car park a walk of 30 minutes return leads to the lake.

Places to Stay & Eat
There are few places to stay in town and there's no budget accommodation. Close to town on the other side of the Duck River, *Bridge Hotel* (☎ 6452 1389) has rooms for $50/60 for singles/doubles. Bistro meals are available every evening with a menu that changes each day.

If you prefer a holiday unit, then stay at *Macvilla Holiday Units* (☎ 6452 1278) in Nelson St. For unit-only, you'll pay $50 to $55 for singles plus $15 for extra adults. Two km south of town on Scotchtown Rd is *Tall Timbers Hotel/Motel* (☎ 6452 2755) which is more like a resort than a motel. The extravagant use of timber in the main building is impressive. Cabins are $60/70 for singles/doubles. Meals are good with an à la carte restaurant and a family bistro. Live bands or a disco provide entertainment on Friday and Saturday nights.

The closest B&B is at Sedgy Creek, six km east of town, where *Rosebank Cottage* (☎ 6452 2660) has two units for $110 to $120 a double.

For light meals there are several coffee shops – try *Birda's Coffee Lounge* at 5 Smith St or *Gloryannas* at 54 Emmett St. At 16 Smith St *Jade Dragon Chinese* is open every evening.

Getting There & Away
Air The airport is three km west of the town. It does not have regular, scheduled passenger flights. If you want to come here by plane, then charter flights can be organised with light-plane companies; try King Aviation (☎ 6452 1886) or Skyways (☎ 6452 2484) at Smithton Airport. They also run scenic flights over the area.

Bus TRC (☎ 6431 3233 or 1800 030 033) runs four buses on weekdays from Burnie to Smithton and return. On Saturday morning, it runs one bus from Smithton to Burnie and the return bus from Burnie operates on Saturday evening. There are no Sunday bus services.

MARRAWAH
Marrawah, at the end of the Bass Hwy, is where the wild Southern Ocean occasionally throws up the remains of ships wrecked on the dangerous and rugged west coast. To visit Marrawah, the most westerly town in Tasma-

nia, it is best to have your own vehicle, but from Monday to Saturday you can get a lift on the mail run from Smithton.

The area has seen minimum disturbance due to European development and was once popular with Tasmania's Aboriginal people. Many signs of Aboriginal inhabitation remain, and particular areas have been proclaimed reserves to protect the remaining relics, including rock carvings, middens and hut depressions. The main Aboriginal sites are at **Mt Cameron West**, near Green Point, at **West Point** and **Sundown Point**.

The township of Marrawah consists of the *Marrawah Tavern* (☎ 6457 1102), which serves counter meals, and a general store selling petrol and supplies. The hotel has no accommodation, but there is a basic *camping ground* at Green Point, two km from Marrawah. This region is good for fishing, canoeing, camping and bushwalking, or for simply getting away from it all. One good walk is to head north from Green Point along the beach to Mt Cameron West which takes about three hours return.

One of Marrawah's major attractions, is it's enormous surf: in February a **wave ski championship** is held and around Easter the state's surfing championship is decided.

Some of the roads past this town are rough vehicle tracks requiring a 4WD vehicle. Based at Marrawah, Blue Wren 4WD Tours (☎ 6457 1307) runs daily tours to the mining town of Balfour and along deserted beaches which are only accessible to 4WDs. Group size is limited to a maximum of five. The tour can be started from Smithton or Stanley if required. Rates are $50 for a half-day and $85 for a full-day tour. This is a good way to see the west coast.

ARTHUR RIVER

The sleepy town of Arthur River, 14 km south of Marrawah, is mainly a collection of holiday houses for people who come here to fish. The town has one kiosk with basic supplies, no regular public transport and, apart from a *camping ground* with basic facilities, only one place to stay. The *Arthur River Holiday Units* (☎ 6457 1288), in Gar-

diner St, has doubles for $55/65. Extra adults pay $10 and children $6.

You can explore the river on your own with Arthur River Canoe Hire (☎ 6457 1312). It hires boats for $15 per hour or $100 per day and canoes from $5 per hour, $30 per day. You can also be transported upriver for a 40-km down-river paddle, which takes two or three days. If necessary, you can be picked up from Smithton or Stanley; bookings are essential for this service because there are no scheduled bus times.

Apart from fishing and cruising on the river, visitors come here to explore the **Arthur Pieman Protected Area**. The many attractions of the protected area include magnificent ocean beaches, waterfalls on the Nelson Bay River, Rebecca Lagoon, Temma Harbour, the old mining town of Balfour, the Pieman River and the Norfolk Ranges. The road as far as Temma is now accessible to standard cars although care is needed after wet weather. South of Temma, it's 4WD-country only. With standard cars you can return to Smithton by following unsealed forestry roads inland past Edith Creek. This is a long, but scenic, drive through forest.

Arthur River Cruises

Paddy and Turk Porteous operate scenic day cruises on the Arthur River (☎ 6457 1158) which depart at 10 am and return at 3 pm. From November to February an evening cruise starts at 5 pm. You sail up the river, feeding sea eagles on the way, to the confluence of the Arthur and Frankland rivers. The cruise runs most days in summer if a minimum of eight people have booked; you can do this direct, or at any Tasmanian Travel & Information Centre. The cost is $38 each, children $15.

HELLYER GORGE

Seven km west of Burnie is the small town of Somerset, at the junction of the Murchison and Bass Hwys. Hellyer Gorge is about 40 km south of Somerset on the banks of the Hellyer River. The Murchison Hwy winds its way through the impressive gorge. At the picnic area by the river, there are two very short walks which provide a welcome break if driving. The River Walk takes only 10 minutes and the Old Myrtle Forest Walk is 15 minutes return.

From Burnie to the Waratah area there is an alternative road which is faster but less scenic. It passes through Ridgley and Hampshire on road B18 and avoids the winding road through the Hellyer Gorge. This has diverted traffic away from the peaceful reserves in the gorge.

About 40 km south of Hellyer Gorge is the CI32 turn off to Cradle Mountain. This is a major highway which was constructed in the 1980s providing a link from the west coast to the northern end of Cradle Mountain national park.

WARATAH & SAVAGE RIVER

The Mt Bischoff mine, near Waratah, was once the world's richest tin mine. Discovered in 1871 by James 'Philosopher' Smith, he soon sold his interest and in 1888 the tin mine opened. Tin is not a high-price metal and the company running the mine invested very large sums of money. Eventually this paid off for the investors and was extremely profitable for the company until 1929 when the mine was leased. The mine continued to be worked in a minor way until 1947. From a population of over 4000 in the 1890s, Waratah almost vanished when the tin ran out.

The nearby development of the low grade iron ore at Savage River in 1968 revived the town and kept it alive. The extracted ore is pumped as a slurry along an 85 km pipeline to Port Latta on the north coast. This is an open cut mine with three pits and in 1990 operations scaled down when the original contracts for ore ceased.

The town's permanent residents were optimistic that there would be another strike. Indeed they were right, in 1983 a rich lead-zinc-silver-copper ore-body was found near the junction of the Murchison Hwy and the link road to Cradle Mountain. By 1989 the Aberfoyle Hellyer Mine (☎ 6466 4108) started operating, and today employs 200 staff supporting the economy.

Waratah is built on both sides of a narrow lake. The townspeople have tried to attract tourists with a **museum** which contains relics of the boom days. It's open daily from 9 am to 4 pm and staffed by volunteers; if closed, you can get the key at the council office on weekdays. Next door to the museum is the **Philosophers Hut**, a reconstruction of the way prospectors lived. There are some signposted walking tracks around town including one to the Power House which is two hours return.

One enterprising business has begun here: Roaring Forties Water collects rainwater from the roof of the community centre and sells it as the purest water in the world. It is an interesting turn of fate that a mining town should become a source of clean water.

Mine Tours

The underground Aberfoyle Hellyer Mine (☎ 6466 4108) is open for group tours; the tours are free but bookings are necessary. Savage River Mines (☎ 6443 4105) are open for inspection and tours on Tuesday and Thursday at 9 am and 2 pm, which must be booked; there is no charge.

Places to Stay & Eat

For accommodation, the 110-year-old *Directors Lodge* (☎ 6439 1191) provides B&B for families or groups of up to five people for $35 per adult plus $20 to $25 per child.

The only other choice in town is the *Waratah Camping Ground* (☎ 6439 1231). In reality, there is no formal camping area; it is suggested you pitch your tent between the council offices or on the lawns beside Lake Waratah. Fees are $9 with amenities or $5 without. Keys to amenities are available at the council offices.

The closest motel is at Savage River, 37 km to the west. The *Savage River Motor Inn* (☎ 6446 1177) has singles/doubles for $40/60 as well as a family rate of $80 for up to two adults and three children.

The *Bischoff Hotel* (☎ 6439 1188) in Main St is the main building remaining from the mining days. It serves daily counter meals.

CORINNA

Corinna, 28 km south-west of Savage River, is at the end of a long and lonely road. It was once a thriving gold-mining settlement of 2500 people, but is now little more than a ghost town. These days it's the scenery and the Pieman River Cruises (☎ 6446 1170) which attract visitors. The cruise passes impressive forests of eucalypts, ferns and Huon pines through to Pieman Heads. Costing $30 ($15 for children), which includes morning tea, the tours on the MV *Arcadia II* depart daily at 10.30 am and return at 2.30 pm. It's definitely best to book;

during summer it can be booked out and in winter it only runs if there are bookings. It's a worthwhile cruise which compares favourably with the better known Gordon River cruises.

The only accommodation in Corinna is at the *Pieman Retreat Cabins* (☎ 6446 1170). Each self-contained cabin can sleep up to six people and the cost is $50 a double and $8 for each extra person. Linen is available at an extra cost. Basic supplies can be bought from the kiosk.

The town is within a state reserve so no pets are allowed.

The West

Nature at its most awe-inspiring is the attraction of Tasmania's rugged and magnificent west. Formidable mountains, buttongrass plains, ancient rivers, tranquil lakes, dense rainforests and a treacherous coast are all features of this compelling and beautiful region, some of which is now World Heritage Area.

Centuries before the arrival of Europeans, this part of Tasmania was home to many of the state's Aboriginal people and some archaeological evidence is more than 20,000 years old. They lived through the last Ice age in the caves along the Franklin River and undoubtedly lived elsewhere inland. In recent times, the Aboriginal people lived primarily along the coast. When Europeans began to enter the region the Aboriginal people were quickly ousted from their home and today there is little evidence of their existence, apart from the remains of their cooking fires and middens.

Prior to 1932, when the Lyell Hwy from Hobart to Queenstown was built, the only way into the west coast was by sea, through the dangerously narrow Hells Gates into Macquarie Harbour to Strahan. Despite such inaccessibility, early European settlement brought explorers, convicts, soldiers, loggers, prospectors, railway gangs and fishers to the region. The 20th century has brought outdoor adventurers, naturalists and environmental crusaders here.

It was over the wild rivers, beautiful lakes and lonely valleys of Tasmania's South-West that battles between environmentalists and government raged. In the 1980s, the proposed damming of the Franklin and Lower Gordon Rivers caused the greatest and longest environmental debate in Australia's history. Subsequently the area has seen the booming of ecotourism in the harbourside town of Strahan.

While debates continue about wilderness versus electricity and national parks versus woodchips, nature has begun to reclaim its

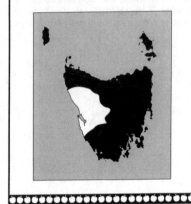

HIGHLIGHTS

- Taking a seaplane flight from Strahan
- Cruising the Gordon River
- Queenstown's lunar landscape
- Exploring the region's rainforests
- Completing the Overland Track

own. The barren hills around Queenstown have begun to show signs of regeneration in recent years, symbolising the reclamation by nature of regions exploited by so-called 'progress'.

Getting There & Around

Buses run along the Murchison Hwy and Lyell Hwy daily during the warmer months and several times a week during winter. Tasmanian Redline Coaches (TRC) (☎ 6471 1011 or 1800 030 033) is the main bus line, with daily services from mid-September to May from Hobart to Queenstown and Strahan. There are also daily services from Burnie and Devonport to Queenstown and Strahan.

From June to mid-September, TRC runs services on Tuesday, Wednesday, Friday and

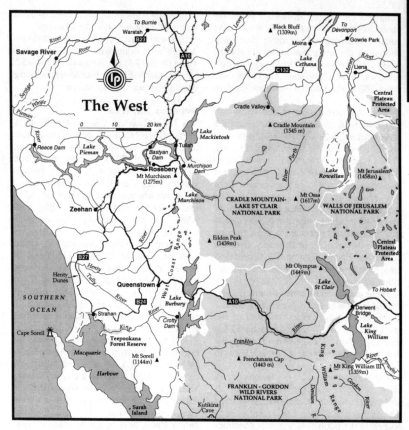

Sunday from Hobart to Queenstown ($33.30) and Strahan ($38.50). Over the same months, services run on Tuesday, Thursday and Sunday from Burnie and Devonport to Queenstown ($27.50) and Strahan ($32.90). TRC operates extra buses on school days from Queenstown to Strahan and Zeehan.

Tasmanian Wilderness Transport (☎ 6334 4442) also runs services to Strahan. It runs one bus every Saturday (all year) from Hobart to Queenstown and Strahan ($35) and returning on Sunday. It also runs one bus every Saturday (all year) from Launceston

through Devonport and Zeehan to Strahan ($40). The return service operates along the same route every Sunday.

TULLAH

Originally this old mining town was in a very isolated area; for much of its history the only access was by foot and later by train. The town was established in 1892 when a lead-zinc-copper-silver ore body was discovered on Mt Farrell and mining continued until the early 1970s when the mine closed.

In 1962 the construction of the Murchison Hwy from Burnie to Queenstown linked

Tullah to the rest of Tasmania. When the mine closed, the town probably would have collapsed but received a reprieve when it was chosen as the accommodation site for the workers for several hydroelectricity schemes. In the 1970s and early 1980s there were 2000 construction workers residing here.

With the completion of the dams and power stations, the workers vanished and the town emptied. Many of the buildings were also removed and the streets were deserted. The remaining residents are now trying to survive on tourism, with the biggest drawcard being the large trout caught in the lakes around the town.

The name, Tullah, comes from an Aboriginal word meaning 'meeting of two rivers' and today these rivers have been flooded with the waters of Lake Rosebery, part of a large hydroelectric scheme. The town offers great views of Mt Murchison and the surrounding ranges.

There are several **scenic drives** passing the major dams and lakes built for hydroelectricity generation. Three km north of the town you can follow a new road for 55 km west to the Reece Dam. The road crosses the dam wall and continues a further 29 km to Zeehan.

The other main road starts five km south of town and heads over the flanks of Mt Murchison towards Queenstown. Known as the Anthony Rd, this has recently been opened to the public (during dam construction it was a private HEC road) and provides some extremely scenic views as it crosses the West Coast Range. From town, minor roads also lead to the Mackintosh and Murchison dams.

From 1908 until the 1960s, the only link Tullah had with the rest of the world was by train. The road eventually replaced the train and in 1977 the residents decided to restore **Wee Georgie Wood**, one of the engines which had operated on the train line. From August to April, the train operates on about two or three days every month (it's always a Saturday or Sunday). Days of operation are published in *Travelways* or ring (☎ 6473

1229) after 6 pm. Fares are nominal – $2 for adults, $1 children or $5 for a family.

One way to see the region around the town is to go horse riding with Tullah Horse Back Tours (☎ 6473 4289). Rides range from $20 for one hour to $60 for four hours; bookings should be made the day before.

Places to Stay & Eat

The *Tullah Lakeside Chalet* (☎ 6473 4121) in Farrell St is located in some of the quarters used by the hydroelectricity construction workers in the 1970s. It has basic rooms from $25 each and often offers even cheaper standby rates after 4.30 pm. There's also a restaurant which is open for breakfast, lunch and dinner every day, plus the Village Cafe where light meals and takeaways are available every day.

Around the corner in Meredith St, *Tullah Lakeside Cottage* (☎ 6473 4165) can be rented for $60 a double plus $15 for extra adults and can hold up to four people. If you prefer B&B, then *Tullah Village Bed & Breakfast* (☎ 6473 4377) in Farrell St charges $25 each; there's a maximum of four guests.

Just north of the main town, beside the highway near the pub, *Wombat Lodge* (☎ 6473 4366) is an attractive two-storey cottage, suitable only for a couple; it costs $50. Next door is the *Bush Nook Tea Room* which is open from 10 am to 4 pm from Tuesday to Saturday. The tired-looking *Tullah Hotel*, next to the Murchison Hwy, has daily counter meals for around $8.

ROSEBERY

• *pop 1640*

Gold was discovered in Rosebery in 1891. Further prospecting revealed rich sulphide deposits and the first mines opened in 1896. Mining started at the same time on Mt Read to the south of Rosebery. By 1899 the Emu Bay Railway from Burnie had reached Rosebery and the lead-silver-copper-gold ore was shipped to Zeehan for smelting. However, when the Zeehan lead smelters closed in 1913 operations also closed in Rosebery, as did the nearby Hercules mine on Mt Read.

In 1920 the Electrolytic Zinc Company bought both mines. It took many years for a mill to be designed and constructed, but in 1936 production resumed at both mines. An aerial ropeway from Mt Read transported the ore from the Hercules mine to Rosebery. In 1986 the Hercule mine was closed and the aerial ropeway collapsed; it can still be seen from the highway.

Today the mine at Rosebery continues to employ around 300 people, and supports the town's economy. For banking there is an ANZ Bank and a Trust Bank which open every week day.

Things to See

Behind the Plandome Hotel, the high school has some interesting remnants from the old mines along its front fence, including a water wheel and railway carriage for steep inclines. The school also contains a mining museum displaying artefacts and old photos; entry is free, ask at the school office.

The picnic area on the south side of town is the start of a walk down the Stitt River. This short walk leads to Park Rd and the **Stitt Falls** just beyond, which are good after recent rainfall. Otherwise there is not much else to see in and around the town.

Sealed roads lead to Williamsford, eight km south of Rosebery. This is the site of an abandoned mining town and also the start of an excellent walk to **Montezuma Falls**. These are over 100 metres high and among the highest falls in the state. The return walk along an abandoned railway line takes about three hours return.

If you prefer a guided walk to Montezuma Falls, Hays Bus Service (☎ 6473 1247) runs trips to the falls for $35 each which includes lunch and takes 3½ hours. Hays Bus Service also runs tours of the **Pasminco Zinc Mine** at 9.30 am, 12.30 pm and 3.30 pm daily. The mine is an underground operation, but the two-hour tour remains on the surface, visiting the above-ground operations. The tour costs $8 per adult, children $5 or family $24. The Hays also have a boat and can take you trout fishing on any of the lakes which are part of the hydroelectric schemes.

Places to Stay & Eat

If you want to stay overnight, *Rosebery Caravan Park* (☎ 6473 1366) in Park Rd has tent sites for $8, on-site vans for $28, cabins for $45 and a small hostel with six bunks for $12 each. Right in the centre of town beside the highway, the *Plandome Hotel* (☎ 6473 1351) has reasonable singles/doubles for $25/38. It serves daily counter meals too. The nearby *Rosebery Hotel* also provides daily counter meals.

If you prefer to hire a cottage, then *Miss Murchison* (☎ 6473 1366) near the caravan park is $60 a double plus $12 for each extra adult and has six beds. Down the hill in Karlson St, *Miners Cottage* (☎ 6473 1796) provides B&B for $70 a double plus $20 for extra adults.

Apart from the two hotels, the only other food available is from *Fitzies Milk Bar* opposite the Plandome Hotel. Fitzies does takeaways and the hamburgers are quite good. The *Rosebery Cake Shop* provides home-baked goodies, but is only open on weekdays.

ZEEHAN
• *pop 1130*

In 1882 rich deposits of silver and lead were discovered over a very wide region around what is today the town of Zeehan. Mining started slowly at first, then in the late 1880s, the silver boom at Broken Hill encouraged a silver rush to Zeehan. The rush soon ended, but the town of Zeehan continued to grow as mining companies sunk shafts and exploited the deeper deposits of rich ore. By 1900 the town had a population of around 8000 and was known as 'Silver City'. In its heyday, Zeehan had 26 hotels, and its Gaiety Theatre seated 1000 people.

Then, like many mining ventures, the ore ran out. Starting in 1908, the major mines started closing and eventually in 1960 the last large mine, 'Oceana', also closed. At that stage, Zeehan was in danger of becoming yet another ghost town.

With the reopening and expansion of the Renison Tin Mine at Renison Bell (17 km towards Rosebery), Zeehan experienced a revival in the late 1960s, becoming the housing base for Renison Ltd. The population increased and the town's future seems assured. A major bush fire in 1981 burnt down many houses prompting a rebuilding programme of parts of the town.

Today Zeehan is the administrative centre for the region run by the West Coast Council. Banking facilities are reasonable with an ANZ Bank and a Trust Bank open every weekday.

Things to See

Buildings that remain from the early boom days include the once famous **Grand Hotel** (now converted into flats), the **Gaiety Theatre**, the **Post Office** (still in use), the **bank** (now occupied by the Trust Bank) and **St Luke's Church**.

For an excellent insight into the workings of a mine, visit the **West Coast Pioneers' Memorial Museum** (☎ 6471 6225) in Main St. This 1894 building was previously the School of Mines; it is open daily from 8.30 am to 5 pm and is free (donations welcome). The museum also features an interesting mineral collection and an exhibit of steam locomotives and carriages used on the early west-coast railways. Upstairs are displays of fauna, Aboriginal artefacts and photographs of mining towns and the people who lived in them.

An excellent way to see more is to complete a circuit walk around town. Starting from the museum, follow Main St west, turn left towards the golf course and walk through **Spray Tunnel**, a former railway tunnel. Turn left again to follow the Comstock track (an old tramway) south to **Florence Dam**. Follow the right track at the fork, winding around Keel Ridge, then descend to the southern end of Main St. It takes about two to three hours to walk and passes a lot of old mine sites. More detailed notes to this walk and others around the mining sites of the west coast are available in *Historic Mines of Western Tasmania* by Duncan How, \$8.95, which can be purchased in bookshops throughout the state.

For a view over the town, you can walk or drive up King Hill. There are plenty of old mining relics further out of town. Four km to the south you will find some old smelters beside the highway. A cairn and display board details their history. For panoramic views you can walk to the top of Mt Zeehan. The track starts near the smelters and follows a vehicle then walking track; it is three hours return.

At Renison Bell, 17 km east of Zeehan, there is a signposted **Battery Mill Walk** starting 300 metres west of the mine entrance. This visits the old mill site where rock from the mine was crushed. A locomotive, railway sidings and old workings are described with the aid of photographic plaques beside the track. Allow about 45 minutes return for a visit.

North-west of Zeehan, a quiet sealed road leads to the **Reece Dam** on the Pieman River, part of the Pieman Hydro Electric Scheme. This road gives access to some rarely visited places like **Granville Harbour** which is down a side road. This is a small camping-holiday place on the west coast with no accommodation or shops. You can camp here. The road to Reece Dam also provides a view of **Heemskirk Falls**; a one-hour return walk leads to the base of the falls.

For fishing enthusiasts, Granville Harbour is a good place for crayfish and Lake Pieman behind the Reece Dam has some fine trout. A gravel road heads west to **Trial Harbour**, the original port for Zeehan, where there are also some good fishing spots.

From Zeehan you could try following the Murchison Hwy (A10) south directly to Queenstown. An alternative, more scenic route is to follow the Henty Rd (B27) to Strahan. This follows an old railway formation for most of the way providing access to the **Henty Sand Dunes**. These cover an extremely large area with sand drifts engulfing the forests. A 45-minute walking track starting from a picnic area leads you through the dunes to the ocean beach.

Places to Stay

At the *Treasure Island West Coast Caravan Park* (☎ 6471 6633), in Hurst St on the northern edge of town, there are camp sites for $11, powered sites for $14, on-site vans for $35 and cabins for $44. The old *Hotel Cecil* (☎ 6471 6221) in the middle of town in Main St has singles/doubles for $30/50, or self-contained holiday units with cooking facilities for $68/70. Counter meals are available every day.

The *Heemskirk Motor Hotel* (☎ 6471 6107), in Main St at the western entrance to town, has motel rooms from $60 for singles plus $12 for extra adults and a holiday unit for up to four people for $85 a double plus $12 for extra adults. It also has counter meals and an à la carte menu with mains for around $15. In Main St, the *Zeehan Motor Inn & Lodge* (☎ 6471 6107) has double rooms for $58 and a hostel that can cater for up to 220 guests for $13 each.

For a light meal go to the *Museum Coffee Lounge* or the *Mid'L Cafe* in Main St. Both are open every day and serve coffee and takeaway food. Around town there are tea-rooms and milk bars.

Getting There & Away

From mid-September to May there is one Tasmanian Redline Bus (☎ 6471 1011 or 1800 030 033) every day which comes via Zeehan en route from Burnie and Devonport to Queenstown and Strahan; there is also a daily return service. During June to mid-September, services run only on Tuesday, Thursday and Sunday along the same route. The TRC agent in Zeehan is Maines Milk Bar in Main St.

On school days TRC runs a special service which leaves at 7.30 am for Queenstown and the return bus leaves Queenstown at 3 pm for Zeehan. Bookings for the school bus must be made at the Queenstown terminal (☎ 6471 1011) before 5 pm on the day before travelling.

Tasmanian Wilderness Transport (☎ 6334 4442) also runs a service via Zeehan. Every Saturday, it runs from Launceston to Devonport and Cradle Mountain then via Zeehan to Strahan. The return bus operates on Sunday from Strahan northward to Devonport and Launceston.

STRAHAN
• *pop 600*

Strahan, 40 km from Queenstown on Macquarie Harbour, is the only town on this rugged and dangerous coast. It has a sheltered harbour which is difficult to access because the entrance through Macquarie Heads, known as 'Hells Gates', is less than 200 metres wide. Though only a shadow of its former self, the town is rich in Aboriginal, convict, logging, mining and conservation history.

For over 35,000 years the Aboriginal people lived here, surviving an Ice age in the caves along the Franklin River. The most visible signs of their occupation are the huge shell middens along the west coast, and the grassy plains which they regularly burnt to catch animals. After such a long history, it took less than 40 years of European settlement for the last Aboriginal people to give up their traditional areas.

For early European explorers, the treacherous seas, lack of natural harbours and the high rainfall discouraged early settlement of the region until Macquarie Harbour was discovered by sailors searching for the source of the Huon pine that frequently washed up on the southern beaches.

In those days, the area was totally inaccessible by land and very difficult to reach by sea, and in 1821 these dubious assets prompted the establishment of a penal settlement on Sarah Island, in the middle of the harbour. Its main function was to isolate the worst of the colony's convicts and to use their muscle to harvest the huge stands of Huon pine. The convicts worked upriver 12 hours a day, often in leg irons, felling the pines and rafting them back to the island's saw-pits, where they were used to build ships and furniture.

With its barbaric treatment of prisoners, Sarah Island became one of Australia's most notorious penal settlements. The most dreaded punishment was confinement on tiny Grummet Island, where up to 40 convicts at a time were held in appalling conditions on what was little more than a windswept rock. Interestingly, Grummet

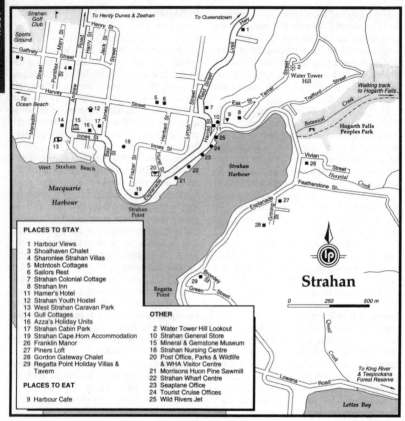

PLACES TO STAY

1 Harbour Views
3 Shoalhaven Chalet
4 Sharonlee Strahan Villas
5 McIntosh Cottages
6 Sailors Rest
7 Strahan Colonial Cottage
8 Strahan Inn
11 Hamer's Hotel
12 Strahan Youth Hostel
13 West Strahan Caravan Park
14 Gull Cottages
16 Azza's Holiday Units
17 Strahan Cabin Park
19 Strahan Cape Horn Accommodation
26 Franklin Manor
27 Piners Loft
28 Gordon Gateway Chalet
29 Regatta Point Holiday Villas &
   Tavern

PLACES TO EAT

9 Harbour Cafe

OTHER

2 Water Tower Hill Lookout
10 Strahan General Store
15 Mineral & Gemstone Museum
18 Strahan Nursing Centre
20 Post Office, Parks & Wildlife
   & WHA Visitor Centre
21 Morrisons Huon Pine Sawmill
22 Strahan Wharf Centre
23 Seaplane Office
24 Tourist Cruise Offices
25 Wild Rivers Jet

Island had been used as a penal colony for women convicts before becoming the place to send the 'worst' male prisoners.

Sarah Island appeared in Marcus Clarke's graphic novel about convict life, *For the Term of his Natural Life*. In 1834, after the establishment of the 'escape-proof' penal settlement at Port Arthur, Sarah Island was abandoned.

As the port for Queenstown, Strahan reached its peak of prosperity with the west-coast mining boom and the completion of the Mt Lyell Mining Company's railway line in the 1890s. At the turn of the century, it was a bustling centre with a population of 2000. Steamers operated regularly between Strahan and Hobart, Launceston and Melbourne carrying copper, gold, silver, lead, timber and passengers. The closure of many of the west-coast mines and the opening of the Emu Bay Railway from Zeehan to Burnie led to the decline of Strahan as a port. The construction of the Lyell Hwy from Hobart to Queenstown in the 1930s completed the port's demise.

In the 1980s the then sleepy town of Strahan became internationally famous as the centre for the Franklin River Blockade.

At that stage, the Hydro Electric Commission (HEC) had already constructed a large dam on the Gordon River and flooded Lake Pedder and was about to construct a series of dams on the Franklin and lower Gordon Rivers. Protesters set off from Strahan in rubber boats and canoes to physically prevent work from proceeding. In the summer of 1982-3, 1400 people were arrested in a widely publicised dispute. The conservationists eventually won and the Franklin River still flows free. This dispute divided Strahan and there were bitter feelings with assaults and violence between the opposing sides.

Eventually the town decided to take advantage of the wilderness at its doorstep and exploit it with tourism. Strahan is now a charming seaside town which draws visitors in droves for cruises on the Gordon River and scenic flights over the area. It really is one of the 'must see' places in Tasmania.

Information
The architecturally unusual and innovative **Strahan Wharf Centre** (☎ 6471 7488) on the waterfront is almost a tourist attraction in its own right. The foyer information area has a river-gravel floor, a superb reception desk built out of Huon pine, and a large information display. Beyond this is the museum section, which presents all aspects of the history of the South-West in a way that really captures the imagination. There are seven themes about people and the wilderness. A good account is given of the Franklin Blockade. You can gain some impression of the display by looking through the glass wall on the harbour side. The centre is open daily from 10 am to 6 pm, 8 pm in summer; entry to the museum section is $4.50, children $3 or a family $9. Tickets remain valid for 24 hours allowing several visits.

There is an office of the Department of Parks, Wildlife & Heritage (☎ 6471 7122) in the old Customs House building close to the town centre. This building also houses the post office, which is also a Commonwealth Bank agency. The Strahan Wharf Centre and Strahan Village General Store have EFTPOS facilities ($200 daily limit).

Things to See
Probably the finest old building on the west coast is Strahan's imposing **Customs House** which now houses the post office and Parks, Wildlife and Heritage visitor centre. Near the Strahan Wharf Centre, **Morrisons Huon Pine Sawmill** (☎ 6471 7378) has a modern display and sales centre. Fortunately the old sawmill next door has not changed and you can gain a fascinating insight into how it operates.

The lookout over the town is **Water Tower Hill**, accessed by following Esk St beside the Harbour Cafe. It's less than one km and you can walk or drive to it. From the top you can see Ocean Beach, Macquarie Harbour and some of the surrounding mountains.

You can spend a pleasant two hours following the foreshore from the caravan park west into Strahan and around to Regatta Point and return. This passes all the major features of the town. Regatta Point was the original terminus for the railway line and the railway station and old wharves can still be seen.

Hogarth Falls is a pleasant 40-minute return walk through the rainforest beside Botanical Creek. The track starts at Peoples Park on the Esplanade, 700 metres east of Hamers Hotel.

The **Cape Sorell Lighthouse**, on the south head of the harbour, is the third largest in Tasmania. A return walk of two to three hours along a vehicle track from the jetty at Macquarie Heads leads to the lighthouse. You will need a boat to cross the heads, or maybe a friendly fisher will take you across.

Opposite the caravan park is the **Mineral & Gemstone Museum** which is open from 10 am to 10 pm. Next to the caravan park, the **West Strahan Beach** with its gently shelving sandy bottom provides safe swimming. Due to rips and undertows swimming at Ocean Beach is not recommended.

Six km from the town is the impressive 33-km **Ocean Beach**, where the sunsets have to be seen to be believed. The beach is one continuous stretch of sand from Trial Harbour in the north to Macquarie Heads in the south. The dunes behind the beach contain the nesting burrows of mutton birds. From mid-September, the mutton birds return from their 15,000 km winter migration and – for the entire summer until April – provide an evening spectacle as they return to their nests at dusk.

The **Teepookana Forest** surrounds the King River to the west of Strahan. You can drive past Regatta Point to the King River and the forest. Here you will see a different aspect of the west coast as the river banks resemble a moonscape from the extensive silting caused by the mining operations further upstream. It graphically illustrates the conflict between uncontrolled mining and conservation. However, it's not all disaster; interpretive signs explain how the river is recovering. A helpful brochure, *Visiting the Teepookana Forest*, is available at the Strahan Wharf Centre.

Fourteen km along the road from Strahan to Zeehan are the **Henty Dunes**, some spectacular sand dunes, many of which are more than 30 metres in height. From the picnic area, you can take a 1½-hour return walk along a track through the dunes and out to Ocean Beach.

Organised Tours & Cruises

River Cruises A traditional way of experiencing the beauty of the Gordon River is on one of the cruises which operate out of Strahan. There are cruises available every day of the year except Christmas Day.

Gordon River Cruises (☎ 6471 7187) operates three large launches, the *James Kelly II*, the MV *Gordon Explorer* and *Wilderness Seeker*. During winter only one or two boats run according to demand, with all three boats running in summer. There are half-day trips (9 am to 1.45 pm) for $44 ($24 for children) including morning tea, or full-day trips (9 am to 3.30 pm) for $62 ($30 for children) including a smorgasbord lunch. The booking office on the wharf has a display of some of the photographs from the

Zeehan Museum which is worth looking at if you are not going to Zeehan.

All trips run up the Gordon River as far as Heritage Landing, where a short walk takes you past a 2000-year-old Huon pine tree. They also visit Sarah Island where some walking tracks, complete with interpretive signs, pass amongst the ruins of the former penal settlement.

World Heritage Cruises (☎ 6471 7174) is a family business with a long association with the harbour; the first trip the family ran across Macquarie Harbour for tourists was in 1896. They operate the MV *Heritage Wanderer*, which charges $36 ($16 for children) for a trip from 9 am to 4.15 pm. Lunch is not included in the price and you can bring your own or eat at the licensed dining area on board. This cruise also visits Heritage Landing and Sarah Island and operates daily from mid-September through to the end of May.

A unique way to see the Gordon River is to sail up it with West Coast Yacht Charters (☎ 6471 7422). For $290 each (children $145) you will be taken on a two-day and two-night sail across Macquarie Harbour and up the river. If this is too much, there is also a 2½-hour crayfish-dinner cruise around Macquarie Harbour for $45 each, children $25. Three-hour fishing trips are also available from 9 am to 12 pm for $35 each, children $20. The yacht is generally available for hire during the warmer period of the year from October through to March.

Seaplane Tours A highly recommended way to see the river and surrounding World Heritage Area is on a seaplane tour with Wilderness Air (☎ 6471 7280). The planes take off from Strahan's wharf every 1½ hours from 9 am onwards and fly up the river to Sir John Falls, where they land so that you can take a walk in the rainforest, before flying back via Sarah Island, Cape Sorell, Hells Gates and Ocean Beach. The 80-minute flight is well worth the $99. Demand for flights is heavy, so it's good to book if possible. The office is diagonally opposite the hotel, just past the Gordon River Cruise

Office. The flight path varies according to weather and the time of day. The seaplanes land much further up the Gordon River than where the launches turn around. There are also some shorter and longer flights around Strahan and over the World Heritage Area.

Jet-Boat Rides With an office on the wharf, Wild Rivers Jet (☎ 6471 7174), operates 50-minute jet-boat rides up the King River for $35, children $22 or $105 for a family of five. The boats can take a maximum of five passengers at a time and run from 9 am to 5 pm daily.

4WD Wilderness Trips A variety of 4WD trips are offered by Strahan Wilderness Tours (☎ 6471 7401). Their trips along Ocean Beach to the Henty Dunes cost $30 each; to nearby Teepookana Forest, $30; to Montezuma Falls near Rosebery, $80 per person and 4½-hour trout-fishing trips are $150 each.

South West Adventure Tours (☎ 6471 7157 or 6471 7462) also runs 4WD tours to the Henty Dunes for $38, to see the sunsets on Ocean Beach ($25), to Teepookana Forest Reserve on the King River ($40) and three-hour fishing tours on Macquarie Harbour for $95. Bookings with both companies can be made at the Wharf Centre.

Horse Riding Trail rides following old cattle tracks, through pine forests and along the west coast beaches, are available with Strahan Trail Rides (☎ 6471 7426). It provides a wide variety of rides; a popular one is the sunset ride which is run daily from October to March. Rides range from one to three hours and cost $30 to $65 per person; bookings are essential.

Places to Stay

Although Strahan has a wide range of accommodation and plenty of it, places are often full, so it's best to book ahead. This is a popular town and prices are generally higher for accommodation than in other parts of the state.

Camping The *West Strahan Caravan Park* (☎ 6471 7239) charges $12 for a camp site for two, and there's also a camping ground with very basic facilities 15 km away at Macquarie Heads.

Hostels At $13 a night for YHA members and $15 for nonmembers, the *Strahan Youth Hostel* (☎ 6471 7255) in Harvey St is the cheapest accommodation in town. It is about a 10-minute walk from the town centre. It also has twin rooms for $36 ($40 for non-members) and some good-value A-frame cabins for $46 a double.

B&B Three km from town, on Ocean Beach Rd, is the historic *Strahan Wilderness Lodge* (☎ 6471 7142), doubles, with a continental breakfast, cost $40/45. The same people also run the *Bay View Cottages* where B&B costs $50 to $70 a double. Unless you have your own transport, staying here can be a bit inconvenient.

Not quite as far out, but still inconvenient without transport, is *Shoalhaven Chalet* (☎ 6471 7400 or 6471 7202) where B&B is $45 to $65 for singles plus $5 to $15 for each extra person. Much closer to town *Harbour Views* (☎ 6471 7143) on the corner of Charles St and the Lyell Hwy provides B&B for $60 a double.

If you don't get seasick then try *West Coast Yacht Charters* (☎ 6471 7422) for a berth on a yacht. They're located beside the wharf and rates are a very reasonable $30 per adult and $10 for children for B&B. As the yacht is used for charters, the late 9 pm check in and early 8 am check out might not be convenient.

A five-minute walk from the hotel, *McIntosh Cottages* (☎ 6471 7358) is an old house divided into two self-contained units, each costing $100 a double. Beside the main highway at 7 Reid St, *Strahan Colonial Cottage* (☎ 6471 7263) is just behind the hotel and very convenient to all facilities. This is reflected in the price which is $115 a double plus $25 for each extra person.

For a memorable stay, you could try the historic *Franklin Manor* (☎ 6471 7311 or

6471 7247), on the Esplanade around the bay, one km from the town centre. During winter there are theme weekends which can be worth attending. The cost of staying in a self-contained suite is $138 to $155 a double. Just as expensive and with less atmosphere is the nearby *Piners Loft* (☎ 6471 7390) in Harrison St with doubles at $140.

Holiday Units *Azza's Holiday Units* (☎ 6471 7253) at 7 Innes St, near the caravan park, is cheap at $45 a double but it is unattractive with many units crammed closely together. On the other side of the same street the *Gull Cottages* (☎ 6471 7227) have two units for $70 a double. Around the corner at 10 Jones St, *Strahan Cabin Park* (☎ 6471 7442) offers portable cabins for $45 a double.

A more interesting place to stay is above Strahan Point at the end of Frazer St. *Strahan Cape Horn Accommodation* (☎ 6471 7169) has reasonably priced units for $45 to $50 for singles and $55 to $70 for doubles. Extra adults cost $15 and a continental breakfast tray is available for $5 per person. It's conveniently located; less than a 10-minute walk back into town.

Sailors Rest (☎ 6471 7237) in Harvey St is only a five-minute walk into town. While the outside of the units are ordinary, inside they are large with good amenities and are $70 a double plus $15 for each extra person. They are good for families as each unit can sleep eight people.

At the corner of Andrew Rd and Gaffney St, *Sharonlee Strahan Villas* (☎ 6471 7224) has units for $99 a double plus $18 for each extra adult.

On the other side of the harbour, *Regatta Point Holiday Villas* (☎ 6471 7103) is located next to some old wharves. It is two km from town by road and has ordinary units with good views for $78 a double plus $11 for extra adults. On the same side of the harbour, but a little closer to town in Grining St, *Gordon Gateway Chalet* (☎ 6471 7165) has even better rooms and views for $90 a double plus $20 for extra adults.

Hotels & Motels *Hamer's Hotel* (☎ 6471 7191) is opposite the wharf right in the middle of town and has comfortable rooms for $40/60, including a continental breakfast. It also has a group of somewhat twee self-contained cottages, recently built in various colonial styles, and these are also close to the waterfront. The most popular (and the most expensive) is the little stone *Sarah's Cottage* on the right. They cost $95-130 a double and some come with a spa.

On top of the hill above the Harbour Cafe at the end of Jolly St, is the *Strahan Inn* (☎ 6471 7160) which has magnificent views over the harbour. Motels rooms of average standard are $99 a double.

Places to Eat

The *Strahan Bakery* in the hotel complex has salad rolls and cakes and at night doubles as a pizza and pasta shop. In the mornings it is open from 7.30 am to 9 am for breakfast and is also used by hotel guests. Diagonally opposite the hotel, the *Harbour Cafe* is open from 6 am to 9 pm daily. It has a breakfast menu which is available until 10 am and then serves takeaways. The building could do with some refurbishment as it is out of character with the rest of the waterfront development.

Hamers Hotel on the Esplanade has been extensively renovated and refurbished in recent years but still serves counter meals at reasonable prices. It's open every day and mains from the *Grill* are $12 to $16. The *Regatta Point Tavern*, which is two km around the bay on the Esplanade, serves counter meals daily with mains around $10. It has an outdoor playground for children and a children's menu.

Overlooking the harbour, the *Macquarie Restaurant* (☎ 6471 7160) in the Strahan Inn has an à la carte menu with mains around $15. At the magnificent *Franklin Manor* (☎ 6471 7311) you can get an excellent à la carte meal with main courses $30 to $36. It's best to book.

Entertainment

During summer the Strahan Wharf Centre

puts on evening performances of the play *The Ship That Never Was*. This is the story of some convicts who escaped from Sarah Island by building their own ship. The play is performed in the amphitheatre beside the centre and is held daily at 7 pm except when special performances are held on Sarah Island. Tickets can be booked at Strahan Wharf Centre and are $7.50, children $5 or $20 for a family. There are about five performances held on Sarah Island over the summer and tickets are $10, children $5 or $25 for a family. A cruise boat leaves at 5 pm for the island and the boat fare and meals are extra.

Getting There & Away

Air Strahan has an excellent airport three km west of town. The only airline that has scheduled flights is Airlines of Tasmania (☎ 1800 030 550) which flies three days a week (Tuesday, Wednesday and Thursday) from Hobart to Queenstown and Strahan, $113 one way. On the same days, it also flies from Strahan to Devonport and Launceston. The timetables regularly change and bookings are essential for all flights.

Bus From mid-September to May, TRC (☎ 6471 1011 or 1800 030 033) has daily services in both directions from Hobart through Queenstown to Strahan. From June to mid-September buses run along the same route on Tuesday, Wednesday, Friday and Sunday. The fare from Hobart to Queenstown is $33.30, and from Queenstown to Strahan it's $5.20.

From mid-September to May, TRC runs a daily bus service in both directions from Burnie and Devonport to Queenstown and Strahan. During June to mid-September, services run on only Tuesday, Thursday and Sunday along the same route. The fare from Burnie to Queenstown is $27.70 with an extra $5.20 from Queenstown to Strahan.

TRC operates extra buses on school days leaving Strahan at 7.20 am for Queenstown and returning from Queenstown at 3 pm. Bookings for the school bus must be made at the Queenstown terminal (☎ 6471 1011) before 5 pm on the day before travelling. The TRC agent is the newsagency in the main street.

Tasmanian Wilderness Transport (☎ 6334 4442) also runs services to Strahan. It runs one bus every Saturday (all year) from Hobart to Queenstown and Strahan arriving at 4.45 pm; the fare is $35 one way or $65 return. The return service to Hobart leaves Strahan every Sunday at 2 pm to arrive in Hobart at 8.10 pm.

It also runs a once-a-week service all year to Devonport and Launceston. On Saturday it leaves Launceston at 8.30 am and travels via Devonport, Cradle Mountain and Zeehan arriving in Strahan at 5.10 pm. The return service leaves Strahan at 2 pm on Sunday and follows the same route without any long stops to arrive in Launceston at 6.45 pm. The fare is $40 one way or $75 return. The Tasmanian Wilderness Transport agent is the Harbour Cafe in the main street.

Hitching If you are hitching, it can be a long wait between vehicles on both the Lyell and Murchison highways, and in winter it gets bloody cold; the bus services are an attractive alternative.

QUEENSTOWN
• *pop 3370*

The final, winding descent into Queenstown from the Lyell Hwy is a memorable experience. With deep, eroded gullies and naked, multicoloured hills, there is no escaping the fact that this is a mining town, and that the destruction of the surrounding area is a direct result of this industry.

The discovery of alluvial gold in the Queen River valley in 1881 first brought prospectors to the area. Two years later, mining began on the rich Mt Lyell deposits, and for nearly a decade miners extracted a few ounces of gold a day from the Iron Blow and ignored the mountain's rich copper reserves. In 1891, the Mt Lyell Mining Company began to concentrate on copper but had trouble raising financial backing. A

WEST

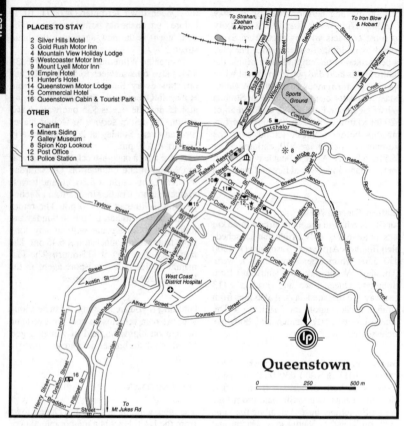

PLACES TO STAY
2 Silver Hills Motel
3 Gold Rush Motor Inn
4 Mountain View Holiday Lodge
5 Westcoaster Motor Inn
9 Mount Lyell Motor Inn
10 Empire Hotel
11 Hunter's Hotel
14 Queenstown Motor Lodge
15 Commercial Hotel
16 Queenstown Cabin & Tourist Park

OTHER
1 Chairlift
6 Miners Siding
7 Galley Museum
8 Spion Kop Lookout
12 Post Office
13 Police Station

Queenstown

lucky discovery of a rich vein of silver rescued the company and in 1895 the first of the Mt Lyell smelters began operating. Copper had become the most profitable mineral on the west coast.

The initial township was at Penghana around the smelters, but a bushfire in 1986 wiped out the shanty town and the residents moved to the newly planned town on the Queen River which became Queenstown.

In 1896, the company built a railway between Queenstown and Strahan to transport copper to the coast. It traversed spectacular terrain and was so steep in some

sections that the rack and pinion system had to be used to assist the two steam engines hauling the train.

At the turn of the century, Queenstown had a population of over 5000 and was the third largest town in Tasmania. It had 14 hotels, there were 28 mining companies working the Mt Lyell deposits, and 11 furnaces were involved in the smelting process. The Mt Lyell Mining & Railway Company eventually acquired most of the mines or leases, and since 1933 has worked the area without a rival.

By the 1920s, after only 20 years of

mining, the rainforested hills around Queenstown had been stripped bare: three million tonnes of timber had been felled to feed the furnaces. Uncontrolled pollution from the copper smelters was killing any vegetation that had not already been cut down, and bushfires raged through the hills every summer, fuelled by the sulphur-impregnated soils and dead stumps, until there was no regrowth left at all. The rains then washed away the exposed topsoil until all that was left was bare rocky hills.

In 1969 the smelters closed and for a long time there was no change to the stark bare hills around the town. In recent years a tinge of green has begun to creep over the hills and, ever so slowly, nature is once again covering the moonscape with trees and forest although it will take centuries for full recovery to happen.

The Mt Lyell mine closed in late 1994 and for a while the town's future looked bleak. In 1995 Copper Mines of Tasmania took over the lease and opened the mines again. Initial results show that ore deeper in the old mine, plus some unmined regions, should provide another 10 years of operation. In line with current practices, a tailings dam has been constructed so that the old method of pumping the waste rock into the Queen River will cease.

However, while mining has had something of a reprieve, it seems to be inevitable that Queenstown's long-term future will rest with other industries, such as tourism which is currently being built up. However, businesses are coming and going as this new industry takes shape.

Orientation & Information

Orr St is the heart of the town; most shops, hotels and businesses are either in this street or very close by. Banks which open from 9 am to 5 pm on weekdays are the Trust Bank, Island State Credit Union and Commonwealth Bank Agency at the Post Office.

The Royal Automobile Club of Tasmania (☎ 6471 1974), in Orr St, has plenty of tourist brochures and helpful staff. You can also get visitor information at the Galley Museum (☎ 6471 1758) on the corner of Sticht and Driffield Sts.

Things to See

The **Galley Museum** started life as the Imperial Hotel and was the first brick hotel in Queenstown. The museum features a large collection of old photographs (recording the history of Queenstown and the west coast), as well as a display of early mining equipment, personal effects and household goods from the town's pioneering days. The museum is open from 10 am to 5.30 pm Monday to Friday, and from 1.30 to 4.30 pm at weekends; admission is $2. It's the first building on the left as you enter Driffield St.

Opposite the museum, the **Miner's Siding** is a public park which features a restored Abt steam locomotive as well as various rock, bronze and Huon pine sculptures. This was Queenstown's centenary project and the sculptures tell the story of the Abt railway to Strahan and the ten decades of mining. At the time the railway line was constructed, it was considered impossible and you can clearly see the teethed rack rail that enabled trains to climb the steep gradients along the line. The siding is located where the train station used to be. The railway line was closed in 1963.

There are good views from **Spion Kop Lookout**, in the centre of town. Follow Hunter St uphill, turn left into Bowes St then sharp left into Latrobe St to the small car park from which a well-paved, short, steep track leads to the summit. The track features a rail adit near the car park and the top of the hill has a pithead on it. The panoramic views of the town are excellent particularly around sunset. If you look at the football oval you will notice that it is cream instead of green. Queenstown's footy team is tough – it plays on gravel, not grass.

Queenstown has a good *Historic Walk* brochure which guides you around the town from the Galley Museum to Spion Kop Lookout. You can pick up the leaflet and map in the museum and most shops and hotels and it is an excellent way to see all the sights.

With the closure of the open-cut mine, you can now go out with Mt Lyell Mine Tours

WEST

(☎ 6471 2388) and view the workings, the remains of the open-cut mine and the museum for $9.50, children $5.50. Mine tours depart from 1 Driffield St at 9.15 am, 2.30 pm and 4.30 pm from October to April. During May to mid-September, tours run at 9.15 am and 4 pm daily.

The newest tourist attraction is the **chair-lift** beside Penghana Rd. Run by Queenstown Ropeways (☎ 6471 2338) it rises 369 metres up the steep side of the valley to a viewing platform from where some short walks lead to an old mine site. Rides cost $4 per person. It sounds good, but similar views can be seen for free from the road to Strahan which crosses the top of the chairlift site.

At **Newell Creek**, nine km south of Queenstown on the Mt Jukes Rd, a platform for visitors gives access to a patch of superb King Billy and Huon pine rainforest. You can continue to follow this road over Mt Jukes to Lake Burbury and the Darwin Dam wall where the bitumen ends. All roads past here are 4WD only and the best way to visit the places further south is with Lyell Tours (☎ 6471 2388) which departs at 8.30 am for the Bird River Rainforest Area. Tours cost $50, children $30.

On the top of the pass on the Lyell Hwy, just before the final descent into Queenstown, a sealed side road leads to the **Iron Blow**. This is the now deserted open-cut mine where mining for the town began in 1883. A short track leads to a lookout over the flooded open cut.

Places to Stay

The *Queenstown Cabin & Tourist Park* (☎ 6471 1332), at 17 Grafton St, about one km from the town centre, has cheap below-average hostel accommodation for $20 a double plus $6 for each extra person. There are also tent sites with power for $11, on-site vans for $30 and cabins for $43; it's about a 10-minute walk south of town along the Queen River.

At 1 Penghana Rd, just over the bridge on the way to Strahan, is the *Mountain View Holiday Lodge* (☎ 6471 1163), which is the former men's quarters for the Mt Lyell Mining Company. The hostel section is pretty basic, but for $10 a night you get your own room and there are cooking facilities. Many of the rooms have been renovated as motel-style units and cost $55 a double.

The *Empire Hotel* (☎ 6471 1699) at 2 Orr St is a lovely old hotel which dominates the entrance to the city centre. It includes an imposing blackwood staircase classified by the National Trust. It is constructed of timber that was sent to England to be turned then shipped back to Queenstown. Clean and pleasant singles/doubles cost $20/35 and, for a little extra, you can get breakfast.

Hunter's Hotel (☎ 6471 1531), further up Orr St with the green and gold front, was built in 1889 and charges $20 including breakfast for singles only. Of similar standard, the *Commercial Hotel* (☎ 6471 1511) in Driffield St provides B&B in basic units for $25/40 for singles/doubles and caters for children, $12.50 each.

Most other places around town are motel rooms. The *Mount Lyell Motor Inn* (☎ 6471 1888), at 1 Orr St is centrally placed and has basic motel suites for $40/50. At the other end of Orr St, the *Queenstown Motor Lodge* (☎ 6471 1866) on the corner of Bowes St has rooms for $50/65.

The *Silver Hills Motor Inn* (☎ 6471 1755) on Penghana Rd has a large number of traditional units for $65/75 for singles/doubles. Just around the corner in Batchelor St, the *Westcoaster Motor Inn* (☎ 6471 1033) has a hotel complex as well as self-contained, multistorey units. Rooms are $110 a double.

Out beside the Lyell Hwy, the *Gold Rush Motor Inn* (☎ 6471 1005) has self-contained units for $99 a double. This was formerly called the Penny Royal Motor Lodge.

Places to Eat

There are plenty of places around town which serve meals and they are all pretty good value. In and around Orr St the *Mount Lyell Motor Inn*, *Empire Hotel* and *Hunters Hotel* all serve counter meals with main courses around $10. Of similar standard and price, is the *Commercial Hotel* in Driffield

St and *Vics Bistro* at the Mountain View Holiday Lodge on Penghana Rd.

Maloney's Restaurant in the Queenstown Motor Lodge offers an à la carte menu which is slightly dearer than the ones in the hotels. The *Westcoaster Motor Inn* has similar prices for upmarket counter meals. The most expensive place in town is *Smelters Restaurant* at the Silver Hills Motor Inn where mains are around $17 from the à la carte menu.

For good cakes and light snacks try *Axel's Takeaway* in Orr St. In Orr St you will also find *Filis Pizza Bar* and *JJ's Coffee Lounge*.

Getting There & Away

Air The airport is six km west of town, beside the road to Strahan. The only airline which has scheduled flights is Airlines of Tasmania (☎ 1800 030 550), which flies three days a week (Tuesday, Wednesday and Thursday) from Hobart to Queenstown and on to Strahan for $113 one way. On the same days there are flights to Devonport and Launceston. Timetables change regularly and bookings are essential for all flights.

Bus From mid-September to May, TRC (☎ 6471 1011 or 1800 030 033) has daily services in both directions from Hobart through Queenstown to Strahan. From June to mid-September, buses run along the same route on Tuesday, Wednesday, Friday and Sunday. The fare from Hobart to Queenstown is $33.30, and from Queenstown to Strahan it's $5.20.

TRC also runs a daily bus service in both directions from mid-September to May from Burnie and Devonport to Queenstown and Strahan. During June to mid-September, services run on only Tuesday, Thursday and Sunday along the same route. The fare from Burnie to Queenstown is $27.70 with an extra $5.20 from Queenstown to Strahan.

TRC operates extra buses on school days, leaving Strahan at 7.20 am for Queenstown and returning from Queenstown at 3 pm. It also runs buses on school days which leave Zeehan at 7.30 am and return from Queenstown at 3 pm. The TRC depot is in Orr St.

Bookings for any school bus must be made at the Queenstown terminal (☎ 6471 1011) before 5 pm on the day before travelling.

Tasmanian Wilderness Transport (☎ 6334 4442) runs one service to Strahan. A bus runs every Saturday (all year) from Hobart to Queenstown, arriving at 3.45 pm and continuing to Strahan; the fare is $35 one way or $65 return. The return service to Hobart leaves Queenstown every Sunday at 3 pm to arrive in Hobart at 8.10 pm.

Hitching If you are hitching, it is usually a long wait between vehicles on the Lyell and Murchison highways. From May to August it can get very cold standing on the roadside; the bus services are an attractive alternative.

LAKE BURBURY

This is a large dam created for hydroelectricity production, and its construction flooded six km of the old Lyell Hwy. The highway was moved further south with a new bridge over the lake and provides some fine views of Frenchmans Cap and the Eldon Range. The dam is on the King River and was part of the compromise that resulted from the Franklin River controversy. Originally Lake Burbury was to be linked into dams on the Franklin River. With the successful stopping of the Franklin River project the King River scheme still proceeded and the Darwin Dam wall had to built to prevent water flowing over into the Franklin River. As with all new dams, the rotting vegetation provides good habitat for the introduced trout. Fishing here is currently very good.

FRANKLIN-GORDON WILD RIVERS NATIONAL PARK

This park is part of the Western Tasmania World Heritage Area and includes the catchments of the Franklin, Olga and Gordon rivers. The most significant peak in the park is Frenchmans Cap which can be seen from the west coast as well as from many places along the Lyell Hwy. This mountain is formed by glacial action and has Tasmania's tallest cliff face.

The park contains a number of unique

plant species and a series of major Aboriginal sites at caves in the Franklin River valley. The most significant is **Kutikina Cave** where 50,000 artefacts have been found from the Aboriginal occupation of 15,000 to 20,000 years ago.

Much of the park consists of deep river gorges and impenetrable rainforest, but the Lyell Hwy traverses its northern end and there are a few signposted short walks which you can take from the road to see what this park contains:

Nelson River – Just west of Lake Burbury, an easy 20-minute return walk through rainforest leads to Nelson Falls. Signs beside the track highlight the common plants of the area and the 35-metre-high falls are excellent.

Donaghys Hill – Four km east of the bridge over the Collingwood River, this 40-minute return walk leads to the top of the hill above the junction of the Collingwood and Franklin Rivers. This has spectacular views of the Franklin River and Frenchmans Cap.

Franklin River Nature Walk – From the picnic ground where the highway crosses the river, a 25-minute return nature trail has been marked through the forest.

The walk to Frenchmans Cap takes three to five days and is the park's best-known bushwalk. It has two shelter huts along the way and lots of lovely, deep mud; you'll find full track notes described in Lonely Planet's *Bushwalking In Australia* by John & Monica Chapman.

Rafting the Franklin

The best way of all to see this park is to raft down its largest and most sensational river, the Franklin. It is a very wild river and rafting it can be hazardous. Experienced rafters can tackle it if they are fully equipped and prepared, or there are tour companies offering complete rafting packages. About 90% of all rafters who tackle the river go with tour companies. Whether you go with an independent group or a tour operator, you should

Rafting the famous Franklin is one of the most thrilling Tasmanian experiences

contact the Department of Parks, Wildlife & Heritage (☎ 6233 6191) for the latest information on permits, current regulations and environmental considerations.

All expeditions should register at the booth at the junction between the Lyell Hwy and the Collingwood River, 49 km west of Derwent Bridge. The trip down the Franklin River, starting at Collingwood River and ending at Sir John Falls, takes about 14 days. From the exit point, you can be picked up by a Wilderness Air seaplane or paddle a further 22 km downriver to a Gordon River cruise boat. It is possible to do just one half of the river. The Upper Franklin takes around eight days from the Collingwood River to the Fincham Track and it passes through the Irenabyss Gorge and you can climb Frenchmans Cap as a side trip. The Lower Franklin takes about seven days from Fincham Track to Sir John Falls and passes through the Great Ravine. The shorter trips are really only practical for tour groups; as the Fincham Track is for 4WD vehicles only and is a long way from the main highways.

Tour companies which arrange complete rafting packages include Peregrine Adventures (☎ 6231 0977), 8 Criterion St, Hobart 7000; Rafting Tasmania (☎ 6227 9516), 63 Channel Hwy, Taroona 7053; and Tasmanian Expeditions (☎ 6334 3477 or 1800 030 230), 110 George St Launceston 7250. An all-inclusive rafting package (the tour operators will transport you to the river) costs around $140 to $180 a day. Departures are mainly from December to March.

Cradle Mountain-Lake St Clair National Park

Tasmania's best-known national park is the superb 1262-sq-km Cradle Mountain-Lake St Clair which is part of the World Heritage Area. The spectacular mountain peaks, deep gorges, lakes, tarns, wild open moorlands, and the reserve's incredible variety of wildlife extend from the Great Western Tiers in Tasmania's north to Derwent Bridge, on the Lyell Hwy in the south. It was one of the most glaciated areas in Australia and includes Mt Ossa (1617 metres), Tasmania's highest mountain, and Lake St Clair, Australia's deepest natural freshwater lake.

The preservation of this region as a national park was due, in part, to the Austrian Gustav Weindorfer, who fell in love with the area and claimed: 'This must be a national park for all time. It is magnificent. Everyone should know about it, and come and enjoy it'. In 1912 he built a chalet out of King Billy pine called Waldheim ('Forest Home' in German), and from 1916 he lived there permanently. Today, eight bushwalkers huts

Leatherwood Honey

Under the canopy of the tall, rainforest trees in the wet, western half of Tasmania, grow the endemic leatherwood trees *(Eucryphia lucida)*. The trees grow to a height of about 20 metres. From December to March the tree is covered in small, white, waxy flowers which have very pale pink stamens. The name 'Leatherwood' comes from the leathery nature of the tree's timber.

Leatherwood honey was first produced commercially in the early 1920s, but it was not until after the war that Tasmanian beekeepers commenced taking large numbers of hives into the leatherwood areas. Today, many thousands of hives are transported by truck or even semi-trailer annually.

Apiarists visit their sites several times during the flowering season to remove full boxes, known as 'supers', and replace them with empty ones for the bees to work on. At the end of the flowering period, all the hives are brought back to their home sites and the honey is extracted from the full supers.

Honey is extracted from the 'combs' inside the supers by spinning and is then packaged for sale and export. The resulting product is a distinctive, aromatic honey which will certainly tempt your taste buds! ■

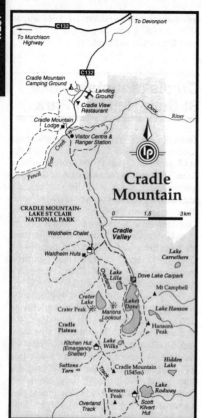

Cradle Mountain

Information

Cradle Valley At the northern park boundary, and built on the verge of an amazing rainforest, the visitor centre and ranger station (☎ 6492 1133) is open year round from 8 am to 5 pm. The centre is staffed by rangers who can advise you about weather conditions, walking gear, maximum and minimum walking groups, bush safety, and bush etiquette. Both the static and audio-visual displays are well worth seeing. In summer, the rangers run many free activities and these are advertised on the board at the centre. Participating in some of these activities is a good way to learn what is so special about this area, what problems people have caused and how they are being solved.

The centre also features an easy – but quite spectacular – 500-metre circular boardwalk through the adjacent rainforest called the **Rainforest-Pencil Pine Falls Walking Track**. This is particularly good for visitors in wheelchairs and for those with youngsters in prams.

Whatever time of the year you visit, be prepared for cold wet weather in the Cradle Valley area – for those who like statistics, it rains on seven days out of 10, it is cloudy on eight days out of 10, the sun shines all day only one day in 10, and it snows on 54 days each year!

Cynthia Bay Cynthia Bay, near the southern park boundary, also has an informative ranger station (☎ (002) 89 1115) where you register to walk the Overland Track in the opposite direction. At the nearby kiosk (☎ 6289 1137) you can book a seat on the small MV *Idaclair* ferry. See Getting Around at the end of this chapter for ferry details. From the same kiosk you can also hire dinghies for a spot of fishing or relaxing on the lake, but make sure you don't fall in – it's freezing!

have been constructed near his original chalet at the northern end of the park, and the area is named Waldheim, after his chalet.

There are plenty of day walks in both the Cradle Valley and Cynthia Bay (Lake St Clair) regions, but it is the spectacular 80-km Overland Track between the two that has turned this park into a bushwalkers' Mecca. The Overland Track is one of the finest bushwalks in Australia, and in summer up to 100 people a day start it. The track can be walked in either direction, but most people walk from north to south (Cradle Valley to Cynthia Bay).

Bushwalking

All walking tracks in this park are signposted and well defined. They are easy to follow but it is still advised to carry a map of the tracks. These can be purchased at the visitor centres.

Cradle Valley From the visitor centre there is an excellent circuit walk following **Pencil Pine Creek** and returning via the **Dove River Gorge**, which takes two hours return. There are also short nature walks and loops around the centre itself.

From the Waldheim Lodge, **Crater Lake** is a popular two-hour return walk. You can also climb Cradle Mountain but this takes a full day to complete, allow seven hours return. The other place from which walks commence is **Lake Dove**. The best walk there is the recently completed circuit of Lake Dove which takes about two to three hours to complete. All other walks involve steep climbs, and the walk to **Mt Campbell** and the **Twisted Lakes** provides great views of Cradle Mountain and the nearby lakes for a four-hour return walk.

Cynthia Bay Region You can follow the management road to **Watersmeet**, then follow the nature trail back to Cynthia Bay; allow one hour return. Most other walks are fairly long such as the track to **Shadow Lake**, four hours return, or the circuit over **Mt Rufus**, seven hours return.

One way to do some good walking is to use the MV *Idaclair* ferry to drop you at Echo Point or Narcissus Hut. The walk back along the lake shore is interesting. From Echo Point it is about three hours and from Narcissus Hut about five to six hours back to Cynthia Bay.

The Overland Track The best time to walk the Overland Track is during summer, when the flowering plants are most prolific, although spring and autumn also have their attractions. You can walk the track in winter, but only if you're very experienced.

The trail is well marked for its entire length and, at an easy pace, takes around five or six days to complete. Along the track, there are many secondary paths leading up to mountains like **Mt Ossa** or other natural features, making it a great temptation to take a few more days to explore the region fully. In fact, the length of time you take is limited only by the amount of supplies you can carry and eight to 10 days is ideal.

Although the walk takes you through wilderness, the track itself is well used and you must expect to meet many walkers each day. Most walk from north to south and this is the recommended direction as you will meet less travellers coming the other way. Each year nearly 5000 people walk the entire track.

There are 12 unattended huts along the track which you can use for overnight accommodation, but you can't rely on them being available. In summer they are usually full, so make sure you carry a tent. Camp fires are banned so you must also carry a fuel stove. You will also need to pay for entry to the national park and a backpackers' permit costing $10 is recommended. This lasts for two months and provides entry to all national parks in the state.

In summer the weather is often fine, but snowfalls and severe storms are also regular features. You must be prepared to camp in snow and walk through cold, wet conditions. A significant number of those who are walking the track for the first time have inadequate equipment and when cold weather occurs the walk becomes a struggle for survival rather than an adventure. The

Lake St Clair map. Labels: Overland Track, Narcissus Hut, Lake Laura, Narcissus Bay, Mount Ida (1253 m), Echo Point, Echo Point Hut, Lake Sappho, Travellers Rest Lake, Mt Olympus (1449m), Lake Petrarch, Cuvier Valley, Lake St Clair, CRADLE MOUNTAIN-LAKE ST CLAIR NATIONAL PARK, Little Hugel, Forgotten Lake, Shadow Lake, Mt Hugel (1403 m), Watersmeet, Mount Rufus (1416 m), Cynthia Bay, Derwent Basin, Pumping Station, Derwent Bridge Chalets, Lake St Clair Wilderness Holidays, Derwent Bridge Wilderness Resort, Derwent Bridge, To Hobart, To Queenstown, A10. Scale 0 2.5 5 km.

Franklin's Overland Journey

In 1842 the Governor of Van Diemen's Land, Sir John Franklin, decided that, with his wife Lady Jane Franklin, he should travel overland from Hobart to Macquarie Harbour on the west coast. At that time over half of the island was still unexplored by Europeans and such a journey was a considerable risk.

The trip started in grand style with Lady Franklin being carried in a palanquin and attended to by a servant. Within three days the entourage had completed 80% of the distance and reached Lake St Clair. The whole journey was planned to take six or seven days but, as modern bushwalkers know, the country of the Franklin River consists of deep gorges and impenetrable scrub.

Heavy rains and the difficult terrain took its toll and the group took 22 days to reach Macquarie Harbour and meet their ship. The troubles were not yet over as winds were unfavourable and the small ship spent a further three weeks trapped in Macquarie Harbour. The group almost starved to death but eventually were able to escape from the harbour and return to Hobart.

A detailed diary was kept of the entire journey and today it makes fascinating reading. The *Narrative of the Overland Journey* by David Burns has been reprinted and is available in many libraries and the bookshops at the major museums. ∎

most dangerous part of the walk is the exposed high plateau between Waldheim and Pelion Creek, near Mt Pelion West. The south-west wind that blows across here can be bitterly cold and sometimes strong enough to knock you off your feet.

The walk itself is extremely varied, crossing high alpine moors, rocky screes, past gorges and through tall forest. A detailed description of the walk and major side trips is given in Lonely Planet's *Bushwalking in Australia* by John & Monica Chapman. For detailed notes of all the tracks in the park, read *Cradle Mountain Lake St Clair and Walls of Jerusalem National Parks* by John Chapman & John Siseman.

If you are walking from Cradle Valley to Cynthia Bay, you can radio from Narcissus Hut for the MV *Idaclair* ferry to come and pick you up; this will save you a 5½ hour walk. In summer, this runs at regular times every day for $15 per person. In other seasons, the boat only operates by demand and there is a minimum fee for using the boat service so it is best to get a group together.

Organised Tours

The company most experienced at running guided bushwalking tours in this national park is Craclair Walking Holidays (☎ 6424 7833), PO Box 516 Devonport, which runs eight and 10-day trips along the Overland

Track for $935 to $1020 per person. This is a good way to walk the track as all packs, sleeping bags, tents, jackets and overtrousers are supplied. The company also runs a wide variety of shorter trips such as four days around Cradle Mountain for $495 per person and seven days around Pine Valley for $785.

There are several other companies which run similar trips. Peregrine Adventures (☎ 6225 0944) has an eight-day Cradle Mountain trek for $850 and Tasmanian Expeditions (☎ 1800 030 230) does an eight-day trip for $880. There are several companies offering short walks, such as Launceston Wilderness Walks (☎ 6334 3477 or 1800 030 230), which has three-day trips for $360, and Tasmanian Outdoor Experience Company (☎ 6334 4442) with three days at Cradle Mountain for $445.

If camping is not for you, then Cradle Huts P/L (☎ 6331 2006) has private huts along the Overland Track. A six-day walk with all meals and sleeping in the huts each night costs $1250 per person.

A less energetic way to see the sights is to go out with Cradle Mountain Scenic Flights (☎ 6492 1132) which operates from the Cradle View Restaurant. A 25-minute trip costs $130 for two or $55 each for three or more people. It also runs longer trips of 65 minutes as far afield as Frenchmans Cap for $120 each.

Places to Stay & Eat

Cradle Valley Region The cheapest place in this area is the *Cradle Mountain Camping Ground* (☎ 6492 1395), 2.5 km outside the national park; it costs $14 a double to camp, plus $7 for each extra adult. It also provides bunkhouse accommodation for $20 per person. Extras like bedding are hired out at exorbitant rates so bring a warm sleeping bag for the cold nights. The camping ground was constructed by national parks staff in 1987 and has been very well designed, providing privacy to all camp sites and areas. Rather than clearing the forest, the natural vegetation has been left between each area. Two large cooking shelters, half-buried in the ground, are provided. The kiosk at the camping ground is open every day for basic supplies.

At Waldheim, five km into the national park, there are eight basic huts, all containing gas stoves, cooking utensils and wood heaters but no bedding. The minimum fees for these cabins are $55 to $75. Check-in and bookings for the huts are handled by the camping ground.

Just on the national park boundary is the luxurious *Cradle Mountain Lodge* (☎ 6492 1303), where doubles in the main chalet cost $85 and basic self-contained cabins are $146 a double. The lodge has good facilities for its guests and anyone is welcome to eat at the excellent restaurant (make sure you book first), visit the Tavern Bar or buy basic groceries and unleaded petrol at the Lodge's general store. Expect prices to be dearer than in other parts of the state; if that's a problem bring everything with you. The Lodge also runs special events in winter such as a three-day food and wine tasting festival in June which includes all breakfasts and dinners. Rates range from $692 to $1100 per person.

The *Cradle View Restaurant*, near the camping ground, serves reasonably priced home-made meals; you can also buy leaded petrol and diesel from outside the restaurant.

Road to Cradle Mountain From Devonport you can pass through Wilmot to Sheffield on the way to Cradle Mountain. Moina is where the two alternative routes meet and there is some high-quality accommodation in this region.

At the corner of Cethana Rd (from Sheffield) and Cradle Mountain Rd you'll find *High Country – Green Gable* (☎ 6492 1318) which provides B&B for a small number of units for $80 to $110 a double. Nearby are self-catering units at *Cradle Country Chalet* (☎ 6492 1401) which come with continental breakfast for $90 a double.

The best known place to stay in the area rivals the Cradle Mountain Lodge. At *Lemonthyme Lodge* (☎ 6492 1112) you can have a room in the main lodge for $80 to $85 a double with breakfast or you can rent one of the chalet-style cabins for $140 to $170 a double. Meals are available every day at the lodge.

Cynthia Bay At the southern end of Lake St Clair, *Lakeside St Clair Wilderness Holidays* (☎ 6289 1137) has several huts, plenty of camp sites and a kiosk that sells basic food supplies and takeaways. It costs $8 for two to camp and $6 per person a night to stay in the bunkhouse, Milligania, which has communal cooking facilities. The other huts are designed for groups and cost $8 per person, with a minimum of $30 for the smaller huts.

A new lodge is under construction near the old pumping station near the dam wall. It includes six self-contained lodges plus a hostel and should be open by the time this book has been printed. Rates are not yet available.

Derwent Bridge & Bronte Park At Derwent Bridge, five km south of Lake St Clair, there's accommodation at the hotel *Derwent Bridge Wilderness Resort* (☎ 6289 1144). Hostel-standard rooms in transportable huts cost $15 per person, and rooms in the hotel are $45/65, including a continental breakfast. The hotel has good, hearty meals at average prices and, with its open fire and friendly staff, is a good place to spend an evening. It's worth visiting just to see the huge barn-like structure of the main hotel – if a possum gets inside it is almost impossible to capture! You can also buy food, basic supplies and maps here, and rent fishing or bushwalking gear. Next to the garage the *Derwent Bridge Chalets* (☎ 6289 1125) has two units of a higher standard, but they are expensive at $99 a double.

If you are after self-contained units, *Bronte Park Highland Village*, (☎ 6289 1126) is just off the highway, 26 km east of Derwent Bridge. It has large units at $60 and $70 a double. It also provides camping for a bargain $5 and charges $12 for a hostel bed. The hotel also has good meals at reasonable prices.

Getting There & Away
Cradle Valley The construction of the link road to the west coast has meant that the national park is now only a short diversion from a highway. All the buses from the north pass the park, but if you're coming from Queenstown, only the weekend services normally come this way.

From mid-September to May, TRC (☎ 6424 5100 or 1800 030 033) runs daily services from Burnie and Devonport, through Sheffield past Cradle Mountain Lodge, then from Zeehan to Queenstown and Strahan. From June to mid-September, it runs services along the same route on Tuesday, Thursday and Sunday. The return bus from Queenstown and Strahan does not come past Cradle Mountain on weekdays but goes directly along the Murchison Hwy to Burnie then Devonport. The weekend services from Queenstown pass Cradle Mountain Lodge on their way to Devonport.

From November to April, Tasmanian Wilderness Transport (☎ 6334 4442) has buses every day from Launceston ($35) and Devonport ($30); from May to October, the buses run on Tuesday, Thursday and Saturday with an extra service returning on Sunday. The Saturday bus continues to Strahan ($40) and returns from there on Sunday.

Cynthia Bay TRC (☎ 6231 3233 or 1800 030 033) has daily services from mid-September to May between Hobart and Strahan

via Derwent Bridge. From June to mid-September, TRC runs buses along the highway on Monday, Wednesday, Friday and Sunday from Hobart to Strahan. The one-way fare from Hobart to Derwent Bridge is $22.70 and the local agent is the roadhouse and petrol station in Derwent Bridge on the Lyell Hwy.

From November to April, Tasmanian Wilderness Transport (☎ 6334 4442) has daily return trips to Lake St Clair from Devonport, Launceston and Hobart. From May to October, the service from Launceston and Devonport runs every Tuesday, and the service to Hobart runs every Monday and Wednesday. During winter and spring, one service runs from Hobart to Lake St Clair and on to Strahan on Saturday and returns from Strahan via Lake St Clair to Hobart on Sunday. Its agent is the kiosk at Lake St Clair. Fares from Launceston to Lake St Clair are $45 one way or $80 return and from Hobart to Lake St Clair $35 one way or $65 return. If you are walking the Overland Track then they have a special $70 fare from both ends of the track.

Getting Around
Cradle Valley During summer, the Tasmanian Wilderness Transport bus can be used to get from the camping ground to Lake Dove for $5. Additionally, Maxwell's (☎ 6492 1400) runs a shuttle bus on demand for $5 per person.

Cynthia Bay Maxwell's also runs an informal taxi to and from Cynthia Bay and Derwent Bridge for $4 (minimum two people), and this operates daily on demand, bookings essential. This meets the regular TRC bus along the highway. The Tasmanian Wilderness Transport bus will also take you to Derwent Bridge for $5.

The MV *Idaclair* (☎ 6289 1137) runs three times daily during summer from Cynthia Bay across Lake St Clair to Narcissus Hut at the northern end. Scheduled times are 9 am, 12.30 pm and 3 pm. You can simply take a return trip on the boat for $20 each, children $12 or use the boat to get to Echo

Top Left: Huon pines reflected in the Gordon River
Top Right: Gordon Dam
Middle: Today's Lake Pedder
Bottom: Pindars Peak, south-west Tasmania

Top: Mt Strzelecki, Flinders Island
Bottom: Boulders on the Flinders Island coastline

Point or Narcissus Hut and walk back to Cynthia Bay. Fares for one-way rides are $15, children $10. Outside summer, the boat runs according to demand and times are posted at the kiosk where bookings can be made.

The South-West

Covering almost one quarter of Tasmania, the south-west is basically a large wilderness area with very few tracks or roads. One road penetrates into the region to service the hydroelectric power scheme that was built in the 1970s. At that stage, very little of the region was known to anyone except hardy bushwalkers, and there were only two national parks: Frenchmans Cap and Lake Pedder. Ironically the power scheme flooded one of the two original parks – the Lake Pedder park.

Since Lake Pedder was destroyed, the map has changed drastically. Almost the entire region is now contained within national parks, and every summer thousands of bushwalkers follow the better-known tracks across the wilderness. While some short walks can be done from the access road, most walks in this region require you to carry all gear for at least a week. There are no huts and only one marked track across the entire region. In spite of developments like the dams, most of the area can still be called wilderness. It is something special to be able to visit one of the few regions of the world where people have not yet had a dramatic impact.

The only road into the region starts from Westerway, which is west of New Norfolk. It passes the entrance to the Mt Field National Park then continues to Maydena, the last town on the road; it has takeaways and a general store. Just past the town is the entrance gate, where park admission fees can be paid. From here the road becomes narrow and winding. At first it passes through tall forests, then traverses open country for 100 km to Strathgordon. The final part of the road has wonderful views of rugged mountain ranges. The road continues a short way past the town to the dam walls, which hold back the water for lakes Pedder and Gordon. The Serpentine Dam on Lake Pedder is very ordinary, while the curved concrete wall of the Gordon Dam is quite spectacular.

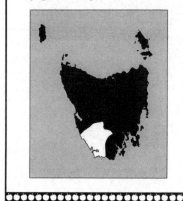

HIGHLIGHTS

- Exploring the World Heritage Area wilderness
- Enjoying the views from Scotts Peak
- Seeing the Gordon Dam wall and power station
- Strolling along the Creepy Crawly Nature Trail
- Flying over the region

About halfway to Strathgordon, a single side road leads south for 40 km to Scotts Peak and this is well worth driving along. The gravel road is in good condition and from the end of it there are excellent views of the major mountains of the South-West National Park.

History

The south-west has not always been wilderness. The original inhabitants were the Tasmanian Aboriginal people, who arrived about 35,000 years ago. At that stage, the world was in the midst of an Ice age and the south-west was covered with open grasslands which were ideal for the hunting of animals. Evidence of Aboriginal occupation

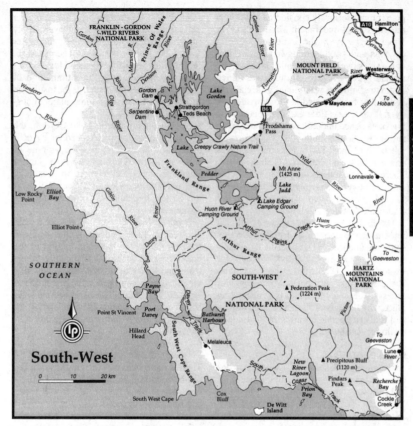

has been found in many of the caves. About 10,000 years ago the Ice ages ended and, with the warmer climate, thick forests began growing across the south-west. The Aboriginal people slowed the growth of the forests with regular burning of the grassy plains, but slowly the forest advanced and by the time the Europeans arrived the only Aboriginal people left in the area lived around the coastline.

The European explorers were, at first, appalled by the landscape. Matthew Flinders, the first to circumnavigate Tasmania, described the south-west with the comment:

'The mountains are the most dismal that can be imagined. The eye ranges over these peaks with astonishment and horror'. Other reports from those who climbed the peaks described the interior as a series of rugged ranges which extended to the horizon – an apt description still applicable today.

Most of the early explorers were surveyors who measured the land and, under great hardships, cut tracks across the area. The tracks were cut to provide access to the west coast, and to open the region for development. A road was built into the area from the north to Gordon Bend, and in the 1880s the government seriously considered building a railway tunnel underneath Mt Anne to Port Davey. However, the expected mineral deposits and good farming lands were few and far between. Huon pine was logged around Port Davey, osmiridium was mined at Adamsfield, tin was mined at Melaleuca and a tiny farm existed at Gordonvale, but overall there was little exploitation and the tracks vanished under the encroaching scrub and forest. So the south-west was left pretty much alone; most Tasmanians regarded it as uninhabitable and dubbed it 'Transylvania'. There is some interesting reading about the early explorers in *Trampled Wilderness – The History of South-West Tasmania* by Ralph and Kathleen Gowlland.

Of all the early developments, all that remains is the tin mine at Melaleuca, a tiny settlement near Port Davey. This is a small-scale operation mining alluvial tin and, for visitors, Melaleuca's most important feature is the small gravel airstrip which provides access to the area. Melaleuca is an interesting place which can be visited on scenic flights, and is also a good starting-point for some of the longer bushwalks.

LAKE PEDDER
At the edge of the south-west wilderness lies Lake Pedder, once a spectacularly beautiful natural lake considered the crown jewel of the region. The largest glacial outwash lake in the world, it was three km by three km square, and its wide, sandy beach made an ideal light-plane airstrip. The lake was considered so important that it was the first part of the south-west to be protected in its own national park.

In 1972, however, this status did not help as it was flooded to become part of the Gordon River hydroelectric development. According to the engineers, they were only 'modifying' the lake by placing 20 metres of water over the top. The flooding was a controversial decision and marked the first major conservation battle in Tasmania. It transpired that it was not even necessary to flood the lake for the hydroelectricity scheme – Lake Gordon is the main dam and

Lake Pedder is simply a back up supply for periods of low rainfall. With the over-supply of other hydroelectric schemes, the water from Lake Pedder has rarely been used. In recent years Tasmania's demand for electricity has decreased with the introduction of conservation measures such as the insulation of houses, and because some major industries have left the state.

Together with nearby Lake Gordon, the Pedder Dam (named Lake Pedder by officials) now holds 27 times the volume of water in Sydney Harbour and is the largest inland freshwater catchment in Australia. The underground Gordon Power Station is the largest hydroelectric power station in Tasmania.

Trout fishing is popular and boats are allowed on Lake Pedder. While there are fewer trout than in the boom period of the dam's first 10 years, the fish caught range from one to 20 kg in size. Tiny boats like dinghies are discouraged as the lake is 55 km long and the frequent storms generate sizeable waves. Boat ramps exist at Scotts Peak Dam in the south and near Strathgordon in the north.

Places to Stay
There are two free camping grounds near the southern end of the lake. The *Lake Edgar Camping Ground* has pit toilets and water and fine views of the area. In wet weather it is less attractive as it's exposed to the cold winds. A better place to camp is the nearby *Huon River Camping Ground* which is hidden in tall forest near Scotts Peak Dam. This has pit toilets, a shelter shed and fresh water.

STRATHGORDON
Built to service Hydro Electricity Company employees during the construction of the Gordon River Power Scheme, the township of Strathgordon is the base from which to visit lakes Pedder and Gordon, the Gordon Dam and the power station. Strathgordon is also becoming a popular bushwalking, trout fishing, boating and water-skiing location. Boats are not allowed on Lake Gordon.

Pedder 2000

The first big conservation issue in Tasmania was the flooding of Lake Pedder in 1972 for a hydroelectric power scheme. This was a unique natural lake being the largest example of a glacial outwash formation in the world. In spite of public protests and the fact that the dam was not really necessary for the power scheme, the project went ahead as it created jobs.

Pedder 2000 is a campaign to reverse the past engineering project by draining the lake and restoring it to its former glory. It has been taken seriously by politicians and there has been a government enquiry, but so far the politicians have not yet committed themselves. Conservationists regard the Pedder 2000 campaign as setting a world precedent for reversing other environmentally destructive projects. It has been shown to be feasible and support is growing for correcting the errors of the past.

Travellers who wish to become involved in the Pedder 2000 campaign should contact the Wilderness Society at 130 Davey St, Hobart 7000 (☎ 6234 9366). ■

OLEGAS TRUCHANAS/WILDERNESS SOCIETY

Lake Pedder prior to its controversial flooding

The **Gordon Power Station** (☎ 6280 1166) can be visited every day except Monday all year. From December to April, tours are run at 10 am and 2.30 pm. In other months, only one tour runs at 11 am. Entry is $5 (children $2.50, family $15). A maximum of 48 people are allowed on any one tour and booking is suggested. The visitor centre at the Gordon Dam site has plenty of information about the scheme, but it neglects to tell you that the scheme was never really necessary.

Places to Stay & Eat

There's a basic free *camping ground* with few facilities at the place once used as the construction workers' quarters. Better places are found beside Lake Pedder, such as the *picnic ground* near the Serpentine Dam and at Teds Beach.

Basic rooms are available at the *Lake Pedder Motor Inn* (☎ 6280 1166), where singles/doubles cost $45/60. Meals are also available from the restaurant and cost around $10 to $15.

SOUTH-WEST NATIONAL PARK

There are few places left in the world as isolated and untouched as Tasmania's south-west wilderness, the state's largest national park. It is the home of some of the world's last tracts of virgin temperate rainforest, and these contribute much to the grandeur and extraordinary diversity of this ancient area.

The south-west is the habitat of the endemic Huon pine, which lives for more than 3000 years – one specimen is reported to be over 10,000 years old – and of the swamp gum, the world's tallest hardwood and flowering plant. About 300 species of lichen, moss and fern, some rare and endangered, festoon the dense rainforest; superb glacial tarns decorate the jagged mountains; and in summer, the delicate alpine meadows are ablaze with wildflowers and flowering shrubs. Through it all are the wild rivers, with rapids tearing through deep gorges and waterfalls plunging over cliffs. Each year more and more people venture into the heart of this incredible part of Tasmania's World Heritage Area, in search of the peace, isolation and challenge of a region virtually untouched since the last Ice age.

The only way to really see the park is to walk across it, something that is only suggested for fit, experienced bushwalkers. You can see a small part of it by following the gravel road from Frodshams Pass on the Strathgordon Rd to Scotts Peak. Not far from the pass the **Creepy Crawly Nature Trail** passes through rainforest beside a creek and is well worth visiting. Further south the road leaves the forest near the base of Mt Anne and wonderful views of many of the mountains in the south-west are obtained in fine weather. Mt Anne towers over the road. To the west lie the Frankland Ranges while to the south is the jagged crest of the Western Arthur Range. The road ends at the Scotts Peak Dam and nearby in the forest, down a side road, is a good (free) sheltered camping area beside the Huon River. There is also another free camping area with very basic amenities at Lake Edgar.

A whole range of escorted wilderness adventures are possible in this area, including flying, hiking, rafting, canoeing, mountaineering, caving and camping. More information on these can be obtained from the National Park Service (☎ 6233 6191). The standard national park entry fee applies even if you're just driving on the road through the park.

Day Walks

From the Scotts Peak Rd you can climb to **Mt Eliza**, a steep, five-hour return walk. Using the same track, you can walk further to climb **Mt Anne**, about eight to ten hours return. A better walk for most around Mt Anne is to follow the recently upgraded track to **Lake Judd**, about four hours return. This provides some fine views of cliffs and mountains without a long steep climb. This track starts nine km south of the car park for Mt Anne and is easily missed as there is no large car park and only a small signpost.

From Scotts Peak the best short walk follows the start of the **Port Davey Track** as it passes through a forest and across the button-grass plain. You can go as far as **Junction Creek**, which takes five hours return, but the first 20 to 30 minutes is the best part. Another short walk nearby is to climb **Red Knoll Hill** by following the road to the top; this provides fine views of the area and takes one hour return.

The road to Strathgordon also provides access to some good walks although none of them are signposted. You should purchase maps and guide books for these walks. **Mt Wedge** is a very popular four-hour return walk and, being located between Lake Pedder and Lake Gordon, provides sweeping views. Past Strathgordon, the Serpentine Dam provides the starting point for a long, steep climb on a poorly marked and muddy track to Mt Sprent, seven hours return. From the Gordon Dam it is possible to follow rough tracks to the **Gordon Splits** and the **Truchanas Pine Reserve**. These walks are only suitable for experienced bushwalkers as the tracks are difficult to follow.

Long Bushwalks

The best-known walk in the park is the

South Coast Track between Port Davey and Cockle Creek, near Recherche Bay. This takes about 10 days and should only be tackled by experienced hikers who are well prepared for the often vicious weather conditions. Light planes are used to airlift bushwalkers into the south-west and there is vehicle access to Cockle Creek at the south-eastern edge of the park. Detailed notes to the South Coast and Port Davey tracks are available in Lonely Planet's *Bushwalking in Australia* by John & Monica Chapman.

There are many other walks that can be done in the park, but you should first complete one of the better-known walks. Contrary to what you might think, the South-Coast Track is not all that hard and is good preparation for the more difficult trips. Most of the other walks are difficult, without marked tracks and require a high degree of bushwalking skills in order to be completed safely and enjoyed. The shortest of these is the four-day circuit of the Mt Anne Range. You will need at least seven days to visit Federation Peak and nine to 12 days are recommended for a traverse of the Western Arthur Range. For detailed notes of these routes and other major walks in the south-west, refer to *South West Tasmania* by John Chapman.

MELALEUCA

This is a tiny location deep in the south-west near Port Davey. The only access to it is by sea, light airplane or by following walking tracks for at least five days. The settlement contains two families who mine alluvial tin on the button-grass plain, along with a semi-resident team of national park staff. There are no shops or any facilities apart from two simple huts for bushwalkers. The major attraction for visitors is the excellent bird hide – quite a substantial building from where you can often see the rare orange-bellied parrot. You can camp at Melaleuca if you bring all your own food and have good bushwalking equipment.

The airstrip is of gravel and is suitable for planes with a maximum of six people. Flights operate on demand from the small airports around the state, with Cambridge airport at Hobart providing the main service. Par Avion (☎ 6248 5390) offers a day in the wilderness which includes time at Melaleuca for $240 per person. If you prefer to stay for several days and don't have your own walking gear, it also provides flights and fully catered camping for $600 for two days and $1094 for four days. Cruises around Port Davey are also available at $788 for two days.

SOUTH-WEST

The Islands

In Bass Strait there are two groups of islands, the Hunter and Furneaux, which guard the western and eastern entrances to the strait. The largest island in the Hunter group is King Island; and in the Furneaux group it is Flinders Island. These were once the transient homes of prospectors, sealers and sailors. Today, these two islands are mainly rural communities offering tourist retreats in natural coastal beauty, rich in marine and other wildlife.

Tasmania also has several other islands although they are all difficult to reach unless you have your own boat. Macquarie Island, 1500 km to the south-east, is the largest and being close to Antarctica has an extremely cold climate. Off the southern coastline of Tasmania are a string of islands which are clearly seen from the South-Coast Track. The largest are De Witt Island and Maatsuyker Island with its lighthouse.

HIGHLIGHTS

- Indulging in the rich cheeses and cream at the King Island Dairy
- Scenery around Cape Wickham
- Enjoying the views from Mt Strzelecki
- Diving for 'Diamonds' in Killiecrankie Bay

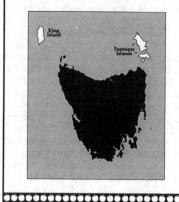

King Island

- *pop 2000*

At the western end of Bass Strait, this small island surrounded by rugged coastline, is 64 km long and only 25 km across at its widest point but its beautiful beaches, rocky coastline and country-town atmosphere more than compensate for its size.

Discovered in 1798, and named after Governor King of New South Wales, King Island quickly gained a reputation as a home and breeding ground for seals and sea elephants. Just as quickly, however, these animals were hunted close to extinction by sealers and sailors known as the Straitsmen.

Over the years, the stormy seas of Bass Strait have claimed many ships, and there are at least 57 **shipwrecks** in the coastal waters around King Island. The island's worst shipwreck occurred in 1845 when the *Cataraqui*, an immigrant ship, went down with 399 people aboard. All lives were lost.

King Island is probably best known for its dairy produce (particularly its rich Brie cheese and cream), although kelp and large crayfish are other valuable exports. Its other main industry was the production of scheelite (used in the manufacture of armaments) until the mine and factory at Grassy closed in December 1990. After several years as a bit of a ghost town, Grassy has recently been sold and accommodation for visitors is currently being developed.

There are many sights to see and things to do on the island. Short walks along beaches, around lakes and through forest will ensure that you will see some of the plentiful wildlife. The calcified forest, kelp industries and rocky coastline are just some of the diverse features of this delightful island. A weekend visit is just not quite enough time to truly experience all the island has to offer.

The main township is **Currie**, which is also the main harbour for the island. It is close to the airport and most of the facilities on the island are located here. The other notable settlements are Naracoopa on the east coast and Grassy Resort to the south-east which has the only other harbour on the island.

When to Go

There is something to do on King Island virtually all year round and it does not have the extremes of temperature change which occurs in other parts of the country. However, summer is the ideal time if you are keen on water sports, while spring and autumn have many pleasant days.

Information

You can write to the King Island Tourist Development Association, PO Box 48, Currie, King Island, 7256 or phone ☎ 6462 1360 or 6462 1666 for further information on what's available. On the island, Top Tours, in Main St, (6462 1245) is a good place for tourist information.

Things To See

King Island has four **lighthouses** to guard its treacherous seas. The one at Currie, built in 1880, is open to visitors in the afternoons on weekends or by appointment for $3 adults and 50 cents for children. The one located at Cape Wickham, built in 1861, is the tallest in the southern hemisphere and, although it's not open, is worth a visit for the coastal scenery which surrounds it. The island's two other lighthouses are at Stokes Point at the most southern point and Cumberland lighthouse south of Naracoopa on the eastern side of the island.

Currie Museum, in Lighthouse St, was originally the lighthouse keeper's cottage and is open on Friday and on weekends from 2 to 4 pm or by appointment. Entry costs $2 for adults. The museum features extensive

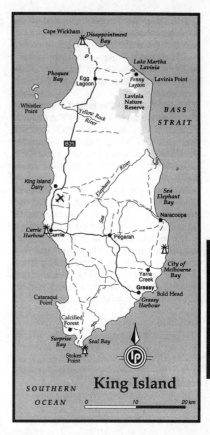

King Island

displays recalling maritime and other local history.

Kelp Industries Pty Ltd, in Netherby Rd, was established in 1975. The factory is the only kelp processing plant in Australia and receives, dries and processes storm cast, **bull kelp** gathered from the rocks and beaches around the island. You can see the kelp being air dried on racks from the road. It is left on the racks for about two weeks, then kiln dried and crushed. It is then shipped to Scotland where it is mixed with kelp from other countries to manufacture a variety of products including sauces, lotions and detergents.

The **Calcified Forest** is located in the south-west part of the island. A short walk of one km from the car park leads onto a viewing platform from where the ancient petrified tree trucks can be seen. Some experts believe these to be up to 30 million years old.

The **Festival of King Island** is held annually in early March. It includes The Imperial 20 Foot Race, an art and craft competition/exhibition, the surfing carnival and the Queenscliff (Victoria) to Grassy Yacht Race. Following on from this is the King Island Show.

You must not go to King Island without visiting the **King Island Dairy** and sampling some of its products. The dairy is located 8 km north of Currie, just north of the airport, and is open weekdays from 10 am to 4 pm and Sunday from 12.30 pm to 4 pm. The dairy is not open on Saturday. The Bries, Cheddar and very thick cream are all available at discounted prices. Salami and other processed meats can also be purchased.

Activities

You can swim at many of the island's long, deserted beaches and freshwater lakes, or **scuba dive** amongst exotic marine life and accessible shipwrecks. Surfing is also popular on King Island.

If you would rather stay dry, you can indulge in golf or **bushwalking**. Fishing is another very popular activity with both surf and freshwater fishing available. There is also plenty of wildlife to observe, such as ducks, quail, wallabies, platypus and seals. Tiger and brown snakes also inhabit the island, and you will see feral pheasants and flocks of wild turkeys. What you won't see are rabbits and foxes. In the summer months, a small colony of fairy penguins comes ashore at dusk at the end of the breakwater at Grassy. Care should be taken not to disturb them or dazzle them with bright lights.

If you're into **bike riding**, then perhaps hiring a mountain bike (Top Tours ☎ 6462 1245) will better suit your needs. It's an excellent way to get around as you can ride all the bush tracks.

King Island Dive Charters (☎ 1800 030 330 or 6461 1133) provides single dives at a cost of $45 per dive or day diving trips for $90. Dive prices include tank, weight-belt, air per dive or on the full-day trips unlimited dives and lunch. It offers **fishing** charters for $300 a half day or $540 a full day which includes bait and handlines as well as lunch. There is room for up to six passengers.

King Island Nature Trail Rides (☎ 6463 1147) offers guided **horse rides** daily, for groups of up to four people. A half-day ride to the beach costs $30 per person and novice and experienced riders are catered for. In fine weather, horse-drawn tours either around the town or out for a country picnic can also be arranged.

Organised Tours

King Island Bushwalks (☎ 6461 1276) runs a short, guided walk along the Yarra Creek Gorge, on demand, which includes afternoon tea for $17.50 adults and $12 children.

Top Tours (☎ 6462 1245), in Main St, Currie, runs guided full-day tours, including lunch, to the north or south part of the island for $50 per person. It does pick-ups from accommodation places in and around Currie. It offers a half-day tour departing at 1.30 pm which includes afternoon tea, the penguins at Grassy and a three-course dinner. It also has a Penguin Parade tour for $15 per person.

Say "Cheese!" on King Island

King Island Coach Tours (☎ 6462 1138) runs full-day tours for $49 per person and half-day tours of Currie on Monday and Thursday for $27 per person including afternoon tea. It also has an evening penguin tour on Monday and Thursday, which departs half an hour before dusk for $22 which includes tea/coffee and nibbles.

Robertsons 4WD Tours (☎ 6462 1470) offers guided day trips and shorter tours around the island for around $50 per person per day which includes morning and afternoon tea and lunch.

Places to Stay

Currie Close to Currie, the *Bass Caravan Park* (☎ 6462 1260), in North Rd, has on-site vans for $40 single and $10 each extra person. Remember, you can't tow your own van over!

In Currie, *Gulhaven Holiday Homes* (☎ 6462 1560), at 11 Huxley St, is a four-bedroom, self-contained unit which sleeps up to eight people. The daily rate is $46 a double and $20 for each extra person. In Main St, the *King Island Colonial Lodge* (☎ 6462 1245) offers B&B at $40/50 for singles/doubles.

The *Boomerang Motel* (☎ 6462 1288), situated high on a bluff, overlooking the 9-hole Currie Golf Course, is moderately priced with singles/doubles at $60/70, which includes a continental breakfast. It has superb ocean views from all rooms and it's only a short walk into town.

King Island A-Frame Holiday Homes (☎ 6462 1260), at 95 North Rd is two km north of Currie and owned by the same people as the caravan park. It offers self-contained units with great sea views; each unit sleeps six people and the cost is $70 a double with $15 for each extra person. The *Island Gem Motel* (☎ 6462 1260), on the same site, is a relatively new addition to the island's accommodation options. It offers single/double rooms at $60/80 including continental breakfast. Picnic hampers are available on request.

Parers Hotel (☎ 6462 1633), in the centre of Currie, provides luxury suites for $65/90

and the main bar has a large open fireplace. Bicycles and golf clubs are available for guests at no extra cost. The hotel provides easy access to shops, the harbour and golf course.

Situated one km west of Currie, *Devil's Gap Retreat* (☎ 6462 1180), in Charles St, is right on the foreshore. The self-contained units have sweeping ocean views and direct access to the beach north of Currie Harbour, but will set you back $100 a double.

Naracoopa On the other side of the island at Naracoopa, the *Naracoopa Lodge* (☎ 6461 1294) has good hostel-style accommodation at $20 a night, with only a short walk to the beach and jetty.

The *Naracoopa Holiday Units* (☎ 6461 1326), in Beach Rd, have a sea-front location close to the fishing jetty. These self-contained units, at $56/74 a single/double, are nestled in their own private gardens on Sea Elephant Bay. *Rocky Glen Retreat* (☎ 6461 1103) is in Lovers Lane, overlooking Naracoopa Beach and Sea Elephant Bay. Here the units cost $65/88, which includes a continental breakfast.

Grassy The town has seen some changes in recent years. Once the mine closed it was a ghost town but the recent selling of the town's buildings has encouraged new tourist development which, at the time of writing, is under construction.

Other For something a little different why not stay on a beef farm. The *Pegarah Host Farm* (☎ 6461 1248) is a working farm property in Grassy Rd, 10 km east of Currie. Here you can experience farm life with family accommodation for $60 a double including continental breakfast. Alternatively, you could stay at the *Yarra Creek Host Farm* (☎ 6461 1276), in Yarra Creek Rd, 27 km east of Currie. This farm adjoins a nature reserve and caters for families or groups of up to five people for $60 a double plus $20 for each extra adult. The price includes continental breakfast.

Another option is to camp in the bush,

ISLANDS

however this is only permitted at Penny Lagoon and Lake Martha Lavinia, the two large freshwater lakes at the northern end of the island. Access is by a sandy track off Haines Rd and the only facilities are bush toilets. The lakes are a favourite water-sport location with the locals and are large enough for sailing dinghies, windsurfers and water skiing. It is advisable to carry in your own freshwater and a stove. Remember also to carry out all your rubbish.

Places to Eat

Currie There are many fine eating places in Currie located within walking distance of most of the accommodation. The *Coffee Shop* serves a selection of light meals and sandwiches and is open daily, while the *King Island Bakery* serves home-made gourmet pies which are an ideal snack on a cold day.

The *Jade Kingdom Chinese Restaurant* is fully licensed and serves Chinese and Malaysian meals, eat in or take away. The King Island Club has *Hoopers Restaurant* and a bistro and is a favourite with the local fishermen with reasonably priced meals. The *British Admiral Family Bistro*, at Parers Hotel, also offers a fine selection of King Island fare and in summer the adjacent beer garden is an ideal spot to soak up the sun.

A little more upmarket is the *Cataraqui Restaurant*, at Parers Hotel. Its à la carte menu offers a wide selection of the Island's local produce. Likewise, the *Fishbowl Restaurant* (☎ 6462 1288) at the Boomerang Motel, is also à la carte and attracts locals and visitors alike with its spectacular ocean views. It also features local seafood and beef, and bookings for non-residents of the motel are essential.

Naracoopa On the other side of the island in Naracoopa, *The Golden Spoon Restaurant* (☎ 6461 1103) provides lunches and morning/afternoon tea/coffee. On a stormy day, it's a great place to enjoy the pancakes, hot chocolates and friendly service while overlooking the coastline from the comfort of a cosy setting. It's also open for dinner, but bookings are necessary.

Things to Buy

There are a number of artists and craftspeople on the island and their wares, ranging from paintings, pottery, kelp and shell craft, can be seen at the **Old Newspaper Office** and the **Boat House Gallery** in Currie. Paintings are also on display at the Golden Spoon Restaurant in Naracoopa.

Getting There & Away

Flying time to King Island is a little under one hour. Aus-Air, Kendall and Airlines of Tasmania all have regular flights to the island. From Melbourne it costs around $124, from Launceston $154, Hobart $202 and Burnie $110.

Most airlines offer package deals to the island which vary depending on the season, but range between $232 and $321 twin share for a two-night stay. Brochures are available from the airlines or most travel agents. Due to the competitiveness of the airlines, pre-paid package deals definitely offer the best value.

Kendall Airlines (☎ (03) 9670 2677) has daily flights from Tullamarine Airport (Melbourne). On weekends a combination of the early morning 7 am Saturday flight and the late afternoon 3 pm flight on Sunday allows you to spend the best part of two full days on the island.

Aus-Air (☎ (03) 9580 6166 or 1800 331 256) runs daily flights from Moorabbin Airport (Melbourne). You can also fly 7.15 am on Saturday and return 3.45 pm Sunday for a weekend trip. The cheapest way to get to Moorabbin is by train to Cheltenham Station and then a taxi to the airport.

Airlines of Tasmania (☎ 6391 8755 or 1800 030 550) have two daily mid-week flights departing from Burnie at 9.10 am and 4.05 pm. The flight departs on Saturday morning at 7.45 am and on Sunday at 2.20 pm. There are flights from Traralgon and Sale in Victoria on Monday, Wednesday and Friday at 1.40 pm.

Getting Around

There is no public transport on the island, however the airlines can arrange airport transfers to Currie for around $12 per person each way and to Naracoopa or Grassy for about $35 per person each way. Hire car companies will meet you at the airport and pre-booking is highly recommended.

Most of the roads on the island are not sealed and there are no road safety signs. Drive carefully around the more remote areas as the roads can be a bit rough and narrow and there are several blind corners. Unless you have a 4WD, take extra care which roads or tracks you take or be prepared to dig yourself out of some sandy and muddy situations.

In Currie, you can rent cars from King Island Auto Rentals (☎ 6462 1297) from around $45 a day plus insurance, or from Howell's Auto Rent (☎ 6462 1282) for around $65 a day including insurance.

Furneaux Islands

FLINDERS ISLAND
• *pop 1010*

Flinders Island is the largest of the 52 islands that comprise the Furneaux Group. It is approximately 60 km long and 20 km wide and is followed in size by Cape Barren and Clarke islands.

First charted in 1798 by the navigator Matthew Flinders, the Furneaux Group became a base for the Straitsmen, who not only slaughtered seals in their tens of thousands but also indulged in a little piracy. Of the 120 or so ships wrecked on the islands' rocks, it is thought that quite a number were purposely lured there by sealers displaying false lights.

The most tragic part of Flinders Island's history, however, was its role in the virtual annihilation of Tasmania's Aboriginal people. Between 1829 and 1834, those who had survived the state's martial law (which gave soldiers the right to arrest or shoot any Aboriginal person found in a settled area) were brought to the island to be resettled. Of the 135 survivors who were transported to Wybalenna (an Aboriginal word which means 'Black man's house') to be 'civilised and educated', only 47 survived to make their final journey to Oyster Cove, near Hobart, in 1847.

On a brighter note, Flinders Island has many attractions for the visitor. Its beaches, especially on the western side, are beautiful, and the fishing and scuba diving are also good. There is no shortage of shipwrecks around the islands, some of which are clearly visible from shore.

A more unusual pastime is fossicking for 'diamonds' (which are actually fragments of topaz) on the beach and creek at Killiecrankie Bay. At one time there were plenty of stones to be found, but there are fewer now, and the locals now dive for them using special equipment.

Flinders Island has some great bushwalks, the most popular being the walk to the granite peaks of Mt Strzelecki which affords some great views of the surrounding area. There are also a number of lookouts on the island, including Furneaux and Walkers Lookouts, almost in the centre of the island, Vinegar Hill in the south and Mt Tanner in the north.

The island's abundant vegetation supports a wide variety of wildlife, including more than 150 species of bird. One of the most well known is the Cape Barren goose. Its protected habitat and increasing numbers mean that it is no longer close to extinction. The other well-known species is the mutton bird which was once hunted in large numbers. Drive slowly on the roads at night otherwise wallabies and other nocturnal wildlife will end up as road kill.

Whitemark is the main administrative centre and Lady Barron, in the south, is the main fishing area and deep-water port. The main industries on Flinders Island are farming, fishing and seasonal mutton-birding.

Summer, spring and autumn are all good times to visit, however a sunny, winter weekend can also be very enjoyable.

Information
You can write to the Flinders Island Tourist

The Cape Barren goose rarely enters water

Committee, P O Box 143, Whitemark, Flinders Island, Tasmania, 7255 (or call ☎ 1800 806 801) for information on the island or have a chat to Thelma Shaik, who runs the Gem Shop at the Interstate Hotel in Whitemark (see Places to Stay in this section). Thelma is a mine of information about the island.

There are only three public telephones on the island. They are located in Whitemark opposite the Interstate Hotel, at Lady Barron in the foyer of the Furneaux Tavern and at Killiecrankie outside the general store. Petrol can be purchased in Whitemark and Lady Barron.

Things to See

The **Wybalenna Historic Site** is all that remains of this unfortunate settlement set up to 'care for' the Aboriginal people removed from mainland Tasmania. Because of its historical significance, this site is rated as the third most important historic site in the State. Close by, the cemetery and memorial chapel, while not part of the site, are looked after by the National Trust. The chapel, which had been restored but has since been vandalised, is sometimes open to visitors.

Nearby, there's the **Emita Museum**, housed in what was the first government school on the island, which displays a variety of Aboriginal artefacts as well as old sealing

and sailing relics. The museum is currently upgrading the display area of the artefacts of the shipwreck of the *Sydney Cove* in 1797. It also has a large display on the mutton bird industry and is open on weekends from 1 to 4 pm, and during summer is also open from 1 to 5 pm weekdays. The museum is staffed by volunteers and entry is by donation.

Trousers Point is definitely worth a visit to explore the rocks and beaches. There are picnic tables, barbecues and toilets in the camping ground under the drooping sheoaks. The colourful rocks surrounding Trousers Point are easily accessible and offer great views of the Strzelecki Peaks. It is a beautiful spot from which to watch the sunset.

Activities

Bushwalking is a popular activity for visitors to the island. *A Walker's Guide to Flinders Island and Cape Barren Island* ($7, available from various shops on the island, including the general store and newsagents at Whitemark) gives information on a number of walks, of varying lengths, which have been graded easy, medium and difficult. **Walks** along beach and coastal heath trails can be linked with hinterland and mountain tracks throughout the island. Alternatively, you can join Furneaux Footprints (☎ 6359 8571) for gentle or more challenging day walks at $40 per person, including snacks and use of a day pack. You provide your own lunch and transport.

The **Strzelecki Track** commences about 10 km south of Whitemark and is approximately four km long. The well-signposted track ascends Mt Strzelecki to a height of 756 metres and, as you can imagine, in good weather the view from the summit over the Furneaux Group islands is spectacular. It is about a three to five-hour return walk, and it is essential that you carry warm clothing, wet weather gear, food and water at any time of the year.

Stretchville Trail Rides (☎ 6359 3572) arrange **horse rides** of two hours or longer on request through the foothills of the Strzelecki Ranges, along the east coast and

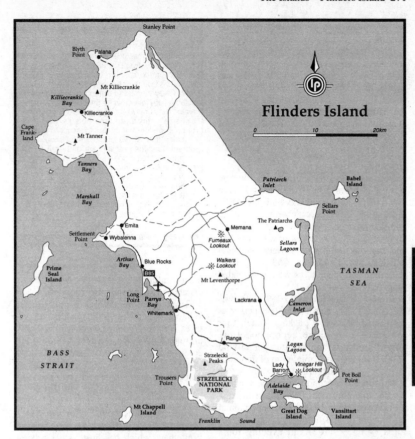

The map shows Flinders Island with locations including Stanley Point, Blyth Point, Palana, Mt Killiecrankie, Killiecrankie Bay, Killiecrankie, Mt Tanner, Cape Frankland, Tanners Bay, Marshall Bay, Emita, Settlement Point, Wybalenna, Prime Seal Island, Arthur Bay, Blue Rocks, Long Point, Parrys Bay, Whitemark, Bass Strait, Trousers Point, Mt Chappell Island, Franklin Sound, Ranga, Strzelecki Peaks, Strzelecki National Park, Lady Barron, Adelaide Bay, Great Dog Island, Vansittart Island, Patriarch Inlet, Babel Island, Sellars Point, The Patriarchs, Memana, Furneaux Lookout, Sellars Lagoon, Walkers Lookout, Mt Leventhorpe, Lackrana, Cameron Inlet, Tasman Sea, Logan Lagoon, Vinegar Hill Lookout, Pot Boil Point.

Flinders Island

0   10   20km

ISLANDS

through the Patriarchs in the north-west for $20 an hour per person.

Rock climbers can find challenging rock stacks or granite walls. Mt Killiecrankie has some very steep granite faces rising from sea level. Although there is a soak at the camp site, you will need to take all your drinking water. The **rock climbs** within Strzelecki National Park and the ridge walk should only be attempted by experienced walkers and climbers.

Rock hounds of another variety can find various localities in which to fossick for the elusive **'Killiecrankie Diamond'**. The Gem Shop in Whitemark and Killiecrankie Enterprises (the general store) can advise on locations where lapidaries can spend some time. The Gem Shop also conducts special **fossicking** tours.

Scuba divers are also catered for on Flinders Island. There are several good **scuba-diving** locations on the northern and western coasts. In many places you can enter from the beach or shelving rocks. The water is warmest between January and April and coldest between June and September. Non-commercial diving licenses for abalone, crayfish and scallops can be obtained from police stations at Whitemark and Lady Barron.

Rock fishing along the southern, northern and north western coasts is good all year. Bait is easily obtained from the rocks and fishing tackle can be purchased from many stores, however you need to bring your own rod. Beach fishing is popular on the eastern coast and from Red Bluff. The North East River also has good fishing.

Organised Tours

If you really want to splash out, Flinders Island Adventures (☎ 6359 4507) in Whitemark have full and half-day 4WD tours as well as Powercat charters for diving and fishing. Prices vary from $375 to $675 and bookings are essential. It also runs day and half-day tours with an environmental and historical flavour for $59 per person, minimum four people, as well as extended tours of up to four days.

Jimmy's Island Tours (☎ 6359 2112) runs day coach tours for around $62 per person as well as a three-day package coach tour including twin-share accommodation, airport transfers and airfares for around $500. Bookings for a minimum of two must be made prior to departure.

Mutton Birds or short-tailed shearwaters, whose migratory path from Japan to Australia covers some 15,000 km, can be found on Flinders Island. Flinders Island Adventures (☎ 6359 4507) run evening tours aboard the Strait Lady from December to March from Lady Barron to see these birds on the small islands in Adelaide Bay.

Places to Stay

Whitemark The *Flinders Island Cabin Park* (☎ 6359 2188), is in Bluff Rd, five km north of Whitemark, right next to the airport. It has two en suite cabins as well as cabins with communal amenities at $25 single and $40 double.

Built in 1911, the *Flinders Island Interstate Hotel* (☎ 6359 2114) is situated in the centre of Whitemark and has rooms for $25/66. Recently renovated in heritage style,

---

Mutton Birds

Each September, the mutton birds return to Flinders and other Bass Strait islands, after a summer in the northern hemisphere, to clean out and repair their burrows from the previous year. They then head out to sea again before returning in November for the breeding season, which lasts until April. Eggs are then laid in one three-day period, and the parents take it in turns, two weeks at a time, to incubate them.

Once their single chick has hatched, both parents feed the fledgling until mid-April, when all the adult birds depart, leaving the young to fend for themselves and hopefully to follow their parents north.

Unfortunately for the well-fed little mutton birds, they make good eating, and once the adult birds leave their nests the 'birders', or mutton-bird hunters, move in. ■

---

it's a comfortable hotel within easy walking distance of shops and other facilities.

Other accommodation in and around Whitemark is mainly holiday units and cottages. *Bulloke Holiday Units* (☎ 6359 9709), in Butter Factory Rd, is a three-bedroom unit costing $56 a double. *Seaview Cottage* (☎ 6359 2011), 5 km south of Whitemark, is a small unit on a farm property which sleeps up to four people. You can rent for $60 a double plus $10 for each extra adult.

Further afield is the *Boat Harbour Beach House* (☎ 6359 6510), 45 km north-west of Whitemark which has hostel-style accommodation for an exorbitant $65 double plus $10 for each extra adult.

Lady Barron The *Lady Barron Holiday House* (☎ 6359 3555), is a three-bedroom unit in Franklin Parade and costs $60 a double. *Yaringa Holiday Units* (☎ 6359 4522), in Holloway St, has two units at $66 a single/double. For the same price and in the same street, you can also stay at *Felicitys Cottage* (☎ 6359 3641).

Overlooking the picturesque Franklin Sound, rooms at the *Furneaux Tavern* (☎ 6359 3521) cost $59 to $78 a double including a continental breakfast. Rooms are spacious and the service is friendly. The Tavern can also provide picnic lunch baskets if you want to go off the beaten track during the day.

Emita *Greenglades Host Farm* (☎ 6359 8506), in Fairhaven Rd, has two rooms with common tea-making and lounge areas. For $45 per person you get full board. Fifteen km north of Whitemark, in Elliot St, *Emita Beach Cottage* (☎ 6359 4539), is within easy walking distance of the beach and costs $66 a double.

Lackrana *Paltarra Holiday House* (☎ 6359 6532) is seven km from Lady Barron near Cameron's Inlet and accommodates up to eight people. The cost is $56 for four persons and $5 for extra adults. *Echo Hills Holiday Units* (☎ 6359 6509), is found 15 km from Whitemark on the east coast, at the foot of the Darling Ranges; the cottages cost $66 a double.

Memana *Carnsdale Holiday Home* (☎ 6359 9718), is 28 km east of Whitemark. This four-bedroom unit costs $60 a double and is situated in a quiet farm setting. *Lisas Cottage* (☎ 6359 6530), is a self-contained home for $66 a double.

Killiecrankie The *Oakridge Holiday Home* (☎ 6359 2160), at Killiecrankie Bay is a three-bedroom home at a flat rate of $50. It's close to the beach and you can't miss its brightly coloured exterior!

Killiecrankie also has a very basic free camping and picnic area with barbecues, toilets and cold showers.

Places to Eat
Whitemark At the *Bakery* in Whitemark, you can buy pies, bread and cold drinks on weekdays. It is also the local pizza place on Friday night. Opposite, *Island Produce* has a selection of fresh food as well as a coffee shop serving light snacks.

Jimmy's Fast Food and Take Away, opposite the Interstate Hotel, is open seven days

a week and serves grills, sandwiches and other take-away meals.

The *Interstate Hotel* (☎ 6359 2114), in the centre of Whitemark, serves a range of moderately priced lunch and dinner counter meals Monday to Friday and dinner on Saturday night in the dining room and public bar. Another place to try for dinner is the *Whitemark Sports Club* (☎ 6359 2220) which has a cosy restaurant with a quality menu. Meals are also available in the bistro throughout the week in summer. The Club has its own bottle shop and bookings for the restaurant are necessary.

Lady Barron *Patterson's Store* is open seven days a week, selling basic supplies. It's also a Post Office, Commonwealth Bank agency and sells fuel.

The *Shearwater Restaurant* (☎ 6359 3521), at the Furneaux Tavern, has a good selection of bistro meals every day. It also has a lovely outlook over Franklin Sound to the distant peaks on Cape Barron Island.

Killiecrankie The only place at which to purchase food is at the *General Store* which has snacks and hot and cold drinks.

Things to Buy
Flinders Island fleece products are available from Killarney (☎ 6359 6509) at Lackrana. You can purchase fine quality yarns and knitwear, some of which is locally spun and dyed. Look for the 'Open' sign on weekdays and most Saturday mornings or phone for an appointment.

Wool-filled quilts and pillows as well as non-allergenic underblankets manufactured from local fleece are available from Mascot (☎ 6359 6526) in Lackrana. Pure and natural wool-filled oilskin and Durapel sleeveless jackets are also manufactured and available. Phone to ensure the owner is available.

Killiecrankie 'diamonds' are actually a semi-precious stone called topaz. Usually they are clear; however some can be purchased with a pale blue or pink colouring. The Gem Shop in Whitemark or the General Store in Killiecrankie sells cut stones for

ISLANDS

around $40 a carat. Uncut stones can also be bought. Both shops offer friendly service and fossick for their own stones.

Getting There & Away

It's only a short flight (less than one hour) part way across Bass Strait to reach Flinders Island. By far the best way to see the island is using one of the many package deals available. These provide return airfares, accommodation and car hire with unlimited kilometres. On a package deal, for two or more nights, the cost savings mean the car hire is almost free compared to paying separately for these services. Costs do vary according to season, but start at around $270 from Launceston and $300 from Melbourne.

Aus-Air (☎ (03) 9580 6166 or 1800 331 256) flies to the island from Melbourne on Monday, Wednesday and Friday at 11 am. Flights depart at 7.15 am on Saturday and 4.30 pm on Sunday.

Airlines of Tasmania (☎ 6391 8755 or 1800 030 550) offers morning and afternoon flights daily from Launceston. It also has flights from Sale and Traralgon in Victoria on Monday, Wednesday and Friday afternoons with a morning flight on Saturday and an afternoon flight on Sunday. Departure times vary.

Getting Around

There is no public transport on the island. Aus-Air provides airport transfers to Whitemark for $12 per person each way and to Lady Barron for $35 per person each way. Hire car companies will meet you at the airport and pre-booking is highly recommended.

There are many unsealed roads on the island so you'll need to drive carefully, particularly around the more remote areas. Unless you have a 4WD, take extra care which roads or tracks you take. You may find yourself in some sandy or slippery places.

In Whitemark, you can rent cars and mini-buses from Bowmans Transport (☎ 6395 2014) for $45 a day. Both Flinders Island Car Rentals (☎ 6359 2168) and Flinders Island Transport Services (☎ 6359 2060) rent cars

from around $50 per day. Furneaux Car Rentals (☎ 6359 3521 or 6359 2112) rent cars and mini-buses starting from $44. The cars are not new and are pretty basic.

Mountain bikes are available for hire from Flinders Island Bike Hire (☎ 6359 2000 or 6359 3506) for $10 per day. You can arrange to collect the bikes from the airport on arrival. Most of the island's roads are fairly level or gently undulating with good grades, although many are gravel.

CAPE BARREN ISLAND

• *pop 50*

Cape Barren Island is located to the south of Flinders Island and is the only other island in the Furneaux Group to have a permanent settlement. Kent Bay on the southern side was the first settlement south of Sydney.

The main settlement on Cape Barren Island, known as **The Corner**, has a small school, church and medical centre. This was the area given over for the resettlement of the Straitsmen from Flinders Island in 1881. Fishing is the main industry, although there are several cattle farms.

Things to Do

For experienced bushwalkers, the circuit walk of the shoreline offers great coastal views including the wreck of the *Farsund*, lovely beaches and interesting rock formations. Mt Kerford at 503 metres offers quite a challenge, while Mt Munro at 687 metres can be tackled from the north. Water is less of a problem here than on Flinders Island, with many fresh water sources available.

For those with a reasonable level of fitness, a day walk to the summit of Mt Munro on a clear day provides spectacular views of the surrounding area. Access is from The Corner, up to Big Grassy Hill and along the ridge to the summit.

Getting There & Away

Flights to Cape Barren Island are infrequent and it would be better to arrange a charter flight from Melbourne or Launceston if you have the numbers. Alternatively you can fly to Flinders Island and then arrange a boat charter to take you across allowing you to cache supplies on the way to your drop-off point. Charters can be arranged through the Furneaux Tavern at Lady Barron on Flinders Island.

Other Islands

SWAN ISLAND
There are not many islands you can rent and be the only guests at reasonably low prices. Swan Island is one of the exceptions. The owners live here and the other house on the island can be rented.

Located just three km off the north east coast of Tasmania this small island is three km long and is dominated by its lighthouse. The lighthouse was built in 1845 and automated in 1986 when the government sold the island. The main attraction of coming here is a get-away-from-it-all experience. For bird lovers it is a real haven with many sea birds nesting here. You can watch the shearwaters and penguins returning to their nests around sunset. The island has several beaches and there is good fishing around the shores and good areas for scuba diving.

Places to Stay
You can stay at the *Swan Island Guest House* (☎ 6357 2211) which is the old lighthouse keeper's quarters. It costs $98 a double plus $40 for each extra adult and holds up to six people. Full board is available for an additional $40 each per day.

Getting There & Away
There is an airstrip for light planes and you can come here on day trips from Cape Portland for $50 to $70 per person which includes lunch. Light planes can also fly here from Bridport or Launceston. Flights can be arranged when you book accommodation with the owners.

MACQUARIE ISLAND
Discovered in 1820 this isolated island in the Southern Ocean is part of Tasmania. It is located 1500 km to the south-east of Hobart and is classified as a sub-Antarctic island. For a long time the only visitors to its rocky shores where there for the purposes of harvesting its abundant wildlife. In 1933 after pressure from Antarctic explorers the island was declared a wildlife reserve. The island contains some important breeding sites with four species of penguin, including the King Penguin, and elephant seals. It has been nominated for World Heritage listing. Currently it is managed by the Department of Parks Wildlife and Heritage. There is a permanent scientific base on the northern end of the island.

Most visitors to the island are scientists in the course of their studies. Ordinary visitors are allowed and they mostly come from cruise ships, the only way to get here is by ship. To protect the wildlife and environment, access is only allowed to specified areas.

Cruises to Macquarie Island are usually part of a general Antarctic tour, which costs between US$2000 and US$6000. If you have the chance to visit Macquarie Island, then do so as it is a unique place.

ISLANDS

Index

MAPS

TEXT

Map references are in **bold** type.

LONELY PLANET JOURNEYS

JOURNEYS is a unique collection of travellers' tales – published by the company that understands travel better than anyone else. It is a series for anyone who has ever experienced – or dreamed of – the magical moment when they encountered a strange culture or saw a place for the first time. They are tales to read while you're planning a trip, while you're on the road or while you're in an armchair, in front of a fire.

JOURNEYS books will catch the spirit of a place, illuminate a culture, recount a crazy adventure, or introduce a fascinating way of life. They will always entertain, and always enrich the experience of travel.

ISLANDS IN THE CLOUDS
Travels in the Highlands of New Guinea
Isabella Tree

This is the fascinating account of a journey to the remote and beautiful Highlands of Papua New Guinea and Irian Jaya. The author travels with a PNG Highlander who introduces her to his intriguing and complex world. *Islands in the Clouds* is a thoughtful, moving book, full of insights into a region that is rarely noticed by the rest of the world.

'One of the most accomplished travel writers to appear on the horizon for many years . . . the dialogue is brilliant' – Eric Newby

LOST JAPAN
Alex Kerr

Lost Japan draws on the author's personal experiences of Japan over a period of 30 years. Alex Kerr takes his readers on a backstage tour: friendships with Kabuki actors, buying and selling art, studying calligraphy, exploring rarely visited temples and shrines . . . The Japanese edition of this book was awarded the 1994 Shincho Gakugei Literature Prize for the best work of non-fiction.

'This deeply personal witness to Japan's wilful loss of its traditional culture is at the same time an immensely valuable evaluation of just what that culture was'
– Donald Richie of the Japan Times

THE GATES OF DAMASCUS
Lieve Joris
Translated by Sam Garrett

This best-selling book is a beautifully drawn portrait of day-to-day life in modern Syria. Through her intimate contact with local people, Lieve Joris draws us into the fascinating world that lies behind the gates of Damascus.

'A brilliant book . . . Not since Naguib Mahfouz has the everyday life of the modern Arab world been so intimately described' – William Dalrymple

SEAN & DAVID'S LONG DRIVE
Sean Condon

Sean and David are young townies who have rarely strayed beyond city limits. One day, for no good reason, they set out to discover their homeland, and what follows is a wildly entertaining adventure that covers half of Australia. Sean Condon has written a hilarious, offbeat road book that mixes sharp insights with deadpan humour and outright lies.

'Funny, pithy, kitsch and surreal . . . This book will do for Australia what Chernobyl did for Kiev, but hey you'll laugh as the stereotypes go boom' – Andrew Tuck, Time Out

LONELY PLANET TRAVEL ATLASES

Lonely Planet has long been famous for the number and quality of its guidebook maps. Now we've gone one step further and in conjunction with Steinhart Katzir Publishers produced a handy companion series: Lonely Planet travel atlases – maps of a country produced in book form.

Unlike other maps, which look good but lead travellers astray, our travel atlases have been researched on the road by Lonely Planet's experienced team of writers. All details are carefully checked to ensure the atlas corresponds with the equivalent Lonely Planet guidebook.

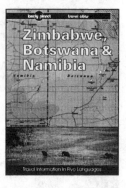

The handy atlas format means no holes, wrinkles, torn sections or constant folding and unfolding. These atlases can survive long periods on the road, unlike cumbersome fold-out maps. The comprehensive index ensures easy reference.

- full-colour throughout
- maps researched and checked by Lonely Planet authors
- place names correspond with Lonely Planet guidebooks
  – no confusing spelling differences
- legend and travelling information in English, French, German, Japanese and Spanish
- size: 230 x 160 mm

Available now:
Thailand; India & Bangladesh; Vietnam; Zimbabwe, Botswana & Namibia

Coming soon:
Chile; Egypt; Israel; Laos; Turkey

LONELY PLANET TV SERIES & VIDEOS

Lonely Planet travel guides have been brought to life on television screens around the world. Like our guides, the programmes are based on the joy of independent travel, and look honestly at some of the most exciting, picturesque and frustrating places in the world. Each show is presented by one of three travellers from Australia, England or the USA and combines an innovative mixture of video, Super-8 film, atmospheric soundscapes and original music.

Videos of each episode – containing additional footage not shown on television – are available from good book and video shops, but the availability of individual videos varies with regional screening schedules.

Video destinations include: Alaska; Australia (Southeast); Brazil; Ecuador & the Galápagos Islands; Indonesia; Israel & the Sinai Desert; Japan; La Ruta Maya (Yucatán, Guatemala & Belize); Morocco; North India (Varanasi to the Himalaya); Pacific Islands; Vietnam; Zimbabwe, Botswana & Namibia.

Coming soon: The Arctic (Norway & Finland); Baja California; Chile & Easter Island; China (Southeast); Costa Rica; East Africa (Tanzania & Zanzibar); Great Barrier Reef (Australia); Jamaica; Papua New Guinea; the Rockies (USA); Syria & Jordan; Turkey.

The Lonely Planet TV series is produced by:
Pilot Productions
Duke of Sussex Studios
44 Uxbridge St
London W8 7TG UK

Lonely Planet videos are distributed by:
IVN Communications Inc
2246 Camino Ramon
California 94583, USA

107 Power Road, Chiswick
London W4 5PL UK

Music from the TV series is available on CD & cassette.
For ordering information contact your nearest Lonely Planet office.

PLANET TALK

Lonely Planet's FREE quarterly newsletter

We love hearing from you and think you'd like to hear from us.

When...is the right time to see reindeer in Finland?
Where...can you hear the best palm-wine music in Ghana?
How...do you get from Asunción to Areguá by steam train?
What...is the best way to see India?

For the answer to these and many other questions read PLANET TALK.

Every issue is packed with up-to-date travel news and advice including:

- a letter from Lonely Planet co-founders Tony and Maureen Wheeler
- go behind the scenes on the road with a Lonely Planet author
- feature article on an important and topical travel issue
- a selection of recent letters from travellers
- details on forthcoming Lonely Planet promotions
- complete list of Lonely Planet products

To join our mailing list contact any Lonely Planet office.

Also available: Lonely Planet T-shirts. 100% heavyweight cotton.

LONELY PLANET ONLINE

Get the latest travel information before you leave or while you're on the road

Whether you've just begun planning your next trip, or you're chasing down specific info on currency regulations or visa requirements, check out the Lonely Planet World Wide Web site for up-to-the-minute travel information.

As well as travel profiles of your favourite destinations (including interactive maps and full-colour photos), you'll find current reports from our army of researchers and other travellers, updates on health and visas, travel advisories, and the ecological and political issues you need to be aware of as you travel.

There's an online travellers' forum (the Thorn Tree) where you can share your experiences of life on the road, meet travel companions and ask other travellers for their recommendations and advice. We also have plenty of links to other Web sites useful to independent travellers.

With tens of thousands of visitors a month, the Lonely Planet Web site is one of the most popular on the Internet and has won a number of awards including GNN's Best of the Net travel award.

http://www.lonelyplanet.com

LONELY PLANET PRODUCTS

Lonely Planet is known worldwide for publishing practical, reliable and no-nonsense travel information in our guides and on our web site. The Lonely Planet list covers just about every accessible part of the world. Currently there are eight series: *travel guides*, *shoestring guides*, *walking guides*, *city guides*, *phrasebooks*, *audio packs*, *travel atlases* and *Journeys* – a unique collection of travellers' tales.

EUROPE

Austria • Baltic States & Kaliningrad • Baltic States phrasebook • Britain • Central Europe on a shoestring • Central Europe phrasebook • Czech & Slovak Republics • Denmark • Dublin city guide • Eastern Europe on a shoestring • Eastern Europe phrasebook • Finland • France • Greece • Greek phrasebook • Hungary • Iceland, Greenland & the Faroe Islands • Ireland • Italy • Mediterranean Europe on a shoestring • Mediterranean Europe phrasebook • Paris city guide • Poland • Prague city guide • Russia, Ukraine & Belarus • Russian phrasebook • Scandinavian & Baltic Europe on a shoestring • Scandinavian Europe phrasebook • Slovenia • St Petersburg city guide • Switzerland • Trekking in Greece • Trekking in Spain • Ukranian phrasebook • Vienna city guide • Walking in Switzerland • Western Europe on a shoestring • Western Europe phrasebook

NORTH AMERICA

Alaska • Backpacking in Alaska • Baja California• California & Nevada • Canada • Hawaii • Honolulu city guide • Los Angeles city guide • Mexico • New England • Pacific Northwest USA • Rocky Mountain States • San Francisco city guide • Southwest USA • USA phrasebook

CENTRAL AMERICA & THE CARIBBEAN

Central America on a shoestring • Costa Rica • Eastern Caribbean • Guatemala, Belize & Yucatán: La Ruta Maya • Jamaica

SOUTH AMERICA

Argentina, Uruguay & Paraguay • Bolivia • Brazil • Brazilian phrasebook • Buenos Aires city guide • Chile & Easter Island • Colombia • Ecuador & the Galápagos Islands • Latin American Spanish phrasebook • Peru • Quechua phrasebook • Rio de Janeiro city guide • South America on a shoestring • Trekking in the Patagonian Andes • Venezuela

ALSO AVAILABLE:

Travel with Children • Traveller's Tales

AFRICA

Arabic (Moroccan) phrasebook • Africa on a shoestring • Cape Town city guide • Central Africa • East Africa • Egypt & the Sudan • Ethiopian (Amharic) phrasebook • Kenya • Morocco • North Africa • South Africa, Lesotho & Swaziland • Swahili phrasebook • Trekking in East Africa • West Africa • Zimbabwe, Botswana & Namibia • Zimbabwe, Botswana & Namibia travel atlas

NORTH-EAST ASIA

Beijing city guide • Cantonese phrasebook • China • Hong Kong, Macau & Canton • Hong Kong city guide • Japan • Japanese phrasebook • Japanese audio pack • Korea • Korean phrasebook • Mandarin phrasebook • Mongolia • Mongolian phrasebook • North-East Asia on a shoestring • Seoul city guide • Taiwan • Tibet • Tibet phrasebook • Tokyo city guide

INDIAN SUBCONTINENT

Bengali phrasebook • Bangladesh • Delhi city guide • Hindi/Urdu phrasebook • India • India & Bangladesh travel atlas • Indian Himalaya • Karakoram Highway • Nepal • Nepali phrasebook • Pakistan • Sri Lanka • Sri Lanka phrasebook • Trekking in the Indian Himalaya • Trekking in the Nepal Himalaya

SOUTH-EAST ASIA

Bali & Lombok • Bangkok city guide • Burmese phrasebook • Cambodia • Ho Chi Minh city guide • Indonesia • Indonesian phrasebook • Indonesian audio pack • Jakarta city guide • Java • Laos • Lao phrasebook • Malaysia, Singapore & Brunei • Myanmar (Burma) • Philippines • Pilipino phrasebook • Singapore city guide • South-East Asia on a shoestring • Thailand • Thailand travel atlas • Thai phrasebook • Thai audio pack • Thai Hill Tribes phrasebook • Vietnam • Vietnamese phrasebook • Vietnam travel atlas

MIDDLE EAST & CENTRAL ASIA

Arab Gulf States • Arabic (Egyptian) phrasebook • Central Asia • Iran • Israel • Jordan & Syria • Middle East • Turkey • Turkish phrasebook • Trekking in Turkey • Yemen

Travel Literature: The Gates of Damascus

ISLANDS OF THE INDIAN OCEAN

Madagascar & Comoros • Maldives & Islands of the East Indian Ocean • Mauritius, Réunion & Seychelles

AUSTRALIA & THE PACIFIC

Australia • Australian phrasebook • Bushwalking in Australia • Bushwalking in Papua New Guinea • Fiji • Fijian phrasebook • Islands of Australia's Great Barrier Reef • Melbourne city guide • Micronesia • New Caledonia • New South Wales & the ACT • New Zealand • Northern Territory • Outback Australia • Papua New Guinea • Papua New Guinea phrasebook • Queensland • Rarotonga & the Cook Islands • Samoa • Solomon Islands • South Australia • Sydney city guide • Tahiti & French Polynesia • Tasmania • Tonga • Tramping in New Zealand • Vanuatu • Victoria • Western Australia

Travel Literature: Islands in the Clouds • Sean & David's Long Drive

THE LONELY PLANET STORY

Lonely Planet published its first book in 1973 in response to the numerous 'How did you do it?' questions Maureen and Tony Wheeler were asked after driving, bussing, hitching, sailing and railing their way from England to Australia.

Written at a kitchen table and hand collated, trimmed and stapled, *Across Asia on the Cheap* became an instant local bestseller, inspiring thoughts of another book.

Eighteen months in South-East Asia resulted in their second guide, *South-East Asia on a shoestring*, which they put together in a backstreet Chinese hotel in Singapore in 1975. The 'yellow bible', as it quickly became known to backpackers around the world, soon became *the* guide to the region. It has sold well over half a million copies and is now in its 8th edition, still retaining its familiar yellow cover.

Today there are over 180 titles, including travel guides, walking guides, language kits & phrasebooks, travel atlases and travel literature. The company is one of the largest travel publishers in the world. Although Lonely Planet initially specialised in guides to Asia, we now cover most regions of the world, including the Pacific, North America, South America, Africa, the Middle East and Europe.

The emphasis continues to be on travel for independent travellers. Tony and Maureen still travel for several months of each year and play an active part in the writing, updating and quality control of Lonely Planet's guides.

They have been joined by over 70 authors and 170 staff at our offices in Melbourne (Australia), Oakland (USA), London (UK) and Paris (France). Travellers themselves also make a valuable contribution to the guides through the feedback we receive in thousands of letters each year.

The people at Lonely Planet strongly believe that travellers can make a positive contribution to the countries they visit, both through their appreciation of the countries' culture, wildlife and natural features, and through the money they spend. In addition, the company makes a direct contribution to the countries and regions it covers. Since 1986 a percentage of the income from each book has been donated to ventures such as famine relief in Africa; aid projects in India; agricultural projects in Central America; Greenpeace's efforts to halt French nuclear testing in the Pacific; and Amnesty International.

'I hope we send the people out with the right attitude about travel. You realise when you travel that there are so many different perspectives about the world, so we hope these books will make people more interested in what they see. These are guidebooks, but you can't really guide people. All you can do is point them in the right direction.'
– Tony Wheeler

LONELY PLANET PUBLICATIONS

Australia
PO Box 617, Hawthorn 3122, Victoria
tel: (03) 9819 1877 fax: (03) 9819 6459
e-mail: talk2us@lonelyplanet.com.au

USA
Embarcadero West, 155 Filbert St, Suite 251,
Oakland, CA 94607
tel: (510) 893 8555 TOLL FREE: 800 275-8555
fax: (510) 893 8563
e-mail: info@lonelyplanet.com

UK
10 Barley Mow Passage, Chiswick,
London W4 4PH
tel: (0181) 742 3161 fax: (0181) 742 2772
e-mail: 100413.3551@compuserve.com

France:
71 bis rue du Cardinal Lemoine, 75005 Paris
tel: 1 44 32 06 20 fax: 1 46 34 72 55
e-mail: 100560.415@compuserve.com

World Wide Web: http://www.lonelyplanet.com